The Collected Writings of Walt Whitman

1872

WALT WHITMAN

The Correspondence

VOLUME II: 1868 – 1875

Edited by Edwin Haviland Miller

 NEW YORK UNIVERSITY PRESS 1961

The Collected Writings of Walt Whitman

GENERAL EDITORS

Gay Wilson Allen and E. Sculley Bradley

ADVISORY EDITORIAL BOARD

Roger Asselineau   *Harold W. Blodgett*

Charles E. Feinberg   *Clarence Gohdes*

Emory Holloway   *Rollo G. Silver*   *Floyd Stovall*

GRATEFUL ACKNOWLEDGMENT IS MADE TO

Mr. Charles E. Feinberg,

WHOSE FINANCIAL ASSISTANCE MADE POSSIBLE
THE ILLUSTRATIONS IN THIS VOLUME AND WHO ALSO
MADE AVAILABLE TO THE PUBLISHER THE RESOURCES
OF THE FEINBERG COLLECTION.

Preface

Since the introduction of the printing press, prefaces have been a part of bookmaking, particularly of works with scholarly pretensions. Favors have been sought and acknowledgments made. Praise has been bestowed in phrases that centuries ago cried for peaceful interment. Authors have struggled to make their clichés meaningful, and sometimes have outwitted themselves in their quest to find novel ways of saying "thank you." Alas! I am no exception. I am powerless to cloak an ancient ritual with new garments. Moreover, to abandon a sanctioned custom would be to claim an independence which is not mine, for many people, some of whom I have not seen, have generously contributed information that enlightened my ignorance.

I am obligated to the following Whitman specialists: Gay Wilson Allen, Harold Blodgett, Sculley Bradley, Edward F. Grier, Clarence Gohdes, Emory Holloway, and F. DeWolfe Miller. To the following curators and librarians I express my gratitude: Miss Anne Freudenberg at the University of Virginia, Dr. John D. Gordan and his staff in the Berg Collection at the New York Public Library, Dr. David C. Mearns at the Library of Congress, Miss Ruth Matzkin of the Camden County Historical Society, and Miss Fannie Rothman of the Fletcher Free Library in Burlington, Vermont. As always, I have been delighted with the co-operation I have received at Harvard University, the Boston Athenaeum, the Boston Public Library, the New York Public Library, and the Simmons College Library.

I can here only reaffirm my words in the first volume as to the kindnesses of Rollo G. Silver and Charles E. Feinberg.

A fellowship from the American Council of Learned Societies gave me the time and the tranquillity necessary to complete this volume.

I am indebted to the following institutions for permission to print Whitman correspondence in their collections: Clifton Waller Barrett Collection, University of Virginia; Berg Collection, New York Public Library; William Andrews Clark Memorial Library, University of California at Los Angeles; Columbia University; Royal Library of Copenhagen, Denmark; Dartmouth College; Estelle Doheny Collection of the

Edward Laurence Doheny Memorial Library, St. John's Seminary; Ralph Waldo Emerson Memorial Association; T. E. Hanley Collection, University of Texas; Harvard University; Historical Society of Pennsylvania; Henry E. Huntington Library; Library of Congress; Oscar Lion Collection, New York Public Library; Minnesota Historical Society; Missouri Historical Society; Pierpont Morgan Library; National Archives, General Services Administration; New York Public Library; Northwestern University; Ohio Wesleyan University; University of Pennsylvania; Rhode Island Historical Society; Syracuse University; University of Texas; Trent Collection, Duke University; Walt Whitman House, Camden; Yale University.

The following individuals have graciously allowed me to print letters: Fred B. Barton, Philo Calhoon, Charles E. Feinberg, Emory Holloway, Mrs. Donald E. Kidd, Oscar Lion, Gilbert S. McClintock, Mrs. Doris Neale, Mrs. Joseph R. Perkins, Jr., Mrs. Francis Frederic Phillips, Rollo G. Silver, Lord Tennyson, Sir Charles Tennyson, Dr. Max Thorek.

E. H. M.

CONTENTS

Introduction

WALT WHITMAN 1868–1875

"Walt Whitman had begun to conquer the world." William Michael Rossetti's publication in England of selections from *Leaves of Grass* early in 1868 introduced Whitman to an international audience. A German poet, Ferdinand Freiligrath, who at the time was in political exile in England, translated a few poems for a German periodical. A group of Irish students and teachers became avid followers of Whitman, and Edward Dowden, later a Shakespearean scholar of note, wrote one of the most judicious of the early critical appraisals. In Denmark Rudolf Schmidt (1836–1899), a poet as well as the editor of *For Idé og Virkelighed* (For Idea and Reality), introduced *Leaves of Grass* to Scandinavians and later translated *Democratic Vistas*. With some misgivings the poet accepted this bowdlerized edition of his poems which through its omissions minimized his tough-mindedness and sexual frankness. Though he later regretted its publication,[1] he never forgot its importance in establishing his reputation. In 1888 Whitman observed to Horace Traubel: "How good that English crowd has always been to me—the whole crowd: I want it to be forever recognized. When the time comes for you to tell your own story . . . you must be careful to do those English fellows justice."[2]

Rossetti's volume had a direct influence upon Whitman's life through Mrs. Anne Gilchrist (1828–1886). The widow of the biographer of William Blake, Alexander Gilchrist, and the mother of four children, she had completed her husband's biography upon his premature death and later prepared a study of Mary Lamb. Intelligent as she undoubtedly was, she was more given to exuberant idealism than to objective analysis. What she admired she soon adored. With her there was no middle ground. Anyone she respected she cloaked in the robes of a hero and paid servile obeisance to his grandeur. As a young woman she had written of Thomas Carlyle: "Surely never before was there in any man the union of such Titan strength and keenest insight, with soft, tenderest, pitying gentleness."[3] After reading Rossetti's volume in 1869, she discovered in Whitman

1. See 403.   2. Traubel, I, 281.
3. Gilchrist, 36–37. Her first child was named Percy Carlyle Gilchrist.

virility fused with feminine sensibility, a hero with the body of a Titan and the soul of a lover. At last she had found the physical and poetic embodiment of her ideal. So impassioned were her letters about Whitman's verse to Rossetti that he advised her to print them anonymously as "A Woman's Estimate of Walt Whitman" (1870), which was the first major defense by a woman of the controversial poet. Hers was an amorous critique, a love letter masquerading as criticism.

In despair because Whitman did not write directly to her—she had a nervous collapse in 1870—she waited and pined. Finally, the "life force" was too much for her. The books which Whitman had sent to Rossetti to transmit to her served as an excuse, and on September 3, 1871,[4] she wrote one of the most extraordinary love letters in the language. This well-bred Victorian lady swept aside conventional amenities to declare her love feverishly and to offer her soul and her body to the poet. She rapturously envisaged herself as the poet's spiritual mate and the mother of a noble progeny. Whitman, understandably, waited over six weeks before he replied to her letter. His brevity and evasiveness did not dampen her passion, nor did his subsequent warning:

Dear friend, let me warn you somewhat about myself—& yourself also. You must not construct such an unauthorized & imaginary ideal Figure, & call it W. W. and so devotedly invest your loving nature in it. The actual W. W. is a very plain personage, & entirely unworthy such devotion.[5]

She, however, was powerless to deny a shattering passion that cried for spiritual and physical satisfaction. He was equally powerless to offer the fulfillment she craved. And so we have an amazing spectacle, the stuff of tragedy for some writers, of comedy to others. The poet who shocked the world because of his anatomical candor and who boldly summoned lovers to embrace him wherever he walked, did not know how to handle a woman whose ardor his verses had inflamed. She exposed her feelings without shame and without stint; he was awed by her emotional excesses —and frightened. He retreated as she pursued. She wanted to come to America to offer herself to him; he preferred to have an ocean between them. In 1875, against Whitman's wishes, she made a fateful decision: in September, 1876, accompanied by three of her children, she came to America. But the story of their meeting and her disillusionment belongs to the next volume.

Meanwhile life in the Whitman family had not changed materially.

4. See 405.   5. See 436.
6. The dates given in one of WW's notebooks (LC #108) and those in the report of an interview with Doyle by the poet's executors are in conflict (CW, VIII, 3–16). There

Jeff and his family were now in St. Louis, and Martha's health continued to deteriorate. George provided a home in Brooklyn for his mother and his brother Eddy. After George's marriage in 1871, about which his possessive mother was never happy, he moved to Camden, and until 1872 Mrs. Whitman remained in Brooklyn, supported by weekly contributions from Walt. Hannah Heyde was in Burlington, Vermont, with a husband she feared but never left. Jesse died in an insane asylum in 1870. Mrs. Whitman was more attached than ever to Walt, her favorite son: Jeff and Martha imposed upon her when they came to Brooklyn; George before his marriage spent too much money on the girls and after his marriage was too economical; Louisa, his wife, was self-centered. There was only Walt. Toward the end of her life the mother dreamed of keeping house for him in Washington.

Until his stroke in 1873 Whitman continued to live in Washington. Employed in the Attorney General's office, he held what amounted to a sinecure. The hours were short, from nine o'clock in the morning until three o'clock in the afternoon, and the work, copying official documents, was not burdensome. Vacations were frequent. Often he hired a substitute when he stayed in Brooklyn for a number of months, and the financial arrangement worked out to his advantage. The salary, at least $1600 annually, enabled him to live comfortably and to accumulate a modest amount. His poetry did not produce large returns, but he sold pieces to magazines for as much as $100, and several of the small editions he personally printed were completely sold out. Whitman himself, however, never admitted in public that during these years he was slowly winning acceptance.

The only unpleasant event was the rift with William D. O'Connor in 1872. Though Whitman, characteristically, remained silent about the matter, as did O'Connor, evidently the abolitionist views of the latter caused a rupture that lasted ten years. O'Connor, whose opinions were explosively extreme, found intolerable the poet's moderateness and lack of sympathy for the Negro.

In Washington Whitman's closest friends were O'Connor, Charles W. Eldridge, and John Burroughs, all of whom were government employees and active champions of his poetry. None of them, however, satisfied his quest for comradeship. This need was filled by Peter George Doyle, a streetcar conductor who was born in Ireland about 1845 and came to the United States as a young man.[6] He served in the Confederate Army and

---

were, evidently, four other men in the Doyle family: Francis M., a policeman, was killed in 1871 (see 418); Michael F. was also a policeman; Edward was a conductor; and James was a laborer.

met Whitman in 1865. Of all the hundreds of soldiers he met, Doyle was
the only one with whom Whitman established a lasting relationship: the
others returned to their homes, to their wives and families. For eight years
Doyle and Whitman saw each other almost daily. Whitman took long
walks with Pete at night, sent "a bouquet" to him frequently,[7] had clothes
made for him,[8] and coaxed the excitable young man out of his depressions.
This was a passionate involvement which filled Whitman with happiness
and despair. He was not happy when he was absent from Pete, but the
poet had to retreat to Brooklyn, where "I think of you very often, dearest
comrade, & with more calmness than when I was there."[9] He feared that
his love was not returned, but was surprised to discover, when he left
Washington for a visit to Brooklyn in 1870, that "you made so much of
having me with you, [and] that you could feel so downcast at losing me.
I foolishly thought it was all on the other side."[10]

Whitman's correspondence with this semi-literate young man was
termed a "delicious volume" by no less a person than William James.[11]
Most of Whitman's letters are presumably extant and are reprinted here,
but, although Whitman preserved great quantities of correspondence,
only a few of Doyle's have survived. Those that remain are chatty, im-
personal, and dull.

As in the first volume, the most moving letters are those which involve
Whitman's affections. The triviality of much of the correspondence with
his mother is relieved by his solicitude for the one woman he could love
without reserve and without fear of involvement. The letters to Doyle
pulsate with the emotion of an older man who is at once paternal (perhaps
maternal, in final analysis) and passionate. And his handling of the un-
wanted ardor of Anne Gilchrist, who assaulted his soul and body with an
aggressiveness which aroused deep fear, provides a fascinating study of a
lover who feared to be loved. Whitman's emotional entanglements during
these years constitute the personal drama of an enigmatic, evasive man.

However, as his letters to other correspondents reveal, Whitman also
participated actively in a campaign to impress upon American and foreign
audiences an image of a neglected and despised poet, of a man who sang
of democracy and received in return only jeers from his countrymen. Tire-
lessly, and repetitively, Whitman informed men like Dowden, Rossetti,
and Schmidt of his trials: no publisher would print his poems; editors of
magazines scorned his works; newspapers were hostile; his books did not
sell. But these were half-truths. His poems were not infrequently printed
in magazines. Whitman received extensive publicity in newspapers

---

7. See 317.   8. See 556.   9. See 304.   10. See 367.
11. *Talks to Teachers on Psychology* (1899), 250.

through his own efforts and those of his friends, among whom there were always journalists. In fact, in the American press Whitman created a new portrait: he minimized "the good gray poet" and emphasized a folksy old man, something of an extrovert given to commonplace sentiments and actions. Needless to add, this journalistic portrait called to mind neither the poet of love, of ideal democracy, and of anguished introspection, nor the author of *Democratic Vistas*. This, his most important prose work, though it did not immodestly say so, was a prose "song of myself," which delineated an idealized version of a democracy cemented by the love of comrades and articulated by a poet who bears family resemblances to Nietzsche's artistic overman and Wagner's mythic heroes. Like many artists in the last one hundred years, Whitman sought simultaneously veneration as a poet-hero and acceptance as a man of the people.

During these years the last great poems, "Passage to India" and "Prayer of Columbus," appeared, but increasingly Whitman produced occasional poetry of no especial merit. Like many poet laureates, Whitman was in greater demand for public appearances as his poetic powers declined. He read poems—not very effectively, unless one accepts his own press releases—at the American Institute in 1871, at Dartmouth College in 1872, and at Tufts College, by proxy, in 1875. The material in his recollections of the Civil War, " 'Tis But Ten Years Since," which was later published as *War Memoranda*, came almost unaltered from the notebooks and diaries which he had preserved. After his paralytic stroke in 1873 Whitman produced few important works: he drew upon old manuscript notes or revised previously published works. Like his body, his inspiration had aged prematurely.

1873 marked, in Gay Wilson Allen's words, "the ebbing tide." First there was the paralytic assault on the (real or imaginary) magnificent physique which he had narcissistically glorified in his early poems and in his letters. The man who had once proudly walked the streets of Brooklyn, New York, and Washington now hobbled with a walking stick. The man who had formerly lived independently as a bachelor now needed the assistance of companions. The man who delighted in his voluble gregariousness with the workers he encountered on the streets and on the ferries even spoke with difficulty for almost a year. Again, as in 1864, Whitman publicly attributed his physical collapse to infections contracted in the wartime hospitals: this was part of the public image. However, the diagnosis of his doctors—"a long continued excessive emotional action generally"[12]—is more convincing. Whitman's body at last proved incapable

---

12. See 531, and Traubel, IV, 472.

of withstanding psychic pressures which, if he understood them, he was unwilling or unable to express: the almost irresistible attraction of that aged lover death; the magnet-like, although probably ambivalent, attraction of his mother; the ardent association with young men, soldiers, workers, and, more particularly, Pete Doyle; his insecurity and lack of gratification in his relations with women and men of his own age.

Not only was the body wracked with pain, which continued for almost three years and left him a semi-invalid, but also the spirit. Martha, Jeff's wife, died of cancer in February, 1873. Just as Whitman began to feel almost exuberant about his chances of recovery from his stroke, his mother, now almost eighty years old, suddenly commenced to fail, and he hastened to Camden a few days before her death on May 23. After the burial he returned to Washington for a few weeks, but he was so depressed that he shortly fled to Camden. There he lived in his mother's room, where "every object of furniture &c. is familiar & has an emotional history."[13] Frequently he sat "in the same big old mahogany chair I gave mother 20 years ago."[14] "I can put up," he wrote to Pete Doyle, "with all but the death of my mother—that is my great sorrow that sticks."[15] Because one day he would feel well enough to go over to Philadelphia and the next day would be prostrated with pain in his limbs and head, his letters sometimes became "perturbed."[16] In October he was so concerned about his physical condition that he drew another will, the third within a year.[17] Above all, he was lonely: George was preoccupied with business affairs; Louisa was kind but led her own life; and he was in a strange environment. "For a fellow of my size, the *friendly presence & magnetism needed*, somehow, is not here."[18] Only as he came to know the pilots of boats, the conductors of streetcars, workers, and neighbors did Camden become tolerable to the lover of comrades.

For months he toyed with the prospect of returning to Washington, but his body stubbornly refused to recuperate. Perhaps in this instance his body acted unconsciously in his interests. In Camden his mother's effects kept her memory and presence near. As devoted as he was to Doyle, the young man caused "perturbations" which once before he had been compelled to escape. Louisa, though she was not so attached as the other sister-in-law, Martha, could provide simple comforts absent in a bachelor's quarters. Besides, Washington no longer engaged his spirits as in the war years; a new generation of political hacks was no more concerned with his ideal democracy than their predecessors. And so, psychologically and physically, he was better off in Camden. Thus, when he was discharged

13. See 524.   14. See 530.   15. See 525.   16. See 531.
17. See 542.

from his governmental post on June 30, 1874, he was more or less reconciled to his new home. In July he bought a cheap lot[19] and laid plans for a "shanty" which he did not acquire until 1884. Letters to Peter Doyle became briefer, and soon he was surrounded by "Camden mechanics." The Delaware River had replaced the Potomac.

The following two years were marked by depressions. Twice he "hurriedly destroyed a large mass of letters & MSS.," he admitted to Ellen O'Connor,[20] because he despaired of his recovery. His letters minutely described his suffering: he was in fact somewhat hypochondriacal. But he published an occasional poem or article. He arranged for the sale of his books and discovered, or imagined that he discovered, that dealers were embezzling the proceeds. In 1875, when he began to improve, he occupied himself with the printing of *Leaves of Grass* and *Two Rivulets*, which were to be issued during the 1876 centennial. The heart of democracy's greatest poet, weary though it was with physical ailments, was once again enkindled when it surveyed with unfailing enthusiasm the achievements of the country's first hundred years: with pride he looked back over the land's growth and found it good, with optimism he looked forward to a future about which he had no fears. He was convinced that the songs of "the outsetting bard of love" were to be part of that future.

18. See 537. 19. See 630. 20. See 580.

This alphabetical list includes all the recipients of extant letters written between 1868 and 1875. The name is followed by the letter number.

Akerman, Amos Tappan, 383
Alcott, A. Bronson, 288
Alden, Henry M., 552, 558
Alden, William Livingston, 298
American Institute, 402
Anderson & Archer, 272
Benedict, Newton, 325
Binckley, John M., 283
Blanch, Charles F., 337, 342
Boston *Daily Advertiser* (?), 450
Botta, Anne C. L., 387, 388, 388.1
Browning, Orville Hickman, 284
Burritt, I. N., 465
Burroughs, John, 322, 434, 448, 501, 514, 528, 532, 582, 614.1, 619, 637, 645, 660, 665, 673, 696
Butts, Asa K., 564, 577, 579
Carlyle, Thomas, 458
Carter, Robert, 674
Channing, Dr. William F., 305
Church, F. P. & W. C., 273, 276, 278, 290, 326, 352, 356
Conway, Moncure D., 269, 281, 361, 366
Dixon, Thomas, 365
Dowden, Edward, 404, 408, 422, 672
Doyle, Peter, 304, 308, 309, 313–315, 317, 318, 323, 346, 348, 349, 367, 369–378, 380, 390, 392, 393, 395, 397, 398, 400, 430–433, 435, 437,

439, 441, 447, 449, 451, 453, 454, 509–511, 513, 516, 518, 519, 521, 523, 525, 526, 530, 534, 536, 537, 542–544, 547–551, 554–557, 559– 562, 567, 568, 570, 572, 573, 575, 578, 581, 583, 585, 590, 593, 595, 597, 599, 600, 602, 604, 606, 608, 611, 612, 615, 617, 620, 621, 624, 626, 628, 630, 631, 633, 635, 636, 638–640, 643, 648, 649, 653, 655, 656, 658, 662, 663, 667, 669, 670, 675–677, 680, 684, 686, 688, 690, 692, 693, 699–707
Edmunds, James M., 464
Einstein, Edwin, 695
Eldridge, Charles W., 320, 455, 512, 515, 527, 539, 541, 545, 546, 565, 642
Ellis, F. S., 403
Elmes, Webster, 452, 522
Emerson, Ralph Waldo, 329
Farwell, Reuben, 668
Felt, Francis B., 498
Field, Walbridge A., 363
Fields, James T., 331, 338
Flood, Jr., John, 327, 333, 385, 385.1(?)
Flower, Cyril, 427
Floyd, A. C., 650
Freiligrath, Ferdinand, 339
French, Mr., 496

*

Additional Letters Not by Whitman

AL	*American Literature*
Allen	Gay Wilson Allen, *The Solitary Singer* (1955)
Allen, *Handbook*	Gay Wilson Allen, *Walt Whitman Handbook* (1946)
Asselineau	Roger Asselineau, *L'Évolution de Walt Whitman* (1955)
Barrett	Clifton Waller Barrett Collection, University of Virginia
Barrus	Clara Barrus, *Whitman and Burroughs—Comrades* (1931)
Berg	Henry W. and Albert A. Berg Collection, New York Public Library
Blodgett	Harold Blodgett, *Walt Whitman in England* (1934)
Bucke	Richard Maurice Bucke, *Walt Whitman* (1883)
Calamus	*Calamus: A Series of Letters Written during the Years 1868–1880 by Walt Whitman to a Young Friend (Peter Doyle)*, ed. Richard Maurice Bucke (1897)
Canby	Henry Seidel Canby, *Walt Whitman: An American* (1943)
CT	Complete Text
CW	*The Complete Writings of Walt Whitman* (1902), 10 vols.
DAB	*Dictionary of American Biography*
DNB	*Dictionary of National Biography*
Doheny	Estelle Doheny Collection of the Edward Laurence Doheny Memorial Library, St. John's Seminary
Donaldson	Thomas Donaldson, *Walt Whitman the Man* (1896)
Feinberg	Charles E. Feinberg Collection
Furness	Clifton Joseph Furness, *Walt Whitman's Workshop* (1928)
Gilchrist	Herbert Harlakenden Gilchrist, *Anne Gilchrist: Her Life and Writings* (1887)
Glicksberg	Charles I. Glicksberg, *Walt Whitman and the Civil War* (1933)
Gohdes and Silver	Clarence Gohdes and Rollo G. Silver, eds., *Faint Clews & Indirections* (1949)

Hanley	T. E. Hanley Collection, University of Texas
Harned	Thomas B. Harned, ed., *The Letters of Anne Gilchrist and Walt Whitman* (1918)
Holloway	Emory Holloway, *Whitman—An Interpretation in Narrative* (1926)
Huntington	Henry E. Huntington Library
In Re	*In Re Walt Whitman* (1893), ed. by Horace L. Traubel, Richard Maurice Bucke, and Thomas B. Harned
Kennedy	William Sloane Kennedy, *Reminiscences of Walt Whitman* (1896)
LC	The Library of Congress
LC #	*Walt Whitman—A Catalog Based Upon the Collections of The Library of Congress* (1955)
Lion	Oscar Lion Collection, New York Public Library
Morgan	Pierpont Morgan Library
Mott	Frank Luther Mott, *A History of American Magazines* (1957), 4 vols.
NEQ	*New England Quarterly*
Nonesuch	Emory Holloway, ed., *Walt Whitman—Complete Poetry & Selected Prose and Letters* (1938)
NYPL	New York Public Library
Pennsylvania	University of Pennsylvania
Perry	Bliss Perry, *Walt Whitman* (1906)
PT	Partial Text
SB	*Studies in Bibliography*
Traubel	Horace Traubel, ed., *With Walt Whitman in Camden* (1906–1953), 4 vols.
Trent	Trent Collection, Duke University
UPP	*The Uncollected Poetry and Prose of Walt Whitman* (1921), 2 vols., ed. by Emory Holloway
WWR	*Walt Whitman Review*

The Correspondence of Walt Whitman

VOLUME II: 1868-1875

1868

266. *To William D. O'Connor* [*1.(?). 1868*]

ADDRESS: William O'Connor, | Light House Bureau.

William—bring in, in your letter to Mr. Rossetti.[1]

I met Mr. Whitman a few evenings since. He has received your letter of December 16th. He duly received the previous ones also, making three letters from you.[2] He is entirely satisfied with your action, & with Mr. Hotten's,[3] in regard to the London selection & reprint, and seems pleased with the condition into which that enterprise has been shaped. He spoke with deep appreciation of you & your letters.

267. *To Edmund Routledge*

ENDORSED: "Letter sent to | Edmund Routledge, | Jan. 17, '68." DRAFT LETTER.

Sent Jan 17, '68 | probably left N. Y. Jan 18, '68
Edmund Routledge: | Dear Sir:

In compliance with request in your name in letter from George Routledge & Sons, New York, of December 28th & my own reply thereto of December 30th,[4] I send you herewith a poem for the Magazine, if found acceptable. For my own convenience & to insure correctness I have had the MS. put in type, & thus transmit it to you in the shape of a printed proof. The price is $120[5] in gold, payable here, and I should like 30 copies of the Magazine, sent me here. It is to be distinctly understood that I *reserve* the right to print it in any future editions of my book. Hoping suc-

---

1868
    1. Perhaps because O'Connor's correspondence with Rossetti had preceded his own, WW encouraged his friend to reply to Rossetti's letter of December 16, 1867. When O'Connor wrote to Rossetti on January 20, he included WW's paragraph with only a few unimportant alterations; see *Rossetti Papers*, 342.
    2. See notes to 257 and 259.   3. See 255 and 269.   4. See 262.
    5. WW accepted $50 in gold; see 271.

cess to the Magazine, & that my piece may be found acceptable for it, I remain

Respectfully &c yours,

Walt Whitman

My address is at Attorney General's Office, Washington City, U. S. A.

268. *To Louisa Van Velsor Whitman*

ATTORNEY GENERAL'S OFFICE,

Washington | Sunday noon | January 26, 1868.

Dearest mother,

Well, I have been out to John Burroughs's again to breakfast this morning—we have a nice hot breakfast, buckwheat cakes, &c.—It seems to be regular thing, almost every Sunday morning—then we sit & talk, & I read the Sunday morning papers till about ½ past 10 o'clock—& then I walk down here to the office, about a mile & a half—Mother, I have not much to write about, only the same old story—

I believe I told you some time ago, I had been applied to by an English magazine "The Broadway," to write something for them—well, I have lately sent them a piece of poetry—if they accept it, I shall get pay for it— The magazine is printed in London, but sold in New York also.[6]

I wrote to Han last Thursday—I suppose you got your letter last Friday[7]—I have not had any word from Jeff yet[8]—

We are having some great speeches made in Congress—This last week, there have been debates in the Senate, & the Republicans seem thoroughly waked up & full of fight[9]—they have had the best of it, so far, in the speeches—some of them were first rate—I am going up to Congress, next week—havn't been yet, this session—I went to Prof. Agassiz' lecture last Friday night[10]—I was very much pleased—

I pass the time very quietly—some evenings I spend in my attic—I have laid in wood, & can have a fire when I want it—I wish you was here— I am already making reckoning of coming home on the next visit—but when it will be, I can't tell—Mother, I would take a morning paper, the Times or something—it would help pass away the time—the debates in

6. See 262. This is the first reference to *The Broadway* in his letters to his mother.

7. Neither letter is extant.

8. Since Jeff and his family had gone to St. Louis at the end of 1867 (see 265), WW expected news of their activities. According to his mother's letter of February 12(?) (Trent), Jeff had received a letter from WW.

9. Congress was debating a supplementary reconstruction bill.

10. According to the Washington *National Republican*, Prof. Alexander Agassiz (1835–1910), the zoologist, lectured at the E Street Baptist Church on January 24 on

Congress are quite interesting now—Well, dear mother, I believe that is all this time.

Walt.

269. *To Moncure D. Conway*

Washington, | February 17, 1868.

My dear Conway,

Your letter of February 1st has just come to hand. I am willing that Mr. Hotten should sell his English publication of my Poems in the United States, on condition of paying me one shilling on every copy disposed of here—& hereby give consent to that arrangement.[11] Furthermore, to save trouble, I hereby fully empower you to decide & act for me in any matters or propositions relating to the book, in England, should any such arise—& what you agree to is agreed to by me. If convenient I should like Mr. Hotten to send me two copies of the book, by mail, immediately. I should also consider it a special favor if you would forward me from time to time any of the English magazines or journals that might contain *noteworthy* criticisms of my poems. But you must allow me to repay you the favor.

William O'Connor is well, and remains employed as before. Ellen O'Connor[12] is absent in Providence, but returns soon—their little daughter has been very ill, but is now convalescing.

Our American politics, as you notice, are in an unusually effervescent condition—with perhaps (to the mere eye-observation from a distance) divers alarming & deadly portending shows & signals. Yet we old stagers take things very coolly, & count on coming out all right in due time. The Republicans have exploited the negro too intensely, & there comes a reaction. But that is going to be provided for. According to present appearances the good, worthy, non-demonstrative, average-representing Grant will be chosen President next fall. What about him, then? As at present advised, I shall vote for him non-demonstrative as he is—but admit I can tell much better about him some five years hence.

I remain well & hearty—occupy the same quite agreeable & quiet berth in the Attorney General's office—and, at leisure, am writing a prose piece or two, (which I will send you, when printed.)[13]

"the succession of organized beings in geological times."

11. In accepting Hotten's proposal as outlined in Conway's letter, WW carefully repeated the agreement. Conway reported that Hotten informed him that "when expenses are paid, you will have a percentage on each copy sold here" (Feinberg; Traubel, II, 284).

12. See 275.

13. WW was preparing "Personalism" for *The Galaxy*. In 281 WW asked Conway to handle the English publication of the work.

I wish to send my sincerest thanks & personal regards to Mr. Rossetti. To have had my book, & my cause, fall into his hands, in London, in the way they have, I consider one of the greatest pieces of good fortune.

Mr. Morley[14] called upon me. Did you get my piece I sent, "Democracy"? I have just received a letter from A. B. Alcott[15]—he was with Mr. Emerson the previous evening, talking.

Remember my request to Mr. Hotten[16] for a couple of copies by mail— also, by your own kindness, any English criticisms of value should such appear.

I have not yet seen the February Fortnightly[17]—nor the book William Blake—but shall procure & read both. I feel prepared in advance to render my cordial & admirant respect to Mr. Swinburne—& would be glad to have him know that I thank him heartily for the mention which, I understand, he has made of me in the Blake.[18]

Indeed, my dear friend, I may here confess to you that to be accepted by those young men of England, & so treated with highest courtesy & even honor, touches one deeply. In my own country, so far, from the organs, the press, & from authoritative sources, I have received but one long tirade of shallow impudence, mockery, & scurrilous jeers. Only since the English recognition have the skies here lighted up a little.

With remembrance & love to you, Rossetti, & all my good friends— I write, for the present, Farewell.

Walt Whitman.

270. *To John Camden Hotten*

ENDORSED: "To John Camden Hotten, | February 18, 1868, (went 19th | probably)." DRAFT LETTER.

Feb 18—1868

Dear Sir:[19]

In response to your letter of the 5th instant, which has just reached me, I have to say that I accept the proposal made in it respecting your English publication of my poems—& hereby agree that you have the privilege of selling that publication in the United States, on payment to me, or my

14. On November 7, 1867 (Feinberg: Traubel, III, 322), Conway had written a note introducing John Morley (see 334).

15. WW was misleading: Alcott wrote on January 9. See 288.

16. See 270.

17. On February 1 Conway called WW's attention to his review of Swinburne's book on Blake in *The Fortnightly Review*, IX (1868), 216–220.

18. Swinburne at the conclusion of *William Blake: A Critical Essay* (1868), 300–303, pointed out similarities between WW and Blake, and praised "Out of the Cradle Endlessly Rocking" and "When Lilacs Last in the Dooryard Bloom'd," which he termed

agent, of a royalty of one shilling, (or 25 cents gold,) upon every copy sold in the U. S.

Of course it is distinctly understood that this grant from me does not affect my copyright here, but that said copyright, in each of its particulars & in the whole, is absolutely fully & exclusively retained by me.

It is not improbable that a very handsome & steady sale of the English volume may be effected here, by the right business manipulation, a moderate, judicious advertising &c. My book has never been really published here at all & the market is in a sort vacant of supplies. I will probably suggest to you something more on these points, in a future letter.

I received yesterday a letter from Mr. Conway, conveying your proposition, to which I mailed an immediate answer, to the same effect as herewith.

Accept my thanks for the *William Blake*.[20] It has not yet come from the post office, but I know it will prove to me a profoundly interesting study, and a handsome gift. It is, in fact, a book I was wanting.

After the reception of the copy you speak of—my own volume—(now probably on its way)—I shall doubtless have occasion to express genuine pleasure—with gratitude both to its editor & publisher.

And now, my dear sir, please accept with my trust in the success of the enterprise my kindest respects to yourself personally.

271. *To Routledge & Sons*   *2.19.1868*

ENDORSED: "Sent to N. Y. | Feb. 19, 1868."
DRAFT LETTER.

Messrs. Routledge: Publishers *Broadway* | Dear Sirs:

By your note of 18th, from New York, just received, I find that Mr. Edmund Routledge, editor, would (I quote) like to keep & use an original poem—three-page poem—sent him from me, but demurs to my first-asked price—that he directs you to offer me 10 pounds—which you can send me, $50: in gold—and that, (the terms being settled, &c.) he will advertise it very largely.[21]

I accept the terms offered—$50 in gold—and you can forward me the

"the most sweet and sonorous nocturn ever chanted in the church of the world." Included in *Songs before Sunrise* (1871) was his famous lyric "To Walt Whitman in America." For the story of Swinburne's veneration of WW and his later recantation, see Blodgett, 103–121.

   19. See 255. Hotten's letter (Feinberg; Traubel, II, 285–286) repeated the financial proposals related by Conway; see 269.

   20. Hotten was the publisher of this critical essay; see 269.

   21. See 267.

am't as soon as convenient. I repeat, that I distinctly reserve the right of printing the piece in a future edition of my poems.[22]

Sending best wishes & respects to editor & publishers, I remain.

272.   *To Anderson & Archer*[23]

ENDORSED: "Sent Anderson & Archer | Feb. 19, 1868." DRAFT LETTER.[24]

ATTORNEY GENERAL'S OFFICE,

Washington, February 19, *1868*

Your letter of 13th[25] was rec'd—

Please find herewith a check for $31:50, which I suppose is the am't of your bill for binding 90 copies, Leaves of Grass, at 35 cts.

Please put up 40 copies in good substantial wrapping envelope, & send me by express. Direct *Walt Whitman, Attorney Gen's Office, Treasury Building, Washington, D. C.*—Please keep the remaining 50 copies till I send some order about them.

You have overlooked one thing. When I called upon you 2d January,[26] we found a discrepancy in the two lists of sheets on hand—yours had it that Sheet B, 2d consisted of only 2wt sheets—while my list had it that Sheet B 2d consisted of 3wt sheets—I wish you to carefully count sheet B 2d & inform me how many there are—as it will decide how many of the deficient signatures of "Drum-Taps" etc.,[27] I will require to finish up the edition. Please acknowledge the reception of this, with check.

(check for $31:50 enclosed)

273.   *To F. P. and W. C. Church*

Washington, | February 21, 1868.

Messrs Church. | My friends,

I have now ready the prose article—(will make, I should think, about 14 printed pages)—which I mentioned to W. F. Church,[28] at an interview here not long since.

I cannot give you any complete description of the piece—but will say

22. WW excised the next paragraph: "Allow [me] to say to Mr. E. Routledge—I profoundly approve your idea & enterprise of a Magazine interlinking the two English-speaking nations, and, persevered in, I have no doubt it will be a triumphant success." See also Traubel, IV, 191.

23. See 256.1.

24. When Professor Holloway made his transcription in 1920, this draft letter was in the Henry Goldsmith Collection.

25. This letter is not known.

26. This reference to visiting Anderson and Archer, who had offices in New York, on January 2 is somewhat puzzling; there is no other evidence that WW was in New

that it takes up the subject of *Democracy* where the article by that name in the *Galaxy* of December, left it—and applies to Individuality—sketches the portrait of the ideal American of the future—also characterizations of the American woman—overhauls the Culture theory, shows its deficiencies, tested by any grand, practical Democratic test—argues that the main thing wanted for the literary, esthetic, & moral areas of the United States is to institute what must result in copious supplies, among the masses, of healthy, acute, handsome Individualities, modernized, & fully adapted to our soil, our days, city & country. The name of my piece is
Personalism.

Don't be alarmed at the (perhaps at first sight) oddity of the word[29]—it is the right title for the article, and will justify itself, & remain.

The piece is a following up of *Democracy*—& is, as a literary performance, I think better than that paper—& will arouse more attention. Of course there is nothing in it which you would demur to print in the magazine.

Are your plans such that you would probably like the piece for your April number? Could you print it positively as the leader? Please give me definite & immediate answers. The piece is all ready.

Walt Whitman.

274. *To Routledge & Sons*

ENDORSED: "Note to Routledge & Sons N. Y. |
Feb. 22 '68." DRAFT LETTER.

February 22, 1868.

Messrs. Routledge, (J. L. Blamire)[30] | Gentlemen:

Your letter reached me this morning, enclosing draft for Fifty Dollars, gold coin, deposit in Bank of New York—of which amount, paid me, for poem, (with reservation to myself of right to print in future book,) you will please consider this the receipt.

Please accept my respects to editor & house—with thanks to yourself for promptness.

York at this time. He was in Washington on December 30 and on January 17; see 261 and 267.

27. The 1867 edition appeared in many forms: *Leaves of Grass* by itself, with *Drum-Taps*, and with *Songs Before Parting*. See Allen, *Handbook*, 173.

28. WW intended to write W. C. Church.

29. Apparently WW coined the word "personalism," which Bronson Alcott introduced into American philosophy; see Allen, *Handbook*, 303. The essay appeared in *The Galaxy*, v (May, 1868), 540–547, though not as the lead article, and was later part of *Democratic Vistas*.

30. See 271.

275. *To Ellen M. O'Connor*

ADDRESS: Mrs. E. M. O'Connor, | at house of Mrs.
Price, | 279 East 55th street, | New York City.
POSTMARK: Washington D. C. | (?).

Washington, | February 24, 1868.

Dear friend,

Your letter reached me this afternoon. I am very glad indeed you
are coming home[31]—I already make calculations not only of resuming our
old talks & good times, but of the much news you will have to tell—also of
seeing little Jenny again—dear child, be sure she is not left out of account—Is Mrs. Channing[32] with you then? I send my friendliest remembrances & good wishes. And to my ever dear friends, Mrs. Price & family
—you know how much I think of them, & estimate them always, with love
& thanks—

It is between two & three o'clock p. m.—We have had a snowy day—
as I look out of my window the ground is white in every direction—William[33] has a bad cold, has not been down to work to-day, but has just come
down town, & is this moment sitting by my desk, reading the extra Evening *Star*—the fight between Congress & the President, about Secretary of
War,[34] rages furiously—The House will doubtless order *impeachment*
—& we are going to have exciting times generally—but I guess no appeal
to arms—

I have heard lately from my dear mother—she is well as usual—
Emma Price can tell you more directly about her, as I hear, (to my
great pleasure) that she has called on mother once or twice lately.[35] I am
well as usual—have not yet rec'd a copy of my English re-print[36]—but hear
that one is on the way—Mr. Swinburne, the poet, has sent me a handsome
copy of his *William Blake*[37] containing certain mention of me, which I will
show you when you come. Hotten,[38] the London publisher, has written me,
very handsomely, offering a fee, on every copy—Rossetti, the editor, has
also written me several letters, very satisfactory—I think you will like your
apartments, after you get used to them—it is a fresh, sweet, new house[39]—
that's a good deal—

31. Mrs. O'Connor had been in Providence, R. I.; see 269.
32. Her sister, Mrs. William F. Channing; see 143. WW visited the Channings in
Providence later in the year.
33. O'Connor had not been well for several weeks. Mrs. Whitman wrote to WW
on February 17: "i was in hopes mrs Oconor had returned for his sake. if he is not very
well it would probably make him more comfortable" (Trent).
34. On February 22 Johnson ordered the removal of Edwin M. Stanton, Secretary of
War. The President had suspended Stanton on August 12, 1867.
35. According to Mrs. Whitman's letter of February 12(?), Emma Price had

And now, dear friend, God bless you & little one, & a safe & speedy return to friends & home.

Walt.

276. *To F. P. and W. C. Church*

Washington, | March 3, 1868.

Messrs. Church. | Dear Sirs:

I sent you "Personalism"[40]—which I suppose you received Monday last. I should consider it a favor from you to have the piece set up as soon as convenient, first proof carefully read & corrected, & then three sets of proofs taken & mailed me here—One set I will read, and return immediately.

I think of offering the article in England,[41] probably to the Fortnightly Review—but of course any thing over there must be strictly subordinated to the appearance of the article here first—that is positive.

Can you let me have the proofs within a week or so?

I think of asking you $100 for "Personalism." I reserve the right of printing it in future book.

How about the little piece "Ethiopia Commenting"?[42] Will it not be practicable for you to print it in the April number? Certain poetical pieces of mine were arranged to appear soon in English magazine[43] & I should like the "Ethiopia" to precede them.

Walt Whitman

277. *To John Camden Hotten*

Washington | March 9, 1868.

Dear Sir:[44]

I thank you for the copy of my poems sent by you. It has just reached me. I consider it a beautiful volume. The portrait, as given in it, is, however, a marked blemish. I was thinking, if you wish to have a portrait, you might like to own the original plate of 1855 which I believe I can procure, in good order, & from which you can print a frontispice more

---

recently visited her during a snow storm (Trent).

36. The English edition of WW's poems was released on February 5; see *Rossetti Papers*, 297.

37. See 269.   38. See 270.

39. The O'Connors were living in the Burroughs' new home.

40. See 273.   41. See 281.   42. See 246 and 326.

43. WW overstated: only "Whispers of Heavenly Death" had been accepted for publication in England.

44. See 255.

creditable—as per impression enclosed. If so, send me word immediately. The price of the plate would probably be $40. gold—or 8 pounds. It would suit just such a volume, & would coincide entirely with the text in note & preface, as they now stand. If I receive your favorable response, I will, if possible, procure the plate, & send it to you by express—on receipt of which, & not before, you can send me the money. (I have sent to New York to see if I can procure the plate, & have not yet received any answer.)[45]

I will thank you to convey to Mr. Swinburne my heartiest acknowledgements for the copy of William Blake, (which has reached me)—& for his kind & generous mention of me in it.[46]

Walt Whitman

278. To F. P. (?) Church

ATTORNEY GENERAL'S OFFICE,

Washington. March 10, 1868

Mr Church. | My dear Sir,

I write a line to jog you about the proofs of *Personalism.* Is it being put in type? For reasons as in former note, I am anxious to have proofs as soon as possible.[47]

Walt Whitman

279. To C. B. Sellinghast

ATTORNEY GENERAL'S OFFICE,

Washington. March 12, 1868.

C. B. Sellinghast.[48] | Dear Sir:

I publish *Leaves of Grass* myself—& send it by mail, post paid, on receipt of the price, $3.

Address.

Walt Whitman
Washington | D. C.

45. For further discussion of the frontispiece, see 287.
46. See 269.
47. See 276. On March 25 W. C. Church reported that WW's second set of proofs had arrived too "late for us to make the corrections & I return it so that you can transfer them to the proofs before sent" (Feinberg).
48. I have not identified Sellinghast.
49. O. K. Sammis wrote to WW on April 6, 1860 (Feinberg), and was mentioned in 42.

280. *To Dr. O. K. Sammis*[49]

ENDORSED (in unknown hand): "Dr. O. K. Sammis."

ATTORNEY GENERAL'S OFFICE,

Washington. March 13, *1868.*

My dear Doctor,

Your note has just come to hand, stating that you intend a visit to Washington, & desire a situation. My friend, if that is your sole object here, & you depend upon any thing of that kind, (unless you have some special friend who has great influence, or offices at his disposal,) I seriously advise you against any such enterprise. I myself have no influence at all, being a mere clerk, & of low grade—& our office is in confusion—the Attorney General having yesterday resigned his place[50]—& it being very probable that the rest of the cabinet will follow before long. They are discharging many of the Department employes, & appointing none. For some months to come, indeed for the ensuing year, every thing will be unsettled & in suspense here[51]—

There is nothing new with me—nor in our family.

Yours, &c.

Walt Whitman

with friendliest regards.

281. *To Moncure D. Conway*   *3.18(?).* [*1868*]

ENDORSED: "went probably | March 18."[52]
DRAFT LETTER.

My dear Conway,

I send the accompanying article[53] in hopes you can do me the favor to dispose of it to an English magazine. The one I first think of is the Fortnightly Review. If not that, some other. I place the whole business, price, &c. in your absolute control. Only understand that the piece is to be pub-

50. Stanbery (see 177) sent a letter of resignation on March 11 and President Johnson acknowledged it on March 12. The correspondence appeared in the Washington *Daily Morning Chronicle* on March 14. Stanbery resigned in order to serve as one of Johnson's counsels during the impeachment proceedings.

51. A reference to the presidential election in the fall.

52. According to Traubel (II, 482), the endorsement read: "Draft of note to Conway about personalism—went March 18, '68. Looked over July 29, 1885."

lished here in the *Galaxy* for May. Some English magazine for May is what would suit best. In haste.

282. *To Edmund Routledge*

ENDORSED: "To | Ed Routledge | March 24 '68."
DRAFT LETTER.

March 22, '68 | (went 24th)

Ed. Routledge

In my note of January 17 last, sending "Whispers of Heavenly Death," I included a request for thirty copies of the magazine, containing the piece, whenever printed. If agreeable therefore, please request the New York house to send by express, at my expense, thirty copies of the "Broadway" containing the piece, to my address, Attorney Gen's office, here.

I propose, before long, to submit to you another piece, for the magazine, if approved.[54]

283. *To John M. Binckley*

ENDORSED: "March 24 | '68 | Note to Mr. Binckley."
DRAFT LETTER.

Washington | March 24, '68

My dear Mr. Binckley,[55]

In reference to the brief conversation between us a few days since, allow me in candor to say, that I should decidedly prefer to retain my present post as Record Clerk, the duties of which I feel that I can fulfil properly—& that I would therefore, as far as my personal choice is concerned, wish to be *not* thought of in view of the pardon clerkship.

53. On May 9 Conway informed WW: "I regret to say I was unable to do anything with the proof of Personalism. I tried several magazines, but they were already made up for their May numbers" (Traubel, IV, 10).

54. Since this is the last extant letter to Routledge, it is not known whether WW actually submitted another poem or article to *The Broadway*.

55. See 245. Binckley, who was in the Attorney General's office, replied on the same day: "Your wishes admit of easy compliance, since Mr Browning has resolved to make a vacancy of the post of pardon clerk" (Feinberg). The numerous changes made in this draft indicate that WW struggled to phrase his refusal tactfully.

56. Orville Hickman Browning (1806–1881) completed the unexpired term of Stephen A. Douglas after his death in 1861. Defeated for re-election in 1862, he established a law firm in Washington, and later actively supported President Johnson, who ap-

Only in case of *urgent wish* on your or Mr. Browning's part, would I deem it my duty to waive the preference mentioned, & obey your commands.

284. *To Orville Hickman Browning*

ATTORNEY GENERAL'S OFFICE,

Washington, April 7, *1868.*

Hon. O. H. Browning,[56] | Attorney General, *ad interim*
Sir:

In obedience to your request, I have carefully examined the papers, presented by Hon. Mr. Cavanaugh,[57] making grave charges against Judge Lyman E. Munson, Associate Justice, U. S. Courts of Montana Territory —& have prepared the following abridgement & abstract of said papers.[58]

Very respectfully,

Walt Whitman,
of A. G. office.

285. *To Abby H. Price*

ADDRESS: Mrs. Abby H. Price, | (new number) |
No. 331 East 55th street, | New York City.
POSTMARK: Washington, D. C. | Apr | 10.

ATTORNEY GENERAL'S OFFICE,

Washington. April 10, *1868.*

My dear friend,

I rec'd your first letter of about a month ago, (March 9)—I enquired of a friend in the revenue office, about the tax under the new law, & whether ruffles would be exempted, &c.[59]—& on or about the 11th

pointed him Secretary of the Interior in 1866. Browning was appointed Acting Attorney General on March 12. At the conclusion of Johnson's administration, he returned to private law practice.

57. James Michael Cavanaugh (1823–1879) was a member from Montana of the House of Representatives from 1865 to 1871.

58. With this letter is a twenty-page document in which WW summarized the affidavits alleging malpractice and the Judge's defense of his conduct. Although the case was apparently never brought to trial, Munson resigned on October 31. For an account of the affair and a digest of WW's report, see *PMLA*, LVIII (1943), 1099–1100.

59. WW had written in 1867 to Mrs. Price, a seamstress, about the possible exemption of ruffles from taxation; see 228.

March, I wrote you, what I had learned—viz: that they were to be exempted—& also all the gossip & news, about the O'Connors, & about myself, literary matters with me, and how I was situated here, and about things in general—*of course* a mighty interesting letter it must have been —and a dreadful loss not to get! for I infer by your second letter April 7, just rec'd, that you did *not* get it—which I deeply regret, for I don't like to be supposed capable of not responding to those that are almost the same as *my own folks*—(I put both the old & new No's on the address—perhaps that made it miscarry,) but let that go—

The changes in the Attorney Gen's office have made no difference in my situation—I have had the good luck to be treated with "distinguished consideration" by all the Attorney Gen's—Mr. Speed,[60] Mr. Stanbery, & the present one Mr. Browning—I couldn't wish to have better bosses—& as to the pleasantness & permanency of my situation here, it is not likely to be affected, as far as at present appears, unless Wade,[61] coming in power, should appoint Harlan,[62] or some pious & modest Radical of similar stripe, to the Attorney Generalship—in which case, doubtless, I should have to tumble out.

My dear friends, I often think about you all—Helen & Emily in particular, & wish I could look in upon you, Sunday afternoons—I warmly thank you for your hospitable offers—Give my best respects to Mr. Arnold & Mr. Price—

I shall have a piece in the Galaxy for May—it will be called "Personalism"—is a continuation of the piece on Democracy—shall have a poem soon, (perhaps in May No.) in the Broadway magazine[63]—

I am well as usual—the Impeachment is growing shaky[64]—it it a doubtful business—I am writing this at my table in office—as I look out it is dark & cloudy with a chill rain, but the grass is green & I see the river flowing beyond. With love,

Walt Whitman

I saw William & Ellen O'Connor last night—told them I should write

---

60. James Speed (1812–1887) was appointed Attorney General in 1864 by Lincoln; because he was opposed to Johnson's policies, he resigned on July 17, 1866.

61. Benjamin Franklin Wade (1800–1878), U. S. Senator from Ohio, was a bitter opponent of President Johnson.

62. James Harlan was the Secretary of Interior who had peremptorily fired WW; see 164. Harlan had resigned in 1866 and had returned to the Senate in the following year.

63. "Whispers of Heavenly Death" appeared in the October issue of *The Broadway;* see 262.

64. On April 9 the prosecution in the impeachment proceedings against Johnson concluded its arguments, and the defense opened.

65. A reference to a lost letter.   66. See 287.

you to-day—Both charged me to send you their love—little Jenny is well & active. I send you a newspaper same mail with this.

286. *To Louisa Van Velsor Whitman*

ATTORNEY GENERAL'S OFFICE,

Washington, | Thursday noon | April 16, *1868.*

Dearest mother,

Well, it is a dark cloudy day, & raining hard—the darkies were to have a great celebration here to-day, in honor of emancipation—they turn out here in real good style, on such occasions—but it is too wet for them to-day—Mr. Stanbery is quite ill, as you see by the papers—The Impeachment trial still goes on—I went up, that day,[65] but it was very crowded, & the air was so bad, I left, & went off & had a real good tramp, way up Georgetown, along the banks of the river—it is beautiful along there, of a fine day—So you see I am still able to get around.

There is nothing new in the office—the same old story—I have rec'd a number of papers from England with notices of my book, there—mostly friendly & favorable—more so than any here[66]—Mother, I am very sorry you have those pains in your face & head[67]—I shouldn't wonder if it was neuralgia—that is a violent inflammation of the nerves of the face & head—Mrs. Mix[68] used to have it very bad—O, I forgot I believe to tell you Mrs. Mix is living yet—she had a very bad spell, but got over it—Mother, I have just got your letter of 14th—& was glad to get it—I havn't seen William Velsor[69] for some time—will tell him when I see him—

Mother, I send a couple of papers same time with this—they are not much, but will do just for a change—poor old Uncle John[70]—he is failing then at last—I suppose George[71] is well, & having good times—I see him every day as I have his picture tacked up on the door of my desk in front—

67. On April 7 Mrs. Whitman said that she was "troubled with the dissiness in my head but to day i feel entirely free from it" (Trent).

68. A Washington acquaintance; see 181.

69. Probably a nephew of Mrs. Whitman, he was listed as a "teamster" in the 1869 Washington Directory. "Jo. Velsor," mentioned in 183 as a driver in the Quartermaster Department, was probably a brother.

70. Not identified.

71. In 1868 George lived with his mother in Brooklyn. He was an inspector for Moses Lane, chief engineer of the Brooklyn Water Works (see 31). On July 8 Mrs. Whitman wrote to WW: "Mr Lane makes strait for george [when there is trouble]. Jeff says george needent be uneasy about being discharged as long as lane is there" (Trent). George continued to build houses on speculation.

Good bye, dearest mother, & take good care of yourself, & dont work too hard.

Walt.

287. To John Camden Hotten

ENDORSED: "To Mr. Hotten | went April 25 '68."
DRAFT LETTER.

April 24   '68

To Mr. Hotten,

I am glad to hear you are having Mr. Conways potograph engraved in place of the bad print now in the book.[72] If a faithful presentation of that photograph can be given it will satisfy me well—of course it should be reproduced with all its shaggy, dappled, rough-skinned character & not attempted to be smoothed, or prettyfied—(if in time I send the following hints)—let the costume be kept very simple & broad, & rather kept down too, little as there is of it—preserve the effect of the sweeping lines making all that fine free angle below the chin—I would suggest not to bring in so fully the shoulders & bust as the photograph does—make only the neck,[73] the collar with the immediately neighboring part of the shirt delineated. You will see that the spot at the left side of the hair, near the temple, is a white blur, & does not belong in the picture. The eyes part, and all around the eyes, try to re-produce fully & faithfully, exactly as in the photograph.

I hope you have a good artist at the work. It is perhaps worth your taking special pains about, both to achieve a successfull picture & likeness, something characteristic, & as certain to be a marked help to your edition of the book. Send me an early *proof of the engraving—*

Thank you for the papers with notices in them[74]—& for your Acade-

72. Hotten wrote about the portrait on April 8 (Yale; Traubel, IV, 308). See also 277.

73. At this point in the draft WW crudely sketched a face, or "autoportraiture," as Traubel says (I, 210).

74. Hotten enclosed on April 8 a number of newspaper notices of the English edition of WW's poems. On April 12, Rossetti also sent clippings (Feinberg; Traubel, II, 123–124).

75. Rossetti informed WW that this review had been composed by a Mr. Robertson, "a Scotchman of acute intellectual sympathies." Rossetti had restored the passages "cut out by a less ardent Editor" (Feinberg; Traubel, II, 123).

76. *Littell's Living Age* printed notices on April 25 from *The London Review of Politics, Society, Literature, Art, and Science* (XVI [March 21, 1868], 288–289), on June 6 from *The Saturday Review* (XXV [May 2, 1868], 589–590), and on June 13 from *The Athenaeum* (April 25, 1868, 585–586); see IX, 4th series (1868), 251–252, 637–640, and 702–703. The critic in *The London Review* observed: "Walt Whitman is, indeed, the Turner of poets. Sometimes you find a mere blurred mass of colour; then an incomprehensible blaze of light; then a piece of apparent commonplace; and then a picture which overawes the beholder."

mia[75] criticism. Please continue to send any special notices. I receive them safely & promptly. The London Review notice is reprinted here in Littell's Living Age.[76] I should like to know who wrote the piece in the Morning Star[77]—it flushed my friends & myself too, like a sun-dash, brief, hot, & dazzling.

I have several things more to say, & will write again soon[78]—Also to Mr. Rossetti[79] to whom, meantime, please offer my friendliest, truest regards.[80]

288. *To A. Bronson Alcott*

ENDORSED: "To Mr. Alcott | April 26 '68."
DRAFT LETTER.

To Mr Alcott, | April 26 '68

Your kind & welcome letter came to hand.[81] Pardon me for not responding sooner. I esteem your friendly appreciation of "Democracy." I have just sent you "Personalism"—which is to be followed, in perhaps a couple of months or so, by another article,[82] addressing itself mainly to the question of what kind of Literature we must seek, for our coming America, &c. In the three articles (to be gathered probably in book) I put forth, to germinate if they may, what I would fain hope might prove little seeds & roots.

I am still living here in Washington—employed in a post in the Attorney General's office, very pleasantly, with sufficient leisure, & almost entirely without those peculiar belongings, that make the Treasury & Interior Dep't &c. clerkships disagreeable. I am, as ever, working on Leaves of Grass—hoping to bring it yet into fitter & fuller proportions. I am well as usual. My dear mother is living & well; we speak of you. I wish you to give my best respects & love to Mr. Emerson—

77. Rossetti also noted that the *Morning Star* "had a very handsome notice . . . but like all literary reviews in that paper a brief one" (Feinberg; Traubel, II, 124).
78. No other communications with Hotten are extant.
79. WW did not reply to Rossetti's letter of April 12.
80. WW deleted the next line of this draft—"I will think about the American agent too, & write"—his answer to Hotten's request on April 8 for the name of "a good agent" in America (Yale; Traubel, IV, 308).
81. This is a reply to Alcott's letter of January 9, in which he praised WW's "Democracy," and added: "I talked last evening with Emerson about your strong strokes at the thoughtless literature and Godless faith of this East" (Feinberg; Traubel, III, 243–244). Alcott noted receipt of WW's letter on April 28: "Say what men may, this man is a power in thought, and likely to make his mark on times and institutions. I shall have to try a head of him presently for my American Gallery: Emerson, Thoreau, and Walt" (*The Journals*, ed. Shepard [1938], 391). On the same day Alcott wrote to WW: "Yet think of the progress out of the twilight since your star dawned upon our hazy horizon!" (Feinberg; Traubel, III, 245). Alcott was so fond of the term "personalism" that he adopted it; see 273.
82. "Orbic Literature"; see 290.

289. To Louisa Van Velsor Whitman   *4.28–5.4. 1868*

ATTORNEY GENERAL'S OFFICE,

Washington | Tuesday afternoon | April 28, *1868*

Dearest mother,

I have received your letter of Saturday 25th this morning, & glad to hear from you indeed—I suppose by this time you have rec'd the letter I sent yesterday 27th[83]—I sent you the Galaxy, but I see by your letter that George had already bought one. I have seen the piece in Thursday's Times[84]—John Swinton sent me one—so you can enclose it to Jeff—I have just received a letter from England, enclosing other notices, &c.—Mr. Conway is very friendly—but my friend Col. Hinton,[85] (in his letter some weeks ago in the Rochester Express,) has given him, Conway, some pretty sharp cuts about his ridiculous anecdotes of me & you too[86]—Still Conway seems to mean all the good he can. But such descriptions of me as, *"he was never known to smile or laugh,"* is altogether too jolly—dont you think so?

Thursday evening 8 o'clock

Well, mother, I will again write a few lines—I have been out most all the afternoon—went up first to the Impeachment trial, & heard Mr. Evarts[87] speak a while, & then left, for it seemed too pleasant outdoors to stay in there—I took a long walk, & ride in the cars away out in the suburbs, & so back to dinner, & now this evening another walk—& have fetched in here at the office, to sit awhile, read the paper &c.—I received to-day another letter from old Mr. Alcott[88]—I sent him the Galaxy with "Personalism"—& he compliments me highly, & speaks of Mr. Emerson

---

83. Apparently not extant.

84. On April 23 "Monadnock" reported under "Affairs in England": "Of course you know that English and French critics admit but one American Poet. Bryant, Longfellow and the rest are only second and third rate English poets—the one American poet is Walt Whitman." The journalist quoted generously from the review of Rossetti's edition in the *Leader* by Edmund Yates (see 504). In a dispatch "From Great Britain" in the New York *Tribune* on May 9, G. W. Smalley commented hostilely on the favorable review of WW in *The Athenaeum*, and concluded: "Mr. Carlyle likens [WW] to a buffalo, useful in fertilizing the soil, but mistaken in supposing that his contributions of that sort are matters which the world desires to contemplate closely." On May 20 O'Connor wrote to Rossetti to inquire about the authenticity of Carlyle's remarks; see *Rossetti Papers*, 355–356.

85. Richard J. Hinton (1830–1901) was born in London and came to the U. S. in 1851. He trained as a printer, and, like James Redpath (see 61), went to Kansas and joined John Brown. In fact, but for an accident he would have been with Brown at Harper's Ferry. A man mistaken for Hinton was hanged. With Redpath he was the author of *Hand-book to Kansas Territory and the Rocky Mountains' Gold Region* (1859). Later he wrote *Rebel Invasion of Missouri and Kansas* (1865) and *John Brown and His Men* (1894). Apparently Hinton had suggested that Thayer & Eldridge print *Leaves of Grass;* see *The New Voice*, XVI (February 4, 1899), 2. Hinton served in the Union Army from 1861 to 1865, and saw Whitman while lying wounded in a hospital, a scene which he described in the Cincinnati *Commercial* on August 26, 1871. After the war Hinton wrote for

too & his friendliness to me—We have had a warm but very pleasant day —I am feeling very well—I only hope, dear mother, you are feeling well & in good spirits.

Friday evening, May 1.

Mother, your letter of Wednesday, 29th, came this forenoon—it was too bad you didn't get mine Tuesday, as I put it in the P. O. myself Monday—So you are not going to move at present—I too remain in the same place, but have been going to move all winter & the spring too—I have been in the office all day to-day—all the rest of the clerks wanted to go up to the Impeachment trial, but I didn't care to go.

I have received another paper from England to-day, with a tremendous big favorable notice of my book, between three & four columns, one of the friendliest notices yet written.[89] The English publisher of my book, Mr Hotten, sends them to me—

Saturday, noon—I am going off for the afternoon—Mr. Stanbery[90] is to speak on the trial, & I may go in & hear him a few minutes, but I guess I shall spend my half-holiday mostly in jaunting around in the open air. Every thing begins to look like summer here—the trees are all green—we are having it pretty warm to-day, but a little hazy—it is now 12 o'clock—the noon-bell has just rung, & I am off for the rest of the day—Take good care of yourself, dear mother—

Sunday afternoon—Mother, you see I am determined to make you out a letter—I have been sitting here in the office all alone, fixing up my new piece[91] for the Galaxy—for I have still another piece, besides those that have already appeared—Two have appeared, & now this is the third one, addressed to the literary classes—I want the Galaxy folks to print it in the July number, but they havn't sent me word yet whether they will or no. It

many newspapers. He defended O'Connor's *The Good Gray Poet* in the Milwaukee *Sentinel* on February 9, 1866. Hinton's article in the Rochester *Evening Express* on March 7 was a lengthy account of WW's "Fame and Fortunes in England and America," with quotations from O'Connor and Burroughs. Obviously pleased, WW sent it to friends, including Rossetti, who acknowledged it on April 12 (Feinberg; Traubel, II, 123). See also Traubel, II, 396; Kennedy, *The Fight of a Book for the World*, 19, 67, 110–111, 242; the Boston *Transcript*, December 21, 1901.

86. WW's friends could not forgive Conway the anecdotes he had related in his article in *The Fortnightly Review*; see 197.

87. William Maxwell Evarts (1818–1901) was chief counsel for Andrew Johnson during the impeachment trial. When WW heard him, he had just presented the opening arguments for the defense. As a reward for his services, Johnson appointed Evarts Attorney General later in the year; see 295. He was Secretary of State from 1877 to 1881 and U. S. Senator from New York from 1885 to 1891.

88. On May 5 Mrs. Whitman replied: "poor old alcot he must be very old seems to me (you remember walt that sunday morning we couldent have him)" (Trent).

89. On April 21 Hotten informed Rossetti that he had just sent WW "a most flattering review" by Charles Kent, the editor of *The Sun* (*Rossetti Papers*, 351).

90. According to the Washington *Daily Morning Chronicle*, Stanbery began his defense of Johnson on May 1 and concluded his address on May 2.

91. See 290.

is a pleasant day—we have had quite a rain storm yesterday afternoon & last night—I am going out at 6 o'clock to O'Connors to tea—Mother, I hope you are having a pleasant Sunday.

Monday forenoon, May 4.

Well, I had a quiet, agreeable sort of Sunday—wrote & read most of the forenoon, & rambled out in the afternoon—& went up to O'Connor's in the evening—he had two or three others there, visitors—O'Connors & Burroughs's are very hospitable to me, the same as they always have been—they are almost the only places I go—I send you a couple of papers same mail with this—I am going to send the MS of my piece to the Galaxy to-day, as I have just rec'd a note from them by mail this morning[92]—I suppose George is well, & busy—I should like to see you all. Love to you, dearest mother—I will write again next Monday.

Walt.

290. *To W. C. and F. P. Church*

Washington | April 30, 1868.

Messrs. W. C. & F. P. Church. | My friends:

I have now just ready an article intended as the third & concluding one to the two already published by you, on "Democracy" and "Personalism."

This is upon the general subject of a needed American *Literature, in the highest sense,* & of our imaginative, mental, &c. growths, home-born, appropriate to & towering high enough for, The States, & faithfully in the interests of their Democratic institutions. I have, of course, treated the subject in my own way—certain parts strong & earnest—but there is nothing in it to make the piece at all improper for the magazine—probably indeed may be found more appropriate & serviceable—more to rouse editorial & critical remark, &c—than the already published articles.

I propose to you to print it in the Galaxy *for July*. It will make from eleven to twelve pages in your new form & type. The name is

92. On May 2 F. P. Church advised that WW's manuscript would have to be received by the end of the following week if the article were to appear in the July issue (Feinberg).

93. On May 15 F. P. Church wrote that, after consultation with Mr. Sheldon (see 292), "I am obliged to come to the conclusion that for the present at least, it is best that it should not be published in The Galaxy" (Feinberg). The essay finally appeared in *Democratic Vistas.*

94. But see 292.

95. Hine (1827–1871) did an early oil painting of WW, the engraving of which was the frontispiece for the 1860 edition of *Leaves of Grass*. In 1889 WW observed of Hine's portrait: "I don't know but the best of all" (Traubel, IV, 378). Hine's reply to WW's letter is not extant, nor is WW's second letter written shortly before June 17. On that date Hine

Orbic Literature.[93]

The price, if satisfactory, will be the same as for each of the previous articles, viz: $100.[94] I reserve the right of printing it in future book. I can send it on immediately.

I think it will be best not to delay too long, as the interest in the thing is now up, something like a serial story. This is the conclusion, & I should like to have it in July number.

Walt Whitman.

291. *To Charles Hine*

ENDORSED: "Chas Hine | sent May 9 '68 | 800 Broadway | N. Y." DRAFT LETTER.

Sent May 9—'68

My dear Charles Hine,[95]

I received with gladness the authentic sign & proof that you are on hand & doing, viz. "Watsons Art Journal"[96] with notice &c.—I am anxious to see the picture. I am sure it must be a thing of beauty, glowing, human, & true. Believe me, my friend, I have not forgotten you, nor your old kindness & friendliness. Also Mrs. Hine & the daughter—to whom I send best remembrances.

As soon as I come to New York again, I will visit you at the studio. In the meantime, I send you by same mail as this a copy of my last edition, also a little book, written by Mr. Burroughs,[97] (a second Thoreau,) and a newspaper, with letter[98]—the book & letter all about my precious self—& I dare say may interest you. If the books are not brought by the carrier, you must send to p. o. for them. I have seen Faris[99] here, but now he has gone back to N. Y. I am working in the Attorney General's office—have a pleasant berth, moderate pay, but sufficient—

I am well, weigh nearly 200, & eat my rations every time. You must write, & let me know whether the books come safe.

wrote: "Be assured of the high estimate I place upon your gift, and the glowing thoughts to which you have given utterance. 'Leaves of Grass' forever! . . . My dear old friend, I love you" (Feinberg). WW visited Hine shortly before his death; see 399–400.

96.   In *Watson's Art Journal*, IX (April 25, 1868), 11–12, appeared " 'Sleep': Painted by Charles Hine." The article described his painting of a female nude, and concluded: "We know no picture of modern date that is in any way comparable with it. It is a work, necessarily sensuous, but utterly devoid of sensuality."

97.   *Notes on Walt Whitman, As Poet and Person* (1867).

98.   Hinton's letter in the Rochester *Evening Express*.

99.   The New York Directory for 1867–1868 listed Henry L. Faris, banker, and John E., broker.

292. *To Messrs. Sheldon & Company*

Washington, | May 18, 1868.

Messrs. Sheldon & Co.[1] | Dear Sirs:

Your note of 16th May, with draft for Seventy-Five Dollars, in pay for article *Personalism*, have safely come to hand.

Please accept thanks, &c. &c.

Walt Whitman.

293. *To Louisa Van Velsor Whitman*   6.6–8. 1868

ATTORNEY GENERAL'S OFFICE,

Washington. | Saturday afternoon | June 6, 1868

Dearest Mother,

I rec'd your letter day before yesterday—& am sorry you are troubled with rheumatism—it must be quite bad—Do you have any one to do the rougher house-work? I hope you have. Mother, every thing is pretty much the same with me—I remain very well, go around a good deal in the open air—we have it pretty hot in the middle of the day, & dusty—but the nights are beautiful—

I know the Mr. Simonson[2] you saw at the post office—he has been a sort of Deputy post master a good many years—Notwithstanding what he says, the Brooklyn p. o. has a very bad name, & a great many money letters sent there never get to their destination—but I should think by what you have said, that the carrier who brings your letters must be a good safe man—

We had the strangest procession here last Tuesday night, about 3000 darkeys, old & young, men & women—I saw them all—they turned out in

1. The April issue of *The Galaxy* announced that Sheldon & Co. had assumed financial control of the journal. The reply to this letter is in the Feinberg Collection. *The Galaxy* in 1868 was more than kind to WW and his friends. In March appeared O'Connor's satirical poem "The Ballad of Sir Ball," 328–333, about the authorship of Florence Percy's (Elisabeth Chase Allen) "Rock Me to Sleep." Of the poem Mrs. Whitman wrote on March 24: "it is signed W. i hope nobody will think you wrote it walt" (Trent). (For this controversy, see AL, XXIII [1951–1952], 330–331.) In April the magazine printed John Burroughs' "Before Genius," 421–426, in which he observed: "If we except 'Leaves of Grass' and Emerson's works, there is little as yet in American literature that shows much advance beyond the merely conventional and scholastic."

2. Joseph M. Simonson.

3. Sayles J. Bowen, a Republican, was elected mayor on June 1 by 74 votes. He was the candidate of Col. J. W. Forney and the Washington *Chronicle*.

honor of *their* victory in electing the Mayor, Mr. Bowen[3]—the men were all armed with clubs or pistols—besides the procession in the street, there was a string went along the sidewalk in single file with bludgeons & sticks, yelling & gesticulating like madmen—it was quite comical, yet very disgusting & alarming in some respects—They were very insolent, & altogether it was a strange sight—they looked like so many wild brutes let loose—thousands of slaves from the Southern plantations have crowded up here—many are supported by the Gov't.

Yesterday I went up to the Presidents to see the reception of the Chinese Embassy—there were eight or nine Chinese, headed by our Mr. Burlingame, who is head of them all, (O'Connor knows him quite well)—you will see the speech made to them by the President, in the papers—I think it is first rate[4]—

Sunday noon, June 7.

I am sitting awhile in the office—we are having a spell of hot oppressive weather—It is generally thought we clerks will get our extra compensation—but I wait to see whether Congress will pass it—if they do I will make you a present, mother dear—So you like the ticket, Grant & Colfax,[5] do you, mother? Well, I do, too—Chase[6] is cutting up, trying to get somebody to nominate him, & doing his best to injure the Republican ticket—He is just the meanest & biggest kind of a shyster—He tried the same game at Lincoln's second nomination—Mother, I send the Chicago News, No. 7[7]—have you rec'd the six others all safe? I have sent them all—

Monday forenoon, June 8. Nothing special to write about this morning, mother. We had a thunder-shower last night & very pleasant this morning—I was up to O'Connors as usual last evening to tea—they are all well. Well, I believe that is all—only to send you my love, mother dear—same to George—write all the domestic news, & about George's work, & the house.

Walt

4. The occasion for these ceremonies was the opening of trade and diplomatic relations with China. Anson Burlingame (1820–1870), U. S. minister to China, was appointed by the Chinese government in 1868 "Envoy Extraordinary and High Minister Plenipotentiary," in which position he was to arrange treaties with the U. S. and other countries.
5. Grant and Schuyler Colfax, Speaker of the House of Representatives, were the Republican candidates.
6. The New York *Times* of June 6 reported on "Mr. Chase and the Presidency—His Views of Party." At this time Samuel P. Chase was chief justice of the U. S. Supreme Court. For WW's relations with Chase, see 28.
7. WW evidently began sending the Chicago *Weekly News* early in May, for on May 5 Mrs. Whitman noted: "Walter i like the chicago news very much. i never saw one before. i wish whenever you have one you would send it to me" (Trent).

294. To Louisa Van Velsor Whitman   *7.10–13. 1868*

ATTORNEY GENERAL'S OFFICE,

Washington, | Friday afternoon, | July 10, 1868.

Dearest mother,

I rec'd your letter this morning. It is too bad you don't get my letters Tuesday, as I send them in ample time Monday—they are in the p. o. here by noon, & the mail don't close till about 6 p. m.—then the letters get in New York by ½ past 5 Tuesday morning—

We have had very hot weather—I thought about you—it is quite oppressive on me this summer—still I get along quite well—get along pretty well nights—but every time the middle of the summer comes round, I think I will never stay through another summer in Washington, if I can help it—

*Saturday noon—11th—*We are having a very hot day—How do you all like the nomination of Seymour and Blair?[8] It is a regular old Copperhead Democratic ticket, of the rankest kind—probably pleases the old democratic bummers around New York and Brooklyn—but every where else they take it like a bad dose of medicine—the democrats are dissatisfied here, the worst kind—

O'Connors have had quite a serious falling out with Mrs. Burroughs[9] —John is away yet—may call upon you on his way home.[10] Mrs. B. is a curious woman—but has been very kind to me—Of course you mustn't let on that you know any thing—only you might mention to him that I often write about the wife's & his kindness to me—but probably it is doubtful if he calls—

Mother, I am sitting here by my window in the office—I dont have the smell of any streets or gutters—but it is burning hot, & hardly any air stirring—fortunately we have moderate nights—& so I manage to get along—

Monday morning 13th

It still keeps hot, & no rain—I was up at O'Connor's a while last evening—Ellen O'Connor is quite sick—has a bad attack of dysentery—the rest are all well—

8. Horatio Seymour (1810–1886), former governer of New York, and Montgomery Blair (1813–1883), Postmaster General in Lincoln's administration.

9. In January, 1868, the O'Connors occupied rented rooms in Burroughs' new house; see Allen, 391. On March 13 Mrs. Whitman asked WW about Mrs. Burroughs: "how does mrs Oconor and she get along. mrs. Oconor thought they would not perhaps" (Trent). Mrs. Whitman alluded to the rift between the O'Connors and the Burroughs on August 19: "i suppose it makes you feel awkard to go to Mr Oconors, their not being friendly and you being friendly to both but when they [the O'Connors] move it will be different. its very disagreable to live in one house and not be on speaking terms" (Trent).

Nothing decided yet about who shall be attorney General[11]—every thing goes on as usual in the office—

Well, mother, I must close—it is now a little after 10—there is a pleasant breeze blowing in from the river, quite refreshing—Good by for the present, & love to you & all, mother dear.

Walt.

295. *To Louisa Van Velsor Whitman*

ATTORNEY GENERAL'S OFFICE,

Washington. | Friday noon, | July 17, *1868.*

Dearest mother,

I have nothing particular to write about, but I thought I would just write a line. I hope you have stood the hot weather, without giving out—& George too I hope he exercises more care about himself, because I think our family is more liable than many to the effects of the great heat & exposure to the sun—I have got along pretty well, but it has been awful hot—& continues so, though as I write here by my window, there has quite a cool breeze sprung up since I commenced writing—Fortunately, I sleep very well nights—there has been only one night I havn't slept comfortably—

We have a new Attorney General, Mr. Evarts, as I suppose you have seen by the papers—He hasn't made his appearance here yet—but is expected soon—I only hope he will be as agreeable for a boss as the others have been—but somehow I don't believe he will—I am really sorry to have Binckley go, for he was a good friend of mine—& Mr. Browning too —Mother, I do hope you will get through this awful spell, all right—it can't last much longer—& George too—Mother, don't look for the next letter till *Wednesday next*—I have had a letter from Jeff[12]—all are well & hearty, except Mat has some cough yet—take care of yourself, dear mother.

Walt.

Your letter has come to-day, mother—John Burroughs has returned— he has a good piece in Putnam's for August[13]—

10. According to Barrus (57), Burroughs visited Mrs. Whitman in late June.
11. Browning was still Acting Attorney General.
12. Jeff wrote at length from St. Louis on July 12: "We are all pretty well, all *very* well except Mat. She has a bad cough—and she has had it so long that I begin to feel quite anxious that she should be rid of it. I have had a doctor examine her lungs two or three times but he says they are not as yet to any extent affected" (Feinberg).
13. "A Night-Hunt in the Adirondacks," *Putnam's Monthly Magazine*, XII (1868), 149–154.

296. To Louisa Van Velsor Whitman   *8.13–17. 1868*

ATTORNEY GENERAL'S OFFICE,

Washington | Thursday noon, | Aug. 13, 1868.

Dearest mother,

Your letter has come this morning—I always read it through, &
then in the afternoon read it through a second time—every little item is
interesting—poor Mat, she has indeed had a narrow escape[14]—to think
how it might have happened by another hair's breadth—We are having
beautiful weather here—quite cool, except in the middle of the day—I am
feeling well as usual—nothing special or new in the office—all seems to go
on smoothly—Mr. Evarts is here—Ashton[15] has gone to New York for a
few days—I have just sent off quite a batch of letters to Hannah—

Saturday 15th—I took a sail down to Alexandria yesterday—it is six
or eight miles—you go down in a steamer, something like the Brooklyn
ferry boats—& to-day I have just been out for nearly two hours—so you
see I am not confined very closely—We have not much to do in the office
—It is beautiful weather again to-day, cool enough, and I feel very well—
It is probable that I shall not take my leave of absence for a few weeks
yet—I will send you good word—

There are a great many clerks dismissed, from the Treasury, War &
other Departments—several hundreds—& more to be dismissed—it makes
a good deal of distress—many have families—as far as appears at present,
I expect to stay on as usual—

It is now about one o'clock—a cool breeze is blowing in from the river
—Mother dear, I hope you are feeling well to-day, & every thing is going
smoothly—I hope George is well, & having good times—I suppose the
house must be most finished—You must tell me all about it, when you
write[16]—

Sunday forenoon—16th—   I am sitting here by myself in the office—
it is warm, but pleasant—It is pretty dull here in Washington now that
Congress is away—

Afternoon—½ past 3—   We have had a hot day so far—had a good
dinner—good roast beef & apple pie—had company to dinner—I have
come around to the office to sit in quiet awhile, by my big open window—
nice old window—I have spent so many quiet comfortable hours by it, I

14. The letters describing Martha's accident are evidently lost; probably WW sent
them to Hannah. On August 10 Jeff wrote to George: "Mat is pretty bad yet, can just get
around a little—very lame—but I think 'twill get away in a week or two" (Feinberg).
15. Assistant Attorney General; see 138.

shall be sorry enough when I leave it—I never get tired looking out, there is river & hills & gardens & trees—can see ten or twelve miles—& boats sailing—I am going up to O'Connors towards 7 o'clock as usual—I am working at my leisure on my little book[17]—I dont know whether I have spoken of it before—in prose—those pieces in the *Galaxy* form portions of it—it is on political & literary subjects—It is a real pleasure to me—the new edition of Leaves of Grass is all ready fixed—so I don't bother with it any more—

Monday forenoon—Aug 17— Well, Mother, I will close up my letter, & send it off to-day—I went out to O'Connors as usual last evening & staid till after 11 o'clock—They have got another house, & move in about a month—We are all quite busy to-day in the office—Mr. Evarts & Ashton are both here now, & we have to fly around—Well I enjoy it just as well when I am busy during office hours, or rather I like it better—the pleasant weather continues—we need rain—dear mother, how are you getting along, & how is the rheumatism?

Love to you & all.

Walt.

297. *To Louisa Van Velsor Whitman*

ATTORNEY GENERAL'S OFFICE,

Washington | Monday forenoon | August 24, 1868

Dearest mother,

I send you some envelopes—they are already stamped—I send you one with Mat's address, & one to Han, so you will have them ready when you want to write. I rec'd your letter of last Wednesday—I hope it will work so that you can have apartments in George's new house, if possible—it must be any thing but agreeable there in Atlantic street, on some accounts, but there is always something—I have not been satisfied with my boarding place[18]—so several weeks ago, I tried another place & room for a couple of days & nights on trial, without giving up my old room—Well, I was glad enough to go back to my old place & stay there—I was glad enough I hadn't given it up—there are some things I don't like, but there are others very good indeed—it is situated in the healthiest, sweetest part

---

16. Mrs. Whitman replied on August 19 that she expected to move into the new house on October 1 (Trent).

17. *Democratic Vistas*, which was printed in 1871.

18. At 472 M Street. See also 300.

of Washington—two of our boarders, clerks, have left—they have lost their places, one in the War, and the other in the State Department—

It is overcast here to-day, but warm—I enjoy it—go around in the open air a great deal, & take things moderate—want to see you, dear mother, very much indeed, but don't think I shall leave till latter part of September—I do hope you are feeling quite well, & not working too hard—

You say you think I like Washington so much[19]—Well I am satisfied here, but not particularly attached to the place—only I think it is better for me as things are, & better all round—if it could only be so that I could come home for a little while, & frequently, I should want nothing more —but one mustn't expect to have every thing to suit perfectly—

I am feeling well as usual—Now that the awful long hot spell is over, I can hardly believe I have stood it so well—& you, too, mother dear, seem to have got along a great deal better than I would have expected— Things are dull enough in Washington, but it suits me just as well—Mr. Evarts has gone home—he has a farm at Windsor, Vermont—his family lives there—he has a large family of children—Ashton is running the office—Love to Georgy & all—Good bye, dear mother.

Walt.

The 50ᶜᵗˢ is for Ed.

298. *To William Livingston Alden*

Washington, | August 27, 1868.

My dear Mr. Alden:[20]

Would the enclosed be considered opportune—& of use to you for *The Citizen?* As it has been printed before, it would *not* be proper to put "For *The Citizen*" over it—but just print it plainly. Of course it is gratuitous—& I accompany it with best respects to yourself. I have not forgotten your kind invitations to furnish an original piece for the paper—& hope one day to have something which will be suitable. I am writing very little lately. Should you print the piece, I wish you to do me the favor to send ten copies by mail to my address here.

Walt Whitman
Attorney General's Office.

19. On August 19 Mrs. Whitman had written: "i dont beleive you ever would be contented any where else. i dont wonder at it for i think you have more true friends there than any other place (i mean those not related to you of course)" (Trent).
20. See 265. According to Prof. Rollo G. Silver, "A Broadway Pageant," which had been published in *Drum-Taps,* was reprinted on September 5 in *The Citizen;* see *AI*

299. *To Louisa Van Velsor Whitman*   *8.30–31. 1868*

ATTORNEY GENERAL'S OFFICE,

Washington. | Sunday forenoon, | August 30, 1868.

Dearest mother—

Well, here I am, sitting alone in the office, Sunday, writing again to you, dear mother. I rec'd your letter last week, all right. It is pleasant weather here, but warm—we had a heavy rain night before last, which laid the dust. There is nothing new with me, or in the office. Mr. Evarts still remains away, up on his farm at Windsor, Vermont, with his family. Ashton runs the office—Mrs. A. returned to Washington last evening, after two months' absence—she left her little boy in New York—she is not well.

The O'Connors expect to move the coming week—They have got a nice little new house, two story, five rooms—it is about four or five blocks from where I live—they pay $30 a month—They are all well as usual—the Burroughs's the same—

You would be amused to see some of the visitors I have now & then— One was a middle-aged, brown-complexioned lady, a great spiritualist & lecturess—she broke off in the midst of the conversation—then after a while told me that she had been spoken to by the spirit of Abraham Lincoln, and begged me to excuse her, as she wanted to talk with *that sperit* —I politely told her I would excuse her under the circumstances—& off she went.

Then another day a tall well-drest man, a perfect stranger, came, & said he had seen a good deal about me in the papers—said he had been an officer in the army—& wanted me to get him a place under government, as he was hard up—I got rid of him as gently as I could—but yesterday he came again & wanted me to let him have $10!—So you see my official life, with all its monotony, is not without a little fun, now & then, for a change.

Then I must tell you that a lady, a Mrs. McKnight,[21] looks & acts quite a good deal like our Mary, has called upon me, a few days since—& I will tell you what for. She is quite a portrait painter, & very ambitious of being a first-rate artist. At present she seems to be tolerably good. Two of her pictures I have seen, are real good—Well she wants to make a portrait of my beautiful countenance for herself to keep, & came to ask me to

VIII (1937), 420.

21. The 1869 Washington Directory listed Mrs. Sarah R. McKnight, artist; see also WW's address book (*LC* #109). Since WW did not subsequently refer to her, it is doubtful that he sat for his portrait.

sit for her—Well I consented—but don't think I shall begin until I return from my leave—So you see I have visitors & applications of all sorts—

Monday forenoon, | Aug. 31.

Well, mother, it is the last day of summer—we have had it very hot & melting here for two or three days—but there is a cool fresh breeze blowing in here, as I finish my letter—it is quite pleasant, as we have had some fine showers lately—I hope this will find you feeling well & in good spirits, dearest mother. Love to Georgy & all—

Walt.

300. *To Louisa Van Velsor Whitman*

ATTORNEY GENERAL'S OFFICE,

Washington. | Monday forenoon, | Sept. 7, 1868.

Dearest Mother—

Your letter came Saturday, with the acc't of the accident & sudden death of little Andrew[22]—poor little child—I believe I have never seen him—it was sad enough—but the poor young one is out of this world of sin & trouble—& I don't know as we have any cause to mourn for him—

Mother, my leave of absence will commence early next week, but I will send you word two or three days before-hand, when I shall come on. I have a good long leave, & want to rest myself as much as possible, & have a change of scene, & a quiet time, & no literary or other work to bother me—only just have a good quiet moderate time, for somehow I feel as if I wanted to throw off everything like work or thought, for a while—& be with my old mammy at least a good part of the time—

Mr. Evarts is still away—O'Connor was to move to-day, but it is showery, & he has postponed it till Wednesday—I was up there last evening, & had tea & spent the evening.

I wrote to Han Saturday last,[23] & enclosed your letter in mine—I am still at Mrs. Benedict's[24] 472 M st.—find it about as good as I could probably get anywhere—most of the boarders have left—I and *another young man* are the only ones left—they were in the Departments, & were

22. This was one of Andrew's sons, whose accidental death at age five was reported in the Brooklyn *Eagle* on September 2; see Allen, 397–398. On May 14 Mrs. Whitman had written of Andrew's wife Nancy, a whore and an alcoholic: "she drinks and every thing else thats bad." Nancy had recently had twins, one of whom had died: "the children is sent out to beg by the day and her brother the one to the court house wants to get the 3 children away from her and have them put in some institution" (Trent; Gohdes and Silver, 196). Mrs. Whitman in this letter and again on June 25 urged her son to support Nancy's brother; WW's replies are lost.

discharged—Many have been discharged within the last two months, & many more the end of this month are expected to be. It makes great misery among some, especially with families—O'Connor & Burroughs still retain their places—

Well, Mother, the summer is pretty well over—they say the folks are coming home from the country, &c—I am glad I didn't take my leave 1st of August, as I expected to, at one time—but was disappointed—When you get this I wish you to write one more letter—but no more till you see me—I think it is going to be a fine day—I am feeling well—

Well, I have a long job of copying to do for Ashton, so I will wind up my letter, & set about it—I shall write once more before I come—Good bye for this time, dear Mother.

Walt.

301. *To Abby H. Price*

ADDRESS: Mrs Abby H. Price, | 331 East 55th street, | bet 1st & 2d av's. | New York City. POSTMARK: (?) | Sep | 8.

Washington, | September 7, 1868.

Dear Abby:

I have leave of absence commencing first of next week, and intend coming on to New York, for a while, to spend the first part of it. Are you so fixed that you can give me a room? You must answer candidly no, if not —please write at once—I am well as usual—nothing very new or important with me. The advent of the new Attorney General, Mr. Evarts, does not seem likely to affect my position here.[25] But there have been many dismissals of clerks in the Departments. The O'Connors are well—the little girl has picked up amazingly—goes about, indeed, as strong & nimble as a grasshopper—

In a late letter, Mother said she had not seen any thing of Helen or Emily for some time—I suppose you have been off in the country.

Love to all—& good bye for the present.

Walt.

---

23. This letter is not known.
24. WW had been living with the Benedicts since February, 1867; see 218.
25. But on October 9 O'Connor wrote cryptically to WW: "I had a long and free talk with [Ashton] about Mat Pleasants and Evarts, in connexion with you, which I must tell you about when we meet. It made me feel quite anxious, but I guess all's right, while Ashton is there. Pleasants is a miserable devil. I wish I had power in that office for a little while. I'd put a spoke in the wheel of his vendetta, which would carry it and him to a safe distance" (Feinberg).

302. *To Abby H. Price*

ADDRESS: Mrs. Abby H. Price, | 331 East 55th
street, | bet 1st and 2d Av's, | New York City.
POSTMARK: Washington, D. C. | Sep | 14.

ATTORNEY GENERAL'S OFFICE,

Washington. | Monday, | Sept. 14, *1868*

Dear Abby,

I shall come on in the train that leaves here in the middle of the
day, to-morrow Tuesday, 15th, & gets in New York at 10 at night—so I
shall be up there by or before 11 to-morrow night—(*to-night* for you reading this.)

I am really pleased that you can accommodate me, & make great
reckoning of being with you, & of my room, &c—but wish [to] have it distinctly understood, in all friendship, that I *pay* for *my room*, &c, just
the same as any body else—*positively* I will not come on any other terms
—& you must just let it be as I say this time—I have lots of money—in fact
untold wealth—& I shall not feel right if you undertake to alter this part
of my programme—I am feeling well & hearty—I wish you to read my
piece[26] in the "Broadway London Magazine," just out—it was written for
you among the rest—In a few hours I shall be with you.

Walt.

303. *To Byron Sutherland*

331 East 55th street, | bet. 1st and 2nd Av's— | New York—

September 20, 1868.

Byron Sutherland, | Dear young man,

I have received your letter of September 12,[27] & was well pleased
to hear from you. I have many times thought of you—for I must tell you,
Byron, I retain just the same friendship I formed for you the short time
we were together, (but intimate,) in 1865.

I think, at that time, I was a clerk in the Interior Department. I was
dismissed from there—but was appointed by the then Attorney General,
Mr. Speed, to a moderate place in his Dep't. I have been in that Dep't.

26. "Whispers of Heavenly Death."
27. Sutherland (see 165 and 167) was now preparing to be a teacher at the State
Normal School at Edinboro, Pa. He wrote after he had seen reviews of WW's poetry in
The New Eclectic Magazine, II (July, 1868), 325–329, 371–375: one was a translation of
Freiligrath's article in the Augsburg *Allgemeinen Zeitung* (see 339), and the other was a
reprint of an English review of the Rossetti edition. In the same issue of the magazine the
editor termed WW "a monstrosity." Sutherland reported details of his academic program
on October 8. Both of his letters are in the Feinberg Collection.
28. The article in the Rochester *Evening Express;* see 289.

ever since—have a pleasant situation—have been promoted—& have now served under four successive Attorney Generals.

It is rather dull in Washington—but I make out quite comfortably—walk & ride around a good deal. Byron, I am still living in the same house, 472 M street, near 12th, where you staid with me a little while in 1865—and where you would be truly welcome to your old friend if you would come & stop with him again.

There is nothing very new or special with me. I have excellent health, eat my rations every time, and am I suppose full as fat and brown and bearded & *sassy* as ever.

I will send you, by same mail with this, a newspaper, with a piece written by a young man, Col. Hinton,[28] a friend of mine, some time since, about me, that may interest you—but he plasters it on pretty thick.

As you see by the heading of this letter I am now in New York. Your letter was sent on to me here. I am on furlough, which expires last of October, when I shall return to Washington. While here I spend much of my time with my dear Mother, in Brooklyn—she is hearty & cheerful, though nearly 73.

My address, for some four weeks to come, will be as at the heading of this letter. After that, at Washington, D. C.

Well, I believe that is all, this time. Byron, I send you my love & friendship, dear soldier boy—and now that we have found each other again, let us try, as far as may be, to keep together.

Walt Whitman

304. *To Peter Doyle*

ENDORSED: "3d letter | Sept 25 | letters sent | 1st
18th Sept. | 2d—22 | 3d—25th | 4th—29 | 5th
Oct 2 | 6th—Oct 6 | 7th Oct 9. | Oct 9—sent papers
to | P. D. Harper's[29] & Star | Charley Sorrell—
Clipper[30] | Wm Sydnor—Sporting Life | Jas
Sorrell[31]—Sporting Life."[32] DRAFT LETTER.

N. Y. | Sept 25 | '68 | 3d letter.

Dear Boy,[33]

I rec'd your second letter yesterday—it is a real comfort to me to get such letters from you, dear friend. Every word does me good. The

29. These "papers" probably included the September 26 issue of *Harper's Weekly*, which contained some of Thomas Nast's brutal cartoons aimed at the Democratic party.

30. New York *Clipper*, "The Oldest American Sporting and Theatrical Journal"; see also 310.

31. The Sorrells were evidently brothers and drivers. William Sydnor was described in an address book as "driver car boy on Pittsburgh's car 7th st" (*LC* #108); see also 311.

32. A weekly sports magazine; see Mott, III, 218.

33. Since WW's first two letters to Peter Doyle are not extant, this is the beginning

Star came all right, & was quite interesting. I suppose you got my second letter last Wednesday. There is nothing new or special to write about to-day—still I thought I would send you a few lines, for Sunday. I put down off hand, & write all about myself & my doings, &c. because I suppose that will be really what my dear comrade wants most to hear, while we are separated.

I am doing a little literary work, according as I feel in the mood— composing on my books. I am having a small edition of the Leaves of Grass for 1867, fixed up & printed. This & some other things give me a little occupation. Upon the whole though I don't do much, but go around a great deal—eat my rations every time, sleep at night like a top, & am having good times so far, in a quiet way, enjoying New York, the society of my mother, & lots of friends. Among other things I spend a portion of the day, with the pilots of the ferry boats, sailing on the river. The river & bay of New York & Brooklyn are always a great attraction to me. It is a lively scene. At either tide, flood or ebb, the water is always rushing along as if in haste, & the river is often crowded with steamers, ships & small craft, moving in different directions, some coming in from sea, others going out. Among the pilots are some of my particular friends— when I see them up in the pilot house on my way to Brooklyn, I go up & sail to & fro several trips. I enjoy an hour or two's sail of this kind very much indeed.[34] My mother & folks are well, & are engaged just these times in the delightful business of moving. I should assist, but have hired a substitute in the shape of a stout young laboring man.

I send you, by mail, a copy of *the Broadway*, with the piece in[35] the same as I had in the car one day. It will not interest you much, only as something coming from me.

of an extensive correspondence. Doyle, however, had written on the day WW had sent his first letter. Doyle's unpublished letter in the Barrett Collection is characteristic:

Washington Sep 18

Dear Walt,
      I could not resist the inclination to write to you this morning. it seems more than a week since i saw you. there is hardly anything of interest transpired since you went away except occasionly some one inquires for the *Magor* or the *General* or some familiar name which no doubt which you have heard so often. Dear Walt, I have examined that book (Pollards History) [*The Lost Cause: A New Southern History of the War of the Confederates* (1866)] and i am very much displeased with it. i find it is quite the opposite from what i was led to believe. i thought it mentioned the movements of the different companys & Regiments. i am sorry that i made such a mistake because the Book is of no interest to me.
      inclosed you will find something from this morning Cronicle. it seems the Washington Papers has you right for once. i am very impatient to hear from you to know that you are doing well. Dave & all the rest of the Rail Road boys is well & sends their best respects. Mother had a very sick headache when i left home this morning. i have to cut this short as i write a part of it while the car is in motion.
      farewell

Peter Doyle

I think of you very often, dearest comrade, & with more calmness than when I was there—I find it first rate to think of you, Pete, & to know that you are there, all right, & that I shall return, & we will be together again. I don't know what I should do if I hadn't you to think of & look forward to.[36]

Tell Tom Hasset,[37] on No. 7, that I wish to be remembered to him particular. Pete, I hope this will find you entirely well of your cold. I am glad to hear that your mother is all right of her cold. This is the time of year when they are apt to be pretty troublesome. I should like to have seen that match played between the Nat. & Olympics.[38]

305. *To Dr. William Francis Channing*

New York, | September 27, 1868.

My dear Dr. Channing:[39]

I yesterday received your kind note. I gladly accept your invitation & hospitality. My leave of absence continues for some time yet, & I should probably like to visit you for a few days, just subsequently to the middle of October—But I will write you a day or two before I come.

I send my best respects & love to Mrs. Channing. As I write we are having a rainy, dark sulky Sunday—after a rainy night. I am well & quietly enjoying holiday.

I wish you & wife to read my last piece[40] in *The Broadway* London Magazine for October. You can get it at any good bookstand.

Walt Whitman.

Doyle referred to the following "Personal" in the Washington *Daily Morning Chronicle* on September 18: "The newspaper gossips have been too fast by several weeks in sending Walt Whitman, the poet, on his recreating tour to Long Island. He has been closely confined to his duties in the Attorney General's office all summer, and only on Wednesday last departed to 'loaf and invite himself' at Montauck Point, on the eastern shore of Long Island. He will be absent several weeks." Probably WW had suggested this somewhat misleading puff to the *Chronicle*. In 1895 Doyle informed Bucke and Traubel: "Walt used often to put a piece in Forney's Washington *Chronicle*" (CW, VIII, 10).

Doyle's second letter on September 23, known through a typescript in the Lion Collection, was signed "Pete the Great" and referred to a visit "to the Theatre to see the Black Crook."

34. At this point WW inserted a direction to himself: "Mention the two letters I have sent."

35. "Whispers of Heavenly Death."

36. WW crossed out the following: "I have been with M. (the lady that was there [in] W[ashington] . . ."

37. Perhaps Thomas Hassett, listed in the Washington Directory as a laborer. The name is spelled Hassett in 314.

38. The Washington Nationals defeated the Olympics 21 to 15 on September 21.

39. Channing (see 143) extended the invitation on September 24 (Feinberg).

40. "Whispers of Heavenly Death."

306. *To William D. and Ellen O'Connor*

ADDRESS: William D. O'Connor, | Light House
Bureau, | Treasury Department, | Washington, |
D. C. POSTMARK: New York | Sep | 28.[41]

New York, | September 27, 1868.

Dear friend,

I received your note,[42] with Ferdinand Freilegrath's[43] address, at Cologne. I have called on Mr. Westermann,[44] who seemed to think, upon the whole, that the best way to reach F. F. would be to direct to him to care of his publisher, J. G. Cotta, at Stuttgart, Germany. I should like to make up a package for F. F.—but most that I want to send him is there in Washington. Still, I may attempt it here. I will write you further about it.[45]

I am having pleasant quiet times here—am occupied a little, & loafe around a great deal—am having fixed up, & bound, (partly printed too,) the remainings of Leaves of Grass, edition 1867—as there are none on hand, & there is a small demand. Am also writing &c a little.

My dear mother I find in unusual health & spirits, for one of her age. We are moving into the new quarters—much more agreeable & roomy, when settled, than the old ones. My brother George is well & hearty. Eddy the same. Mother sends her love to you & Nelly.

I received yesterday a kind note from Dr. Channing,[46] offering me hospitality at Providence. I shall gladly accept—shall certainly make them a visit of a few days before I return to Washington.

I am rooming at Mrs. Price's, but spend a great part of every day with Mother, always taking dinner there. The journey to & fro, & especially crossing the ferry, & resuming my acquaintance with the pilots, is quite a part of my pleasure here.

I had quite an interview *tete-a-tete* with John Swinton a few nights ago. He is much more deeply impressed with *Leaves of Grass* than I had supposed—said that the more he read it, the more it imprest him with the meanness & superficiality of all current literature & journalism—went on in a strain that would have answered your & John Burroughs's extremest demands, &c.[47]

Swinton has lately been posting himself about William Blake, his

41. A draft of this letter, in the Feinberg Collection, appears on the verso of 308.
42. O'Connor's letter of September 16 (Feinberg; Traubel, II, 431–432).
43. See 339.
44. Bernard Westermann, publisher and importer of books, whose office was at 440 Broadway.
45. See 312.   46. See 305.
47. The enthusiasm of Swinton (see 37) for WW was unbounded. On September 25 he wrote: "I am profoundly impressed with the great humanity, or genius, that expresses itself through you. I read this afternoon in the book. I read its first division which I never before read. I could convey no idea to you of how it affects my soul. It is more to me than all other books and poetry" (Feinberg; Traubel, II, 339). See also 307.

poems—has the new London edition of W. B. in two vols.[48] He, Swinton, gives me rather new information in one respect—says that the formal resemblance between several pieces of Blake, & my pieces, is so marked that he, S, has, with persons that partially know me, passed them off temporarily for mine, & read them aloud as such. He asked me pointedly whether I had not met with Blake's productions in my youth, &c—said that Swinburne's idea of resemblance &c was not so wild, after all. Quite funny, isn't it?[49]

Tell John Burroughs I send him my love, & I wish you to let him have an opportunity of reading this letter, if he desires to. Charles Eldridge the same.

Is Ashton there, & well—& what news in the office?

To Nelly.

Dear Nelly.

I am writing this in my room at Mrs. Prices. We had rain all last night, and now a rainy, cloudy, dark Sunday. I was down late to breakfast this morning—had a good breakfast though—nobody home but Mrs. Price & Mr. Arnold[50]—I like the latter more than formerly—after breakfast we sat leisurely & had a good chat—subject, the Roman Catholic religion—anent of Mrs. Rein's sister & adopted sister being Catholics. When I rose I said I was going up to my room to write to you & William—there were warm expressions from both—Mrs. Price charged me to give her love to you, to William, & to Jeannie—Mr. A. said "Give my love to Mrs. O'Connor, she is a woman I like—Mr. O'Connor I believe I have never seen." Good bye for the present, dear friends.

Walt.

307. *To John Swinton*   [*9.28(?). 1868*]

ENDORSED (in unknown hand): "Mem sent to John Swinton | for publication by WW."

(qu?) To make a *Personal* item or ¶ for "*Minor Topics.*"[51]
qu? To commence for instance
        "With the bright, crispy autumn weather,

48. *Songs of Innocence and of Experience* and *Poetical Sketches*, published by Pickering and edited by R. H. Shepherd, appeared in 1868; see Geoffrey Keynes, *A Bibliography of William Blake* (1921), 268–269.

49. On October 9 O'Connor commented: "Swinton's discovery of the resemblance in form between Leaves of Grass and Blake's poetry, is in my humble opinion, a mare's nest of the first water. (Irish!!) The resemblance is extremely superficial—about as much as between the Gregorian chant, bellowed by bull-necked priests with donkey lips, and a first-class, infinitely varied, complex-melodied Italian opera, sung by voices half-human, half-divine" (Feinberg).

50. A friend of the Prices (see 12).

51. The news item appeared under "Minor Topics" in the New York *Times* on Oc-

WALT WHITMAN again makes his appearance on the sidewalks of Broadway," &c &c

(three or four lines on *personnel* as lounging along)

---

item   the obstinacy,[52] pertinacity or continuity of Leaves of Grass & of the personality of W. W. in current Literature notwithstanding all attacks & objections

---

The poems have been republished in England, & are being translated by Freiligrath for publication in Germany.[53]

---

allude to the proposed prose work—"Democratic Vistas."

Cant you put in the idea of an obstinate, tenacious, determined *living man*, appearing with a will, in our easy-going imitative literature.

308. *To Peter Doyle*   9.29. [1868]

ENDORSED: "4th letter."[54] DRAFT LETTER.

Sept 29.

Dear boy Pete,

It is splendid here to-day, & I am feeling first-rate. We have had quite a dark & rainy spell—but now the prospect is good weather, clear sky, bright sun, coolish, & no dust. I shall spend an hour or two on the river to-day. Your letter of 27th,[55] Sunday, came this morning. Also two *Stars*, 25th & 26, the latter with Hinton's speech, the other containing an item about me.[56] The previous *Star* arrived with your note of 23d, written just as you were going to see the Black Crook[57]—& next morning another Star came. Peter, you are a good boy, & shall have your reward in Heaven, if not on earth.[58]

tober 1. Swinton followed the outline proposed by WW, and even quoted at places. The first sentence was WW's except for the substitution of "New York" for "Broadway." Swinton wrote: "The pertinacity of the existence of these 'leaves' is certainly remarkable in the face of all attacks and objections; and his admirers can only attribute it to the appearance in our easy-going, imitative literature of an obstinate, tenacious, determined *living American man.*" The Washington *Star* reprinted the article on October 2. See also *WWR*, VI (1960), 72–73.

52.   WW put a question mark above this word.

53.   This was an exaggeration of Freiligrath's intention, or wishful thinking; see 339.

54.   At the top of WW's letter he struck out this sentence: "To me they tell every thing."

55.   Doyle's chatty letter (Morgan) was filled with references to his comrades: "Walt you cant think [how] much pleasure i derive from our letters. it seems to me Very often that you are With me and that i am Speaking to you."

56.   The *Star* on September 26 reported that Hinton spoke on women's rights before the Universal Franchise Association. On the preceding day the newspaper contained a report on the payment WW received from *The Broadway Magazine:* "It is needless to add that no other poet, except Tennyson, commands such a price in England." The Washing-

Now how about that cold? I see you went to work Saturday. You seem to be under the weather more than I thought. Dear comrade, I hope this will find you all right & well as ever. I suppose you are working this week. Yesterday I spent most of the day in Brooklyn helping the folks to finish up the moving business. Got through just after dark. I have not been to any amusements yet. Somehow I dont seem to care about them,[59] & I go around enough during the day. There is considerable political excitement here—banners swung across the streets almost every block, & big transparences in front of the different headquarters. I have seen several splendid torch-light processions, & outdoor meetings, &c. Of course the great majority in New York & Brooklyn is for Seymour & Blair.

To Jim Sorrell:[60] Dear Jimmy: You may not understand it, what that lady said about the bedfellow business, but it's all right[61] & regular—besides, I guess you understand it well enough. Jimmy, dear boy, I wish you was here with me—we could have such good times. I send you my love—& to Charley[62] the same—Mention how Charley's young one is getting along—

I will now bid you good bye for this time, my loving friend, & God bless you, dear comrade, & keep you all right. I will write a line to No. 6,[62.1] & will speak to the other boys in my next.

---

309. *To Peter Doyle*   *10.2. [1868]*

ENDORSED: "5th letter | Oct 2. | To Pittsburgh[63] | To Harry Hurt."[64] DRAFT LETTER.

Oct 2

Dear boy and Comrade[65]

You say it is a pleasure to you to get my letters—well, boy, it is a

ton *Daily Morning Chronicle* on September 26 also noted that WW had received "fifty pounds in gold." According to his letter of October 9, O'Connor had inserted the item in the *Star:* "It made a great sensation in Washington, and your stock went up enormously" (Feinberg).

57. *The Black Crook* opened at the National Theatre in Washington on September 7 and ran until September 26. The play, produced according to the advertisements at a cost of $20,000, included a Parisian ballet and "Transformation Scenes, Incantation Scenes, Cascade Scenes of Real Water, Amazonian Armor."

58. Originally WW wrote: "Dear Pete, every word you write is most welcome. I suppose you got a letter from me last Saturday, as I sent one the day before."

59. WW deleted: "just to go by myself."

60. Doyle wrote on September 27: "Jim Sorrill Sends his love & best respects & says he is alive & kicking but the most thing that he dont understand is that young Lady that said you make such a good bed fellow" (Morgan). See also notes to 313.

61. WW at this point excised: "to a dot—Jimmy dear boy, Jim."

62. Sorrell's brother.   62.1. The conductor or driver on car 6.

63. See 311.   64. See the following letter.

65. Since this draft consists of scraps of paper pasted together, with vague directions to transpose passages, the text as here given is of necessity conjectural.

real pleasure to me to write to you—I just write off-hand, whatever comes up, and, as I said before, mostly about myself & my own doings. [There have been some] tremendous fires—the one [in] Brooklyn—eight or ten first-class steam engines[66]—Tell Harry on No 11,[67] he would see quite a change in the Fire Dep't.[68] Pete, if you see Pittsburgh either tell him the following, or let him have this letter, & then return it to you. Write how David Stevens[69] is, & write how he is getting along.[70]

I have more than I can attend to here. I find myself surrounded by friends, many old ones, some new ones, some young & attractive, & plenty of invitations & amusements. I have received an invitation from a gentleman & wife, friends of mine, at Providence, R. I.,[71] and shall go there & spend a few days latter part of October. How about the cold? I hope it is well. Dear Pete, with all my kind friends here & invitations, &c., though I love them all, & gratefully reciprocate their kindness, I finally turn to you, & think of you there.[72]

Well, I guess I have written enough for this time. Dear Pete, I will now bid you good bye for the present. Take care of yourself, & God bless you, my loving comrade. I will write again soon.

310. *To Henry Hurt*   *10.2.* [*1868*]

ENDORSED (by R. M. Bucke?): " '68." DRAFT
LETTER.

Oct 2.

Dear friend Harry Hurt,[73]

I thought I would just drop you a line for yourself—but no doubt you keep fully posted about me by my letters to Pete, as I am willing you or any of my particular friends who wish to, should read them. (He knows who I would be willing should read them—I leave it to him)—Harry, you would much enjoy going round N. Y. with me, if it were possible, & then

66. On October 2 the New York *Times* reported that there had been five fires in stables during the week. A fire on October 1 in the stables of Tunis G. Bergen, a Brooklyn official acquainted with WW (see 7), had caused damage estimated at $1,000.
67. On September 27 Doyle informed WW that Harry wanted information about the New York Fire Department (Morgan).
68. After this sentence appeared two notes which WW apparently planned to expand in the letter: "Political meeting, at Cooper Institute—the great Hall, mostly under ground—conductor—pistol incident in Brooklyn."
69. A driver. In an entry dated September 7, 1874, in an address book (*LC #*108), WW recorded a visit from Stevens, who was at that time a driver in Philadelphia.
70. The latter part of this sentence originally read: "& remember me particular. He is a young man . . ."
71. See 305.
72. What was evidently to be the next sentence was stricken: "I wish we could be together on the last trip this evening, & have an hour with each other afterward as usual." WW also excised the following: "Political excitement—banners stretched across the

how much I should like having you with me. This great city, with all its crowds, & splendor, & Broadway fashion, & women, & amusements, & the river & bay, & shipping, & the many magnificent new buildings, & Central Park & 5th Avenue, & the endless processions of private vehicles & the finest teams I ever saw, for miles long of a fine afternoon—altogether they make up a show that I can richly spend a month in enjoying—for a change from my Washington life. I sometimes think I am the particular man who enjoys the show of all these things in N. Y. more than any other mortal—as if it was all got up just for me to observe & study. Harry, I wish when you see Ben. Thompson, conductor, you would say I sent him my love, & have not forgot him. Let him read this letter. I send him a newspaper, the N. Y. Clipper. I have marked the piece about the Five Points.[74] I went down there myself just for fun, three nights ago, with a friend of mine, a policeman, & that account in the Clipper is a very good description—only not half rank enough. I wish you to tell John Towers, conductor, I sent him my love, & we will see each other again one of these days. I send him a Clipper also with an acc't of the Five Points—Harry, you let one of them lend you the paper, & read the acc't—it will amuse you—I was there two hours—it was instructive but disgusting—I saw one of the handsomest white girls there I ever saw, only about 18—blacks & white are all intermingled—

311. *To Lewis Wraymond*   [*10.2(?). 1868*]

ENDORSED (by R. M. Bucke?): "Oct. 68." DRAFT LETTER.

Dear Lewy,[75]

I will write you just a line, to let you know I have not forgotten you. I am here on leave, & shall stay nearly all this month. Duffy is here,

streets, &c—processions—"

73. Henry Hurt, like Doyle, worked for the Washington and Georgetown Railroad Company. Hurt's reply to this letter on October 5, written on the company's stationery, had the self-conscious stiltedness of a clerk: "I am pleased to Know that you are enjoying your leave of absence so much; may you continue to do so until you return. Your favor of 2d inst. to me, and papers for others were duly received, and I am requested by the recipients to return their thanks for the same" (Feinberg). According to the Washington *Chronicle* of January 15, 1874, at that time he was the treasurer of the company.

74. The October 3 issue of the *Clipper* contained Paul Preston's article "On the 'Five Points,'" part of a series entitled "Reminiscences of a Man about Town." Preston recalled the depravities of the inhabitants, the mixture of races, and the squalid bars and whorehouses in this "plague spot," which surrounded the intersection of Worth, Park, and Baxter streets in lower Manhattan.

75. Lewy Wraymond (or Raymond), also called "Pittsburgh," worked for one of the Washington railroads; see Doyle's letter to WW on September 27 (Morgan). This draft was written on the verso of the preceding letter.

driving on Broadway & 5th av. line. He has been up the Hudson river this summer driving hotel coach. He is the same old Duffy. I have heard that William Sydnor on 65, was laid up sick. I wish to hear about him, & whether he is well, & again at work. If you see him, tell him I have not forgot him, but send him my love, & will be back in Washington again. Tell Johnny Miller[76] there is still a sprinkling of the old Broadway drivers left. Balky Bill,[77] Fred Kelly, Charley McLaughlin, Tom Riley,[78] Prodigal, Sandy, &c. &c. are still here. Frank McKinney[79] & several other old drivers are with Adams Express. Staging is rather dull.

312. *To William D. O'Connor*

ADDRESS: William D. O'Connor, | Light House Bureau, | Treasury Department, | Washington, | D. C. POSTMARK: New York | Oct | 4 | 1:30 PM.

New York, | October 4, 1868.

Dear friend,

I suppose you received my letter of September 25.[80] The letters to me from A. G. office, (I suppose sent by you,) have probably all come right. I have received some five or six. Please continue to send them the same way. If the envelopes run out, please prepare some more, same form. When you write, tell me what news in the A. G. office. Is Ashton well? Is he running the office? Say to him I sent my love—& that, here north, as it seems to me, the Grant & Colfax tide is rising higher & higher every day.

Did you see John Swinton's warm ¶ about my illustrious self in *N. Y. Times*, 1st instant?[81] Give my best love to John Burroughs, & show him this note to read. J. B., dear friend, I wish I could have you here, if only just to take a ride with me for once up & down Broadway, on top a stage, of a fine afternoon.[82]

I send my love to Charles Eldridge—By a wretched oversight on my part I missed an appointment with him at Fifth Av. Hotel, when he passed through New York.

William, I shall send Freiligrath a small package, containing a copy

76. A Washington driver.

77. In writing to WW about old New York drivers on June 21, 1874, William H. Taylor, himself a former driver or son of one, referred to "William Baun alias (Bawlkey Bill)" (Feinberg).

78. Frederick Kelly, Charles McLaughlin, and Thomas Riley were listed as New York drivers.

79. Francis McKinney, a driver, was cited in the New York Directory of 1869–1870.

80. WW intended to write September 27; see 306.

81. In the draft letter after this sentence appeared the following: "John seems lately possest with L. of G. as with a demon. I have found two or three others—a Mr. Norton, of Boston, is one. He is an educated man, a Boston metaphysical thinker." WW also in-

of *L. of G.* with John's *Notes*, a *Good Gray Poet* &c. in a couple of days from here, by the European Express. I wish, if you feel like it, you would prepare a letter to F. F. to go by mail—following the package.[83]

Nelly, my dear friend, I send you my best love—in which my mother joins me—We are all well. Half my leave has already expired—& the other half will be soon over.

Affectionately

Walt.

313. *To Peter Doyle*   *10.6.* [*1868*]

ENDORSED: "6th letter." DRAFT LETTER.

Oct 6

Dear Pete,

There is nothing special with me to write to you about. The time slips away mighty quick. It seems but a day or two since I left Wash, yet I am now on the fourth week of my furlough. Last night was about the greatest political show I ever saw, even in New York—a grand Democratic meeting & torch-light processions. I was out in the midst of them, to see the sights. I always enjoy seeing the city let loose, and on the rampage, as it was last night to the fullest extent. I cannot begin to tell you how the Democrats showed themselves by thousands & tens of thousands. The whole city was lit up with torches. Cannons were fired all night in various parts of the city. As I was on my way home in a 2d av. car between 12 & 1 o'clock we got blocked in by a great part of the returning procession. Of course we had to just stand & take it. I enjoyed it hugely from the front platform. They were nearly an hour passing us, streaming both sides. In the procession were all sorts of objects, models of ships, forty or fifty feet long, full-manned, cars of liberty with women, &c &c. The ranks spread across the street, & every body carried a blazing torch. Fireworks were going off in every direction. The sky was full of big balloons, letting off rockets & Roman candles, 'way up among the stars. The excitement,

terpolated in the draft: "Tell Charles Eldridge."

82. The draft letter ends at this point. However, above the salutation appeared the following: "ask about the office—Ashton—has Andy Kerr returned—my new desk." Kerr (see 187 and 190), a clerk in WW's office, probably had gone to Pittsburgh; see address book (LC #108).

83. For Freiligrath, see 306 and 339. Again, as with Rossetti (see 266), O'Connor was to act as WW's emissary. On December 2, in a letter to his daughter, Freiligrath joyfully noted receipt of a thirty-two page letter from O'Connor as well as the books WW mentioned in this letter: "Der Schreiber ist natürlich ein enthusiastischer Verehrer des sonderbaren Kauzes" (*Briefe* [1910], 167–168). According to one of WW's address books (LC #109), the package was sent to Freiligrath on November 11.

the rush, & the endless torches, gave me great pleasure. Ever & anon, the cannon, some near some distant. I heard them long after I got to bed. It sounded like a distant engagement. I send you the Herald with a sort of account of the show, but it doesn't do half justice to it.[84] The speeches were of no account at all.

I suppose you got a letter & paper from me Saturday, Oct 3. I rec'd your welcome letter of Oct 1,[85] also the Star.[86] I read Mr. Noyes[87] western letters with pleasure. So you have something new in RR—new officers & rules. The RR business here is very different. They go through these long routes on the rush—no mercy to cattle. The 3d av. RR. lost 36 horses in one day last summer, one of those hot days. We are having pleasant weather just now, seems like Indian summer. So long, dear Pete. From your loving comrade.

314. *To Peter Doyle*   *10.9. [1868]*

ENDORSED: "7th letter." DRAFT LETTER.

Oct 9

Dear Pete,

It is splendid here this forenoon—bright and cool. I was out early taking a short walk by the river—only two squares from where I live. I received your letter of last Monday[88]—also the *Star* same date—& glad enough to hear from you—the oftener the better. Every word is good—I sent you a letter, on the 6th, which I suppose you rec'd next day. Tell Henry Hurt I received his letter of Oct. 5 all right, & that it was welcome. Political meetings here every night. The coming Pennsylvania & Ohio elections cause much talk & excitement. The fall is upon us. Overcoats are in demand. I already begin to think about my return to Washington. A month has nearly passed away. I have received an invitation from a gentleman & his wife, friends of mine, at Providence, R. I.[89] & shall probably go there & spend a few days, latter part of October.

---

84. Doyle concurred in WW's opinion in his letter of October 9: "i think your description of the Procession beats theirs all to pieces" (Lion). The article in the *Herald* was lengthy (almost a page and one-half) but factual and colorless: "It were an unending task to describe in detail this monster procession."

85. A partial text of Doyle's letter on October 1 appeared in the catalog of the Swann Auction Galleries, April 4–5, 1951: "I showed your letter to Jimmy Sorrill & it tickled him very much as he did not know that i told you what he said about that young lady. He sends his best love . . . . & all the rest of the boys sends love. . . . I expect you will get tired of so much scribling as its done with a lead pencil & very often in the car." See also 308.

86. The first draft of the conclusion to this letter read: "I remain well, work a little, & loafe around a good deal, sometimes on the river, or occasionally on Broadway, or take a ride on top of the stage, &c. Well, Pete, that is all this time from . . . For life your loving comrade. So long—Your loving comrade." (I have recorded only the final version of

I am grateful to these young men on the RR. for their love & remembrance to me—Dave,[90] & Jim & Charley Sorrell, Tom Hassett, Harry on No. 11.

Every day I find I have plenty to do—every hour is occupied with something. Shall I tell you about it, or part of it, just to fill up? I generally spend the forenoon in my room, writing &c., then take a bath, fix up & go out about 12, & loafe somewhere, or call on some one down town, or on business, or perhaps if it is very pleasant & I feel like it, ride a trip with some driver-friend on Broadway from 23d street to Bowling Green, three miles each way. You know it is a never-ending amusement & study & recreation for me to ride a couple of hours, of a pleasant afternoon, on a Broadway stage in this way. You see everything as you pass, a sort of living, endless panorama—shops, & splendid buildings, & great windows, & on the broad sidewalks crowds of women, richly-dressed, continually passing, altogether different, superior in style & looks from any to be seen any where else—in fact a perfect stream of people, men too dressed in high style, & plenty of foreigners—& then in the streets the thick crowd of carriages, stages, carts, hotel & private coaches, & in fact all sorts of vehicles & many first-class teams, mile after mile, & the splendor of such a great street & so many tall, ornamental, noble buildings, many of them of white marble, & the gayety & motion on every side—You will not wonder how much attraction all this is, on a fine day, to a great loafer like me, who enjoys so much seeing the busy world move by him, & exhibiting itself for his amusement, while he takes it easy & just looks on & observes.[91] Then about the Broadway drivers, nearly all of them are my personal friends. Some have been much attached to me, for years, & I to them. But I believe I have already mentioned them in a former letter. Yesterday I rode the trip I describe with a friend, on a 5th Avenue stage, No. 26—a sort [of] namesake of yours, Pete Calhoun.[92] I have known him 9 or 10 years. The day was fine, & I enjoyed the trip muchly. So I try to put in something in my letters to give you an idea of how I pass part of my time, & what I see here in N. Y. Of course I have quite a

these lines.)

87. Crosby Stuart Noyes (1825–1908) was editor of the Washington *Star* from 1867 until his death. On September 30 his newspaper printed his account of "Chicago."

88. Doyle's letter of October 5 (Lion) contained gossip about Washington.

89. The invitation from the Channings; see 305.

90. David Stevens, a driver or a conductor.

91. William James printed this paragraph up to this point, and commented: "Truly a futile way of passing the time, some of you may say, and not altogether creditable to a grown-up man. And yet, from the deepest point of view, who knows the more of truth, and who knows the less,—Whitman on his omnibus-top, full of the inner joy with which the spectacle inspires him, or you, full of the disdain which the futility of his occupation excites?" (*Talks to Teachers on Psychology* [1899], 252).

92. Cited in two address books (LC #108, 109); the former is dated September, 1870. See also 390.

variety—some four or five hours every day I most always spend in study, writing, &c. The other serves for a good change. I am writing two or three pieces.

I am having finished about 225 copies of Leaves of Grass bound up, to supply orders. Those copies form all that is left of the old editions. Then there will be no more in the market till I have my new & improved edition set up & stereotyped, which it is my present plan to do the ensuing winter at my leisure in Washington.[93]

Mother is well, I take either dinner or supper with her every day. Remember me to David Stevens & John Towers.[94] Tell Harry on No 11 I will go [to] the Hall again & see if I can find that man in the Sheriff's office.[95] I send you my love, & *so long* for the present. Yours for life, dear Pete, (& death the same).

315. *To Peter Doyle*   *10.14.* [1868]

ENDORSED: "8th letter." DRAFT LETTER.

Oct. 14

Dear boy Pete,

There is great excitement here over the returns of yesterday's elections, as I suppose there is the same in Washington also—the Democrats look blue enough, & the Republicans are on their high horses.[96] I suppose Grant's success is now certain. As I write, the bands are out here, parading the streets, & the drums beating. It is now forenoon. To-night we will hear the big guns, & see the blazing bonfires. It is dark & cloudy weather here to-day. I was glad to get your letter of Friday, 9th which is the last[97]—also a Star at same time. Also this morning, Star and Express to 12th. I suppose you rec'd mine of the 9th & the papers. I am about as well as usual. Mother is well, & my brothers the same. I am going to-morrow to Providence, R. I., to spend a few days. Should you write any time within four or five days after receiving this, direct to me *care of Hon. Thomas Davis, Providence, R. I.*[98]

My friend O'Connor is quite unwell, and is absent from Washington

93. The next edition of *Leaves of Grass* appeared in 1871–1872.
94. Like Stevens, a driver or a conductor.
95. See 309.
96. After Pennsylvania went Republican in the elections held on October 13, the New York *Times* remarked editorially on the following day: "This splendid civil triumph of Gen. Grant is only surpassed by his brilliant military achievements."
97. The letter contained gossip about Washington friends (Lion).
98. See 149 and 317.
99. O'Connor described in his letter of October 9 the physical and emotional exhaustion which forced him to leave Washington on September 30 to vacation at James-

away down on the New England coast.[99] I received a letter from him yesterday. I believe I told you I was finishing up about 230 copies of my book, expecting to sell them. I have had them finished up & bound &c. but there is a hitch about the sale, & I shall not be able to sell them at present. There is a pretty strong enmity here toward me, & L. of G., among certain classes—not only that it is a great mess of crazy talk & hard words, all tangled up, without sense or meaning, (which by the by is, I believe, your judgment about it)—but others sincerely think that it is a bad book, improper, & ought to be denounced & put down, & its author along with it. There are some venemous but laughable squibs occasionally in the papers. One said I had received 25 guineas for a piece in an English magazine, but that it was worth all that for any one to read it. Another, the *World*, said "Walt Whitman was in town yesterday, carrying the blue cotton umbrella of the future."[1] (It had been a drizzly forenoon)—So they go it. When they get off a good squib, however, I laugh at it, just as much as any one.

Dear Pete, I hope this will find you well & in good spirits. Dear boy, I send you my love. I will write you a line from Providence. So long, Pete.

Walt

I have been debating whether to get my leave extended, & stay till election day to vote—or whether to pair off with a Democrat, & return (which will amount to the same thing.) Most likely I shall decide on the latter, but don't know for certain.[2]

316. *To William D. O'Connor*

ADDRESS: William D. O'Connor, | care of | Dr. W. F. Channing, | p. o. box 69 | Providence, | R. I. POSTMARK: New York | (?) | 14 | (?).

New York, | October 14, 1868.

Dear friend,

I only write to say that I have received your welcome letter of the

---

town, R. I.: "My purpose was to kill two birds with one stone—get well and fix up the 'Carpenter,' but I fear neither are likely to be effected. I feel wretchedly unwell, and can't think of composition" (Feinberg).

1. The New York *World*, October 3; the quotation is accurate except for the insertion of "carrying." On October 8 the *World*, probably borrowing from the New York *Times* of October 1, announced "Freiligrath's" translation, and two days later the newspaper reported that "Walt. Whitman visited THE WORLD office yesterday."

2. WW excised: "Remember me to Coley, John Towers, Jim Sorrell, Dave Stevens, & all the boys."

9th, from Jamestown—& that—as Mrs. Paulina Davis has been here, & has, in her own & husband's behalf, kindly invited me, & indeed made the arrangements—I shall come on to Providence, to-morrow, 15th—they to meet me at the depot, & take me home as their guest—from whence I shall report to you, & to Dr. & Mrs. Channing forthwith—& fulfil my promised visit to them also, before I return here—which will be about 21st or 22d.

Affectionately

Walt.

317. *To Peter Doyle*   *10.17.* [1868]

ENDORSED: "9th letter." DRAFT LETTER.

Providence R. I. | October 17.

Dear Pete,

According to announcement in my last, I have made a movement & change of base, from tumultuous, close-packed, world-like N. Y., to this half-rural, brisk, handsome, New England, third-class town. I came on here last Thursday. I came as guest of Thomas Davis, formerly M. C. from this city—arrived between 8 and 9 o'clock at night—found his carriage at the depot waiting for me—at the house (a sort of castle built of stone, on fine grounds, a mile & a half from the town) a hearty welcome from his hospitable wife, & a family of young ladies & children—a hot supper, a tip-top room &c. &c.—so you see, Pete, your old man is in clover. I have since been round the city & suburbs considerably. I am going down to Newport before I return. Invitations &c. are numerous. I am, in fact, already dividing myself between two hospitalities, part of the time with Mr. & Mrs. Davis, and part with Dr. & Mrs. Channing, old acquaintances of mine in another part of the city. I stopt last night at the house of the latter. It is on a high & pleasant hill at the side of the city, which it entirely overlooks. From the window of my room, I can look down across the city, the river, and off miles upon miles in the distance. The woods are a real spectacle, colored with all the rich colors of autumn. Yesterday it was beautiful & balmy beyond description, like the finest Indian summer. I wandered around, partly walking, partly in a carriage, a good part of the day. To-day there is an entire change of scene—As I sit

3. Apparently not extant.

writing this—what do you think, Pete?—great flakes of *snow* are falling, quite a thick flurry—sometimes the wind blows gusts—in fact a real snow storm has been going on all the forenoon, though without the look or feeling of actual winter as the grass & foliage are autumnal, & the cold is not severe yet. Still it [is] disagreeable & wet & damp & prevents me from going out. So I will make it up by writing a couple of letters—one to mother,[3] & one to you, telling you about things. Providence is a handsome city of about 70,000 inhabitants—has numerous manufactories in full operation—every thing looks lively. From the house up here, I can hear almost any time, night or day, the sound of factory bells & the steam whistles of locomotives half a mile distant. Then the lights at night seen from here make a curious exhibition. At both places I stop, we have plenty of ripe fresh fruit and lots of flowers. Pete, I could now send you a bouquet every morning, far better than I used to, of much choicer flowers.

And how are you getting along, dearest comrade? I hope you are well, & that every thing is going on right with you. I have not heard from you for a good while, it seems.[4] I suppose you got my last letter, 14th, from N. Y. I expect to return to N. Y. about the 22d. Should you feel to write after receiving this, you might direct to 331 East 55th st. as before. I am well as usual. I am luxuriating on excellent grapes. I wish I could send you a basket. At both places I stop they have vineyards, & the grapes are very good & plenty this year. Last night, when I went up at 11 o'clock to my room, I took up three great bunches, each as big as my fist, & sat down and eat them before I turned in. I like to eat them this way, & it agrees with me. It is quite a change here from my associations & sur-roundings either in Washington or New York. Evenings & meal times I find myself thrown amidst a mild, pleasant society, really intellectual, composed largely of educated women, some young, some not so young, every thing refined & polite, *not* disposed to small talk, conversing in earnest on profound subjects, but with a moderate rather slow tone, & in a kind & conciliatory manner—delighting in this sort of conversation, & spending their evenings till late in it. I take a hand in, for a change. I find it entertaining, as I say, for novelty's sake, for a week or two—but I know very well that would be enough for me. It is all first-rate, good & smart, but too constrained & bookish for a free old hawk like me. I send you my love, dear Pete. *So long*. Will write from N. Y. soon as I return there.

W W

4. Doyle had written on October 14 (Barrett).

P.S. Just after 12 o'clock—noon—as I am just finishing, the storm lightens up—I am sure I see a bit of blue sky in the clouds—yes, the sun is certainly breaking out.

318. *To Peter Doyle*

ENDORSED: "10th letter." DRAFT LETTER.

Providence, R. I. | October 18, 1868

Dear boy & comrade,

I sent off a letter to you yesterday noon, but towards evening Mr. Davis brought me up from the p. o. yours of the 15th,[5] which I was so glad to get that you shall have an answer right off. After the flurry of snow I told you of yesterday morning, we had a pleasant clear afternoon. I took a long walk, partly through the woods, and enjoyed it much. The weather was pretty cold & sharp, & remains so yet. As I left my overcoat in Washington, I have been compelled to get something here—so I have bought me a great iron-grey shawl, which I find very acceptable. I always had doubts about a shawl, but have already got used to mine, & like it first rate. In the evening, I went by invitation to a party of ladies & gentlemen—mostly ladies. We had a warm, animated talk, among other things about Spiritualism. I talked too, indeed went in like a house afire. It was good exercise—for the fun of the thing. I also made love to the women, & flatter myself that I created at least one impression—wretch & gay deceiver that I am. Then away late—lost my way—wandered over the city, & got home after one o'clock.[6]

The truth is, Peter, that I am here at present times mainly in the midst of female women, some of them young & jolly—& meet them most every evening in company—& the way in which this aged party comes up to the scratch & cuts out the youthful parties & fills their hearts with envy is absolutely a caution. You would be astonished, my son, to see the brass & coolness, & the capacity of flirtation & carrying on with the girls—I would never have believed it of myself. Brought here by destiny, surrounded in this way—& as I in self defence would modestly state—sought for, seized upon & ravingly devoured by these creatures—& *so* nice & smart some of them are, & handsome too—there is nothing left for me—is

---

5. Doyle's letter, dated "Oct 14—4," mentioned the death of a cousin and a plot to assassinate the president: "all the boys sends their love— | Pete X X" (Barrett).
6. WW's directions for transposing material are confusing at this point. Possibly in

there—but to go in. Of course, young man, you understand, it is all on the square. My going in amounts to just talking & joking & having a devil of a jolly time, carrying on—that's all. They are all as good girls as ever lived. I have already had three or four such parties here—which, you will certainly admit, considering my age & heft, to say nothing of my reputation, is doing pretty well.

I go about quite a good deal—this is as handsome a city, as I ever saw. Some of the streets run up steep hills. Except in a few of the business streets, where the buildings are compact—in nine-tenths of the city, every house stands separate, & has a little or quite a deal of ground about it, for flowers, & for shade or fruit trees, or a garden. I never saw such a prosperous looking city—but of course no grand public buildings like Washington.

This forenoon I have been out away down along the banks of the river & cove, & making explorations generally. All is new to me, & I returned quite tired. I have eat a hearty dinner. Then I thought I would come up & sit a while in my room. But as I did not feel like reading, I concluded to write this precious screed. Fortunate young man, to keep getting such instructive letters—aint you? It is now four o'clock & bright & cool, & I have staid in long enough. I will sally forth, on a walk, & drop this in the P. O. before supper. So long, dear Pete—& my love to you as always, always.

W

319. *To Ellen M. O'Connor*

ADDRESS: Mrs. E. M. O'Connor, | care of | Charles W. Eldridge, | Internal Revenue Bureau, | Treasury Dept. | Washington, D. C. POSTMARK: Providence | Oct | 19.

Providence, R. I. | October 19, 1868.

Dear Nelly,

I will just write you a line or two, anyhow. I am stopping the last three days here with Doctor and Jeannie[7] & having a very pleasant time indeed—only Jeannie has had something of a bad spell—but is quite bright & comfortable this morning, & presided at breakfast. William is here—

the letter he sent he deleted this sentence, which interrupted his gossip about the ladies.
7. Channing's wife was Mrs. O'Connor's sister.

which adds much indeed to the pleasure of my visit—William has not recovered from an annoying cold, yet does pretty well—I have seen Mrs.
Whitman,[8] & like her—have seen her & talked &c. three times—have seen
Miss Nora Perry[9]—am going this afternoon to Thomas Davis's to stay
two or three days, & then return to New York—whence in two or three
days more, to Washington.

Mother is quite well for an old woman of 74—speaks of you[10]—is now
in her new quarters—much roomier & pleasanter. Sister Martha & her two
little girls have come on from St. Louis, and are now living with
mother.[11] George & Eddy are well. Mrs. Price & her girls are well & in
good spirits—I am enjoying my vacation agreeably, but moderately—as
becomes a gentleman of my size & age.

Give my love to Mr. and Mrs. Ashton—also to Charley—also to dear
little Jeannie—It will not be long, Nelly, before I shall be with you all
again. Best love to you, dearest friend.

Walt.

My last letter to William was also to you—though I suppose you did
not see it yet.

320. *To Charles W. Eldridge*

Providence, R. I. | October 20, 1868.

Dear Charley,

If the next *Sunday Morning Chronicle*[12] contains a "personal"
about me, would you do me the favor to get half a dozen copies, & keep
for me? I shall doubtless return about the 26th—as my leave expires that

8. Sarah Helen Whitman (1803–1878), the American poet and fiancée of Edgar Al-
lan Poe, to whom he wrote the second "To Helen." Her collected poems appeared in 1879.
WW presented an inscribed copy of *Leaves of Grass* to her during or shortly after his
Providence visit. In a letter to WW on November 23, O'Connor, who was a close friend of
Mrs. Whitman, transcribed some of her comments in a recent letter to him: "The great,
the good Camerado! The lover of men! . . . How strange it seems to me now that I
should have been so near him without knowing him better! How many questions that I
asked you about him would have needed no answer, if I had but have read his book then
as I have read it now" (Feinberg; Traubel, III, 505).
9. According to *DAB*, Miss Perry (1831–1896) was a poet, journalist, and author of
juvenile books.
10. On October 23 Mrs. O'Connor wrote most urgently to Mrs. Whitman to make a
visit to Washington: "I want you to come and see how you like Washington, because you
know I have always had a hope that you would come here to live" (Feinberg).
11. See 324.
12. The following notice in the Washington *Sunday Morning Chronicle* was
WW's public version of his vacation:
"After an absence of some weeks, Walt Whitman, the poet, is just returning, we hear,

day. (I wished to stay to vote, but have paired off with a vehement Seymourite, an old friend of mine.) I suppose Nelly received a letter I sent her yesterday, to your care.

I am writing this in my room at Mr. & Mrs. Davis's. I came here yesterday, after three most agreeable days with Dr. Channing & Jeannie. As I write, we are expecting a call from William O'C. as he promised yesterday to come over & see Mrs. D. and myself, & spend an hour or two. This afternoon, after dinner, Mr. Davis whom I like, & get along with first rate, is going to take me out to ride, down to the Point, as I wish to see more of the harbor & bay. I am treated on all sides with the greatest hospitality & courtesy—& yet left just as free as I wish to be. It is beautiful fall weather to-day. I go back to New York & Brooklyn on Thursday next.

I am profoundly impressed with Providence, not only for its charming locality & features, but for its proof & expression of fine relations, as a city, to average human comfort, life, & family & individual independence & thrift—*After all, New England for ever!*—(with perhaps just one or two little reservations)—With love to you, Charley—& repeated again to dear Nelly.

> Yours truly
>
> > > Walt.

P.S.—Later—2 o'clock—William & Dr. Channing have been over here—staid to dinner—We had quite a gay time—indeed quite a little dinner party—William & Doctor, Mr & Mrs. Davis, Nora Perry, George Davis,[13] Katy Hinds,[14] & illustrious self—We are just through—Doctor has gone home, not wishing to leave Jeannie too long—William still remaining—I go presently on the drive with Mr. D.—and also to deposite this letter in P. O.

> > > W.

to his residence and employment in this city. Besides visiting his mother at Brooklyn, and recuperating down Long Island and at Providence and Newport, he has spent quite a while 'loafing at his ease' in New York, among the streets, docks, throngs on Broadway, and upon the waters adjacent to that great metropolis, abandoning himself to one of his favorite spells of studying and enjoying the life and scenes there, not for pleasure alone, but to give color to his characteristic poetry. Mr. Whitman, however, we may say in passing, it is understood among his friends, has been for some time and is now principally engaged on a poem, or a series of poems, intended to touch the religious and spiritual wants of humanity, with which he proposes to round off and finish his celebrated 'Leaves of Grass.' He has also, we hear, completed several magazine pieces for publishers in London, a quarter where his productions appear to be in demand. A small prose book by him, 'Democratic Vistas,' will probably appear the ensuing winter. As we understand, Mr. Whitman returns to Washington all the more robust and healthy from his vacation, and with the prospect and purpose, in the leisurely way usual for him, of considerable literary work in the future."

13. Probably George K. Davis, a jeweller, undoubtedly related to the Davises.
14. Mentioned as a friend of Mrs. Price in 207.

321. *To Abby H. Price*

ADDRESS: Mrs. Abby H. Price, | 331 East
55th street, | between 1st and 2d Avenues |
New York City. POSTMARK: (?) | Oct | (?)1 | (?).

Providence, R. I. | October 21, 1868.

Dear Abby,

I shall return to New York to-morrow, Thursday[15]—leaving here at ½ past 12, noon, and getting in N. Y. about 8—& intend to go on to Washington on Monday next, 26th. I have been at the Channings's—Jeannie is quite unwell—but bears it like the heroine she is—William O'Connor is there—I am now at Mr. & Mrs. Davis's—Am treated with the greatest hospitality & courtesy every where. Yesterday Mr. Davis took me out riding—went down to Fields' Point, off the bay—& thence to the domain & factories of the Spragues,[16] & so to Olneysville &c &c—as interesting a ride & exploration as I ever had in my life—

I have seen Mrs. Whitman—& like her. We had yesterday here to dinner & spend the evening Nora Perry, Wm O'Connor, Dr. Channing, &c—To-day Mrs. Davis had intended to take me out riding, but it is threatening rain, wind east, & skies dark—So it will have to be given up. I like Mr. Davis much. I am very glad I made this jaunt & visit—Love to you, Helen, Emily, & all.

Walt.

322. *To John Burroughs*

Providence, R. I. | October 22, 1868.

Dear friend,

I have been thinking about you this morning, and will write a few lines, though without any thing special to communicate. My vacation is nearly done, & in four or five days more I shall be back in Washington. I have been here in Providence the past week, as guest of Thomas Davis, a manufacturer here, & formerly M. C.—have had a good time generally, in a quiet way—am going on to New York this afternoon, & shall be back in Washington on the 27th—

William O'Connor[17] is here in Providence—I have been with him a good deal—he is not very well, but goes around—Will finish my letter in New York, & mail it thence to-morrow.[17.1]

Walt.

15. WW was staying with the Prices on this visit to New York.
16. Amasa and William Sprague, manufacturers; see 323.
17. Before he returned to Washington, O'Connor called on WW's mother in Brooklyn; see letter from Mrs. Whitman to WW dated November 4(?) (Trent).

323. *To Peter Doyle*   [*10.23(?). 1868*]

ENDORSED: "11th letter." DRAFT LETTER.

Dear Pete,

Well here I am back again in New York—Have had a pleasant trip down east—went down the bay there after I wrote you last—& also a visit around among the factories of Rhode Island. Some of them are very large—regular little towns. The Spragues, two brothers, employ 7000 workmen in their factories alone. Some of the owners are men of immense wealth. I write this early in the forenoon, sitting in my room in 55th street, after breakfast. As to getting my leave extended so that I might stay to vote, I have settled (as I spoke of in a former letter)[18] to pair off with a friend of mine here who was going to vote for Seymour, and return on time. The weather is cool & clear to-day. I shall probably not make out much [of] a letter to you this time, Pete, as I feel rather stupid yet this morning. I guess I slept too hard, or perhaps, as they say, I got up wrong end foremost. But I thought I would write one more letter, for the last. I believe it is about the eleventh. I hope you have enjoyed reading them as much as I have writing them—for that, I *have* enjoyed. You too have done first rate, & have sent me as many as I have you, and good letters too. I am now going out down town, & across to Brooklyn, to spend a few hours with my mother. I don't know whether I told you that my sister with her two young children from St. Louis, arrived the night before I left N. Y. & will stop with mother this fall & winter—her health is not very good.[19]

I shall return 26th. Take care of yourself. Dear Pete, we will soon be together again.

324. *To Thomas Jefferson Whitman*

New York, | Sunday forenoon, Oct. 25 | 1868.

Dear brother Jeff,

I suppose you rec'd the letter[20] I wrote four or five days ago from Providence, R. I. I came back Thursday night, & was over home on Friday. I received your letter. Matty has had an examination of her

---

17.1 The sale at the American Art Association on March 11, 1924, listed a one-page letter to Burroughs on October 23, which stated that WW intended to spend a few days in New York before he returned to Washington.

18. See 315.   19. See 324.   20. This letter is not extant.

lungs,[21] by Dr. A. D. Wilson, 30 Gates Av. near Clinton av. I had not seen Dr. W.—it was the Thursday before I returned—yesterday I went down to see Dr. Enos,[22] waited some time, but did not see him—I intended to make an appointment, & go down with Mat but, as I say, came away without seeing him—Then I went up to Gates av. & found Dr. Wilson in, & had a long talk with him about Mat. The impression he made upon me was that he is a man who knows his business thoroughly, very candid, & probably a little disposed to state things on the most unfavorable side, rather than the other—He said he could tell better in ten or twelve days— one of Mat's lungs is affected—thinks there is no imminent danger at all —thinks that the physician in St. Louis who advised a change from there here, couldn't have had any knowledge of Brooklyn climate or situation —nevertheless thinks that the journey & a temporary change will be very salutary, & do her good—advised whiskey, wine, condensed milk, &c— did not advise any drug medicines—was evidently interested, & took hold of the case not merely as a matter of business—After seeing him & talking [to] him, I abandoned the idea of consulting Enos—at least for the present.

My idea is that Matty has the possibilities of consumption in her system—but that with ordinary good luck, she can & will get over it. She has good spirits, is very comfortably situated—has a good, cheerfull, warm room, with southern exposure—has a good stove, gas, &c—Upon the whole, as to personal surroundings, &c she could not be happier in them—for Mother, & George, & Ed too, think & do every thing that the tenderest mother & brothers could—George is very kind—Mat realizes it all perfectly, & is herself very kind & affectionate as indeed she always was.

Mother & all wish you to arrange without fail to come on, on or before 1st December[23]—before, if convenient—Mother is well, but shows her old age more & more. I return to Washington to-morrow, as my leave is up. The little girls are hearty as ever. Best love—

Walt.

21. Martha's condition (see 295) had not improved. On September 6 Jeff had informed George that her doctor had recommended "a visit east," and on September 8 he wrote: "The doctors all unite in declaring that Mat has no disease of the lungs—it is all in the bronchial tubes of the throat" (Feinberg). She remained in Brooklyn until the middle of December. See also 328.

22. Dr. DeWitt C. Enos at 16 Clinton Avenue.

23. Jeff arrived in Brooklyn about November 20; see 328.

24. To George on September 8 Jeff had complained that "the house is damp and I cannot seem to better it. I have spent abt $125 on it trying to fix it" (Feinberg).

25. His landlords; see 218.

26. WW had submitted "Ethiopia Commenting" to *The Galaxy* on September 7, 1867; see 246. If he sent the poem "to another quarter," it has not as yet been discovered.

27. Flood was a streetcar conductor in New York, known, according to an unidenti-

It is certain that her cough is not near as bad here as it was in St. Louis, in that house.[24]

325. *To Mr. and Mrs. Newton Benedict*   *10.25.1868*

[*Writing from New York, WW informed the Benedicts*[25] *of the date of his return to Washington.*]

326. *To F. P.(?) Church*

ATTORNEY GENERAL'S OFFICE,

Washington. Nov. 2, *1868*

My dear Sir,

As you have not found the little piece "Ethiopia Commenting"[26] available, allow me to withdraw it—Indeed I have already sent it to another quarter.

327. *To John Flood, Jr.*

TRANSCRIPT.

ATTORNEY GENERAL'S OFFICE,

Washington, D. C., Nov. 22, *1868.*

Dear Jack Flood.[27]

I received your welcome letter, and was happy to know that you had not forgotten me—for I have thought of you many times since. I returned here from New York about four weeks ago, and have been and

fied notation on his letter to WW, as "Broadway Jack." According to dated entries in an address book (LC #109), WW saw Flood on September 30 and October 5, and rode with him on his Second Avenue car; Flood had been a conductor for ten years. After WW's return to Washington, there was a brief correspondence, consisting of four extant letters from WW (see also 333, 385, and 385.1) and one from the young man. Flood, somewhat better educated than some of WW's other conductor friends, wrote on January 11, 1869: "Sir, It is with great pleasure that I sit down with pen in hand to address a few lines to you." He informed WW that he had lost his position on New Year's Eve and that he was now seeking another job: "I shall still continue to correspond and can never forget your kind friendship towards me. . . . Your True and Ever intimate friend" (Yale). According to the first listing of his name in the New York Directory, in 1872–1873, he was at that time either in the milk business or a milkman.

now am working in this office as usual—am well and hearty, and don't hurt myself with hard work. Our hours are from 9 till 3.

You speak of coming here and paying me a visit. Dear boy, I hope you will come truly, for it would be a great comfort to me if we could be together again. I don't know whether it would be very pleasant to you here, Jack, for this is a stupid place compared to New York—but we would have each other's society, and that would be first rate.

There's not much excitement in Washington—at least none that I take any interest in. Politics and politicians carry the day here—but I meddle with them very little. In a couple of weeks more, Congress will meet, and then the city will be quite lively.

I am out a good deal in the open air, as I have plenty of leisure time. It is fine scenery around Washington—plenty of hills, and a noble river. I take a ride on the cars out to Georgetown west, or Navy Yard east, once in a while of a pleasant afternoon, or Sunday—but I tell you I miss New York. We had a long spell of splendid weather. But now it is colder, with some snow a couple of days since. Jack, you must write often as you can—anything from my loving boy will be welcome—you needn't be particular about the writing—you might write in the car with pencil, when you have any time. I will write to you too. I will now close for this time. Dear Jack, I send you my love.

Walt Whitman.

328. *To Louisa Van Velsor Whitman*

ATTORNEY GENERAL'S OFFICE,

Washington. Nov. 24, 1868.

Dearest Mother,

I suppose you got my letter last Saturday, 21st—All goes along at present the same old story—nothing new in the office—I shall be glad when Grant comes in, & a new Attorney Gen'l appointed—if I weather

28. Evarts was one of Johnson's appointees.
29. His landlady.
30. On November 18 Mrs. Whitman reported that Jeff was on his way from St. Louis to Brooklyn (Trent).
31. On November 11(?) Mrs. Whitman wrote: "matty is improving but far from well. the doctor is doctoring her throat with great success. i think he has performed two moderate opperations on her throat, but o dear if you could hear her talk it would make me hoarse to talk a steady stream as she does when any one comes on to see her" (Trent). After Jeff's family left, Mrs. Whitman complained, on December 14(?), that they had not paid for any "provisions" while they stayed in Brooklyn: "i did really think they had ought

it out till then—though I am well enough off, at present, & probably safe—I don't think there is any show for Mr. Evarts[28] remaining here after Grant comes in—

We are having a splendid spell of weather again, after the storm of Saturday last—To-day it is very fine—I should like to be with you on Thanksgiving, Thursday—I shall take dinner at my boarding house— Mrs. Benedict[29] told me yesterday to bring any of my friends to dinner I wanted to—I still have the same room—I make a fire mornings, & have it quite comfortable—

Is Jeff home?[30] Martha must keep up good spirits—I have no doubt she will get all right again[31]—I approve what you advised her about the wine —it is as George said, you can't get any real pure port wine—I shall keep watch of the place in Western Pennsylvania I spoke of, & if they have any genuine wine, as I was informed they would in January, I shall get some for Martha—

Has George done any thing about the Portland av. house, yet?[32] Write to me all the news. Your letter came last week, & was welcome. I am quite busy to-day—have several jobs of work in the office that keep me hard at it—

Love to you, dearest mother—& to all—

I have had to scratch off my letter in a hurry, but I wanted you to have something, according to promise in my last.

Walt.

329. *To Ralph Waldo Emerson*

ATTORNEY GENERAL'S OFFICE,

Washington Nov. 30, 1868.

Dear Mr. Emerson:

On the eve of sending the enclosed piece[33] abroad, I have taken a notion to first offer it to the *Atlantic*—and, if not too great a liberty, to solicit your services for that purpose.

to give me some [money] but let every thing go but i would ask more than 100$ to go through the same again (*burn this letter*)" (Trent).

32. Mrs. Whitman added a postscript to her letter of December 14(?): "george has commenced his house. they are digging the cellar" (Trent).

33. WW sent "Proud Music of the Sea-Storm" (later called "Proud Music of the Storm"), which Fields (see 331) promptly accepted for *The Atlantic Monthly*; see XXIII (February, 1869), 199–203. In 1888 Traubel asked WW why he had appealed "to Emerson as a mediator": "For several reasons, I may say. But the best reason I had was in his own suggestion that I should permit him to do such things for me when the moment seemed ripe for it" (Traubel, II, 22).

I would be much obliged if you would take it in to Mr. Fields the first time you go to Boston—show him this letter—If available at all, I propose it for about the February number of the magazine. The price is $100, & 30 copies of the number in which it may be printed—and I will ask Mr. Fields to do me the favor to send me an answer within a week from the time he receives the piece—or perhaps he can give his decision at once on receiving it.

      With best respect & love,

Walt Whitman.

      The piece appears in printed form because I have had it put in type for my own convenience, and to insure greater correctness—I forgot to say, above, that I scrupulously reserve the right to print this piece in future in my book—(which, however, will not be for several months.)

W. W.

330. *To John Harrison Littlefield*

ATTORNEY GENERAL'S OFFICE,

Washington. Dec. 1, 1868.

Mr. Littlefield.[34] | Dear Sir:

      I have been very much occupied, since I saw you—& wish you to accept my apoligies for not coming to see you, & sit, &c. I appreciate your courtesy, & invitation—& hope to be soon more at leisure, & in the vein for sitting.

Walt Whitman

---

    34. Littlefield (1835–1902) advertised himself in the Washington Directory of 1869 as an artist and publisher; see also *Mallett's Index of Artists* (1948). The Republican publishers of the Washington *Daily Morning Chronicle* in 1868 were offering to new subscribers Littlefield's steel engraving of Grant.

    35. James T. Fields (1817–1881) succeeded James Russell Lowell as editor of *The Atlantic Monthly*. After Emerson (see 329) delivered the poem to him, Fields sent $100 to WW on December 5 (Traubel, II, 22). He informed WW on December 14 that if he was to get the poem into the February issue it would be impossible to send proof to Washington (Traubel, II, 211). This was the second of WW's poems to appear in *The Atlantic Monthly;* "Bardic Symbols" (see 16–17) was published in 1861.

    36. Unaccountably, WW lined through the rest of the draft.

    37. Dr. Thayer (1817?–1882) was professor of anatomy at the University of Vermont Medical School. According to John Brooks Wheeler, *Memoirs of a Small-Town Surgeon* (1936), 284–289, Thayer performed most of the operations in Burlington during the 1860's; "he kept no books and never sent a bill . . . he lived and died a poor man." For this information I am indebted to Miss Fannie Rothman, librarian of the Fletcher Free Library in Burlington.

    Relations between Hannah Heyde and her husband and between Heyde and the Whitmans remained the same. On March 3 Mrs. Whitman informed WW of the receipt of

331. *To James T. Fields*

ENDORSED: "To | J. T. Fields | Dec. 8, '68."
DRAFT LETTER.

sent | Dec 8, '68

J. T. Fields,[35] | Dear Sir:

Your letter has come to hand, with the check for $100, as payment in full for the piece "Proud Music of the Sea-Storm"—leaving me, however, the right to print it in future book. Please when ready send me proof, which I will return forthwith. Please send me,[36] by express, 30 copies of the number, when ready, to my address here.

With thanks & best respects,

332. *To Dr. Samuel W. Thayer*

ENDORSED: "sent to Dr. Thayer, | Dec 8, '68."
DRAFT LETTER.

sent | Dec 8, '68

Dr. Thayer,[37] | Dear Sir:

Won't you do me the very great favor to write me a few lines regarding the condition of my sister, Mrs. H. L. Heyde. I am sure, from what I hear, that it is mainly to your medical skill, and your kindness as a good man, that she got through her late illness. She seems by her letters to be left in an extremely nervous state. Doctor, please write me as fully as you think proper. Though we have never met personally, I have heard of you from my mother & sister. I must ask you to keep this letter, and the whole matter, strictly confidential, & mention it to no

"the most awful" letter from Heyde (Trent), and on March 6 she mentioned writing "a pressing letter to hannah urging her to come and make us a visit" (Trent). Nothing of course happened; after her marriage Hannah never left her husband. On March 24 Mrs. Whitman noted "a letter or package from charley heyde, three sheets of foolscap paper and a fool wrote on them" (Trent). Later in the year, on November 4(?), Mrs. Whitman wrote that Hannah was ill (Trent). On November 13 Hannah herself wrote to WW about excruciating pain in her thumb: "Charlie was very ugly. He would not get a nurse. . . . Dr. Thayer I believe thinks all my thumb wont get well. I feel very anxious about it. dear brother write to Dr. Saml. B. Thayer . . . but dear brother of all things in [the world?] I beg you to not let Charlie know I have wrote to you & run a great risk. . . . be pleasant to Charlie while I am sick on my account" (Trent). On November 24 Hannah wrote to her mother about her illness, somewhat more calmly than she had to her brother, perhaps because her letter was part of Heyde's (Trent). According to Mrs. Whitman's letter of December 5(?), Heyde wrote to her about "a very stupid letter from Walt addressed to han which he humanely concluded not to deliver to her" (Trent). About December 8 Heyde reported to Mrs. Whitman the amputation of Hannah's thumb, refused to "withdraw" his remarks about WW, and explained: "I have no desire to annoy or give you unnecessary concern. . . . Besides Han's illness, I was exceedingly annoyed at the unnecessary, miserable condition of our domestic affairs" (Trent).

person. My sister in a late letter, wished me to write you & thank you for your great kindness to her.[38]

333. *To John Flood, Jr.*

ENDORSED (by WW): "2d." DRAFT LETTER.

sent | Dec 12 '68

Dear Jack,

I send you a few lines, though there is nothing new or special with me. I am still working here in the same place, and expect to be here all winter—(yet there is such a thing as a man's slipping up in his calculations, you know.) My health keeps good, & work easy. I often think of you, my loving boy, and think whether you are all right & in good health, & working on 2d avenue yet.

I suppose you received the letter I sent you. I got yours November 15, & sent you a letter about the 20th or 21st[39] I believe. I have not heard from you since.

Congress began here last Monday. I have been up to see them in session. The halls they meet in are magnificent. The light comes all from the roof. The new part of the Capitol is very fine indeed.[40] It is a great curiosity to any one that likes fine workmanship both in wood & stone. But I hope you will come here & see me, as you talked of[41]—Whether we are indeed to have the chance in future to be much together & enjoy each other's love & friendship[42]—or whether worldly affairs are to separate us—I don't know. But somehow I feel (if I am not dreaming) that the good square love is in our hearts, for each other, while life lasts.

As I told you in my previous letter, this city is quite small potatoes after living in New York. The public buildings are large & grand. Most of them are made of white marble, & on a far grander scale than the N. Y. City Hall; but the oceans of life & people, such as in N. Y. & the shipping &c, are lacking here. Still a young man ought to see Washington once in his life, any how. Then I please myself with thinking it will be a

38. After listening to Traubel read this letter in 1889, WW commented on Heyde: "He is a cringing, crawling snake: uses my sister's miseries as a means by which to burrow money out of her relations. . . . I think if Charlie was a plain everyday scamp I'd not feel sore on him: but in the rôle of serpent, whelp, he excites my active antagonism" (Traubel, III, 500).

39. November 22; see 327.

40. On November 30 O. H. Browning, Secretary of the Interior, informed Congress of the completion of the exterior marble work on the Capitol; see *Documentary History . . . of the United States Capitol Buildings and Grounds* (1904), 1266.

41. WW excised the following: "No doubt you are all right, Jack, but should ever sickness or any thing trouble you, you must send me word." WW inserted similar sentiments after the first paragraph and then lined through the passage.

pleasure to you to be with me. Jack, I want you to write to me often as you can.

334. *To John Morley*

ENDORSED: "letter to Mr. Morley | reach'd London | probably New Year's | day"; "went by steamer Dec 19 | reach'd London | New Year's."
DRAFT LETTER.

Dec. 17, '68.

John Morley,[43] | Dear Sir:

I send you an original piece of mine, in hopes it will be found available for say the March Number of your magazine. The price is 4 pounds—$20—in gold—and four copies of the number in which it is printed, sent me by mail.

Please send me an answer, with decision, by next or succeeding mail. My address is Attorney Gen's office, this city.

335. *To George Palmer Putnam*

ATTORNEY GENERAL'S OFFICE,

Washington Dec. 17, 1868.

Mr. Putnam.[44] | Dear Sir:

Would the enclosed piece be available to you for say the March number of your monthly?

The price is $45—and 30 copies of the number in which it may be printed.

I have had it put in type for my own convenience, & to insure greater correctness.

May I ask you the favor to send me your decision within a week?

Walt Whitman

I reserve the right of printing the piece in future book.

42. WW originally wrote "loving society."
43. John Morley (1838–1923), a statesman as well as a man of letters, was editor of *The Fortnightly Review* from 1867 to 1882. He had visited WW in February; see 269 and Morley's *Recollections* (1917), II, 105. Morley replied on January 5, 1869, that he could not print WW's poem ("Thou vast Rondure, Swimming in Space") until April: "If that be not too late for you, and if you can make suitable arrangements for publication in the United States so as not to interfere with us in point of time, I shall be very glad" (Feinberg; Traubel, I, 216). Unaccountably, the poem did not appear in print.
44. George Palmer Putnam (1814–1872) was founder and publisher of *Putnam's Monthly Magazine*. In January Putnam had printed O'Connor's "The Carpenter," XI (1868), 55–90, and one of Burroughs' essays in August (see 295). It is not known which poem WW submitted.

336. *To a Soldier*[45]   [*1868?*]

. . . I am leading a quiet, monotonous life, working a few hours every day very moderately. Have plenty of books to read but few acquaintances. I spend my evenings mostly in the office.

---

45. For this unidentified ex-soldier, see 160.

1869

337. *To Charles F. Blanch*

ATTORNEY GENERAL'S OFFICE,

Washington. Jan. 20, 1869.

Charles F. Blanch.[1] | Dear Sir:

Your note enclosing $3:50 has just been received. I have enveloped & sent you by to-day's mail, a copy of "Leaves of Grass," as desired. I have also sent a magazine, containing a piece of mine.

Walt Whitman

338. *To James T. Fields*

ATTORNEY GENERAL'S OFFICE,

Washington. Jan. 20, 1869.

James T. Fields.[2] | Dear Sir:

The package of February magazines, sent on the 16th, arrived safely yesterday. Accept my thanks. I am pleased with the typographical appearance, correctness, &c. of my piece.[3]

I enclose a piece, "*Thou vast Rondure, Swimming in Space*," of which I have to say to you as follows. It is to appear in the April number of the *London Fortnightly Review*.[4] Having just received a note from the editor of that Review, Mr. Morley, in which he intimates that he has no objection to its appearing simultaneously in America, I thought I would show it to you. Very possibly, you will not care any how to print a piece which is to appear elsewhere. Should that, however, be no objection, and should you consider the piece available for your purposes, the price is $20. Of course it would have to go in your Number for April. I reserve the right of printing in future book.

Respectfully, &c

Walt Whitman

1869
1. I have not identified this correspondent.   2. See 331.
3. "Proud Music of the Sea-Storm." WW inserted a blurb about the poem in the Washington *Star* of January 18; see Holloway, *American Mercury*, XVIII (1929), 483–485.
4. See 334. The poem did not appear in either magazine. It later was incorporated into *Passage to India*.

339. *To Ferdinand Freiligrath*

ATTORNEY GENERAL'S OFFICE,

Washington, Jan. 26, 1869.

Dear Mr. Freiligrath:[5]

I have sent you to-day by ocean mail, a copy of my latest printed *Leaves of Grass*—not knowing whether you have received the package forwarded for you by a friend[6] of mine last November. I should be well pleased indeed to hear from you. My address is,

Walt Whitman,
Washington, D. C.
U. S. America

340. *To Louisa Van Velsor Whitman*   2.2–8. [*1869*]

ATTORNEY GENERAL'S OFFICE,

Washington. 18 | Tuesday, 2d Feb.—

Dearest mother—

I am still troubled with a severe cold in my head—I suppose it is that which causes me to have these bad spells, dizziness in the head—I have them a great deal lately; sometimes three or four in an hour[7]—

The 20 per cent bill came up again in Congress yesterday, & was rejected again[8]—I don't think there is much chance for it—It looks as though we are going to have snow—feels cold & raw—I am sitting at my desk in the office writing this—there is not much to do to-day in the office—

Wednesday afternoon. It commenced snowing yesterday noon, & stormed all day, & a rain at night—I have been out to-day—not any work hardly in the office—still I have to be around—it is a dark & muddy day

5. A German poet and translator and friend of Longfellow (1810–1876). His review in the Augsburg *Allgemeinen Zeitung* on April 24, 1868 (reprinted in his *Gesammelte Dichtungen* [1871], IV, 86–89), was among the first notices of WW's poetry on the continent. (A translation of the article appeared in *The New Eclectic Magazine*, II [July, 1868], 325–329; see also Allen, *Walt Whitman Abroad* [1955], 3–7.) Freiligrath had promised his readers "some translated specimens of the poet's productions," not a complete translation. O'Connor and WW were applying pressure. A sympathetic article on WW in the New York *Sontagsblatt* of November 1, 1868, mentioned Freiligrath's admiration for the American poet. A translation of this article, which WW had a Washington friend prepare, is now in the Feinberg Collection.

6. O'Connor; see 306 and 312.

7. Evidently WW had written of his "bad spells" in an earlier (lost) letter, for on February 4 his mother wrote: "i was sorry, Walter, you have them bad spells with your head. it must be very bad indeed, there is a kind of linement called cloroform linement. it dont affect one in the least, that is to stupify, but it is thought to be good for the neu-

here—a young man has just been in with a photograph of me—his mother had bought it at a place here, & sent it to me for me to write my name—I gratified him—They have taken a very good little photo of me here lately[9]—I will send you one before long—It is now three o'clock, & the colored man has commenced to clean up—so I will vamose—

Great excitement here among the politicians—Cant tell who will be the new Attorney General under Grant—but don't think Mr. Evarts will continue on—still I don't know—

Saturday forenoon. | Feb. 6th.

Mother, your letter has just come this forenoon—You must not worry about Han[10]—one can't tell any thing about it—but it is probable things go on with them just as they always did—I believe I shall write to Han again—shall not say any thing about Heyde, of course—

We have had a cold snap here—but this forenoon it is very pleasant, bright, & comfortable enough—I did not have any bad spells in the head yesterday—nor, so far, to-day—My cold in the head has been extremely bad, & is not well yet—Went up to Ashton's Thursday evening to spend the evening with some company—had supper about 9 o'clock.

I get along pretty well at the old boarding house—I suppose it is about as well as I could do any where—I make a fire these cold mornings, to wash & dress by—it has been very cold lately—

Monday forenoon | Feb. 8.

Well, mother, I will finish my letter & send it off—I thought to send it yesterday, Sunday, but did not come down to the office. All goes on the same with me—it is now about 11 oclock, and very pleasant—I am rather busy to-day with work in the office—but nothing to hurt—I have had a present of the most beautiful red rose you ever see—I have put it in a little glass of water, on my desk—Love to you, dearest mother, & George & all.[11]

Walt.

one of the 50cts is for Ed.

ralghy and rheumatism" (Trent). An entry in an address book (LC #109) would indicate that he went in January to Dr. Charles H. Bowen (see 238).

8. A new bill intended to raise the salaries of governmental clerks by ten per cent (substituted for the "20 per cent bill") was defeated in the House of Representatives on February 1. On the following day the New York *Times* commented: "The clerks were at it once more to-day."

9. A "capital photo" taken by Alexander Gardiner was mentioned in the Washington *Star* on January 18.

10. On February 4 Mrs. Whitman complained about Hannah's failure to write to her: "sometimes i get so worried about her that it makes me quite unhappy" (Trent).

11. During the spring George was building houses in Brooklyn and, because of the tight money situation, was having trouble arranging construction loans. Jeff advanced $3,000, for which he was to receive a mortgage, and on March 15 Mrs. Whitman asked WW to lend George $600 (Trent). Though no correspondence on the subject between WW and his family is extant, Jeff's letter of March 25 confirms the fact that WW as-

341. *To Abby H. Price*

ADDRESS: Mrs. Abby H. Price, | 331 East
55th street | bet 1st and 2d av's | New York City.
POSTMARK: Washington, D. C. | Apr | 8(?).

ATTORNEY GENERAL'S OFFICE,

Washington. April 7, 1869.

Dear Abby,

Here I am in the same office, at the same desk, writing to you
again—though the interval I know has been too long—but I will try not
to let so long a time elapse in future.

There is not much difference with me, in any respect—I have been, &
am quite well, considering—though I have had trouble from a cold during
the winter & spring—My situation in the office continues the same—The
new Attorney General, Mr. Hoar,[12] treats me very kindly—He is from
Concord, Mass. & is personally intimate with Emerson. Washington has
been swarming with office-seekers[13]—about half of whom have left—
thousands *in disgust*—it is quite a curiosity to see them around the Departments, in the hotels, and at the White House & Capitol—

The O'Connors are well as usual—William is still in the Treasury
Dep't—I spent last Sunday evening with them, at their house—

I am still boarding at the same place—I expect to bring out the final
edition of my book the ensuing summer[14]—stereotyped—(*positively last
appearance* for the season &c) as the play bills say—

Abby, I have been waiting till I felt in the mood to write a long, *good*
[inter]esting letter to you [all?][15]—but it's no use waiting—so I write
this. Don't be mad at me because I have been so negligent—You all have
my love & "best respects" to boot—how I should like just to come in &
spend the afternoon & evening with you—& Helen & Emily[16]—& then

sisted his brother (Feinberg), and on December 7 Mrs. Whitman informed WW that
George was repaying $200 (Trent).

During 1869 the lot of the Whitmans underwent no changes. Heyde still wrote nasty
letters, and Hannah promised, when she got around to writing, a visit to Brooklyn. Martha's health did not improve markedly. Though George provided a new home for his
mother, she complained that "these gals and amusements takes the greenbacks" (Summer, Trent). Mary Van Nostrand in October moved in "bag and baggage" with Mrs.
Whitman. Evidently Ansel Van Nostrand failed in business, Mrs. Whitman wrote on October 19, "got a drinking," and "come near dying with the deleru tremen" (Trent). WW
remained "the same good old standby" (June 30, Trent).

12. Ebenezer Rockwood Hoar (1816–1895) was Attorney General from 1869 to 1870
and was later a member of the U. S. House of Representatives. Evidently during the last
month of Johnson's administration WW had some uncertain moments as to his future. For
on February 17 his mother asked: "walt what is it you alluded to that was disagreable in
the office" (Trent). In his additions to the second edition of *Notes on Walt Whitman, As
Poet and Person* (1871), 123, Burroughs wrote cryptically: ". . . and afterward, (1869,)
he is subjected, in another Department, to trains of dastardly official insolence by a dig-
nitary of equal rank [to Harlan], from whom he narrowly escapes the same fate."

13. Because of Grant's new administration.

14. In a publicity blurb in the Washington *Sunday Chronicle* on May 9 (reprinted

have a good bouncing argument with Mr. Arnold, about finances, patriotism, &c &c—*What do you think of Grant*—his doings—especially some of his diplomatic appointments—Washburn,[17] for instance?

Good bye, dear friends—Love to you all.

Walt.

342.   *To Charles F. Blanch*

ATTORNEY GENERAL'S OFFICE

Washington, June 4, 1869

Dear Sir:[18]

Your letters have been received. I cordially accept your appreciation & sympathy.

I send you, same mail with this, a copy of my book, as requested—Also a copy of Mr. Burroughs's "Notes," which I have procured. Also a late photograph, accompanied by a picture taken in 1855, very good at the time. Also a late newspaper.

Since the book, there have been several pieces of mine, in magazines.[19] I will endeavor to procure them, (or some of them,) & forward you.

I send you my thanks & good will.

Walt Whitman

343.   *To Charles Warren Stoddard*

Washington, | June 12, 1869.

Charles W. Stoddard,[20] | Dear Sir:

Your letters have reached me.[21] I cordially accept your appreciation, & reciprocate your friendship. I do not write many letters, but

by Holloway, *American Mercury*, XVIII [1929], 482–483), WW spoke of his plans for the summer: a new edition of *Leaves of Grass*, "the collection, revised, and including his new verses on religious themes," and *Democratic Vistas*. These works did not appear until 1871.

15. There is an ink blot here.

16. On April 7 Mrs. Whitman informed her son that "Emily price is going to get married . . . his name is law an artist in the cheap picture line" (Trent).

17. Elihu Benjamin Washburne (1816–1887) served as Grant's Secretary of State for a few days and then resigned to become minister to France.

18. See 337.

19. After WW's letter to Blanch on January 20, only "Proud Music of the Sea-Storm" (see 331) had appeared in a magazine.

20. Stoddard (1843–1909) published *Poems*, edited by Bret Harte, in 1867. His most famous book, *South-Sea Idyls* (1873), is mentioned in 362. He was a journalist, a lecturer at the Catholic University of America from 1889 to 1902, and for a brief period Mark Twain's secretary.

21. Stoddard's first letter was written on February 8, 1867, when he was about 24; he requested (or beseeched) an autograph. When he wrote again on March 2, 1869, he was in Honolulu, and passionately implored an answer. Fascinated with the "Calamus" theme, Stoddard began a correspondence with Burroughs; see Barrus, 48. See also 362.

like to meet people. Those tender & primitive personal relations away off there in the Pacific Islands, as described by you, touched me deeply.[22]

In answer to your request,[23] I send you my picture—it was taken three months since. I also send a newspaper.[24]

Farewell, my friend. I sincerely thank you, & hope some day to meet you.

Walt Whitman

344. To Alfred Pratt

ATTORNEY GENERAL'S OFFICE,

Washington. July 1, 1869.

Dear Alfred Pratt,[25]

I am still here in Washington, & work in the same office—My health is good, & there is nothing specially new or important with me since I wrote you last. I have received your letters. Dear boy, I would like to see you, that we might be together once more, even if but for a little while—I have thought I would try to journey out your way,[26] for a few days—but it dont seem practicable just at present—

I hope you are well—you must write me a good long letter all about your affairs & yourself—all will be interesting—

I send you my love, & to your parents also[27]—Tell them I hope yet to meet them—Good bye, dear young man—I too have not forgotten those times when you lay sick in the hospital—& our love for each other—such things are not easily forgotten—Some day I will try to come out there, & we will see each other again.

Walt Whitman

I send you a newspaper with a piece in about me,[28] that may interest you. I send it same mail with this.

Good bye, my loving boy[29]—

22. In his letter Stoddard described his entry into a typical native village: "The native villagers gather about me, for strangers are not common in these parts. I observe them closely. Superb looking, many of them. Fine heads . . . Proud, defiant lips, a matchless physique, grace and freedom in every motion. I mark one, a lad of eighteen or twenty years who is regarding me. I call him to me, ask his name, giving mine in return. He speaks it over and over, manipulating my body unconciously, as it were, with bountiful and unconstrained love. I go to his grass-house, eat with him his simple food. Sleep with him upon his mats, and at night sometimes waken to find him watching me with earnest, patient looks, his arm over my breast and around me" (Feinberg; Traubel, IV, 268). (Note the similarity between Stoddard's description and the conclusion of the "Calamus" poem "When I Heard at the Close of the Day.") After listening to Traubel read this letter, WW commented: "Occidental people, for the most part, would not only not understand but would likewise condemn the sort of thing about which Stoddard centers his letter" (IV, 269).

23. This phrase did not appear in the draft; otherwise there are no significant

345. *To Abby H. Price*

ADDRESS: Mrs. Abby H. Price, | 331 East
55th street, | bet 1st and 2d Av's. | New York City.
POSTMARK: Washington, D. C. | Jul | 16.

ATTORNEY GENERAL'S OFFICE,

Washington. July 16, 1869.

Dear Abby,

Every thing here goes on pretty much the same with me. My health has been good since I last saw you. It is very monotonous here, & I sometimes feel like pulling up stakes in desperation—Abby, I have little to write about, only I wanted to write you something—I hear from you occasionally by mother's letters—What a good girl Helen is, to go and make those nice calls on mother[30]—I am grateful to her for so doing, & hope she will continue always—the same good affectionate Helen—& indeed I am sure she always will be—

It is very hot weather here—to-day it is 96 or '7—I am sitting here at my desk in the office—there is quite a breeze pouring in the window, but it is a warm wind—half our clerks are away on vacation. I shall leave Washington soon after the middle of August—then I will see you all, & we will have some good talks.

Good bye, dear Abby—I send my love to Emily,[31] & all—The O'Connors are well—Jenny[32] grows like every thing.

Affectionately

Walt.

346. *To Peter Doyle*   *8.21.* [*1869*]

Brooklyn, N. Y. | Saturday evening—Aug 21.

Dear Pete—

I have been very sick the last three days—I dont know what to

alterations.

24. WW probably sent the Washington *Sunday Chronicle* of May 9; see 342.
25. See 164.1.
26. The Pratts lived in Williamson, N. Y.
27. WW omitted mention of Alfred's wife, whom he had married in 1868; see 355.
28. Probably the Washington *Sunday Chronicle* of May 9.
29. At the bottom of the page, within a little square, is printed in pencil in another hand, "For | Mother."
30. According to Mrs. Whitman's letter of July 14, Helen Price had visited her on the preceding day. Probably WW wrote because Helen was "wondering all the time why you dont write to her" (Trent).
31. Again (see 342) WW did not refer to his mother's report that "emmily will be married this fall" (Trent).
32. The O'Connors' daughter.

call it—it makes me prostrated & deathly weak, & little use of my limbs.[33] I have thought of you, my darling boy, very much of the time. I have not been out of the house since the first day after my arrival. I had a pleasant journey through on the cars Wednesday afternoon & night—felt quite well then. My Mother & folks are all well. We are in our new house—we occupy part & rent out part. I have a nice room, where I now sit writing this. It is the latter part of the afternoon. I feel better the last hour or so. It has been extremely hot here the last two days—I see it has been so in Washington too. I hope I shall get out soon. I hanker to get out doors, & down the bay.

And now, dear Pete, for yourself. How is it with you, dearest boy— and is there any thing different with the face?[34] Dear Pete, you must forgive me for being so cold the last day & evening. I was unspeakably shocked and repelled from you by that talk & proposition of yours—you know what—there by the fountain. It seemed indeed to me, (for I will talk out plain to you, dearest comrade,) that the one I loved, and who had always been so manly & sensible, was gone, & a fool & intentional mur- derer stood in his place. I spoke so sternly & cutting. (Though I see now that my words might have appeared to have a certain other meaning, which I didn't dream of, insulting to you, never for one moment in my thoughts.) But I will say no more of this—for I know such thoughts must have come when you was not yourself, but in a moment of derange- ment—& have passed away like a bad dream.

Dearest boy, I have not a doubt but you will get well, and entirely well—& we will one day look back on these drawbacks & sufferings as things long past. The extreme cases of that malady, (as I told you before) are persons that have very deeply diseased blood, probably with syphilis in it, inherited from parentage, & confirmed by themselves—so they have no foundation to build on. *You* are of healthy stock, with a sound constitution, & good blood—& I *know* it is impossible for it to continue long. My darling, if you are not well when I come back I will get a good room or two in some quiet place, (or out of Washington, perhaps in Baltimore,) and we will live together, & devote ourselves altogether to the job of curing you, & rooting the cursed thing out en- tirely, & making you stronger & healthier than ever. I have had this in my mind before, but never broached it to you. I could go on with my work

33. WW's health had begun to deteriorate; note also 340. Yet in his puff in the Washington *Sunday Chronicle* on May 9, he had written: "On the verge of becoming half a centenarian, he retains his accustomed health, eats his rations regularly, and keeps his weight well toward 190 pounds"; reprinted in *American Mercury*, xviii (1929), 482.

34. According to Dr. Bucke, Doyle was suffering a skin eruption popularly known as "barber's itch" and was taken by WW to Dr. Charles Bowen for treatment; see *CW*, viii, 40–41n. Doyle's suicidal response to the skin irritation was undoubtedly associated

in the Attorney General's office just the same—& we would see that your mother should have a small sum every week to keep the pot a-boiling at home.

Dear comrade, I think of you very often. My love for you is indestructible, & since that night & morning has returned more than before.

Dear Pete, dear son, my darling boy, my young & loving brother, don't let the devil put such thoughts in your mind again—wickedness unspeakable—murder, death & disgrace here, & hell's agonies hereafter[35] —Then what would it be afterward to the mother? What to *me?*—

Pete, I send you some money, by Adam's Express—you use it, dearest son, & when it is gone, you shall have some more, for I have plenty. I will write again before long—give my love to Johnny Lee,[36] my dear darling boy, I love him truly—(let him read these three last lines)—Dear Pete, *remember*—

Walt

347. *To William D. O'Connor*

ADDRESS: Wm. D. O'Connor, | Light House Board, | Treasury Dep't. | Washington, | D. C.
POSTMARK: New York | Aug | 23 | (?).

Brooklyn, | August 23, 1869.

Dear William O'Connor:

I was very ill after my arrival here—& made worse by the heat—but have recovered[37]—& to-day, Monday, feel about the same as formerly. Mother is well, & sends her love to you all—mother asked a great deal about Nelly, and also about Jenny—

My brother George is remarkably well & robust this summer—he was out in all the excessive heat of the three latter days of last week, & came home every evening to his supper, unflagging, & full of strength & fun—I quite envied & admired him—especially as I felt deathly weak—indeed despicable—but, as before said, I think I am all right again now—

I have not been out yet—havn't heard any news of special interest, literary or other—havn't seen Mrs. Price—but shall begin to explore, this week—& will report in my next—

with deep-seated feelings of guilt.
35. In this uncharacteristic injunction, WW was no doubt exploiting Doyle's Catholicism.
36. Probably a laborer or a conductor. The 1869 Directory listed, however, a number of John Lees.
37. But see the following letter.

Dear Nelly, I had an unusually pleasant journey that afternoon & evening in the cars—felt quite well—enjoyed my lunch, the cold tea, &c —got in at Jersey City a few minutes after 10, not a bit tired—Nothing very new from my sisters Mat or Hannah—Eddy is as usual—

Jenny, my darling, I must not forget to put in a line for you too, & send my love—

William,[38] do you see how Mrs. Stowe[39] & the Atlanticites are getting cuffed & smitten front & rear, anent of the Byron resurrectionism? The papers are all having articles about it—& all condemn the Atlantic article.

                                                             Walt.

My address is | 101 Portland av. | opp. Arsenal | Brooklyn, New York.

348. *To Peter Doyle*

                                              Brooklyn, | September 3, 1869.

Dear Pete,

I thought I would write you a letter to-day, as you would be anxious to hear. I rec'd your letter of Aug. 24, & it was a great comfort to me. I have read it several times since—Dear Pete, I hope every thing is going on favorably with you. I think about you every day & every night. I do hope you are in good spirits & health. I want to hear about the face.[40] I suppose you are working on the road.

There is nothing new or special in my affairs or doings. The weather is pleasant here—it is pretty cool & dry. My folks all continue well— mother first rate, & brothers ditto. I do not have such good luck. I have felt unwell most every day—some days not so bad. Besides I have those spells again, worse, last longer, sick enough, come sudden, dizzy, & sudden sweat—It is hard to tell exactly what is the matter, or what to do. The doctor says it is all from that hospital malaria, hospital poison absorbed in the system years ago—he thinks it better for me in Washington than here.

About one third of the time I feel pretty well. I have taken three or four of my favorite rides on Broadway. I believe I described them to you in my letters a year ago. I find many of my old friends, & new ones too, & am received with the same warm friendship & love as ever. Broadway is more crowded & gay than ever, & the women look finer, & the shops

---

38. Someone, probably O'Connor, placed a large asterisk over this paragraph.

39. Harriet Beecher Stowe entered the Byron controversy with a vigorous, melodramatic article in *The Atlantic Monthly*, XXIV (September, 1869), 295–313. "The True Story of Lady Byron's Life" was based on an interview and some notes that Lady Byron, critically ill at the time, gave to her in 1856. She attacked the biographical studies of Thomas Moore and Countess Guiccioli, and almost deified "the most remarkable woman that England has produced in the century." Mrs. Stowe's bias and her Uncle-Tom's-cabin morality contributed little enlightenment to the subject.

richer—then there are many new & splendid buildings, of marble or iron —they seem to almost reach the clouds, they are so tall—some of them cost millions of dollars.

Staging in N. Y. has been very poor this summer—9 or $10, even on the big Broadway lines—Railroading has also been slim. New York is all cut up with railroads—Brooklyn also—I have seen Jimmy Foy[41]—he was over to Brooklyn, looking for work on a road. He was well & hearty, & wished to be remembered to you. They pay $2½ on many of the roads here, & 2¼ on the rest. The work is pretty hard, but the hours not so long as in Washington.

There is all kinds of fun & sport here, by day & night—& lots of theatres & amusements in full blast. I have not been to any of them—have not been to see any of my particular women friends—though sent for, (the papers here have noticed my arrival)—have not been down to the sea-shore as I intended—In fact my jaunt this time has been a failure— Better luck next time—

Now Pete, dear, loving boy, I don't want you to worry about me—I shall come along all right. As it is, I have a good square appetite most of the time yet, good nights' sleep—& look about the same as usual, (which is, of course, lovely & fascinating beyond description.) Tell Johnny Lee I send him my love, & hope he is well & hearty. I think of him daily. I sent him a letter some time ago, which I suppose he rec'd about Aug. 26, & showed you[42]—but I have not had a word from him. Lend him this letter to read, as he will wish to hear about me.

God bless you, dear Pete, dear loving comrade, & Farewell till next time, my darling boy.

Walt.

101 Portland av. opposite the Arsenal, Brooklyn, New York

349. *To Peter Doyle*

Brooklyn, | Friday afternoon, Sept. 10, 1869.

Dear Pete—dear son,

I have received your letter of the 8th to-day—all your letters have come safe—four altogether. This is the third I have sent you (besides that one by Adams' Express, Aug. 23d.)[43]

Though O'Connor's reply to WW is lost, he expressed his opinion of the article with his usual vigor to Rossetti on August 28: "One would fancy Mrs Stowe demented to issue this old foul romance, without one scrap of evidence, and pregnable on every side" (*Rossetti Papers*, 460).

40. The skin eruption mentioned in 346.
41. A railroad worker, cited in one of WW's address books (LC #109).
42. The letter is not known.
43. Apparently lost. It probably contained the money order mentioned in 346.

Pete, you say my sickness must be worse than I described in my letters
—& ask me to write precisely how I am. No, dearest boy, I wrote just as
it really was. But, Pete, you will now be truly happy to learn that I am
feeling all right, & have been mainly so for the last four days—& have
had no bad spells all that time. Yesterday I thought I felt as strong &
well as ever in my life—in fact real young & jolly. I loafed around New
York most all day—had a first-rate good time. All along Broadway hundreds of rich flags & streamers at half-mast for Gen. Rawlins'[44] funeral—
From the tall buildings, they waved out in a stiff west wind all across
Broadway—late in the afternoon I rode up from the Battery to look at
them, as the sun struck through them—I thought I had never seen any
thing so curious & beautiful—On all the shipping, ferry boats, public
buildings &c. flags at half mast too. This is the style here. No black
drapery, for mourning—only thousands of flags at half mast, on the water
as well as land—for any big bug's funeral.

To-day I am all right too. It is now towards 3—Mother & I have just
had our dinner, (my mammy's own cooking mostly.) I have been out all
the forenoon knocking around—the water is my favorite recreation—I
could spend two or three hours every day of my life here, & never get
tired—Some of the pilots are dear personal friends of mine—some, when
we meet, we kiss each other (I am an exception to all their customs with
others)—some of their boys have grown up since I have known them, &
they too know me & are very friendly.

Pete, the fourth week of my vacation is most ended. I shall return
the middle of next week.

Give my love to Johnny Lee—let him read this letter, & then return
it to you. Dear Jack, I rec'd your affectionate letter of Sept. 5th.

Pete, I have seen Tom Haslett[45]—he is well—he is working extra on
Broadway & 42d st. RR. He does not think of going home till Christmas.
Jimmy Foy has not got work yet.

I suppose you got "Kenilworth" I sent.

Well, boy, I shall now take a bath, dress myself & go out, cross the
river, put this letter in the p. o. & then ramble & ride around the City,
awhile, as I think we are going to have a fine evening & moonlight &c.

Good bye, dear son—We will soon be together again.

Walt.

44.   General John Aaron Rawlins (1831–1869) was Grant's aide-de-camp during
the Civil War and Secretary of War in 1869.
45.   Perhaps WW intended to write "Hassett," the Washington conductor mentioned in 304.
46.   Probably associates in the Attorney General's office.
47.   The "Parton affair" has never been adequately explained. This letter, with the
accompanying documents (reproduced in Traubel, III, 237–239), was WW's version,
written at the insistence of O'Connor when the story "was bandied about Washington—

350. *To Washington Friends*

Brooklyn | September 13, 1869.

My friends,[46]

I shall return to Washington either on *Wednesday* next, 15th or *Thursday*, 16th—Shall probably come in the train which gets in at 10:15 p. m.

Walt Whitman

351. *To William D. O'Connor*

ENDORSED (by O'Connor): "Parton Matter."
ADDRESS: Wm. D. O'Connor, | Light House Board, | Treasury Dep't. | Washington City. POSTMARK: [*indecipherable*].

ATTORNEY GENERAL'S OFFICE,

Washington, Sept 28, 1869.

Dear William O'Connor:

As you were interested in Mr. Parton's[47] money-borrowing item about me, I enclose you the receipts signed & given me by his Attorney at the time, (June, 1857.) The sum borrowed by me of Mr. Parton was Two hundred dollars. He had, just before, kindly volunteered the loan himself, without the least request or hint from me. I then declined, but afterward borrowed the money, & gave a short-time Note. I felt soon, & feel now, that it was a great impropriety on my part, & it has caused me much compunction & real unhappiness since. Any how when the time for paying the note came, I had no money. Mr. Parton then put the matter in the hands of his Attorney, Mr. Oliver Dyer, who sued. My recollection is that I confessed judgment, & proposed to Mr. Dyer that he should receive payment in goods. He came by appointment to my room in Classon avenue, Brooklyn, June 17, 1857, talked over the matter, behaved very kindly, positively accepted there & then, & conveyed away, goods to the amount of One hundred and eighty one dollars, and receipted for them, on account. He also, for the balance, conditionally accepted other goods, (which he also conveyed away with him,) on the agreement between us that if they, when more deliberately examined, proved acceptable, they would requite the balance, & the debt would be considered paid; other-

got into the papers" (III, 235). Involved according to WW were the "venom, jealousies, opacities . . . [of] a woman" (III, 235–236), probably Parton's wife, the poet Fanny Fern; yet she was the first woman to praise WW publicly (*New York Dissected*, 146–154, 162–165). Parton (1822–1891) was a journalist and, according to *DAB*, "the most successful biographer of his generation." Shortly before WW had borrowed money, Parton had published his first best seller, *The Life of Horace Greeley* (1855). See Oral S. Coad, "Whitman vs. Parton," *The Journal of the Rutgers University Library*, IV (1940), 1–8; Allen, 209–210; Mott, II, 352–353.

wise they would be returned, & the balance would still stand against me. These goods he retained, and subsequently told me that they had proved acceptable, and consented to give me a receipt in full, & satisfaction paper —but, (I think,) said the latter would require the signature of Mr. Parton. This was a meeting either in the street, or on the Brooklyn ferry. On meeting him afterwards in a similar way, once or twice, I mentioned the matter of a receipt in full, but never pressed it—never procured such receipt, nor the original note either.

I consider the debt *paid*—(though if I had wealth, to-day, I should certainly pay it over again, in cash.) Among the goods rendered I remember an oil painting, an original, of marked beauty & value, by Jesse Talbot,[48] illustrating a scene from Pilgrim's Progress, worth from four to five hundred dollars. This I put, if I remember right, at one hundred dollars. I presume Mr. Dyer or Mr. Parton has it yet.

The enclosed receipt, marked 1,[49] was, on turning over the goods, written by me & signed, by Mr. Dyer, who then remarked that he would also give me one in more technical form, and wrote, signed, & handed me the receipt marked 2[50]—I presume, (but do not know for certain,) that Mr. Dyer considers the debt fully paid.

(The balance of thirty five dollars mentioned, besides the one hundred & eighty one includes sixteen dollars as Mr. Dyer's fee, or more probably costs of suit, over & above the original two hundred.)

Walt Whitman

352. *To F. P. and W. C. Church*

ATTORNEY GENERAL'S OFFICE,

Washington. Nov. 15, 1869.

Messrs Church, | Dear Sirs:

I write a line with reference to my piece "Brother of All with

48. Jesse Talbot (1806–1879) was a Brooklyn genre painter.

49. This document, written by WW and signed by Dyer, noted the receipt of $181 and the balance of $35 due.

50. The second document, in Dyer's hand, was headed: "Supreme Court Kings County. | James Parton | vs | Walt Whitman."

51. George Peabody (1795–1869), merchant and philanthropist, died in London on November 4, and his body was returned to Danvers, Mass., in January, 1870. He founded and endowed the Peabody museums at Yale and Harvard. The poem, now entitled "Outlines for a Tomb (G. P., Buried 1870)," appeared in *The Galaxy*, IX (1870), 75–76.

52. Rossetti sent on July 13 what O'Connor termed a "precious enclosure," extracts from Anne Gilchrist's correspondence with the English critic. In his letter Rossetti described Mrs. Gilchrist: "The writer is a lady of earlyish middle age, & more than common literary cultivation. She is a person of remarkably strong sense, firm perception, solidity of judgment, with a rather strong scientific turn. My impression is that hitherto she has cared very little about *poetry*. . . . If I had been asked how this lady would receive Whitman's poems, I should have replied—'She will glance into them, set them aside in

generous hand," (commemorative of George Peabody,)[51] handed to W. C. Church here three or four days since. I suppose it ought to appear, if at all, in the January Number.

Please send me proof forthwith. Direct to me this office.

Walt Whitman

353. To William M. Rossetti

Washington, | December 9, 1869.

Dear Mr. Rossetti,

Your letter of last summer to William O'Connor[52] with the passages transcribed from a lady's correspondence have been shown me by him, and a copy lately furnished me, which I have just been re-reading. I am deeply touched by these sympathies & convictions coming from a woman, & from England, & am sure that if the lady knew how much comfort it has been to me to get them, she would not only pardon you for transmitting them to Mr. O'Connor, but approve that action.[53] I realize indeed of such an emphatic & smiling *Well done* from the heart & conscience of a true wife & mother, & one too whose sense of the poetic, as I glean from your letter, after flowing through the heart & conscience, also comes through & must satisfy Science, as much as the esthetic, that I had hitherto received no eulogium so magnificent.[54]

I send by same mail with this, same address as this letter, two photographs, taken within a few months. One is intended for the lady (if I may be permitted to send it her)—and will you please accept the other with my respects & love? The picture is by some criticized very severely indeed, but I hope you will not dislike it, for I confess myself to a (perhaps capricious) fondness for it as my own portrait over some scores that have been made or taken at one time or another.

I am still at work in the Attorney General's office. My p. o. address

her own mind as eccentric unavailable sort of work, & never touch the book again.' And see how utterly I should have been mistaken. The result fairly astonishes me" (Feinberg). Writing to Rossetti on August 28, O'Connor was obviously deeply moved, though he did not know "the dear lady's name," and he noted that, after reading the extracts, WW's "Olympian front was surcharged with a tender pensiveness" (*Rossetti Papers*, 459–460).

53.   In his letter to O'Connor, Rossetti said: "I have not told her that I communicate her letters to any one" (Feinberg). But in his diary on July 23 he noted that he had informed Mrs. Gilchrist of his action (*Rossetti Papers*, 404). Mrs. Gilchrist began to expand her comments in September, and on November 19 Rossetti "finished transcribing Mrs Gilchrist's paper on Whitman"; see *Rossetti Papers*, 411, 415, and *Letters of William Michael Rossetti*, ed. Gohdes and Baum (1934), 27–45. At the time WW wrote to Rossetti, he probably had received the new version.

54.   Though WW did not realize that Mrs. Gilchrist's passion included his person as well as his poetry, this letter, which Rossetti gave to her, served to inflame her ardor. See her letter to Rossetti on January 1, 1870 (*Rossetti Papers*, 497).

remains the same, here. I am, & have been, quite well & hearty. My new editions, considerably expanded, with what suggestions &c. I have to offer, presented, I hope, in more definite, graphic form, will probably get printed, the coming spring. I shall forward you early copies.

I send my love to Moncure Conway,[55] if you see him. I wish he would write to me, soon & fully. If the pictures don't reach you, or if they get injured on the way, I will try again by express. I wish you to read or loan this letter to the lady—or, if she wishes it, give it to her to keep.

Walt Whitman

354. *To William D. O'Connor*   [*12.23. 1869*]

ENDORSED (by O'Connor): "Dec. 23, 1869."

William

I wish to send a little box of grapes to Nelly—please go down to the Central Produce store on the N. side Avenue bet. 10th & 11th sts & get them when you go to dinner—

Walt

---

55. On January 9 Rossetti informed WW that he had conveyed "your cordial message" to Conway, who had recently returned from Russia (Feinberg; Traubel, 1, 380).

1870

355. *To Alfred, N. M., and John B. Pratt*

ATTORNEY GENERAL'S OFFICE,

Washington. Jan. 20, 1870.

Dear son & comrade Alfred Pratt:[1]

I have received your letter of the 14th. So you are going to Kansas, & it would seem you think of settling there—so it may be we shall not see each other—but I wish you to write to me, & let me know how it goes with you—& I hope, dear boy, you will continue to remember me with a love which time shall not fade out.

My dear friends, | N. M. and J. B. Pratt,

I appreciate your kindness & your hospitable invitations, & I am sure it would be a good change & a comfort to me to come out & see you, & be with you a few days, surrounded with new scenery, & a farm life—it is what I should enjoy of all things—and I hope things may work so that I can come one of these days—if so, I will send you word, in advance—The picture of the dear daughter will be welcome—I should also like another of my dear loving boy Alfred, as soon as he gets any late ones, if he does so—

So good bye & God bless you, my dear friends, & my love to all.

Walt Whitman

356. *To W. C. and F. P. Church*

ATTORNEY GENERAL'S OFFICE,

Washington. Feb. 8, 1870.

W. C., & F. P. Church. | My friends:

I send you a page & a half piece—"*A warble for lilac-time*"[2]—if available for the April Galaxy. If not, for the May number.

Yours truly

Walt Whitman.

1870
1. See 164.1. On January 14 Alfred spoke of his departure for Kansas, and John offered to send a picture of his "daughter," whom Alfred had married in August, 1868: "She ways about 100 lbs and is as handsome as a picture." (A picture of Alfred and his wife at the time of their marriage is in the Feinberg Collection.) He concluded: "please write soon to your unworthy friends" (Feinberg). On March 15 John informed WW that Alfred had left on January 25 and had settled in "Douglass," Kansas (Yale). This was apparently the last letter in the correspondence.
2. It appeared in the May issue, *The Galaxy*, IX (1870), 686.

93

357. *To Andrew and Thomas Rome*

ATTORNEY GENERAL'S OFFICE,

Washington. March 15, 1870.

Andrew & Thos. Rome,[3] | Dear friends,

I suppose the MS. of "Passage to India" came safe, last week—to be put in type as requested—with p. o. order for $10—I write now merely to ask you to *read the proof carefully by copy—correct carefully*—& then send me *two proofs*—put it through as soon as convenient.

Walt.

I have a piece in next Galaxy[4]—about three or four sticks full—about Spring—I wish you would just copy it in your paper & send me 10 copies—

358. *To The Editors*, The Overland Monthly

ENDORSED: "Overland | Monthly | sent April 4 '70."
DRAFT LETTER.

ATTORNEY GENERAL'S OFFICE,

Washington. April 4, 1870

Editors Overland Monthly:[5]

Would the accompanying piece, "Passage to India," be available to you, to be printed as leading article in either the June or July number of the "Overland"? The price is $200, and I should like 20 copies of the number—I reserve the right to print it in future book. My address is at this office.

Very respectfully,

3. The Romes were old Brooklyn friends. In their printing establishment WW set up the first edition of *Leaves of Grass*.

4. "Warble for Lilac-Time."

5. On April 13 Bret Harte replied for *The Overland Monthly:* "I fear that the 'Passage to India' is a poem too long and too abstract for the harty and material-minded readers of the *O. M.*" (Feinberg; Traubel, I, 28). Though WW liked "The Outcasts of Poker Flat" (Traubel, IV, 208), he felt that "somehow when [Harte] went to London the best American in him was left behind and lost" (Traubel, I, 28). In a newspaper interview in 1879, WW objected to Harte's "ruffians and delirium tremens specimens. . . . I think it is an outrage. He seems to me to have taken Dickens' treatment of the slums of London and transferred it to California." See *AL*, XIV (1942–1943), 146.

6. Sutherland (see 165) was now teaching at Jamestown, N. Y. In reply to WW's request for further information about his life, the former soldier observed on April 8: "You remember me in 1865 a green vain(?) lad of Eighteen—without, even, an imperfect knowledge of the rudimentary English branches, I came home from Washington and

359. *To Byron Sutherland*

TRANSCRIPT.

ATTORNEY GENERAL'S OFFICE,

Washington. April 4, 1870

Dear young man:[6]

Your affectionate letter of March 30 has reached me, and has given me much comfort—for our acquaintance in this city at the last of the war, & our being with each other so closely those two or three days & nights before you went away, have left a loving remembrance of you which will never be effaced. I am well as usual—still work in this office—still board at the same house in M Street—& I suppose hold my own generally about the same as when we were together—I suppose you have progressed a good deal & I want to hear all about it—everything about you & your fortunes will be interesting—& the sight of you, dear friend, & to have you with me again, would be more welcome than all. I will not write a long letter this time—but send you my love—& charge you to write more regularly in future.

Walt Whitman

360. *To Benton H. Wilson*

DRAFT LETTER.

April 15—1870.

Dear Benton Wilson,[7] | Dear loving comrade,

As I have just been again reading your last letter to me of December 19, last, I think I wrote to you on receiving it, but cannot now remember for certain. Sometimes, after an interval, the thought of one I much

applied myself, as soon as possible, to school and to study . . . My life since we parted that July day upon the Treasury steps, has been one of hard work and little recreation—I find on looking back to that time, that I am not so pure or trusting—that the world isint quite so fair and beautiful as it seemed then—That the world is not precisely a green pasture for unsophistocated human lambs to skip in—That I like dreaming less, and work or excitement better—That I have lost a great deal of Ambition, and gained a like quantity of stupidity—That I dont know nearly so much as I once supposed I did" (Feinberg).

7. For WW's earlier correspondence with this ex-soldier, see 230. In his letter of December 19, Wilson reported that he had moved to Greene, N. Y., but was still selling melodeons and sewing machines (Feinberg). On May 15 Wilson informed WW of his father's death two weeks earlier and related that his son "Little Walt . . . is quite a boy now . . . and gets into all kinds of Mischief." Benton's father, who "was insane at times," had written to WW on January 17, 1867, and on March 30, 1868 (Feinberg). Evidently Benton wrote to WW for the last time on June 23, 1875, when he wanted to know "what I can do to contribute to your comfort and happiness" (Berg).

love comes upon me strong & full all of a sudden—& now as I sit here by a big open window, this beautiful afternoon, every thing quiet & sunny—I have been, & am now, thinking so of you, dear young man,[8] & of your love, or more rightly speaking, our love for each other—so curious, so sweet, I say so *religious*—

We met there in the Hospital[9]—how little we have been together—seems to me we ought to be some together every day of our lives—I don't care about talking, or amusement—but just to be together, & work together, or go off in the open air together—Now it is a long while since we have been together—& it seems a long while since I have had a letter. Don't blame me for not writing oftener.

I know you would feel satisfied if you could only realize how & how much I am thinking of you, & with what great love,[10] this afternoon. I can hardly express it in a letter[11]—but I thought I would just write a letter this time off-hand to you, dearest soldier, only for love to you—I thought it might please you.

Nothing very new or different in my affairs. I am still working here in Atty Gens office—same posish—have good health—expect to bring out new editions of my books before very long—how is the little boy—I send my love to him, & to your wife & parents.[12]

361. *To Moncure D. Conway*

ATTORNEY GENERAL'S OFFICE,

Washington. April 22, 1870.

Dear Mr. Conway,[13]

I send (in the mail for printed matter,) same time as this, duplicate printed copies of a poem I have written, "Passage to India," in which I endeavor to celebrate in my own way, the modern engineering masterpieces, the Pacific Railroad & the Suez Canal—in fact the great modern

8. Originally WW wrote "dearest young man."

9. WW struck out the following: "How good it was that we met—I remember the times we used to sit there in the Ward in Armory Square Hospital."

10. The first reading was: "with what peculiar great love."

11. At this point, obviously groping for words, WW wrote but then deleted: "O if we could only be together now even if only   Dear Boy, dear, dear friend, my dear soldier—dear comrade."

12. In 1888 WW commented to Traubel about this letter: "I can't live some of my old letters over again. . . . Comradeship—yes, that's the thing: getting one and one together to make two—getting the twos together everywhere to make all: that's the only bond we should accept and that's the only freedom we should desire: comradeship, comradeship" (Traubel, II, 370–371).

13. Conway continued to act as WW's agent in England; see 269. He was not able to sell the poem to an English journal; see 366. Burroughs observed in the second edition

material practical energy & works—& then make of them as heights & apices whereby to reach freest, widest, loftiest spiritual fields. But you will see what I have written. It will make from 12 to 14, 15, or 16 ordinary pages.

Can I take the liberty of asking you to seek to dispose of the piece, if eligible, to some London magazine? It will not be printed here in any magazine—I reserve the right to print it in future book. The price, time, selection of magazine, and in fact all the points of that sort, I leave absolutely to you—

My address remains as before at this office & city. Nothing new or very different with my affairs. I remain in good health & spirits.

With love, as ever,

Walt Whitman

362. *To Charles Warren Stoddard*

Washington | April 23, 1870

Dear Charles Stoddard,

I received some days since your affectionate letter, & presently came your beautiful & soothing South Sea Idyll which I read at once.[14]

Now, as I write, I sit by a large open window, looking south & west down the Potomac & across to the Virginia heights. It is a bright, warm spring-like afternoon. I have just re-read the sweet story all over, & find it indeed soothing & nourishing after its kind, like the atmosphere. As to you, I do not of course object to your emotional & adhesive nature, & the outlet thereof, but warmly approve them—but do you know (perhaps you do,) how the hard, pungent, gritty, worldly experiences & qualities in American practical life, also serve? how they prevent extravagant sentimentalism? & how they are not without their own great value & even joy?[15]

It arises in my mind, as I write, to say something of that kind to you—

of his *Notes* (1871), 123: "The manuscript of *Passage to India* was refused by the monthly magazines successively in New York, Boston, San Francisco, and London."

14. Stoddard's letter of April 2 began dramatically: "In the name of CALAMUS listen to me!" He was sending "a proze *idyl* wherein I confess how dear [barbarism] is to me" (Feinberg; Traubel, III, 444–445). "A South-Sea Idyl," which appeared in *The Overland Monthly*, III (September, 1869), 257–264, related, with thinly veiled homosexual overtones, Stoddard's relations with a sixteen-year-old native boy Kána-ána. It was reprinted as Part One of "Chumming with a Savage" in *South-Sea Idyls* (1873).

15. WW was obviously trying to check the seething emotion of this young man who was about to sail for Tahiti: "I know there is but one hope for me. I must get in amongst people who are not afraid of instincts and who scorn hypocracy. I am numbed with the frigid manners of the Christians; barbarism has given me the fullest joy of my life and I long to return to it and be satisfied" (Feinberg; Traubel, III, 444–445).

I am not a little comforted when I learn that the young men dwell in thought upon me & my utterances—as you do—& I frankly send you my love—& I hope we shall one day meet—

—I wish to hear from you always,

Walt Whitman

363. *To Walbridge A. Field*[16]

Brooklyn May 11, 1870

Sir:[17]

The hurt on my hand has not healed.[18] Allow me to take permission till Saturday next. I shall try to report at the office on Monday next.

Respectfully

Walt Whitman
By A. H. P.[19]

Hon W A Field.

364. *To William D. O'Connor*

ADDRESS: William D. O'Connor, | Light
House Board | Treasury Dep't, | Washington | D. C.
POSTMARK: Brooklyn N. Y. | May | 11.

Brooklyn May 11, 1870

Dear William,

My hand has been pretty bad, but looks more encouraging to-day. I don't think there is anything very serious, but it has caused me much

16. The letter, now in the National Archives, is docketed: "Walt Whitman | Brooklyn, N. Y. | May 11. Recd May 12, 1870 | Asks extension of his leave | of absence—| May 12. Answered unofficially."

17. Walbridge A. Field (1833–1899) was the Assistant Attorney General from 1869 to 1870. Later he was chief justice of the Massachusetts Supreme Court.

18. Late in April or early in May, WW cut his thumb, which became infected, and he returned to Brooklyn for about two weeks. The thumb healed slowly, for his mother referred to it anxiously in letters written on June 1 (Trent), June 8(?) (LC), June 22 (Trent), and June 29 (Trent).

19. Abby H. Price wrote this letter and the following one for WW.

20. Anne Gilchrist's "A Woman's Estimate of Walt Whitman" appeared in the May issue of the Boston *Radical*, VII (1870), 345–359, reprinted in *In Re*, 41–55, and Harned, 3–22. In an undated letter, probably written early in June, 1870, Mrs. Whitman commented: "that Lady seems to understand your writing better than ever any one did before as if she could see right through you. she must be a highly educated woman" (Trent). On June 13 Heyde wrote of the article: "Yet you percieve, even the praise she bestows is qualified with the general recoil, which all natures of true human sensibility experience, at your (mistaken) barbarism. The louse and the maggot know as much about procreation as you do, and when you unveil and denude yourself, you descend to the level of the dog, with the bitch, merely" (Trent; Gohdes and Silver, 226).

Since O'Connor promised Rossetti to have Mrs. Gilchrist's essay "fitly given to the world" (Gilchrist, 187), he probably arranged for its publication in *The Radical*, which suffering, since I have been here. If the "Radical"[20] has come, send me a copy immediately. Address to No 101 Portland avenue, opposite Arsenal. Mother is well as usual. We both send love to you and Nellie. I expect to be back next Monday.

Walt Whitman
By AHP.[21]

365. *To Thomas Dixon*[22]

ENDORSED: "Thomas Dixon | 15 Sunderland | st."
DRAFT LETTER.

June 30 | '70

I must first render you thanks for the box of books, as they have at last reached me in good condition—The delay in their arrival is unaccountable. But they are welcome, and will all be read in due time, and with sincere gratitude to the donor. Both your letters also reached me, and were cordially welcomed. I should have acknowledged them at date, only that for many weeks I have been disabled from writing & from any clerical work, by reason of a wound in the right hand, which is now better.

There is nothing new or noteworthy in my own affairs. I still remain in the Attorney General's office here—still enjoying good health. I keep fashioning & shaping my books at my leisure, & hope to put them in type the current year.

You speak of my prose preface to first "Leaves of Grass." I am unable

was printed in Boston by Samuel H. Morse, and which included among its contributors at least two of WW's friends, Conway and Alcott; see Mott, III, 78. The former co-editor of the journal, Joseph B. Marvin, was now a clerk in the Treasury Department and was acquainted with WW; see 645.

21. Abby H. Price.

22. Thomas Dixon, an uneducated corkcutter of Sunderland, England, was one of WW's early English admirers. In 1856 he had bought copies of *Leaves of Grass* from a book peddler; one of these copies was later sent by William B. Scott to Rossetti. Dixon vigorously supported cultural projects and was in effect the ideal laborer of Ruskin, who printed many of his letters to the corkcutter in *Time and Tide* (1867). See *Autobiographical Notes of the Life of William Bell Scott*, ed. W. Minto (1892), II, 32–33, 267–269; Blodgett, 15–17; *The Works of John Ruskin*, ed. E. T. Cook and Alexander Wedderburn (1905), XVII, lxxviii–lxxix.

On the basis of the lengthy correspondence of this impassioned man now preserved in the Feinberg Collection, it seems clear that Dixon must have written to WW in 1869 or earlier and asked him to inquire about the whereabouts of his sister. (WW's reply is apparently lost.) They exchanged photographs at this time, Dixon's being dated October, 1869. In Dixon's first extant letter, December 23, 1869, he wrote: "I love nearly all the Men thou lovest, and all the Books and thoughts that seem congenial to me, long hath been so to me. I gaze at the Sea while I eat my food and think of thee. . . . and often while I gaze thereon I think of thee, and how thou loves that Sea, and how to thee it hath been more then to me." On January 9, 1870, Dixon informed Rossetti that he was to send it you, having not a copy left. It was written hastily while the first edition was being printed in 1855—I do not consider it of permanent value.[23] I shall send you, (probably in the mail that follows this—certainly very soon,) a piece written some while since by me on "Democracy"[24] —in which Mr. Carlyle's "shooting Niagara" is alluded to. I shall also send an article by an English lady,[25] put in print here, that may interest you.

I am writing this at my desk in the Treasury building here, an immense pile, in which our office occupies rooms. From my large open window I have an extensive view of sky, Potomac river, hills & fields of Virginia, many, many miles. We are having a spell of that oppressive heat which so much falls upon us here.

366. *To Moncure D. Conway*

Washington, | July 21, 1870.

My dear friend,

I have just received your letter of the 7th inst. I appreciate your kindness in the matter of the poem.[26] I send herewith a verbatim copy of Emerson's note,[27] as requested.

Nothing very new or special with me, these days. I am well as usual— am still employed in the Attorney General's Office. A new edition of my book will be printed this fall, with another small volume in prose.[28] You shall have early copies, may-be in sheets.

Farewell for the present. I send you my love—Write whenever you can.

Walt Whitman

---

enclosing a copy of WW's portrait, and that WW had sent "a very nice letter of sympathy for *Mother's death*, and of friendship to me" (*Rossetti Papers*, 508). In June, Dixon sent books which included Mazzini, Carlyle, and various works on oriental religion. He asked for WW's opinion of them on July 27, 1871. The fervor of the corkcutter was evident in his letter of September 8, 1874: "Ruskin is also working hard too to help on a nobler life, and one not much unlike the one you also long to see. so many souls laboring for one end must someday effect the accomplishment of the 'Golden Days' so long sung, so long toiled for, prayed for—and fought for!!" When WW wrote again to Dixon in 1876 (the letters are not known), the latter resumed the correspondence with his customary intensity. "I see thee now while I write this," he wrote on February 16, 1876. "I look into thine eyes. I grasp thy hand. Thou grasps it hard, thou looks upon me with a smile. I hear thee say: 'All is peace now, young man, the Storm is indeed past. I live once again in the Souls and memories of these Hero's and all is Well!'" Later in the same year, on June 17, he reported that in addition to selling and circulating many copies he had placed WW's poem in the town libraries at Shields, Manchester, New Castle, Warrington, Liverpool, and Plymouth. "So you see," he concluded modestly, "the little band's been a Working one."

23. Dixon had requested this preface on May 28. After Traubel read this letter in 1888, WW commented: "I may have underrated the preface: it appears to have some very likely friends" (Traubel, II, 311).

24. See 246.

367. *To Peter Doyle*   7.30–8.2. [1870]

ADDRESS: Peter Doyle, | conductor, | Office |
Wash. & Georgetown City RR. Co. | Washington |
D. C. POSTMARK: New York | Aug | 2 | 10:30 PM.

Brooklyn, | Saturday afternoon, July 30.

Dear Pete,[29]

Well here I am home again with my mother, writing to you from
Brooklyn once more. We parted there, you know, at the corner of 7th st.
Tuesday night. Pete, there was something in that hour from 10 to 11
oclock (parting though it was) that has left me pleasure & comfort for
good—I never dreamed that you made so much of having me with you,
nor that you could feel so downcast at losing me. I foolishly thought it
was all on the other side. But all I will say further on the subject is, I
now see clearly, that was all wrong.

I started from the depot in the 7:25 train the next morning—it was
pretty warm, yet I had a very pleasant journey, & we got in New York by
5 o'clock, afternoon. About half an hour before we arrived, I noticed a very
agreeable change in the weather—the heat had moderated—& in fact it
has been pleasant enough every day since. I found mother & all as well as
usual. It is now Saturday between 4 & 5 in the afternoon—I will write more
on the other side—but, Pete, I must now hang up for the present, as there
is a young lady down stairs whom I have promised to go with to the ferry,
& across to the cars.

Sunday—6 p. m.

Pete, dear boy, I will write you a line to-day before I go. I am going
over to New York to visit the lady I went down to the ferry with—so you

25. See 364.
26. See 361. Conway's letter is not known.
27. WW's transcription of Emerson's famous letter of 1855 (see 10) is with the
letter to Conway.
28. *Democratic Vistas*.
29. During this extended leave, from July 27 to October 15, WW was to see
through the presses three works, the fifth edition of *Leaves of Grass*, *Passage to India*,
and the much-delayed *Democratic Vistas*. The electroplates for these works were made
by Smith & McDougal, and J. S. Redfield was the publisher, though his name did not
appear on the title pages; see Allen, 583–584.
A few days before WW left Washington, he made one of his most enigmatic entries
in a notebook on July 15: "TO GIVE UP ABSOLUTELY & for good, from this present hour,
this FEVERISH, FLUCTUATING, useless undignified pursuit of 164—too long, (much too
long) persevered in,—so humiliating—It must come at last & had better come now—(It
cannot possibly be a success) LET THERE FROM THIS HOUR BE NO FALTERING, NO GET-
TING [*erasure*] at all henceforth, (NOT ONCE, under any circumstances)—avoid seeing
her, or meeting her, or any talk or explanations—or ANY MEETING WHATEVER, FROM THIS
HOUR FORTH, FOR LIFE" (LC; *UPP*, II, 96). For interpretations, see Allen, 421–425, and
Asselineau, 192–193, who concludes that feminine pronouns were substituted for mascu-
line. "164" was undoubtedly intended to conceal Doyle's initials, P (16) D (4).

see I am quite a lady's man again in my old days—There is nothing special to write about—I am feeling in first-rate spirits, & eat my rations every time.

Monday, Aug 1

The carrier brought quite a bunch this forenoon for the Whitman family, but no letter from you. I keep real busy with one thing & another, the whole day is occupied—I am feeling well quite all the time, & go out a great deal, knocking around one place & another. The evenings here are delightful and I am always out in them, sometimes on the river, sometimes in New York—There is a cool breeze & the moon shining. I think every time of you, & wish if we could only be together these evenings at any rate.

Tuesday—Aug 2.

Well, Pete, you will have quite a diary at this rate. Your letter came this morning—& I was glad enough to get word from you. I have been over to New York to-day on business—it is a pleasure even to cross the ferry—the river is splendid to-day—a stiff breeze blowing & the smell of the salt sea blowing up, (sweeter than any perfume to *my* nose)—It is now 2 o'clock—I have had my dinner & am sitting here alone writing this—Love to you, dear Pete—& I wont be so long again writing to my darling boy.

Walt.

368. *To William D. O'Connor*   *8.2.* [*1870*]

ADDRESS: Wm. D. O'Connor, | Light House Board, | Treasury Dept. | Washington, D. C. POSTMARK: New York | (?) | (?).

Brooklyn | Aug. 2.

Dear friend,

I write a line just to give an account of myself. I am well as usual, & in good spirits. My Mother, brother George, & all, are well. I came through finely on the RR. last Wednesday—& found myself received very agreeably just as I crossed Jersey flats, approaching New York, by an entire *change in the weather*—the distressing heat gone—& in its place summer atmosphere, of course, but moderate enough—which has continued every day since. I enjoy it all, home here, day & night—especially the nights—which are fine.

30. At this time William Swinton was professor of English at the University of California; see 37.

31. On July 30 the New York *Tribune* referred to Dr. Holmes's assertion that Boston, "our Literary Head Center," could claim writers like O'Connor.

32. Emily Price had married in 1869; see 342.

33. The 1869 Washington Directory listed George S. Smith, a driver. However, in

I hear that Wm Swinton[30] is here, from California. Your name was just mentioned on the editorial page of last Saturday's (I believe Saturday's) *Tribune.*[31] I have seen Mrs. Price, she is ill with asthma. Her daughter Emily[32] has had a fine little baby boy, now about a month resident in this mad world—(I write about the baby for Nelly and Jenny)—My sister Martha & the children have migrated from St. Louis to St. Paul, (Iowa) for a few weeks. They are as well as usual.

I am quite busy flying around—the printers & stereotypers commence on my *immortal work* to-morrow—My dear, dear friend, I hope you are well & in good spirits—I send you my love—also to Charles Eldridge, if he is there—the package of letters & paper came promptly—& I will heartily thank you to continue watching the letters &c. and forwarding them to me in same manner—

Please enclose this in your next letter to Nelly—Nelly, my darling, I hope you are having comfortable times, & that all goes well—& Jennie too—I think often about you both—& send you my best love—in which I am joined by my Mother.

Walt.

369. *To Peter Doyle*   8.3–5. [*1870*]

ADDRESS: Peter Doyle, | conductor, | Office | Wash. & Georgetown City RR. Co. | Washington, | D. C. POSTMARK: New-York | Aug | 5 | 130 P.M.

Brooklyn | Wednesday night Aug 3.

Dear Pete,

Dear son, I received your second letter to-day, also the Star. I sent you a letter Tuesday evening, which I suppose you have received. As I am now sitting in my room & have no desire to go to bed yet, I will commence another. Give my best respects to George Smith[33]—also to Pensey Bell & his brother George[34]—also to Mr. Shedd[35]—and in fact to all my railroad friends, whenever they inquire after me—

Dear son, I can almost see you drowsing & nodding since last Sunday, going home late—especially as we wait there at 7th st. and I am telling you something deep about the heavenly bodies—& in the midst of it I look around & find you fast asleep, & your head on my shoulder like a chunk

an entry dated October 13, 1868, in an address book (LC #108), WW referred to Smith as a driver on the Fifth Avenue "stage" in New York.

34. The 1869 Directory listed at the same address George A. Bell, a conductor, and Horace Bell, a messenger.

35. Henry Shedd, the driver of the streetcar (#14) on which Doyle was the conductor.

of wood—an awful compliment to my lecturing powers. All the talk here now is either the war on the Rhine,[36] or the murder of old Mr. Nathan,[37] or some other murder—for there are plenty of them—I send you a couple of papers with pieces about them. Say whether they come safe.

I believe that is all for to-night, as it is getting late—Good night, Pete —Good night, my darling son—here is a kiss for you, dear boy—on the paper here—a good long one—

Thursday—4th—I have been out all the forenoon & until about 2 o'clock—had some business in New York, which I attended, then came back & spent an hour & a half on the river, with one of the pilots, a particular friend of mine—saw the yachts, several of them, including the America out practising, for the great race that comes off Monday[38]—the Dauntless was out yesterday—& the Cambria went down three days ago— the America is the handsomest little craft I ever laid eyes on—I also saw Henry Ward Beecher[39] & had some talk with him—I find myself going with the pilots muchly—there are several that were little boys, now grown up, & remember me well—fine hearty fellows—always around the water— sons of old pilots—they make much of me—& of course I am willing—

10 o'clock at night—As this is lying here on my table to be sent off to-morrow, I will imagine you with your arm around my neck saying Good night, Walt—& me—Good night, Pete—

Friday morning Aug 5. All well—fine weather & I feel in good spirits —I am just going out, & across to New York.

Walt.

We had a heavy shower here yesterday afternoon, 4th—the weather is not too hot here.

370. *To Peter Doyle*   *8.7–10.* [1870]

Brooklyn | August 7.

Dear boy Pete,

It is a beautiful quiet Sunday forenoon. I am feeling first rate, & have had quite a good day so far. After breakfast I went out & sat a long while on the porch in front, reading the Sunday paper, enjoying the cool & shade—& besides some real sweet music—A young widow next door, a

36. The New York *Times* of August 3 reported the "first battle" of the Franco-Prussian War, the capture of Saarbruck by the French.
37. According to the New York *Times*, Benjamin Nathan, a wealthy broker and one of the founders of Mount Sinai Hospital in New York, was murdered in his home on July 29. For days the newspaper carried lengthy accounts of the unsolved murder.
38. The Queen's Cup Race was held off Staten Island on August 8. The *Dauntless* finished second, the *America* fourth, and the *Cambria* eighth. On August 9 the New York *Times* observed: "The contest was probably attended by more public and wide-spread enthusiasm than any American sporting event that has ever occurred, either on land or water."

friend of mother's, has been in her parlor the last three hours, singing and practising—she has a voice not powerful & ornamental as the opera ladies, but with that something, pleasing & tender, that goes to the right spot—sings good old hymns & songs—I have enjoyed it greatly—you would too—

It is now between ½ past 10 & 11—The distant bells are slowly ringing—Otherwise it is pretty quiet—The last two hours I have been up here reading my proof. I have four or five hours of this every day, which gives me something to do—an employment like.

Pete, I have just taken out your last letter, & read it over again—I went out on a kind of little excursion by myself last night—all alone—It was very pleasant, cool enough, & the moon shining—I think of you too, Pete, & a great deal of the time—

Tuesday afternoon 9th

I was out yesterday a great part of the day on the river to see the yacht race[40]—over a thousand spectator boats, big, little, & middle sized—many of them all drest with flags, bright colored streamers &c. streaming over the green waters, beneath the sunshine & bright blue sky—a grand sight—& the beautiful yachts & pleasure boats, lots & lots of them, with immense white sails, like great wings, tearing along in the breeze—the bay each side alive with people on the boats—150,000 people they say—the shores & hills covered for miles too—I was out again last night. It was fine—

Your welcome letter of the 8th has come this morning, dear loving son, & has pleased me, as always. That accident on the bridge was indeed terrible[41]—that bridge is a disgrace to Washington, any how—Pete, I wish you to tell Mr. & Mrs. Nash[42] & your cousin, & all, I send them my best respects—Also Henry Hurt—also Andy Woolridge[43] on 7th st—

Wednesday afternoon | 10th—

Dear son, yours of 9th came this forenoon—I feel quite unhappy about your bad luck again—reported by some damned fool, & taken off by a worse damned fool—But you keep a good heart, Pete—school will keep some how—I have no room to write more at present—Dear loving son, I want to keep writing frequently.

Walt.

39. The celebrated clergyman (see 12).   40. See 369.

41. The Washington *Daily Morning Chronicle* of August 7 noted an accident on the Chesapeake & Ohio Railroad at White Sulphur Springs, Greenbrier County, W. Va., in which twelve people were killed.

42. Mr. and Mrs. Michael Nash, Washington friends to whom WW referred frequently in his letters to Doyle. Mr. Nash was an old resident of the city (see 559).

43. Probably Andrew J. Wooldridge (not Woolridge), listed as a druggist in 1873.

just going out—Bub, just in the nick of time before I sealed this letter, as I had finished dressing to go out, mother sung out to me from the foot of the stairs—& I got your good welcome third letter. Pete, you are doing first-rate. I guess Pleasants[44] was after something stronger than Kissengen[45]—Tell Dr. Milburn[46] I dont find any place in N. Y. or Brooklyn to compare with his, for the mineral drinks—But I am living more to suit me in the grub line, this weather—not so much meat—mother's cookery, & quite a good deal of fruit &c.—A lovely broil'd steak & perfect coffee this morning—I wish you had been on hand, young man—

371. *To Peter Doyle*   8.12. *[1870]*

Brooklyn, | August 12.

Dear son,

Yours of yesterday 11th has just this minute come, & I wish to write a few lines so that you may get them before Sunday. I have not time to write much, as it is now about 5 p. m. Dear son, I hope you will not feel discouraged at the situation, even if it comes to the worst. It is now thought that business generally throughout the country is ready to revive as soon as the hot season is done, & that every thing will be brisker this fall than any time since the war. Dear Pete, whatever happens, in such ups & downs, you must try to meet it with a stout heart. As long as the Almighty vouchsafes you health, strength, & a clear conscience, let other things do their worst—& let Riker[47] go to hell. You are better off to-day to be what you are, than to be him, with his $10,000 a year—poor thin-livered cuss that he is—

My darling son, I will send you $5 every Saturday, should you be idle —as I can easily spare that, & you can depend upon it—it wont go far, but it may take the edge off.

Many, many loving kisses to you, dear son—for I must close, or I shall lose to-night's mail.

Walt.

372. *To Peter Doyle*

Brooklyn, | August 22, 1870.

Dear Pete,

I have not heard from you now for nine days. Your letter of 13th (last Saturday week,) in which you said the orders were for you to go to

44. Chief clerk in WW's office (see 187). He died later in the year or early in 1871 (see 383).
45. A mineral water.
46. J. P. Milburn & Co., druggists: "Proprietors and Manufacturers of Milburn's

work next day, was the last I have received. I took it for granted that you went to work, & have been at it since—& I hope all is right with you—but why have you not written? Dear son, if not to work I wish to send you a little money.

Every thing goes well with me—that is, every thing goes as well as can be expected—I am feeling first-rate—I am down the bay often, & sometimes spend nearly all day on the sea-shore a few miles down—I am all sunburnt & red, & weigh *severeal* pounds more than when I left Washington—A friend who hasn't seen me for a good while said this morning—"Why, Walt, you are fatter & saucier than ever"—but I will close by sending my love, to my darling son—& to him I shall always be the same old

Walt.

373. *To Peter Doyle*   *8.25–26.* [*1870*]

Brooklyn, August 25.

Dear son,

I will begin a letter for you to-day, & probably finish it to-morrow, & send it off, so that you will have it by or before Sunday. The heat is again upon us here, days—but the nights are pleasant. It is now Thursday afternoon, between 3 and 4—& I am writing this in my room in Portland av. Pete, one month of my leave exactly is up to-day. I have been out quite a while to-day, over to New York, to the printing office, & seeing to one thing & another. It was sweaty work. On my way back, I went up in the pilot house & sailed across the river three times—a fine breeze blowing. Then home—took a bath—ate my dinner—& here I am all alone, most stript, taking things as cool as possible, & writing this letter.

Pete, your letter of 23d came yesterday, & the one written partly that night & partly 24th came this forenoon. Those are the only letters I have received since the one of 13th telling me the orders were for you to go to work next day, (Sunday.) I have been uneasy ever since to hear. The letter rec'd this morning gives me the first definite information how things have turned out. Dear son, I want you to try to cast aside all irritating thoughts & recollections, & preserve a cheerful mind. That is the main part of getting along through the toil & battle of life—& it is a good deal habit.[48]

I was away a good part of last week, down the bay—went away each time early in the morning, & got home after dark. I am having quite jovial times. I went to Wallack's theatre one night lately with a friend who

UNRIVALED POLAR SODA WATER."

47. Silvanus S. Riker, president of the Washington & Georgetown Railroad, for which Doyle worked.

48. WW was disturbed by Doyle's mood swings; note also 346.

wanted to see a piece called "Fritz"[49]—a miserable, sickish piece. I was glad enough to get out in the open air away from such humbug. I am still feeling gay & hearty. I work several hours a day keeping things straight among the printers & founders, on my books. They are being cast in electrotype plates. I will tell you more about it when we meet. Well, Pete, I guess this will do for to-day. I think of sallying forth, soon as the sun gets pretty well down, & crossing to New York to loafe around two or three hours.

Friday afternoon | August 26.

Well I went over to New York last evening—up town to see some friends—come home about 11—just in time to escape a thunder shower. It is splendid to-day—I have been over all day working, quite busy—& have just got home & had my dinner—it is now about 4—It is quite pleasant riding here in Brooklyn—we have large open cars—in good weather it is real lively—I quite enjoy it—

Pete, give my respects to Mr. & Mrs. Nash, & to your cousin—also to Jenny Murphy[50]—not forgetting the boys on the road—also Wash Milburn[51]—God bless you, & good bye for this time, my own dear loving boy.

Walt.

374. *To Peter Doyle*

ADDRESS: Peter Doyle | Conductor | Office | Wash. & Georgetown City RR. Co. | Washington, | D. C. POSTMARK: New-York | Sep | 2 | 6:30 P.M.

Brooklyn | September 2, 1870.

Dear Pete,

I received your welcome letter of Aug. 27th—and also 31st, enclosing Ned Stewarts[52]—When you write tell Ned I am here in Brooklyn, loafing around—& that I send my love. Pete, there is nothing particular to write about this time—pretty much the same story—every day out on the bay awhile, or going down to Coney Island beach—and every day from two to four or five hours in the printing office—I still keep well & hearty, & the weather is fine—warm through the middle of the day, & cool mornings & nights—

49. J. K. Emmet appeared in Charles Gayler's *Fritz, Our German Cousin* at Wallack's Theatre from July 11 to September 10; see Odell, VIII, 564–565.

50. Not identified.

51. W. C. Milburn, either the son or the brother of Dr. J. P. Milburn (see 370).

52. Probably Edward C. Stewart, who wrote an undated letter on February 12. WW also referred to him in an address book (LC #109).

53. WW referred to the "Fred Gray association"; see 40 and Introduction to Volume I. According to the New York Directory of 1870–1871, Charles H. Russell lived

I fall in with quite a good many of my acquaintances of years ago[53]—the young fellows, (now not so young)—that I knew intimately here before the war—some are dead—& some have got married—& some have grown rich—one of the latter I was up with yesterday & last night—he has a big house on Fifth avenue—I was there to dinner (dinner at 8 p. m.!)—every thing in the loudest sort of style, with wines, silver, nigger waiters, &c. &c. &c. But my friend is just one of the manliest, jovialest best sort of fellows—no airs—& just the one to suit you & me—no women in the house—he is single—he wants me to make my home there—I shall not do that, but shall go there very frequently—the dinners & good wines are attractive—then there is a fine library.

Well, Pete, I am on the second month of my furlough—to think it is almost six weeks since we parted there that night—My dear loving boy, how much I want to see you—it seems a long while—I have rec'd a good letter from Mr. O'Connor,[54] & also one from John Rowland[55] who is in the office for me. Nothing new in office—Well, Pete, about half our separation is over—the next six weeks will soon pass away—indeed it may be only four, as John Rowland told me he might wish to go away—

Good bye for the present, my loving son, & give my respects to any of the boys that ask about me.

Walt

375. *To Peter Doyle*

ADDRESS: Peter Doyle | conductor, | Office |
Wash. & Georgetown City RR. Co. | Washington |
D. C. POSTMARK: New-York | Sep | 6 | (?).

Brooklyn, | September 6th 1870.

Dear son,

I see by your letter of the 4th that you are working as usual. I sometimes fancy I see you—and 14—and Mr. Shedd—going up or down the Avenue—or at the end at Georgetown—or Navy Yard—the old familiar route & scenes—the Circle, the President's House—Willard's—7th street—Capitol Gate—the Hill—&c. &c. &c.

at 417 Fifth Avenue. Russell's occupation was not cited, and he was not listed in the following year.

54. Not extant.

55. A clerk in the Attorney General's office (see 216). On September 24 Rowland received through A. J. Falls $50, "on account, for service as substitute for Walt Whitman." A later receipt, dated October 18 and prepared by WW himself after his return to Washington, read: "Received from W. W. seventy dollars additional, making One hundred & twenty dollars—in full of all demands" (Feinberg).

I keep pretty busy, writing, proof-reading, &c. I am at the printing office several hours every day—I feel in capital health & spirits—weigh several pounds heavier—but, as a small drawback, & something new for me, find myself needing glasses every time I read or write—this has grown upon me very rapidly since & during the hot weather, & especially since I left Washington—so I read & write as little as possible, beyond my printing matters, &c—as that occupies several hours, & tires my eyes sometimes.

We are having splendid fall weather, both days & nights. Last night I was out late—the scene on the river was heavenly—the sky clear, & the moon shining her brightest—I felt almost chilly at last with the cold—& so put for home. One of the prettiest sights now is to see the great German steamers, and other ships, as they lay tied up along shore, all covered with gay flags & streamers—"dress ship" as they call it—flaunting out in the breeze, under a brilliant sky & sun—all in honor, of course, of the victory of the German armies[56]—all the spars & rigging are hid with hundreds & hundreds of flags—a big red-white-& black flag capping all—

Of course you may know that the way the war turns out suits me to death—Louis Napoleon fully deserves his fate—I consider him by far the meanest scoundrel (with all his smartness) that ever sat on a throne. I make a distinction however—I admire & love the French, & France as a nation—of all foreign nations, she has my sympathy first of all.[57]

Pete, I was just reading over your last letter again. Dear son, you must try to keep up a good heart. You say you do—but I am afraid you are feeling, (or have felt,) somewhat unhappy. One soon falls into the habit of getting low spirited or deprest & moody—if a man allows himself, he will always find plenty to make him so—Every one [has] his troubles, disappointments, rebuffs, &c. especially every young & proud-spirited man who has to work for his living. But I want you to try & put a brave face against every thing that happens—for it is not so much the little misfortunes of life themselves, as the way we take them & brood over them, that causes the trouble.

About the "*tiresome*,"[58] all I have to say is—to say nothing—only a good smacking kiss, & many of them—& taking in return many, many, many, from my dear son—good loving ones too—which will do more credit to his lips than growling & complaining at his father.

Walt

56. Napoleon III was deposed and the French army surrendered on September 2.
57. For WW's changing attitude toward the Franco-Prussian war, see 377. In the New York *Evening Mail* on October 27, the Washington correspondent reported: "At the commencement of the present war in Europe [WW] was strongly German, but is now the ardent friend of the French, and enthusiastically supports them and their Republic" (Glicksberg, 116*n*.). Note also "O Star of France."

376. *To Peter Doyle*

ADDRESS: Peter Doyle, | Conductor, | Office |
Wash & Georgetown City RR. Co. | Washington, |
D. C. POSTMARK: New-York | Sep | 9 | 6 P.M.

Brooklyn | September 9, 1870

Dear son,

I wrote you a letter last Tuesday, 6th, which I suppose you have rec'd. The last I have from you was yours of Sunday, 4th. I am still here in Brooklyn, quite busy with the printing. I have rec'd a letter from John Rowland who is working for me in the office, complaining that he has to work too hard—I should think by his letter he means to back out of his bargain with me—if so, it will be a bad loss & inconvenience to me—But I shall not fret about it—whatever happens. It is likely that this will shorten my leave, & that I shall have to come back & do my work myself, about the end of the month.

Dear Pete, I hope you are having good times, & are in good spirits. We are having quite coolish weather here. The drivers wear their over-coats mornings & evenings. As I sit here writing Friday afternoon, it is cloudy & threatens rain. I am going over to New York in an hour or so, & shall leave this in the P. O., and then go around awhile—possibly going to Niblo's Theatre, as they play Shakespeare's "Julius Caesar" to-night, with Davenport & quite a bunch of stars in the piece[59]—

Son, I am afraid I shall not make out much of a letter this time—but you take it so hard when I don't write, I thought I would send a few lines —they would be better than nothing—

God bless you, my loving boy—& farewell for this time.

Walt.

377. *To Peter Doyle*   *9.15–16. 1870*

ADDRESS: Peter Doyle | Conductor, | Office |
Wash. & Georgetown City RR. Co. | Washington, |
D. C. POSTMARK: New-York | Sep | 16(?) | (?).

Brooklyn, | September 15, 1870.

Dear Pete,

Your letters of 10th and 12th have come safe, & are welcome— dear son, I see you are hard at work & appear to be in lively spirits—I am

58. Since Doyle's letters to WW in 1870 are lost, it is impossible to explain this paragraph.

59. WW did not see this play on September 9, since that was the one evening in the week on which it was not presented. The cast included E. L. Davenport as Brutus. Laurence Barrett as Cassius, and Walter Montgomery as Marc Antony.

glad to hear you practice with the Arithmetic—I wish you to try & do a little with it every day—practice makes perfect—you will see how soon & how clear it will all come to you—If you have the Geography or Atlas, look into that a little too—one needs to have an idea of the world too.

I am concerned to hear of the death of Amos Dye—poor Amos—he was one of the first (I don't know but the very first) of the railroad men there I got acquainted with, & rode with—Pete, if there is any further subscription for Mrs. Dye, I authorize you to put me down for $5—I will either send the money, or give it to her when I return—

I shall return in about three weeks. I am now in the eighth week of my furlough—it is seven weeks last Tuesday night since we parted there at the corner of 7th street. Well, Pete, dear loving boy, I must now close for to-day.

Walt.

late Friday afternoon | Sept. 16.

Dear son, I have time to add only a few words, in order to put it in the mail this evening—I am working a while every day at my printing yet—but I go around considerable—still go out in the bay—& enjoy myself among my friends here—& in riding around, &c—The weather is very fine, both days & nights. I don't know whether I told you how I stand now about the war—suffice it to say, that as things have gone on, & as the case stands, I find myself now far more for *the French* than I ever was for the Prussians[60]—

Then I propose to take my first drink with you when I return, in celebrations of the pegging out of the Pope & all his gang of Cardinals & priests—& the entry of Victor Emanuel into Rome, & making it the capital of the great independent Italian nation.[61]

Good bye till next time, darling boy.

Walt.

378. *To Peter Doyle*   9.23. [1870]

Brooklyn | Friday, Sept. 23.

Dear Pete,

Your letter of last Sunday & Monday came safe—was glad to see you so cheerful & feeling well, as seemed plain by the tone of the letter.

60. Note 375.

61. The New York *Times* of September 15 reported that the Papal troops were evacuating various towns and Papal states. On September 21 the forces of Victor Emmanuel entered Rome without bloodshed, after "the Pope forbade any resistance."

62. Baalam Murdock, a conductor, was mentioned in an address book: "went to school several years but with little profit" (*LC* #108).

63. Perhaps the Rev. F. E. Boyle; see also 78. An address book (*LC* #109), how-

All goes right with me. I am feeling well, & business matters move along as favorably as could be expected, taking all things in consideration. The weather is elegant—We had rain here too last Saturday & Sunday—& since then it has been clear & bright—I am out dashing around every day —fetch up home every night somewhere between 10 & 1 oclock, quite tired. The river & bay get more & more beautiful, under these splendid September skies, the green waves & white foam relieved by the white sails of the crowds of ships & sail craft—for the shipping interest is brisker this fall than it has been for twelve years.

Say to Harry Hurt, Mr Shedd, Pensey & George Bell, Baley Murdock,[62] George Smith, Dr. & Wash. Milburn, or any of the railroad boys, or other friends that may inquire after me, that I send them my best respects—not forgetting my friends Mr. & Mrs. Nash—also Father Boyle[63]— (By the bye, Pete, I have taken a great fearful drink of whiskey, in honor of the news that arrived night before last of Victor Emanuel entering Rome—I couldn't wait.)

Later—afternoon—It is now between 3 and 4—I have been pitching in heavy to a great dish of stewed beef & onions mother cooked for dinner—& shall presently cross over to New York & mail this letter—shall probably go to some amusement with a friend this evening—most likely Buckleys Serenaders[64]—

Pete, dear son, I hope this will find you all right, & every thing lovely— It will not be long now before I shall be back—Till then, take care of yourself, my loving son.

Walt.

379. *To John T. Trowbridge* 9.24. *[1870]*

107 north Portland av | Brooklyn, N. Y. | Sept. 24.

My dear friend,[65]

I am here a while on leave—am in good health as usual—have been engaged in electrotyping a new edition of my book in better form—You sent me word a year or more ago of some Boston publisher, or bookseller, who was willing (or perhaps wished) to sell my book[66]—Who was it?— I should like to have some such man there—to sell the book on commission, & be agent, depositor, &c—He will be under no expense, of course &

ever, listed an A. F. Boyle of Washington, a journalist.

64. G. Swayne Buckley's minstrel troupe appeared in Brooklyn in August in travesties of operas; Odell, however, does not record performances in September.

65. See 102.

66. On July 20, 1867, Trowbridge had suggested W. H. Piper as "a good man to retail the book" (Feinberg; Traubel, III, 506).

will only receive the books from me on sale—I wish to put his name in an advertisement list of agents—

Please answer forthwith—direct to me here.

Yours as ever

Walt Whitman

No objection to a couple of such Boston bookselling places—as agencies. Love to the son, dear boy.[67]

380. *To Peter Doyle*   9.[*30. 1870*]

Brooklyn, | Friday afternoon, | Sept. 29.[68]

Dear Son,

I am sitting here in my room, having just eat a hearty dinner with my mammy, (who has this month entered on her 76th year,[69] but to my eyes looks young & handsome yet.) It is a dark & cloudy day, & the rain is just now pouring down in torrents. It is a great disappointment to many, as Farragut's funeral celebration[70] was to come off to-day, & all the military, & Departments here, & hundreds of societies, orders, schools &c. had prepared to turn out—& most of them did turn out, this forenoon, only to get soaked with rain, & covered with mud—I saw one crack battalion, all so spruce & handsome, with white pants, & silver gray coats, & every thing so bright & trim when they marched down—& an hour & a half afterwards, they looked like draggled roosters that had been pumped on—

We have had weeks and weeks of the very finest weather up to early this morning, & now it is the worst kind to be out in. Still we want rain so very much, one dont feel to complain.

Pete, I rec'd your last letter, the 26th—it was a good long, lively letter, & welcome—you write about the Signal Corps—Allen[71] deserves credit for persevering & studying—& I hope he will do well—& think he will too —for he is sober, & tries to get ahead—any how he is a young man I like —Thornett[72] is a very intelligent manly fellow, cute, plucky, &c—he has one fault, & a bad one—that is he will drink, & spree it—which spoils all— True it is none of my business, but I feel that it would be perhaps the mak-

67. Windsor Warren Trowbridge (1864–1884); see Gohdes and Silver, 75*n*.
68. WW intended to write "Sept. 30," which was Friday; see note on Farragut below.
69. Mrs. Whitman was born September 22, 1795.
70. The burial rites of Admiral David Glasgow Farragut (1801–1870) were held in New York on September 30. All business activity was suspended, and the ceremonies, according to the New York *Times*, "surpassed in their imposing character anything of the kind ever seen in this City, with the exception of the obsequies of the murdered President

ing of him, if he would give it up, & find his pleasure in some other way—Pete, should you see Allen again, give him my love—& the same for Thornett also—

Did you mean for me to write what I think of your joining the Signal Corps? But are you proficient enough in studies? I heartily advise you to peg away at the arithmetic—do something at it every day—arithmetic is the foundation of all such things—(just as a good stone wall is the foundation for a house)—become a good arithmetician first of all—& you *surely will, if you keep pegging away a little every day*—how much leisure you have after all, that might be used for study—I don't mean all your leisure, but say one hour out of every three—then keep looking over the geography—when I come back I will bring a little pocket dictionary—with 15 minutes writing every day, & correcting by the dictionary I would warrant you becoming a correct speller & real handsome writer in a year or less—& when one is a fair arithmetician & spells & writes finely, so many things are open to him.

As things stand at present I expect to be back by or before next Sunday.[73]

Walt.

381. *To William D. O'Connor*   *10.10.* [*1870*]

ENDORSED: "Answ'd Oct 12." ADDRESS: Wm. D. O'Connor, | Treasury Department, | Light House Board, | Washington, | D. C. POSTMARK: New-York | Oct(?) | (?) | 6 PM(?).

107 north Portland av. | Brooklyn, Oct. 10.

My dear friend,

I shall return to Washington next Saturday, 15th—William, it would be a favor if you would secure me a room to lodge & quarter in[74]—(look at the Dyer Hotel—it is a one-horse place, but might answer—or the Union hotel at Georgetown)—just needed for temporary purposes, (unless I find it sufficiently inviting to make me a "permanency")—

I do not feel to be very particular—only it would be so much off one's mind to have a specific point to make for—Write to me, so that I may get

Lincoln."

71. Perhaps George Allen, mentioned in 525.
72. Alfred Thornett, like Doyle, was a conductor; see LC #109. Evidently he later entered the Signal Corps, since in another address book (LC #108) WW gave his address as "Obs. Sig. Serv. U. S. A., Mt. Washington, N. H."
73. WW altered his plans; see the following letter.
74. Evidently WW had given up his room with the Benedicts.

the letter Friday, 14th—or else meet me at the depot at 10 Saturday evening, if eligible—

All goes "as well as could be expected" with me—that's the phrase you know in parturition cases—& have not I been just delivered—& of triplets?[75]—I am hearty in health, & good spirits, Mother is well—also George —& in fact the whole Whitman family.

Have not heard a word from you or Nelly, since your letter—Has Nelly returned yet? Where is Charles Eldridge? I write this in my room home, early afternoon—Mother & I having had tete-a-tete dinner—so good & quiet—& this bright mellow October weather around us—I am now off for a couple of hours on the river & bay.

Walt.

382. *To William D. O'Connor*   *10.14.* [*1870*]

ENDORSED: "Answered"(?). ADDRESS: Wm. D.
O'Connor, | Treasury Department, | Light House
Board | Washington, | D. C. POSTMARK:
New-York | (?) | (?).

Brooklyn | Friday afternoon | Oct. 14

Dear William O'Connor,

I have just rec'd your letter. To make the matter certain won't you take thirty or forty minutes & go down to the St. Cloud—look at the rooms, & pick out one for me?—positively engaging it—You know what is good as well as I do, (I mean for me)—I shall want a room at least for a few weeks—& perhaps for the winter—& for that season one is not so particular about the location—(But perhaps you have already engaged for me at St. C. a specific room.)

lovingly

Walt.[76]

75. *Leaves of Grass, Passage to India,* and *Democratic Vistas.*
76. "Sigma" noted in the New York *Evening Mail* on October 27 the poet's return to Washington, "where Walt Whitman fitly belongs, both in his *personnel* and what his works represent." The correspondent also reported that WW now supported the French, liked and defended Grant, and placed "little stock in 'woman's rights.'"

1871

383. *To Amos Tappan Akerman*

DEPARTMENT OF JUSTICE

Washington. Jan. 9, *1871.*

Hon. A. T. Akerman,[1] | Attorney General.

Sir:

I hereby respectfully make application for the office of Pardon Clerk, now vacant in the Department of Justice.

I have served in the Department under Attorney Generals Speed, Stanbery, Browning, Evarts, Hoar, & yourself—am familiar with the general routine of the office (am the oldest in continuous service of any of the present clerks)—think I could soon learn the special duties of the pardon desk—and hope I should conscientiously seek to perform them, both with regard to their great official, and still greater moral obligations.

I would refer to Mr. Speed and Mr. Stanbery, Attorneys General, & Mr. Ashton, Assistant Attorney General, under whom I have acted as clerk, some of them for several years—and to Mr. Pleasants,[2] late Chief Clerk—and if agreeable to you, or desirable, would bring written testimonials from them.

Very respectfully,

Walt Whitman

Should it not be convenient to grant the foregoing application I respectfully ask to be promoted to a fourth-class clerkship, to date from 1st of February, 1871.[3]

Walt Whitman

1871
1. Akerman (1821–1880) served in the Confederate Army and was Attorney General from 1870 to 1871.
2. See 187.
3. The letter is endorsed: "Received Jany 10, 1871 | Dated Jany 9 1871 | From Walt Whitman Clerk | Subject: Asks for position of pardon clerk | Action. [*unfilled space*] | Filed June 2, 1871."

384. *To James S. Redfield*

TRANSCRIPT.

Washington | Jan. 29, 1871

My Dear Redfield,[4]

The $25 you sent me last week duly arrived, for which please accept this Receipt, & my thanks.

Walt Whitman
Solicitor's office Treasury

385. *To John Flood, Jr.*   *2.23.* [*1871*]

DRAFT LETTER.

Feb. 23.

Dear son,[5]

I received yours of the 9th—and was right glad to hear from you, and to get such an affectionate letter. We have had gay times here this week, with what they call the "Carnival"—it continued two days & nights. The nights were the best. Every thing was lit up, and it was like a scene of enchantment. The crowds of spectators were countless. Hundreds and even thousands mixed in, the second afternoon & night in fancy dresses, or wore masks—& went around having fun. Lots of women were out, some of them as full of sport as the men—The principal street here is very wide, I should think three times as wide as Broadway. This was the scene of operations. All the vehicles were turned off, then at certain hours let on again for a while, for driving & races—there were some splendid horses— Less drinking than you would have supposed—No musses, & no acci-

4. Redfield, a publisher at 140 Fulton Street, New York, was a distributor of WW's books in the early 1870's. On March 23, 1872, Redfield accepted 496 copies of *Leaves of Grass:* "I am to account to him (for all that I may sell) at the rate of One Dollar & Fifty Cents a copy, (1.50)" (Feinberg). (The receipt, written by WW, originally read $1.60, but was corrected to the lower figure when the receipt was dated in another ink.) When WW prepared his will on October 23, 1872, he noted that Redfield had 500 copies of the fifth edition of *Leaves of Grass,* 400 copies of *As a Strong Bird on Pinions Free,* and 500 copies of *Democratic Vistas* (Trent). Redfield later established a London outlet for *Democratic Vistas* and *Leaves of Grass* with Sampson, Low, Marston, Low, and Searle, who, on March 28, 1873 (Feinberg), transferred Redfield's account for the remaining books to WW. On February 12, 1875, when his firm was in bankruptcy, Redfield noted that the balance due WW ($63.45) "will have to go in with my general indebtedness. I think my estate will pay 50 cents on the dollar: hope so at any rate." He suggested that Doolady (see 252) and the new Boston firm of Estes & Lauriat might agree to handle his books. He noted, however, that most book dealers were unwilling to sell WW's books, either because of inadequate sales or because of the poet's reputation in respectable circles: "It is only here and there a speckled sheep, like J. L. R., turns up who—not to put too fine a point upon it—don't care a d--n for Mrs Grundy, who would take you in"

dents. I send you a paper. Last night however was a murder, a man I knew well by sight, a gambler called "Sonny James"[6] was killed.

With me all goes about the same. I work about 6 hours every day, mostly writing—am well & hearty, travel around out doors quite a good deal—& keep up a cheerful heart.[7] Johnny,[8] you say you should like to see me—Well, no more than I should to see you, my darling[9] boy. I wish we were together this minute, & you had employment so we could remain with each other, if you would feel satisfied to be so.[10]

Have[11] you got work of any kind there in Brooklyn? Write to me, Jack,[12] & let me know all particulars.[13] Love to you, dear son,[14] & good bye for this time.

385.1 *To John Flood, Jr.(?)*   *3.8. [1871?]*

DRAFT LETTER.

Wednesday evening | March 8

Dear son,

I thought I would write you just a short letter, if no more, as you are in my mind this evening. I sometimes come to the office nights, to read, it is so quiet—and now I am sitting here at my desk, with a good lamp, all alone. So I thought of my dear boy, and will send a few words, though nothing particular to say.

Johnny, I wish you would write to me when you receive this, whether you have got work yet. Dear son, if you feel to come on here on a visit, you come with me—you shall not be under any expense for board and lodging.

Johnny, I send you my love, & good night for this time—the mail closes at 8, & it is some after 7 now.

(Feinberg).

5. See 327. The date of this letter is based on WW's reference to Flood's unemployment: on January 11 Flood wrote that he had been "discharged" on New Year's Eve (Yale). WW's first salutation was, "Dear boy." The frequent alterations in this letter are interesting: WW softened his affectionate terms, and attempted to make the relationship that of a father and son.

6. Joseph "Sonny" James, a well-known Washington gambler, was killed in a brawl by Horatio Bolster, an ex-prizefighter.

7. At first WW wrote: "& keep up pretty good spirits."

8. WW at this point deleted "Jack" and "my darling."

9. The first reading was "my loving boy."

10. The qualifying clause was an afterthought.

11. The following was struck out at the beginning of this paragraph: "Should you feel like coming on here . . . Wha . . . Are you doing any th[ing]."

12. WW excised "Johnny" and "my dear son."

13. The next sentence was deleted: "Don't make any move without . . ."

14. "Boy" was altered to "son."

386. *To Abby H. Price*

ADDRESS: Mrs. Abby H. Price | 331 East
55th street | bet 1st and 2d av's. | New York City.
POSTMARK: Washington | Apr | 22 | D. C.

Washington | April 21, 1871.

Dear Abby,

I have seen Major Saxton,[15] & handed him your note, & the accompanying paper—he said he knew the 4th Auditor personally, & would see him about it, & would probably write to you within three or four days. So Arthur[16] is home, & you are all well—what with the baby[17] & all you women—what jolly times you must have—I wish I could just drop in and take part in them—

With me, nothing very new or special—I am well & hearty—feel first-rate the greater part of the time—and as to streaks of the other kind of feeling, I am thankful they are so few—for you know I am getting to be an old fellow—though my temperament for buoyancy & fun I believe increases instead of diminishes—I shall take my vacation considerably earlier than usual, this summer—so it wont be long before I shall see you all.

Love to all—not forgetting the baby.

Walt.

Abby, Willard Saxton's address is | 1st Comptroler's office | Treasury Dep't.

386.1 *To Cora L. V. Tappan*

Washington, D. C., May 5, 1871.

My Dear Madam and Friend:[18]

I was expecting to visit New York early this month, and intended to call and thank you for your beautiful and valued gift of Hesperia—but finding I shall not go now for two or three weeks, I write to acknowl-

15. Major Samuel Willard Saxton, who served in the Union Army from 1862 to 1866, was later employed in the Treasury Department.
16. Arthur Price was in the Navy; see 194.
17. Emily's baby; see 368.
18. WW was acquainted with Mrs. Tappan, then Mrs. Hatch, in 1857; see 12. One of the sections of her collection of poems entitled *Hesperia* was dedicated to "Walt Whitman, the Poet of Nature." This letter was discovered by Professor F. DeWolfe Miller.
19. Mrs. Botta (1815–1891) was a teacher, a poet, and a sculptor. Her "literary"

edge the receipt of the poem and to say that when I come on, I shall personally call and pay my respects.

Walt Whitman

387. *To Anne Charlotte Lynch Botta*

DEPARTMENT OF JUSTICE

Washington. May 13, *1871.*

Mrs. Botta,[19] | My dear Madam,

In answer to your request of some days since, I send you the MS. of a small piece I have written, to be printed forthwith in the June Galaxy.[20]

According to your request, I also send a picture.

Walt Whitman

388. *To Anne Charlotte Lynch Botta*

TRANSCRIPT.

May 19, 1871

Please remit to me here, a check for $25. in pay for "O Star of France."

388.1 *To Anne Charlotte Lynch Botta*

DEPARTMENT OF JUSTICE

Washington | June | 6, *1871.*

Mrs. Botta: | My dear Madam:

I sent you by mail about three weeks ago, (in compliance with your request of April 13,) the MS. of one of my poems, "O Star of France"— also a photographic portrait. Please let me know whether they arrived safely.

With greatest respect.

Walt Whitman

evenings in New York are mentioned in Bayard Taylor's *John Godfrey's Fortunes.* According to the *Memoirs of Anne C. L. Botta* (1894), 14, Poe gave his first public reading of "The Raven" at her home. Her evaluation of WW's poetry appeared in her often reprinted *Handbook of Universal Literature* (1885 ed.) 535: "Walt Whitman . . . writes with great force, originality, and sympathy with all forms of struggle and suffering, but with utter contempt for conventionalities and for the acknowledged limits of true art."

20. On April 10 F. P. Church had accepted "O Star of France" for the June issue of *The Galaxy* (Feinberg).

389. *To Ellen M. O'Connor*

ENDORSED: "June 8, 1871 | Ans'd." ADDRESS:
Mrs. E. M. O'Connor, | 1015 O street near 11th |
N. W.

Washington, | June 8, 1871.

I have received your kind note, dear, dear friend—I shall be with you all again next Sunday evening without fail, soon after 7.[21]

Nelly, I have procured from New York one of the Brady Photos,[22] (the one with the hand up, which you liked) and am having it framed, to present to you. Understand that, like the new year's Bible, the Photo is a gift, with my best love, to you & William—to pass on to dear Jeannie.

Walt Whitman

390. *To Peter Doyle*   *6.21–[23]. 1871*

Brooklyn | June 21, 1871

Dear Pete,

I arrived home last night between 11 and 12, all safe & sound—found mother up, waiting for me—It was dark & stormy, as rain had set in about 9—had quite a pleasant journey—took a chair in the reserved seat car, 50 cts extra—plenty of room & a very easy riding car—Thought while I was sitting up here now in my room waiting for dinner I would write a line to boy Pete—

Thursday forenoon

The weather is very fine now here—plenty cool enough—I went over to New York yesterday afternoon & evening—took a ride up & down Broadway—am now laying off & taking it easy in my room—find it very pleasant here—fall just as natural into habits of doing nothing—lie on the sofa & read the papers—come up punctually to my meals—sleep a great deal—& take every thing very quietly—

Friday—Pete, I will finish this scribbling letter, & send it off, so you will get it for Sunday—I am feeling well & enjoying myself doing nothing, spending a great deal of time with my mother, & going out a few

21. WW visited the O'Connors regularly on Sunday when he was in Washington.
22. Perhaps No. 45 in *100 Whitman Photographs*, ed. Henry S. Saunders (1948).
23. On April 26 William Foster (1837–1873), a former New York conductor, accosted a woman and her daughter in a street car, and was rebuked by their companion, Avery D. Putnam. When Putnam got off, Foster, who was drunk, killed him with a car-hook. The murder was reported in the New York *Times* on April 28. Pete Calhoun (see 314), one of WW's friends, was the driver of the car. Because of appeals for commuta-

hours every day on the river or over to New York—I hope you are feeling all right, & that every thing is lovely—I believe that is all this time—

Love to you, dear son, & you must keep a good heart through all the tribulations & botherations, not only of railroading but life generally.

I find that Foster,[23] the "car assassin," is an old driver & conductor that I knew quite well—he was a very good man, very respectable, only a fool when drunk—it is the saddest case I know, he has three fine children —the public is down upon him savage—& I suppose no hope for him.

Walt

391. *To Ellen M. O'Connor*   *6.29.* [1871]

ENDORSED: "Ans'd." ADDRESS: Mrs. E. M.
O'Connor, | 1015 O street, N. W. | Washington |
D. C. POSTMARKS: New York | Jun | 29 | 6(?) PM;
Carrier | Jun | 30 | 3 AM.

107 north Portland | av. | Brooklyn, | June 29.

Dear Nelly,

I will just write you a line to let you know I am here in Brooklyn, & well & hearty. Mother is well as usual, & sends love to you & William, & to Jeannie. My sister Martha at St. Louis was not in good health at last accounts.

Helen Price was here & spent part of the day—She is looking finely— they are all as usual—it *was* John Arnold[24] that died—he was a complete wreck—death was a boon & relief in the case—

I have heard from Mrs. Howells[25]—I have seen Beulah,[26] she is a fine young woman, a handsome healthy blonde—she is at the fine establishment of Wilcox & Gibbs,[27] on Broadway—her sister Lou is married—I shall soon see Mrs. Howells, & then I will tell you further—Beulah asked much about you & William, and Jeannie—

Nothing special with me or my affairs. As it turns out, my death by railroad smash permeated the lower orders, (I suppose at second & third hand) & the *rectification* in many cases never reached them. So I hardly stir out in New York, but what I am called upon to certify, &c.—

I am daily on the water here—it is inspiriting, & surpassingly beautiful—Every fine day the bay swarms with yachts, large & small—they are

tion, including one from Putnam's widow, Foster was not hanged until March 21, 1873. On March 21 and 22 the New York *Daily Graphic* devoted pages to pictures and stories of Foster's last hours.
24. Not the John Arnold (see 6) who was a friend of the Prices.
25. A friend of the O'Connors; see 95.   26. Evidently Mrs. Howells' daughter.
27. Distributors of sewing machines.

literally in scores—I never tire of looking on them—All the young fellows yacht here—

Dear William, how are you? and dear Charles Eldridge, how are you? My true love to you both—Jeannie, my darling, a kiss for you—good bye, Nelly dear—

Walt

392. *To Peter Doyle*   *6.30.* [*1871*]

ADDRESS: Peter Doyle, | Conductor, | Office Wash. & Georgetown | City RR. Co. | Washington, | D. C. POSTMARK: New York | Jun | 30 | (?).

Brooklyn | June 30.[28]

Dear boy,

I rec'd your letter of Tuesday last, & was glad to hear every thing was going on all right. I am well, & still enjoying myself in a quiet way— I have been home every evening since I come—but out quite a good deal in the day—the weather is splendid here—plenty cool enough. This has got to be a great place for boating—All the rich men have their yachts, and most every young man belongs to a boat or yacht club—sometimes of a pleasant day, especially Sunday, you will see them out all over up & down the bay in swarms—the yachts look beautiful enough, with white sails & many with white hulls & their long pennants flying—it is a new thing to see them so plenty.

11 o'clock | Friday forenoon.

Pete, I am sitting in my room home, finishing this—have just had a bath, & dressed myself to go over to New York, partly on business— shall go down & put this in the P. O. here—shall walk down as it is a very pleasant forenoon—

When you write tell me if you have read Charles Reade's novel of "Foul Play"[29]—if not, I have one here I will send you—

Dear son, I believe that is all this time—I send my love, dear son, & a good loving kiss—I think of you every day—Give my best regards to all

---

28. This letter cannot have been written in 1872 (the year assigned by the executors), for then WW read a poem at Dartmouth College on June 26 and visited Hannah at Burlington, Vt., on June 30; see 455. Note also the similar material in this and the preceding letter.

29. *Foul Play*, by Charles Reade and Dion Boucicault, was published in Boston in 1868.

30. Michael C. Hart was listed as a printer in the Washington Directory of 1869,

enquiring friends, & inform them I expect to be back in about three weeks—

Good bye, my darling boy—from your comrade & father,

Walt.

393. *To Peter Doyle*

Brooklyn, | July 7, 1871

Dear Pete,

Well here I am still, pretty much the same thing, doing nothing & taking things easy. By your letter I see that you too are jogging along about the same, on your car, with an occasional let up—Often in my jaunts around the city, or on the bay, I wish you were with me, as you would enjoy it much—I have seen Mr. Hart,[30] formerly of the Chronicle—he is about the same in appearance as formerly—Pete, I will not write much this time, as I am feeling somewhat dull and stupid this forenoon—We had a fine shower last night, and there is some breeze—but it is pretty warm and oppressive—

Pete, here is a loving kiss for you, dear son, and much, much love for you, as ever, from your affectionate comrade & father—

Walt.

394. *Alfred, Lord Tennyson to WW*

Aldworth, Blackdown, Haslemere,
Surrey, England, July 12, 1871.

My dear Sir,[31]

Mr. Cyril Flower wrote to me some time ago to inform me that he had brought your books with him from America, a gift from you, and that they were lying in my London chambers; Whereupon I wrote back to him, begging him to bring them himself to me at my country house, and I have been accordingly, always expecting to see him, but he never came, being detained by law business in town. I have now just called at my London lodgings, and found them on the table. I had previously met with

and was the person to whom WW sent publicity puffs for insertion in the Washington *Daily Morning Chronicle;* see Doyle's letter to WW on October 5, 1868 (Lion). Hart was listed as an editor in the New York Directory of 1871–1872.

31. This was Tennyson's first letter to WW. WW wrote to Tennyson in 1871, or late 1870, probably shortly after the visit of Cyril Flower (see 427) in December, 1870, but the letter is not extant (see Donaldson, 223). According to WW's reply (see 443), Tennyson wrote a second letter on September 22, 1871, also apparently lost.

several of your works and read them with interest and had made up my mind that you had a large and lovable nature. I discovered great "go" in your writings and am not surprised at the hold they have taken on your fellow countrymen.[32]

Wishing you all success and prosperity, and with all thanks for your kind gift which I should have acknowledged earlier, had I received it sooner, I remain

Ever yours, very truly,

A Tennyson

I trust that if you visit England, you will grant me the pleasure of receiving and entertaining you under my own roof.

395.   *To Peter Doyle*   *7.14.* [1871]

ADDRESS: Peter Doyle, | Conductor, | Office Wash. & Geo. City RR. Co. | Washington, | D. C. POSTMARK: New York | Jul(?) | 14 | 1:30.

Brooklyn, | Friday, July 14.

Dear Pete,

It is pretty much the same with me, as when I wrote my former letters—still home here with my mother, not busy at any thing particular but taking a good deal of comfort—It has been very hot here, but one stands it better here than in Washington, on account perhaps of the sea-air—I am still feeling well, & am out around every day.

There was quite a brush in N. Y. on Wednesday[33]—the Irish lower orders (Catholic) had determined that the Orange parade (protestant) should be put down—mob fired & threw stones—military fired on mob—bet. 30 and 40 killed, over a hundred wounded—but you have seen all about it in papers—it was all up in a distant part of the city, 3 miles from Wall street—five-sixths of the city went on with its business just the same as any other day—I saw a big squad of prisoners carried along under guard—they reminded me of the squads of rebel prisoners brought in Washington, six years ago—

The N. Y. police looked & behaved splendidly—no fuss, few words,

32. Sylvester Baxter reported that in April, 1881, WW had informed Trowbridge and himself of his discouragement about his "poetic mission" at the time Tennyson's letter arrived. See Rufus A. Coleman, "Trowbridge and Whitman," *PMLA*, LXIII (1948), 268.

33. With the headline "War at Our Doors," the New York *World* reported: "The ides of March have come and gone. In spite of the efforts of the clergy, the municipal authorities, and all good citizens, New York has been disgraced by a street fight in 1871 over the merits of an Irish battle fought and won in 1690." The journal devoted two full pages (in an eight-page issue) to the incident, and announced that 45 had been killed and 105 wounded.

but *action*—great, brown, bearded, able, American looking fellows, (Irish stock, though, many of them)—I had great pleasure in looking on them—something new, to me, it quite set me up to see such chaps, all dusty & worn, looked like veterans—

Pete, dear son, I rec'd your two letters, & was glad to get them—

Mother has been quite sick, & I have been sort of nurse, as she is here alone, none of my sisters being home at present—she is much better this morning, under my doctoring—

Pete, I see by your letters that every thing goes on right with you on the road—give my best regards to my friends among the drivers & conductors—Dear son, I shall now soon be coming back, & we will be together again, as my leave is up on the 22d[34]—I am now going to take a bath & dress myself to go over to New York. Love to you, my dearest boy, & good bye for this time—

Walt.

396. *To William D. O'Connor*   *7.14. [1871]*

ENDORSED: "Answ'd July 16 | 71." ADDRESS: Wm. D. O'Connor, | Treasury Department, | Light House Bureau, | Washington, | D. C. POSTMARK: New York | (?) | 14 | 1:30 PM.

Brooklyn, | 107 North Portland av. | July 14.

Dear friend,

There is nothing special to write about, yet I will send you a line. I wrote to Nelly between two & three weeks ago[35]—with a line to you and Charles Eldridge—which I suppose came all right at the time. I have been having a comfortable time, absolutely doing nothing, sleeping a good deal, eating & drinking what suits me, and going out a few hours a day, a good part of the time on the water. Mother has had an attack of illness, somewhat severe, the last few days—& I have been sort of nurse & doctor—(as none of my sisters are home at present)—result is that Mother is very much better this morning—

John Burroughs[36] has called on me—looking well.

I must tell you that the *Westminster*[37] for July has for the 2d article of the number a long article of 33 or 4 pages, headed

34. Because of his mother's illness, WW had his leave extended, and returned to Washington on July 31; see 397 and 400.

35. See 391.

36. Burroughs was one of WW's staunchest defenders in print during this period; see his "More about Nature and the Poets," *Appleton's Journal*, IV (Sept. 10, 1870), 314–316, and Barrus, 58. Burroughs issued the expanded second edition of his *Notes* in 1871.

37. An unsigned article by Edward Dowden (see 404) in *The Westminster Review*, XCVI (1871), 33–68. A few weeks later WW was still pleased with the review; see 399, 401.

"The Poetry of Democracy: Walt Whitman"
and capped with the names of the three last issued books—rather quiet
in tone, but essentially very favorable & appreciative—undertakes to de-
fine the character of democratic art & poetic literature, as discrimi-
nated from aristocratic—quotes freely from all my books—will please you,
I think.

Wednesday's brush in N. Y. you have seen in the papers[38]—in five
sixths of the city, it was curiously almost unfelt, every thing went on the
same—30 or 40 killed and a hundred wounded—yet it all falls very
languidly on our people—we have supped full of horror of late years—the
Policemen looked & behaved splendidly—I have been looking on them &
been with them much, & am refreshed by their presence—it is something
new—in some respects they afford the most encouraging sign I have got—
brown, bearded, worn, resolute, American-looking men, dusty & sweaty
—looked like veterans—the *stock* here even in these cities is in the main
magnificent—the heads either shysters, villains or impotents—Love to
Nelly, Charles Eldridge & Jeannie—

Walt

397. *To Peter Doyle*   *[7.16]–7. [21.1871]*

By the sea-shore, Coney | Island, Sunday 3 p. m.
Dear Pete,
    I will write you a few lines as I sit here, on a clump of sand by the
sea shore—having some paper in my haversack, & an hour or two yet, before I start back. Pete, I wish you were with me the few hours past—I
have just had a splendid swim & souse in the surf—the waves are slowly
rolling in, with a hoarse roar that is music to my ears—the breeze blows
pretty brisk from south-west, & the sun is partially clouded—from where
I sit I look out on the bay & down the Narrows—vessels sailing in every
direction in the distance—a great big black long ocean steamship streak-
ing it up toward New York—& the lines of hills & mountains, far, far
away, on the Jersey Coast, a little veiled with blue vapor—here around
me, as I sit, it is nothing but barren sand—but I don't know how long I
could sit here, to that soothing, rumbling murmuring of the waves—&
then the salt breeze—

Pete, if you are still working, and all is going on smooth, you can send
me that $50—you might get Mr. Milburn to send it to me by post-office

38. See 395.   39. See next letter.
40. The date has been lined through and "21?" (correctly) substituted in another
hand.

order—give it to him, with this envelope, & ask him to go to p. o. & send a p. o. order to me—it will save you the trouble—But Pete, dear boy, if any thing has turned up in mean time, you needn't send it, as I can get along otherwise[39]—

I am doing very well, both in health & *business prospects* here—my book is doing first rate—so every thing is lovely & the goose hangs high— Your loving comrade & father

Walt.

Friday July 20.[40]

Dear son, I wrote the preceding nearly a week ago, intending to finish & send it then—Nothing very new or special with me—Mother has been quite unwell, gets better, & then worse again—I have applied for a few days further leave—The weather here remains nearly perfect—we have had but three or four uncomfortably hot days the past five weeks—every day a fine breeze smelling of the sea—

397.1 *To an Unidentified Correspondent*   *7.19.* [*1871?*][41]

Brooklyn | 107 north Portland av. | July 19.

My dear sir,

You can get any or all my Books at J. S. Redfield, 140 Fulton street, upstairs, N. Y.

Walt Whitman

398. *To Peter Doyle*   *7.24.* [*1871*]

Brooklyn | Monday forenoon, July 24.

Dear Pete,

I rec'd the $50 to-day all right, and a real help to me—I have money, but cannot have the use of it just now—so this comes first rate—

I spent yesterday down on the sea-shore—was all by myself—had a splendid good day—took my dinner with me—went down in the boat 12 miles in the morning, & back in a big open horse car, toward evening, through the fields & woods—very pleasant indeed—staid a long while in the water—weather perfect—Mother is better to-day—she has been

41. The year is established by two facts: WW was in Brooklyn at this time, and Redfield was now the distributer of his books (see 367).

pretty sick, with several ups & downs—I am as well as a fellow can be—eat & sleep tremendous—Shall stay here a week or so longer—shall be back first part of next week if nothing happens—

Well, Pete, I believe that is all this morning—Good bye, my darling son, and a long, long kiss from your loving father

Walt

399. *To William D. O'Connor*   7.26. *[1871]*

Brooklyn | Wednesday forenoon, | July 26.

Dear William O'Connor,

I take it by the enclosed from Rossetti[42] that he has sent me the *Westminster* by mail to Washington, & that it is now there, probably in the A. G. office. You go down & see, & get it to read. (May be in p. o.)

Mother's health is about reëstablished if nothing unfavorable occurs.[43] I shall return to Washington early next week. I start this afternoon for New Haven for one day only—an emergency—an artist friend of mine is very low there with consumption—is in fact dying—& has expressed the most earnest wish to see me[44]—We have been, & are, having a cold easterly rain storm here—I enclose, on loan, the last two photos of my most sweetly philosophic & fascinating self—(for you to gaze upon till I return)—

The *Swinburne Hilliard* article has been copied in the *World*,[45] *Home Journal*, &c. &c.

Not a word of the *Westminster* article—The ungodly, (sorely tried,) will of course endeavor to ignore it, & leave it entirely unmentioned & uncommented on, if possible—but that will *not* be possible—It is a powerful essay—I have been reading it over carefully a second time—It strikes the true chords—even the name "*The Poetry of Democracy*" &c—is it not pregnant? from your loving old

Walt

---

42. See 401.

43. Probably because of Mrs. Whitman's health, Jeff and his family visited her in the fall. Martha and her children went to Camden to see George's wife Louisa, whom he had married on April 14. On October 10 Mrs. Whitman wrote to WW: "george and loo [Louisa] and Jeff insists on my breaking up houskeeping. they dident only insist but almost commanded me. i told them i should remain here this winter (if i lived). they none of them want edd, walter, and they would soon get tired of paying his board and we aint much expence to any but you, walter dear, for any thing but houseroom" (Trent; Gohdes and Silver, 203–204).

44. Charles Hine (see 291). On August 4 Mrs. Hine informed WW of her husband's death: "I think after your visit to him that his hold on life seemed to give way and his yearnings were all accomplished" (Feinberg; Traubel, III, 330). Mrs. Hine, who visited Mrs. Whitman on August 22, thought it "strange" that WW did not write (Trent).

400. *To Peter Doyle*   *7.28.* [*1871*]

Brooklyn | July 28.

Dear son,

I shall return on Monday next, in the 12:30 train from Jersey city
—(the train I usually come in)—Pete, I have rec'd your letter of 26th—
Mother seems to-day full as well as usual—I continue all right—I have
been on to New Haven, about 75 miles from here—a former friend of
mine[46] is in a dying condition there, from consumption, & expressed such
a strong desire to see me, that I went on—I thought he would die while I
was there—he was all wasted, to a skeleton, faculties good, but voice
only a low whisper—I returned last night, after midnight—

Well, bub, my time here is short—I have had a good quiet visit—the
best in some respects yet—& I feel satisfied—My darling son, we will
very soon be together again—

Your loving comrade

Walt.

401. *To William Michael Rossetti*

Brooklyn | N. Y. | July 28 | 1871.

W. M. Rossetti: | Dear Sir & friend:

Please accept these copies of my latest edition. Please have conveyed to *the lady*[47] the set enclosed for her. John Burroughs sends second
edition of his "Notes"[48]—Your letter of 8th July[49] has reached me—I hope
to write you more fully & answer it from Washington city—My address is
still there—(& always, always glad to hear from you, my friend.)

I am still blest with the greatest health, & have been enjoying this fine
summer here exceedingly. My *"Leaves of Grass"* I consider substantially
finished, as in the copies I send you. To *"Democratic Vistas"* it is my plan
to add much, if I live. I have read carefully the article in the *Westmin-*

According to Mrs. Whitman's letter of September 30, Mrs. Hine had received a "dona-
tion" from WW (Trent). See also 400.

 45. The New York *World* of July 24 reprinted Lucy Fountain's article, "An Evening with Swinburne" (retitled "Swinburne at Home") from the August *Galaxy*, XII
(1871) 231–234, in which Swinburne's favorable comments on WW were reported. I
cannot explain the reference to "Swinburne Hilliard" unless Hilliard was the real name of
the author.

 46. See 399.

 47. Anne Gilchrist. Rossetti noted receipt of the books on October 8 (Feinberg;
Traubel, III, 376–377).

 48. The second edition, with new supplementary notes, was printed by Redfield.

 49. Actually July 9 (Feinberg; Traubel, I, 132–133).

ster.[50] If you learn for certain who wrote it, I should be glad to know—It is a profound & eloquent essay—& I am proud to be the subject of it—I have received much comfort from your country—*here* little but refusal or coldness.

I conclude by sending best respects & love. Indeed, my friend, I wish to hear from you oftener.[51]

Walt Whitman

402. *To the Committee on Invitations, American Institute*

DRAFT LETTER.

DEPARTMENT OF JUSTICE

Washington. Aug 5, *1871*

Messrs. George Payton, Chas. E. Burd, and James B. Young,
Committee on Invitations.[52]

Dear Sirs:

I have read your letter of 1st inst. containing invitation to deliver an appropriate original poem at the opening of the 40th Annual Exhibition of the American Institute, Sept. 7, & stating terms, &c. I accept with pleasure, & shall be ready without fail to deliver the poem at time specified.

Address me here, if any thing further.

50. On July 9 Rossetti had sent WW a copy of *The Westminster Review.* He conjectured that the author was Edward Dowden, and had called attention to the "highly respectful references" to WW in H. Buxton Forman's *Our Living Poets* (1871), 11, which also included two prefatory quotations from WW.

51. Rossetti informed WW on October 8 (Feinberg; Traubel, III, 376) that he was preparing "a vol. of Selections from American Poets," which appeared in 1872 as *American Poems* with a dedication to WW, "the greatest of American poets."

52. The Committee of the American Institute had written on August 1 "to solicit of you the honor of a poem on the occasion of its opening, September 7, 1871—with the privilege of furnishing proofs of the same to the Metropolitan Press for publication with the other proceedings. . . . We shall be most happy, of course, to pay traveling expenses & entertain you hospitably, and pay $100 in addition" (Feinberg; Traubel, I, 326).

The newspaper coverage of WW's appearance was extensive: the Washington *Daily Morning Chronicle* published the poet's account on September 7; the New York *Evening Post* reprinted the poem, later entitled "After All, Not to Create Only," and called WW "a good elocutionist"; he was also praised in the New York *Sun* and the Brooklyn *Standard;* the New York *Tribune* printed excerpts from the poem on September 8 and later a devastating parody by Bayard Taylor (reprinted in his *Echo Club* [2nd ed., 1876], 169–170); the Springfield *Republican* published the poem on September 9. In reply to the criticisms of the poem, WW prepared the following for submission to an unidentified newspaper: "The N. Y. *World's* frantic, feeble, fuddled articles on it are curiosities. The *Telegram* dryly calls it the longest conundrum ever yet given to the public" (Yale). See also Traubel, I, 328–329; Holloway, *American Mercury,* XVIII (1929), 485–486; and Allen, 433–435.

403. *To F. S. Ellis*   [*8.12(?).1871*]

ENDORSED: "went by | steamer | Aug 12, '71."
DRAFT LETTER.

F. S. Ellis,[53] Publisher,

33 King st. Covent Garden, | London:

I take the liberty of writing at a venture to propose to you the publication in a moderate-priced volume, of a full edition of my poems, Leaves of Grass, in England under my sanction. I send by same mail with this, a revised copy of L. of G. I should like a fair remuneration or percentage.

I make this proposition not only to get my poems before the British public, but more because I am annoyed at the horrible dismemberment of my book there already & of something worse.[54]

Should my proposal suit you, go right on with the book. Style of getting it up, price, rate of remuneration to me, &c. I leave entirely to you. Only the text must be sacredly preserved, verbatim.[55]

Please direct to me here, as soon as convenient.

404. *To Edward Dowden*

DRAFT LETTER.

Washington D. C. | Aug 22, 1871.

Dear Mr. Dowden,[56]

I have received your kind letter, & your review in the Westminster, & thank you heartily. I wish to write you at more length, & may

On September 11 John W. Chambers, secretary of the Institute, thanked WW "for the magnificent original poem" (Feinberg; Traubel, IV, 484).

53. Ellis replied on August 23: since there were poems in *Leaves of Grass* which "would not go down in England," he believed that it would "not be worth while to publish it again in a mutilated form" (Feinberg; Traubel, II, 447). On the following day he sent another note and a specially printed copy of Swinburne's *Songs before Sunrise* (Feinberg; Traubel, II, 448).

54. WW referred to his dealings with his English publisher Hotten (see 255 and 421).

55. Following this passage, WW deleted: "literal—and all your English carefulness in proof-reading, must by cap?"

56. Dowden (1843–1913), professor of English literature at the University of Dublin, sent a copy of his article with a letter on July 23: "I ought to say that the article expresses very partially the impression which your writings have made on me. It keeps, as is obvious, at a single point of view, & regards only what becomes visible from that point. But also I wrote more cooly than I feel because I wanted those, who being ignorant of your writings are perhaps prejudiced against them, to say 'Here is a cool, judicious, impartial critic who finds a great deal in Whitman—perhaps, after all, we are mistaken' " (Feinberg; Traubel, I, 134). Note also Dowden's comments to Burroughs, in Barrus, 67. On three occasions in 1870 Dowden had written to Rossetti about his difficulties in having his article published; see *Rossetti Papers*, 517–518, 519, 520. In 1888 WW observed to Traubel: "Dowden is a book-man: but he is also and more particularly a man-man: I guess that is where we connect" (I, 299).

do so before long. I take real comfort in the thought that I have such friends in Ireland, including yourself. I wish to hear more of Mr. Tyrrell,[57] whom you speak of.

Walt Whitman

405.   *Anne Gilchrist to WW*   9.3–6. [1871]

September 3

Dear Friend[58]

At last the beloved books have reached my hand[59]—yet now I have them, my heart is so rent with anguish, my eyes so blinded, I cannot read in them. I try again and again but too great waves come swaying up & suffocate me. I will struggle to tell you my story. It seems to me a death struggle. When I was eighteen I met a lad of nineteen[60] who loved me then, and always for the remainder of his life. After we had known each other about a year he asked me to be his wife. But I said that I liked him well as my friend but could not love him as a wife should love & felt deeply convinced I never should. He was not turned aside, but went on just the same as if that conversation had never passed. After a year he asked me again, and I, deeply moved by & grateful for his true steady love, and so sorry for him, said yes. But next day, terrified at what I had done & painfully conscious of the dreary absence from my heart of any faintest gleam of true tender wifely love, said no again.[61] This too he bore without desisting & at the end of some months once more asked me with passionate entreaties. Then, dear friend, I prayed very earnestly, and it seemed to me that I should continue to mar & thwart his life, so was not right if he was content to accept what I could give. I knew I could lead a good and wholesome life beside him. His aims were noble, his heart a deep beautiful true Poet's heart, but he had not the Poet's great brain. His path was a very arduous one and I knew I could smooth it for him—cheer him along it. It seemed to me God's will that I should marry him. So I told him the whole truth and he said he would rather have me on those terms than not have me at all. He said to me many times, Ah, Annie, it is not you who are so loved that is rich, it is I who so love. And I knew

<hr>

57. R. Y. Tyrrell, a fellow of Trinity College and "an excellent Greek scholar," had recently delivered a public lecture on WW's poetry; see Traubel, I, 135, 225.

58. This, one of the most pathetic love letters ever written, marks the beginning of the correspondence between a woman whose passion compelled her to an aggressiveness that could but put fear into her beloved's heart, and a man who impotently surveyed the effects of the ardor that his own verse inspired.

59. See 401. On September 3 Rossetti replied affirmatively to Mrs. Gilchrist's query as to the propriety of writing directly to WW; see *The Letters of William Michael Rossetti*, ed. Gohdes and Baum (1934), 80.

this was true, felt as if my nature were poor & barren beside his. But it was not so, it was only slumbering—undeveloped. For, dear friend, my Soul was so passionately aspiring—it so thirsted & pined for light it had not power to reach alone & he could not help me on my way. And a woman is so made that she cannot give the tender passionate devotion of her whole nature save to the greater conquering soul stronger in its powers though not in its aspirations than her own, that can lead her forever & forever up and on. It is for her soul exactly as it is for her body. The strong divine soul of the man embracing hers with passionate love—so alone the precious germs within her soul can be quickened into life. And the time will come when men will understand that a woman's soul is as dear and needful to his & as different from his as her body to his body. This was what happened to me when I had read for a few days, nay hours, in your books. It was the divine soul embracing mine. I never before dreamed what love meant: nor what life meant. Never was alive before. No words but those of "new birth" can hint the meaning of what then happened to me.

The first few months of my marriage were dark & gloomy to me within, and sometimes I had misgivings whether I had judged aright, but when I knew there was a dear baby coming my heart grew lighter, and when it was born, such a superb child—all glooms & fear forever vanished. I knew it was God's seal to the marriage, and my heart was full of gratitude and joy. It was a happy and a good life we led together for ten short years, he ever tender and affectionate to me—loving his children so, working earnestly in the wholesome bracing atmosphere of poverty—for it was but just possible with the most strenuous frugality & industry to pay our way. I learned to cook & to turn my hand to all household occupations, found it bracing, healthful, cheerful. Now I think it more even now that I understand the divineness & sacredness of the Body. I think there is no more beautiful task for a woman than ministering all ways to the health & comfort & enjoyment of the dear bodies of those she loves: no material that will work sweeter & more beautifully into that making of a perfect poem of a man's life which is her true vocation.

In 1861 my children took scarlet fever badly: I thought I should have lost my dear oldest girl. Then my husband took it—and in five days it carried him from me. I think, dear friend, my sorrow was far more

60. Alexander Gilchrist.
61. Mrs. Gilchrist's passion led her to distort reality: she was engaged to Gilchrist for three years before her marriage, and at the time of her engagement she wrote ecstatically to her friend Julia Newton: ". . . guess that your friend is very happy, for she loves and is beloved by one who can fulfil her aspirations, realize her ideal of a true marriage, one who is her friend and helper, as well as her lover. . . . I know not how to describe him to you, dear Julia, except by telling you that he is altogether, both in intellect and heart, great, noble and beautiful" (Gilchrist, 30).

bitter though not so deep as that of a loving tender wife. As I stood by him in the coffin I felt such remorse I had not, could not be more tender to him —such a conviction that if I had loved him as he deserved to be loved he would not have been taken from us. To the last my soul dwelt apart & unmated & his soul dwelt apart unmated.[62] I do not fear the look of his dear silent eyes. I do not think he would even be grieved with me now. My youngest was then a baby. I have had much sweet tranquil happiness, much strenuous work & endeavour raising my darlings.

In May 1869 came the voice over the Atlantic to me. O the voice of my Mate: it must be so—my love rises up out of the very depths of the grief & tramples upon despair. I can wait—any time, a lifetime, many lifetimes—I can suffer, I can dare, I can learn, grow, toil, but nothing in life or death can tear out of my heart the passionate belief that one day I shall hear that voice say to me "My Mate. The one I so much want. Bride, Wife, indissoluble eternal!" It is not happiness I plead with God for—it is the very life of my Soul, my love is its life. Dear Walt. It is a sweet & precious thing this love—it clings so close, so close to the Soul and Body, all so tenderly dear, so beautiful, so sacred; it yearns with such passion to soothe and comfort & fill thee with sweet tender joy; it aspires as grandly, as gloriously as thy own soul, strong to soar, soft & tender to nestle and caress. If God were to say to me—see—"he that you love you shall not be given to in this life—he is going to set sail on the unknown sea—will you go with him—" never yet has bride sprung into her husbands arms with the joy I would take thy hand & spring from the shore.

Understand aright, dear love, the reason of my silence. I was obeying the voice of conscience. I thought I was to wait. For it is the instinct of a womans nature to wait to be sought—not to seek. And when that May & June I was longing so inexpressibly to write I resolutely restrained myself, believing if I were only patient the right opening would occur. And so it did through Rossetti. And when he, liking what I said, suggested my printing something, it met and enabled me to carry into execution what I was brooding over. For I had and still have a strong conviction that it was necessary for a woman to speak—that finally and decisively only a woman can judge a man, only a man a woman, on the subject of their relations. What is blameless, what is good in its effect on her, *is* good—however it may have seemed to men. She is the test. And I never for a moment feared any hard words against myself because I know these things are not judged by the intellect but by the unerring instincts of

62. A year after her husband's death she wrote to her sister-in-law: "Alec's spirit is with me ever—presides in my home, speaks to me in every sweet scene; broods over the peaceful valleys; haunts the grand wild hill tops; shines gloriously forth in setting sun, and moon and stars" (Gilchrist, 126).

the soul. I knew any man could not but feel that it would be a happy and ennobling thing for him that his wife should think & feel as I do on that subject—knew that what had filled me with such great & beautiful thoughts towards men in that writing could not fail to give them good & happy thoughts towards women in the reading. The cause of my consenting to Rossetti's urgent wish that I should not put my name (he so kindly solicitous yet not altogether understanding me & it aright) was that I did not rightly understand how it might be with my dear Boy if it came before him.[63] I thought perhaps he was not old enough to judge and understand me aright: nor young enough to let it altogether alone. But it has been very bitter & hateful to me this not standing to what I have said as it were, with my own personality, better because of my utter love and faithfulness to the cause & longing to stand openly & proudly in the ranks of its friends; & for the lower reason that my nature is proud & as defiant as thine own and immeasurably disdains any faintest appearance of being afraid of what I had done.

And, my darling, above all because I love thee so tenderly that if hateful words had been spoken against me I could have taken joy in it for thy dear sake. There never yet was the woman who loved that would not joyfully bare her breast to wrest the blows aimed at her beloved.

I know not what fiend made me write those meaningless words in my letter, "it is pleasantest to me" &c., but it was not fear or faithlessness—& it is not pleasantest but hateful to me. Now let me come to beautiful joyous things again. O dear Walt, did you not feel in every word the breath of a woman's love? did you not see as through a transparent veil a soul all radiant and trembling with love, stretching out its arms towards you? I was so sure you would speak, would send me some sign: that I was to wait—wait. So I fed my heart with sweet hopes: strengthened it with looking into the eyes of thy picture. O surely in the ineffable tenderness of thy look speaks the yearning of thy man-soul toward my woman-soul? But now I will wait no longer. A higher instinct dominates that other, the instinct for perfect truth. I would if I could lay every thought and action and feeling of my whole life open to thee as it lies to the eye of God. But that cannot be all at once. O come. Come, my darling: look into these eyes and see the loving ardent aspiring soul in them—easily, easily will you learn to love all the rest of me for the sake of that and take me to your breast for ever and ever. Out of its great anguish my love has risen

63. "A Woman's Estimate of Walt Whitman" appeared anonymously; see 353 and 364. In a letter on July 19, 1869, Rossetti had urged Mrs. Gilchrist to "suppress" her name; see *Letters of William Michael Rossetti*, 31.

stronger, more triumphant than ever: it cannot doubt, cannot fear, is strong, divine, immortal, sure of its fruition this side the grave or the other. "O agonistic throes," tender, passionate yearnings, pinings, triumphant joys, sweet dreams—I too know you all. But, dear love, the sinews of a womans outer heart are not twisted so strong as a mans: but the heart within is strong & great & loving. So the strain is very terrible. O heart of flesh, hold on yet a few years to the great heart within thee if it may be. But if not all is assured, all is safe.

This time last year when I seemed dying I could have no secrets between me & my dear children. I told them of my love: told them all they could rightly understand, and laid upon them my earnest injunction that as soon as my mother's life no longer held them here, they should go fearlessly to America, as I should have planted them down there—Land of Promise, my Canaan, to which my soul sings "Arise, Shine, for thy light is come & the glory of the Lord is risen upon thee."

After the 29th of this month I shall be in my own home, dear friend—it is at Brookbank, Haslemere, Surrey. Haslemere is on the main line between Portsmouth & London.

Good-bye, dear Walt,

Anne Gilchrist.

Sept. 6.

The new portrait also is a sweet joy & comfort to my longing, pining heart & eyes. How have I brooded & brooded with thankfulness on that one word in thy letter "the comfort it has been to me to get her words,"[64] for always day & night these two years has hovered on my lips & in my heart the one prayer: dear God, let me comfort him! Let me comfort thee with my whole being, dear love. I feel much better & stronger now.

406. *To John Swinton*

DEPARTMENT OF JUSTICE,

Washington. Sept. 14, 1871

My dear John Swinton:

I have rec'd your note & enclosures. I have several things to write or talk to you about—but at present I only enclose these two slips—& I wish you would see that one is offered to *Evening Post*, & the other to any

64. See 353.
65. Since the press had not reported his speech before the American Institute sympathetically (see 402), WW wanted Swinton (see 37), who was no longer editor of the New York *Times*, to place an "official" but anonymous reply in the newspapers named. I have not found the notices. At Yale (see 402) there is a detailed answer to the newspaper attacks on this poem which WW prepared for an unidentified newspaper.
66. The firm was established in Boston in 1863. Though it introduced such authors as Dante Gabriel Rossetti, William Morris, Joaquin Miller, Oscar Wilde, Robert Louis

paper you think best—perhaps either *Commercial Adv[ertiser]* or the *Standard.*[65]

I am well as usual.

W. W.

if pub. please send me a paper—

407. *To Roberts Brothers*[66]

DRAFT LETTER.

DEPARTMENT OF JUSTICE

Washington | sent Sept. 17, | *1871*

I send herewith the copy of my American Institute Poem. It will be plain sailing, if you have a careful printer & proof reader. I think an ordinary 12 mo would be best, and send you a sample, my idea of size of page, and sort of pamphlet-volume to be made. As to size of type for the poem, if English solid would not be too large, I would like to have that. If you think it too large, take the next smaller size. In binding let the edges remain uncut, & bind in the kind of paper according to sample. See sample of title on cover. Send the revised proofs to me by mail, directed to this city, and I will promptly return them.

My percentage &c. I leave to you to fix—I should expect two or three dozen copies. I reserve the copyright to myself.

That the papers have freely printed & criticized the piece will much help, as it awakes interest & curiosity, & many will want to have it in good form to keep. The demand will grow. I have no authority to speak for them, but I think the American Institute will want several hundred copies, & that the pamphlet will have a sale at all their public Exhibitions & Fairs. They always have book stands at them.

It ought to be put in hand immediately, & out soon.

408. *To Edward Dowden*

Washington, U. S. | Sept. 19, 1871.

My Dear Mr. Dowden:

The gentleman who will hand you this is John Burroughs,[67] a very valued friend of mine, who is about to start for Europe, and thinks of visiting Dublin, & making a call on you.

Stevenson, and Emily Dickinson, it became famous for the works of Louisa May Alcott. *After All, Not to Create Only* was the only work of WW that the firm published. It has been suggested that Bronson Alcott persuaded Roberts to undertake the work; see Raymond L. Kilgour, *Messrs. Roberts Brothers, Publishers* (1952), 107. The house merged with Little, Brown and Co. in 1898.

67. Burroughs wrote to WW from London on October 3–4, after he had visited St. Paul's, where he had a staggering revelation, not unlike Henry James's in a Parisian gallery: "I saw for the first time what power & imagination could be put in form & design

I have rec'd your letter of Sept. 5,[68] & hope to write you further—
Believe me I deeply appreciate all you send me—

Walt Whitman

409. *To an Unidentified Correspondent*   *10.17. 1871*

[*Writing from Washington, WW mentioned where copies of the
first edition of* Leaves of Grass *were probably available.*] . . . The last
edition of my poems complete I publish and sell myself.

410. *To Anne Gilchrist*[69]

Washington City, U. S. | November 3, 1871.

Dear friend,[70]

I have been waiting quite a long while for time & the right mood to
answer your letter[71] in a spirit as serious as its own, & in the same un-
mitigated trust & affection. But more daily work than ever has fallen
upon me to do the current season, & though I am well & contented, my
best moods seem to shun me. I wished to give to it a day, a sort of Sabbath
or holy day apart to itself, under serene & propitious influences—confident
that I could then write you a letter which would do you good, & me too.
But I must at least show, without further delay, that I am not insensible
to your love. I too send you my love. And do you feel no disappointment
because I now write but briefly. My book is my best letter, my response,
my truest explanation of all. In it I have put my body & spirit. You understand this better & fuller & clearer than any one else. And I too fully
& clearly understand the loving & womanly letter it has evoked. Enough
that there surely exists between us so beautiful & delicate a relation, accepted by both of us with joy.[72]

Walt Whitman

—I felt for a moment what great genius was in this field. . . . I had to leave there & sit
down. . . . My brain is too sensitive. I am not strong enough to confront these things
all at once . . . It is like the grandest organ music put into form" (Feinberg; Traubel,
I, 89–90). WW wrote in the margin: "Splendid off hand letter from John Burroughs–
? publish it." On October 8 Rossetti referred to a visit three days earlier from Burroughs:
"I like his frank manly aspect & tone" (Feinberg; Traubel, III, 377). Burroughs visited
Dowden in November; see *Fragments from Old Letters, E. D. to E. D. W., 1869–1892*
(1914), 16–17.
   68.   In this letter Dowden cited a number of Dublin admirers, and concluded: "One
thing strikes me about everyone who cares for what you write—while your attraction is
most absolute, & the impression you make as powerful as that of any teacher or *vates*, you
do not rob the mind of its independence, or divert it from its true direction. You make
no slaves, however many lovers" (Feinberg; Traubel, I, 224–225). Dowden replied to
WW's letter on October 15 (Feinberg; Traubel, III, 41–42).
   69.   For forgeries of this letter, see *WWN*, IV (1958), 92–93.

411. *Anne Gilchrist to WW*   [*11.27.1871*]

ENDORSED (by Bucke?): "27 Nov '71."

Dear Friend

Your long waited for letter brought me both joy & pain; but the pain was not of your giving. I gather from it that a long letter which I wrote you Sept. 6th[73] after I had received the precious packet, a letter in which I opened all my heart to you, never reached your hands: nor yet a shorter one which, tortured by anxiety & suspense about its predecessor, I wrote Oct. 15,[74] it, too, written out of such stress & intensity of painful emotion as wrenches from us inmost truth: I cannot face the thought of these words of uttermost trust & love having fallen into other hands. Can both be simply lost? Could any man suffer a base curiosity, to make him so meanly treacherously cruel? It seems to cut and then burn me.

I was not disappointed at the shortness of your letter & I do not ask nor even wish you to write save when you are inwardly impelled & desirous of doing so. I only want leave and security to write freely to you. Your book does indeed say all—book that is not a book but, for the first time, a man complete, godlike, august, standing revealed the only way possible, through the garment of speech. Do you know, dear Friend, what it means for a woman, what it means for me to understand these poems. It means for her whole nature to be then first kindled; quickened into life through such love, such sympathy, such resistless attraction, that thenceforth she cannot choose but live & die striving to become worthy to share this divine mans life—to be his dear companion, closer, nearer, dearer than any man can be—for ever so. Her soul stakes all on this. It is the meaning, the fulfilment, the only perfect developement & consummation of her nature—of her passionate, high, immortal aspirations—her Soul to mate with his for ever & ever. O I know the terms are obdurate—I know how hard to attain to this greatness, the grandest lot ever aspired to by woman. I know too

70. See Mrs. Gilchrist's letter, 405.
71. WW had not as yet received Mrs. Gilchrist's second letter, written on October 23: ". . . but spare me the needless suffering of uncertainty on this point & let me have one line, one word, of assurance that I am no longer hidden from you by a thick cloud—I from thee—not thou from me: for I that have never set eyes upon thee . . . love thee day & night. . . . I am yet young enough to bear thee children, my darling, if God should so bless me. And would yield my life for this cause with serene joy if it were so appointed, if that were the price for thy having a 'perfect child' " (LC; Harned, 65–66).
72. After Traubel read this letter aloud in 1889, WW spoke at some length of the "passionate love" of his friends which "offset the venomous hate" of his critics: "The substance of that letter—its feel: what it starts out to say to her: oh! with a few words taken out and put in—it would do for any of you!" (Traubel, III, 514).
73. See 405.
74. The letter was dated October 23 (LC; Harned, 65–66).

my own shortcomings, faults, flaws. You might not be able to give me your great love yet—to take me to your breast with joy. But I can wait. I can grow great & beautiful through sorrow & suffering, working, struggling, yearning, loving so, all alone, as I have done now nearly three years—it will be three in May since I first read the book, first knew what the word love meant. Love & Hope are so strong in me, my souls high aspirations are of such tenacious, passionate intensity, are so conscious of their own deathless reality, that what would starve them out of any other woman only makes them strike out deeper roots, grow more resolute & sturdy in me. I know that "greatness will not ripen for me like a pear." But I could face, I could joyfully accept the fiercest anguish, the hardest toil, the longest, sternest probation, to make me fit to be your mate—so that at the last you should say "this is the woman I have waited for, the woman prepared for me: this is my dear eternal comrade, wife—the one I so much want." Life has no other meaning for me than that—all things have led up to help prepare me for that. Death is more welcome to me than life if it means that—if then, dear Sailor, thou sailing upon thy endless cruise, thou takest me on board—me, daring all with thee, steering for the deep waters, bound where mariner has not yet dared to go: hand in hand with thee, nestled close—one with thee. Ah that word enough[75] was like a blow on the breast to me—breast that often & often is so full of yearning tenderness I know not how to draw my breath. The tie between us would not grow less but more beautiful, dear friend, if you knew me better: if I could stand as real & near to you as you do to me. But I cannot like you clothe my nature in divine poems & so make it visible to you. Ah foolish me! I thought you would catch a glimpse of it in those words I wrote—I thought you would say to yourself "perhaps this is the voice of my mate" & would seek me a little to make sure if it were so or not. O the sweet dreams I have fed on these three years nearly, pervading my waking moments, influencing every thought & action. I was so sure, so sure if I waited silently, patiently, you would send me some sign: so full of joyful hope I could not doubt nor fear. When I lay dying as it seemed, still full of the radiant certainty that you would seek me, would not lose [me], that we should as surely find one another there as here. And when the ebb ceased & life began to flow back into me, O never doubting but it was for you—never doubting but that the sweetest, noblest,

---

75. See the last sentence in 410.   76. See 405.

77. Because WW did not reply immediately to this letter, Mrs. Gilchrist recopied it and sent it in December.

78. Schmidt, editor of *For Idé og Virkelighed* (see Introduction), wrote to WW on October 19: "I intend to write an article about yourself and your writings in the above named periodical which is very much read in all the Scandinavian countries. . . . I

closest, tenderest companionship ever yet tasted by man & woman was to begin for us here & now. Then came the long long waiting, the hope deferred: each morning so sure the book would come & with it a word from you that should give me leave to speak: no longer to shut down in stern silence the love, the yearning, the thoughts that seemed to strain & crush my heart. I know what that means—"if thou wast not gifted to sing thou wouldst surely die." I felt as if my silence must kill me sometimes. Then when the Book came but with it no word for me alone, there was such a storm in [my] heart I could not for weeks read in it. I wrote that long letter[76] out in the Autumn fields for dear life's sake. I knew I might and must speak then. Then I felt relieved, joyful, buoyant once more. Then again months of heart-wearying disappointment as I looked in vain for a letter—O the anguish at times, the scalding tears, the feeling within as if my heart were crushed & doubled up—yet always afterwards saying to myself "if this suffering is to make my love which was born & grew up & blossomed all in a moment strike deep root down in the dark & cold, penetrate with painful intensity every fibre of my being, make it a love such as he himself is capable of giving, then welcome this anguish, these bitter deferments: let its roots be watered as long as God pleases with my tears."[77]

Annie Gilchrist.

50 Marquis Road | Camden Sqr. N. W. | London

412. *To Rudolf Schmidt*

DEPARTMENT OF JUSTICE

Washington Dec. 7, 1871

Rudolf Schmidt,[78] | Dear Sir:

I have received, (through Mr. Clausen)[79] your letter of 19th October, from Kopenhagen—& I cheerfully forward you my poems "Leaves of Grass," & a small prose work of mine, "Democratic Vistas." I also enclose several articles & criticisms written about my books in England & America within the last ten years.

May I say, there is something about your letter & application that has deeply pleased me. How I should like to know your country & people—&

therefore take the liberty to ask you, if you should not be willing to afford some new communications of yourself and your poetry to this purpose" (LC).

79. Carl F. Clausen, termed in Schmidt's letter "my old friend and countryman," corresponded with Schmidt after he left Denmark in 1860; see *Orbis Litterarum*, VII (1949), 34–39. The Directory in 1870 listed him as a draughtsman and in 1872 as a patent agent. He died of consumption in the middle 1870's; see LC #108.

especially you yourself, & your poet Björnson[80]—and Hans Andersen. How proud I should be to become known to you all.

Pray let me hear from you—and if the books & papers reach you safely. Please accept my best, brotherly good will.

Any thing by mail will reach me addressed

Walt Whitman
Washington, D. C.
U. S. of America.

413. *To W. H. Piper & Co.*

DEPARTMENT OF JUSTICE

Washington. Dec. 8, 1871.

W. H. Piper & Co.[81] | Dear Sirs:

Please send me acc't. & remit am't. sold—25 per cent off—of

25	Copies	"Leaves of Grass" @	$2.50
25	"	"Passage to India" @	1.
25	"	"Democratic Vistas" @	.75

sent you on sale, & receipted by you Nov. 3, 1870.

Respectfully, &c.

Walt Whitman

414. *To Louisa Van Velsor Whitman*   *12.25. [1871]*

ADDRESS: Mrs. Louisa Whitman | p. o. Box 218, | Brooklyn, New York. POSTMARK: Washington | Dec | 25 | D. C.

DEPARTMENT OF JUSTICE

Washington. 187 | *Dec. 25*[82]—*Evening ½ past 6—*
Well, mama dear, Christmas day is finished, & I thought I would

---

80. Björnstjerne Björnson (1832–1910), Norwegian poet, dramatist, and novelist, was co-editor of Schmidt's journal. In his reply on January 5, 1872, Schmidt observed: "Hans Christian Andersen would perhaps not make you very great joy, if you did know him personally. Björnson would be your man" (Syracuse; Traubel, IV, 103). Schmidt later altered his opinion of Björnson; see notes to 594.

81. In a letter on July 20, 1867, Trowbridge (see 102) had said that William H. Piper & Co., booksellers in Boston, were willing to take 50 copies of the new edition of *Leaves of Grass*, and that he could personally recommend the firm (Feinberg; Traubel, III, 506). The firm was advertised as WW's Boston agent in books published in 1871 and 1872. Later WW authorized Asa K. Butts & Co. to collect the money Piper owed to him; see 564 and 577.

82. In 418 WW reported that he had sent three letters to his mother the preceding week, of which this was the first.

just send you a line—We have had a mild day, as warm as spring—I took dinner at O'Connor's by invitation—we had an excellent dinner—I am invited to Dr. Channings[83] this evening, but I hardly feel like going, & shall not go—They are very clever people, & have invited me to Newport next summer—

I am writing this in the office, (alone in my own room)—I have just time to catch the mail—I hope you have had a nice Christmas, mama dear—May be George & Lou are with you—(I hope you will all take a glass of the Spanish wine)—

I believe I told you in my last that I wrote to Martha and Han—Good bye, mama dear, for this time, & Love to you & Lou & all—

Walt.

Mother, I will send the order in my next—The bells are all ringing for 7 oclock church—there is a chime of bells in one of the churches—they are playing an old hymn tune—it sounds good—it is a beautiful moonlight night—

415. *To Anne Gilchrist*

Washington, | U. S. | Dec. 26, '71.

Dear friend,

Your late letter has just reached me—& I write at once to at least say specifically that both your letter of Sept. 6 and that of Oct. 15[84] safely reached me—this that comes to-day being the third.

Again I will say that I am sure I appreciate & accept your letters, & all they stand for, as fully as even you, dear friend, could wish—& as lovingly & *bona fide*.[85]

Walt Whitman

---

83. William F. Channing, the doctor whom WW visited in Providence in October, 1868.

84. In 411 Mrs. Gilchrist wrote anxiously about her earlier letters, actually written on September 3–6 and October 23. "Baffled & almost despairing," she sent two copies of her November letter; see her letter of January 24, 1872 (LC; Harned, 74).

85. In her reply on January 24, Mrs. Gilchrist said: "Your few words lifted a heavy weight off me. Very few they are, dear friend: but knowing that I may give to every word you speak its fullest truest meaning, the more I brood over them the sweeter do they taste. Still I am . . . restless, anxious, impatient, looking so wistfully toward the letters each morning—above all, longing, longing so for you to come—to come & see if you feel happy beside me: . . . Only so can you judge whether I am indeed the woman capable of rising to the full height of this great destiny, of justifying & fulfilling your grand thoughts of women" (LC; Harned, 72–73).

416. *To Louisa Van Velsor Whitman*

DEPARTMENT OF JUSTICE

Washington | Dec. | *27 1871.*

Dearest mother,

There is nothing special to write about to-day. The new Attorney General Mr. Williams[86] has been in once or twice—he is a tallish, western sort of man, wears a stove-pipe hat—is rather spare & a little round shouldered—sallow complexion—long legged—seems quite plain in his talk— Ashton says he is a good man—we will see—He takes his seat about the 10th Jan.

½ past 10, forenoon—Mama, your letter has just come—It is too bad to have such a puppy as Stanton[87] annoying you—He is one of the Heyde sort, it always seemed to me—Mother, write to me how it turns out—whether they leave or not—

I see you have it very changeable there too—After the severest cold spell ever known here so early, we are just now having it mild & warm enough for spring—it rained here this morning, but is now bright & pleasant—

I suppose Lou[88] will be with you now—I should like first rate to just drop in on you all—

I continue to get letters &c from abroad about my book—I believe I told you I got one the other day from Denmark, from the editor[89] of the principal magazine there. He is preparing a review & partial translation of my writings—

Mama dear, I hope you will have a pleasant holiday week, what's left of it—Don't let Stanton annoy you, the dirty scamp—Love to you, dearest mother, & to George & Lou & all.

Walt.

Write by next Sunday if convenient, & tell me if the order comes safe—

Mother, give the enclosed $1 to the letter-carrier, if you think proper—

86. George Henry Williams (1820–1910), U. S. Senator from Oregon, served as Attorney General from 1871 to 1875. Williams dismissed WW on June 30, 1874 (see 627).

87. The Stantons lived downstairs. George "turned 'em out for impudence to mother" (see 424).

417. *To Louisa Van Velsor Whitman*   *[12.28–29. 1871?]*[90]

DEPARTMENT OF JUSTICE

Washington. 187 | Thursday night—½ past 8

Dearest mama,

I will write you a line, to begin my letter, before I leave the office—I have been sitting here alone for a couple of hours, having a good time, all by myself, nobody in the building besides me, but the watchman—Mama dear, I suppose you got the order in my last—I have also sent you the old Franklin Almanac—write if it arrived safe. There is nothing new or special—I am well, & only hope your cold is better—I sometimes think a bad cold is about as aggravating as any thing one can have—

I saw Grant to-day on the avenue walking by himself—(I always salute him, & he does the same to me.)

Friday forenoon ½ past 11

I have been hard at work all the forenoon—it is a cloudy day here, threatening rain—Mama dear, I don't seem to think of any thing to write about this morning—Love to you—& to George & Lou if they are there.

                                                            Walt.

I send you a couple of Washington papers.

88. Louisa and George had come from Camden to visit Mrs. Whitman.
89. Rudolf Schmidt.
90. WW wrote to his mother three times during this week, and George and Louisa were in Brooklyn at the time (see 418).

1872

418. *To Louisa Van Velsor Whitman*

DEPARTMENT OF JUSTICE

Washington. 187 | Monday noon—Jan. 1, 1872.

Well, mother dear, New Year has begun—it is the funniest one yet —there is a fog as dark as Egypt here, sometimes you cant see a rod before you—it has been so for two days steady—very muddy, & spells of drizzling rain—I am well & hearty—

I am just informed that I am to be transferred over to the Treasury Building, into the Solicitor of the Treasury's office (it is in the Department of Justice—is a branch of it)[1]—Mr. Williams, the new boss, wishes to bring some friend of his here—I do not know that I shall dislike the change—I can tell better all about it in a week or two—

I have applied for a good long leave of absence, to commence about Feb. 1st—I shall probably get it, but without pay, (or with only a small part pay)—I am willing to take a leave without pay—I want to come home for a while, both to be home, & to see about the new edition of my books— I am real well & fat & hearty this winter—but I believe I have got a little set against one thing & another here, (especially the grub,) & I want a change for a couple of months very much—

Mama dear, I want to hear about your last week—& George & Lou —I sent three letters to you last week, & papers—I knew that policeman Doyle[2] that was shot dead here—he was Peter Doyle's brother—I was at

1872
1. WW moved to the new office before January 23; see 423. The official transfer was not prepared until March 10, 1873 (National Archives).
2. Francis M. Doyle was murdered on December 29, 1871, by Mrs. Maria Shea, known as "Queen of Louse Alley," when he went to her home to recover a stolen watch and chain. According to the Washington *Daily Morning Chronicle*, Doyle, a native of Ireland, was 38, had a wife and three children, and lived at 340 K Street. He had been on the police force for four or five years, and had served during the War for three years as a fireman on the "U. S. Wabash." Among the manuscripts at Yale is a draft of an article which WW prepared for a Washington newspaper to answer criticisms of Doyle for his "arrest of a little boy, for theft." WW doubted that "the true interests" of the public were "aided by this attempt to make martyrs and heroes of the steadily increasing swarms of juvenile thieves & vagabonds who infest the streets of Washington."

the funeral yesterday—it was in the papers I sent you—love to you, dear mama—

Walt.

I forgot to say Arthur Price[3] is here, on the iron-clad *Mahopac*—the vessel is at the navy-yard—expects to sail soon—I am going down this afternoon to go on board the ship & see him—he is well & hearty.

419. *To Louisa Van Velsor Whitman*   *1.3.* [*1872*]

Wednesday noon—Jan 3.

Dearest mother,

Your letter of Sunday night came this morning—it seems indeed "after a storm comes a calm"—You must have had quite an exciting week—still I think it must have been kind of good to have had George and Lou home—was Lou as kind and helpful as ever? About being alone, if you feel as I do about it, it is a satisfaction to be by one's self, as you grow old—(though perhaps not too much)—I was glad to hear about little Jim & Georgey[4]—I am glad the Stantons are gone—they would only have been a continual nuisance—

Mama, I shall come home, (if nothing happens more than at present known) and stay two months, & then return here to my place—I shall write in good time before—

Mama dear, you must try to take as much comfort as you can—I hope Gracie[5] comes in frequently—& Mrs. Mormon too—(she seems to me a good neighbor)—

Walt.

This is the 2d letter this week—

3. Abby Price's son (see 423).

4. If WW was replying to the undated letter of Mrs. Whitman (Yale), his remarks about Andrew's children were inappropriate, for his mother described how George—"i think he is a very bad boy indeed"—came to beg, and also informed her son that Nancy, Andrew's wife, "said in the letter i could take george if i wanted too." According to a letter from Mannahatta, Jeff's daughter, to her grandmother on October 26 (LC), George was killed in an accident later in the year.

5. Grace B. Haight. Evidently WW forgot, or did not know, that Mrs. Haight, the daughter of the Bruces (see 423), was in Independence, Iowa, whence she wrote to Mrs. Whitman on February 7 (LC). After her return to Brooklyn, she wrote to WW's mother on September 22 (LC) and to WW on September 26 (LC). The Bruces and Mrs. Haight visited Mrs. Whitman at Camden the day after Thanksgiving; see Mrs. Whitman's letter to WW on December 3 (LC).

420.   *To Louisa Van Velsor Whitman*   [*1.5. 1872*][6]

DEPARTMENT OF JUSTICE

Washington 187 | Friday evening—after 6—
Mama dear, I believe I must send you a line for Saturday though
I have little or nothing to write about—I am sitting here alone in the
office, writing by my lamp—I went over to Baltimore last evening for a
little trip—saw Mr. Emerson—he lectured there—John Burroughs wanted
to go over & hear him—it was not interesting to me at all[7]—but we had a
pleasant little jaunt—got back about ½ past 11—Nothing different in the
office—I [expect][8] to go over in the Treasury Building, in the office of
the Solicitor of the Treasury, as I told you—the new Attorney Gen'l Mr.
Williams has assigned me there—but several important bits of work have
had to be done just now, & today & yesterday I have had to do them—
(as the old ladies say "I guess they'll miss me a good deal more than they
'spected")—so I have been held on to here so far—
Mama dear, I hope this will find you well of your cold—and that you'll
have a good Sunday—
Congress convenes again next Monday—I met a man who saw Jeff
about nine days ago in St. Louis. Good bye for this time, dear mother—
Walt.

421.   *To Rudolf Schmidt*

Washington, D. C. United States. | January 16, 1872.
Dear sir:[9]
Supposing that the books & papers I sent you in response to your
letter have safely arrived, I thought I would now write you a few lines.
What I have to submit & say, I will just say without ceremony—confident
you will receive it in the same spirit in which it is written.
I sent you (by Mr. Clausen) my poems "Leaves of Grass"—and little

6. According to the Baltimore *American*, Emerson lectured at the Peabody Institute
on January 2 (Tuesday) on the subject "Imagination and Poetry." Yet WW wrote as
though he had heard Emerson on Thursday, January 4. See Rusk, *Letters of Ralph
Waldo Emerson*, VI, 187–197. WW conveyed to Emerson an invitation from Charles
Sumner; see Rusk, VI, 193.
7. Note also WW's comment on the Emerson lecture in 422. Not surprisingly,
Burroughs' reactions were almost identical: he too believed that Emerson failed to perceive "the needs of the American people today" (Barrus, 65–66).
8. WW wrote "except."
9. In this letter WW was furnishing information Schmidt sought for his article;
see 412. This and the following letter contain almost identical statements of WW's con-

prose work "Democratic Vistas"—also a piece I recited at opening of an Exhibition of Industry in New York;[10] adding several criticisms, sketches, &c. about the books & about myself, written by different persons from different points of view. These will furnish you with sufficient material for your examination, digest, &c.

The main object of my poetry is simply to present—sometimes by directions, but oftener by indirections—the Portraiture or model of a sound, large, complete, physiological, emotional, moral, intellectual & spiritual *Man*, a good son, brother, husband, father, friend & practical citizen—& *Woman* also, a good wife, mother, practical citizen too—adjusted to the modern, to the New World, to Democracy, & to science. My verse strains its every nerve to arouse, brace, dilate, excite to the love & realization of health, friendship, perfection, freedom, amplitude. There are other objects, but these are the main ones.

The central purpose of "Democratic Vistas" is to project & outline a fresh & brawny race of original American Imaginative authors, with *moral purpose*, Hegelianism, underlying their works, poems—and with Science & Democracy—also thoroughly *religious*—(not ecclesiastical or sectarian merely.)

And now an item for your proposed review:

When you are composing your review, I would like to have you bring in, in a proper place, the following mentioned facts[11]—that neither my poetic "Leaves" or "Democratic Vistas" is cordially accepted in the United States—nor do the chief literary persons or organs of the country admit the poems as having any merit, or recognize the author as a poet at all— that he has once indeed been ignominiously ejected from a moderate government employment at Washington by special order of a Cabinet officer there, for the sole & avowed reason that he was the writer of the book; that up to this time no American publisher will publish it (the author printing the various editions himself)[12]—that many of the booksellers refuse to keep it for sale—that the swarms of versifiers and writers of book notices in America are quite generally banded against this new man (myself) and that his position, in his own country, both as to literary

ception of his works.

10. "After All, Not to Create Only."

11. Once again WW restated what was by this time a somewhat shop-worn charge —a poet systematically persecuted by governmental authority and by American newspapers and journals. In his desire to appear in the role of a martyr, he consistently neglected mention of the coverage he received in the press. Even Traubel, in 1889, dissented from WW's opinion; see IV, 61–62. In addition, sales were better than he admitted; see 424.

12. Again WW omitted reference to the 1860 edition published by Thayer & Eldridge.

recognition & worldly prosperity, has been, and remains to-day, under a heavy & depressing cloud.

Of course you will at the same time hardly need to be told that I take all this very coolly—that my book is written in the sun & with a gay heart —for these surely, fully belong to me. But I think a good foreign review of my works would be more complete by giving those facts—would be hardly complete without them—for they are *the substantial facts*, notwithstanding a few exceptions.

Meanwhile, abroad, my book & myself have had a welcome quite dazzling. Tennyson writes me friendly letters, inviting me to become his guest. Freilegrath[13] translates & commends my poems. Robert Buchanan,[14] Swinburne, and all the great English & Dublin colleges, affectionately receive me & doughtily champion me. And while I, the author, am without any recompense at all in America, the English pirate-publisher, Hotten,[15] derives a handsome annual income from a bad & defective London reprint of my Poems.

I wish you to speak of the purpose of "Democratic Vistas." (It is at present in danger of falling still-born here.)

I should be glad to hear more from you, your magazine—Denmark too. For all, accept my friendliest good wishes.

    Direct

> Walt Whitman
> Washington, D. C.
> Solicitor's Office Treasury,
> United States America

Later—Upon reading over my letter within, previous to mailing it, I had almost decided not to send it—as a part of it may be open to the imputation of a complaining spirit, & querulousness—Yet as nothing can

13. WW's misspelling.

14. Robert Buchanan (1841–1901), English poet and critic, had lauded WW in *The Broadway Annual* in 1867 (see 262), and in 1872 praised WW but attributed his poor reception in England to the sponsorship of W. M. Rossetti and Swinburne. See Blodgett, 79–80, and Allen, 445–446. Swinburne's recantation later in the year may be partly attributable to Buchanan's injudicious remarks.

15. See 255. Mark Twain, incensed by the pirated edition of *The Innocents Abroad*, damned "John Camden Hottentot"; see Delancey Ferguson, *Mark Twain: Man and Legend* (1943), 163.

16. Feinberg; Traubel, I, 224–225, III, 41–42.

17. See 404.   18. *The Westminster Review*.   19. See 408.

20. Dowden omitted the names of his friends in his transcription; these are supplied from the draft letter.

21. On September 5 Dowden described Cross as a clergyman who "has I dare say taken you in more thoroughly than any of us" and his brother John as a clergyman "who finds his truth halved between John H. Newman (of Oxford celebrity) & you" (Feinberg; Traubel, I, 224–225).

22. Elizabeth D. West, daughter of the dean of St. Patrick's in Dublin, was one of Dowden's students and an author. She became Dowden's second wife in 1895, and after his death published *Fragments from Old Letters—E. D. to E. D. W., 1869–1892* (1914).

be further from my real state of mind, (which is *more* than satisfied, & delightedly grateful for my literary fortunes & reception by the world,) I will let it go.

422. *To Edward Dowden*

TRANSCRIPT.

Washington Jan 18, 1872.

Dear Mr Dowden,

I must no longer delay writing, & to acknowledge your letters of Sept 5 and Oct 15 last.[16] I had previously (Aug 22)[17] written you very briefly in response to your friendly letter of July 23d, the first you wrote me, accompanying copy of the Review.[18] All—letters & Review—have been read & reread. I am sure I appreciate you in them. May I say you do not seem to stand afar off, but very near to me. What John Burroughs[19] brings adds confirmation. I was deeply interested in the acc'ts given in the letters of your friends. I do not hesitate to call them mine too.[20] Tyrell, Cross, your brother,[21] Miss West,[22] Todhunter,[23] O'Grady[24]—Yeats,[25] Ellis,[26] Nettleship.[27] Affectionate remembrance to all of them. You especially, and Mrs. Dowden, & indeed all of you, already, I say, stand near to me. I wish each to be told my remembrance (or to see this letter if convenient).

I like well the positions & ideas in your Westminster article—and radiating from the central point of assumption of my pieces being, or commencing "the poetry of Democracy." It presents all the considerations which such a critical text & starting point require, in a full, eloquent, & convincing manner. I entirely accept it, all & several, & am not unaware

23. Dowden characterized Dr. John Todhunter (1839–1916) as "a man of science, & a mystic—a Quaker." Todhunter later held a chair in English literature at Alexandria College in Dublin, and wrote *Study of Shelley* (1880), in which he termed Shelley, Hugo, and WW the three poets of democracy. See Blodgett, 180.

24. Standish James O'Grady (1846–1928), a lawyer and later a celebrated Irish poet, published, under a pseudonym, "Walt Whitman: the Poet of Joy," *The Gentleman's Magazine*, xv, n.s. (1875), 704–716, in which he concluded: WW "is the noblest literary product of modern times, and his influence is invigorating and refining beyond expression." See Blodgett, 180–182, and Hugh Art O'Grady, *Standish James O'Grady—The Man & the Writer* (1929).

25. John Butler Yeats (1839–1922), the artist and father of the poet.

26. Edwin Ellis (1841–1895), an artist and poet, shared a studio in London with Yeats. See *Letters of Edward Dowden and His Correspondents* (1914), 43.

27. John Trivett Nettleship (1841–1902), a painter, had recently published *Essays on Robert Browning's Poetry* (1868). He was a friend of W. M. Rossetti and a contributor to the 1876 appeal for funds for WW; see *Rossetti Papers*, 339, and Blodgett, 37. J. B. Yeats reported that Nettleship had spent almost his last three guineas to purchase a copy of *Leaves of Grass* which "had not been bereaved of its indecencies"; see *Letters of Edward Dowden and His Correspondents* (1914), 44.

that it probably afforded, if not the only, at least the most likely gate, by which you as an earnest friend of my book, & believing critic of it, would gain entrance to a leading review—Besides, I think the main theme you exploit is really of the first importance—and all the rest can be broached & led to, through it, as well as any other way.

I would say that (as you of course see) the spine or verteber principle of my book is a model or ideal (for the service of the New World, & to be gradually absorbed in it) of a complete healthy, heroic, practical modern *Man*—emotional, moral, spiritual, patriotic—a grander better son, brother, husband, father, friend, citizen than any yet—formed & shaped in consonance with modern science, with American Democracy, & with the requirements of current industrial & professional life—model of a Woman also, equally modern & heroic—a better daughter, wife, mother, citizen also, than any yet. I seek to typify a living Human Personality, immensely animal, with immense passions, immense amativeness, immense adhesiveness—in the woman immense maternity—& then, in both, immenser far a *moral conscience*, & in always realizing the direct & indirect control of the divine laws through all and over all forever.

In "Democratic Vistas" I seek to make patent the appalling vacuum, in our times & here, of any school of great imaginative Literature & Art, fit for a Republican, Religious, & Healthy people—and to suggest & prophesy such a Literature as the only vital means of sustaining & perpetuating such a people. I would project at least the rough sketch of such a school of Literatures—an entirely new breed of authors, poets, American, comprehensive, Hegelian, Democratic, religious—& with an infinitely larger scope & method than any yet[28]—

There is one point touched by you in the Westminster criticism that if occasion again arises, might be dwelt on more fully—that is the attitude of sneering denial which magazines, editors, publishers, "critics" &c. in the U. S. hold toward "Leaves of Grass." As to "Democratic Vistas" it remains entirely unread, uncalled for here in America. If you write again for publication about my books, or have opportunity to influence any forthcoming article on them, I think it would be a proper & even essential part of such article to include the fact that the books are hardly recognized at all by the orthodox literary & conventi[on]al authorities of the U. S.—that the opposition is bitter, & in a large majority, & that the author was actually turned out of a small government employment &

28. Note the similar material in 421.
29. Burroughs wrote twice to Dowden about WW's possible tour of Europe; see Barrus, 74, 77.
30. On September 30, 1871, Joaquin Miller (1839–1913) had concluded his letter: "I am tired of books too and take but one with me; one Rossetti gave me, a 'Walt Whitman'—Grand old man! The greatest, and truest American I know, with the love of your

deprived of his means of support by a Head of Department at Washington solely on account of having written his poems.

True I take the whole matter coolly. I know my book has been composed in a cheerful & contented spirit—& that the same still substantially remains with me. (And I want my friends, indeed, when writing for publication about my poetry, to present its gay-heartedness as one of its chief qualities.)

I am in excellent health, & again & still work as clerk here in Washington.

I saw John Burroughs very lately. He is well. He showed me a letter he had just rec'd from you.

I wish more & more (and especially now that I realize I know you, & we should be no strangers) to journey over sea, & visit England & your country.[29]

Tennyson has written to me twice—& very cordial & hearty letters. He invites me to become his guest.

I have rec'd a letter from Joaquin Miller.[30] He was at last accounts in Oregon, recuperating, studying, enjoying grand & fresh Nature, & writing something new.

Emerson has just been this way (Baltimore & Washington) lecturing. He maintains the same attitude—draws on the same themes—as twenty-five years ago. It all seems to me quite attenuated (the *first* drawing of a good pot of tea, you know, and Emerson's was the heavenly herb itself—but what must one say to a *second*, and even *third* or *fourth* infusion?) I send you a newspaper report of his lecture here a night or two ago. It is a fair sample.[31]

And now, my dear friend, I must close. I have long wished to write you a letter to show, if nothing more, that I heartily realize your kindness & sympathy, & would draw the communion closer between us. I shall probably send you any thing I publish, and any thing about my affairs or self that might interest you. You too must write freely to me—& I hope frequently—

Direct

> Walt Whitman
> Solicitor's Office Treasury
> Washington D C
> U. S. America.

son. Joaquin Miller" (Feinberg; Traubel, I, 107). In an entry in his journal dated August 1, 1871, Burroughs recorded WW's fondness for Miller's poetry; see Barrus, 60. WW met Miller for the first time later in 1872; see 455.

31. Emerson's lecture on January 16 was reported at length the next day in the Washington *Daily Morning Chronicle*.

423. *To Louisa Van Velsor Whitman*   1.23–24. [1872]

Tuesday evening—Jan 23—

Mother, I wrote yesterday in my letter that I had a bad cold— I felt quite disagreeable yesterday, but went to bed early, & had a good sleep—to-day, Tuesday, I have felt all right.

It has been snowing some here to-day—I have been out walking though —it is not cold—As I write this, I am sitting here in the office, (Treasury solicitor's) at 8 o'clock—have been reading & writing all by myself—

Mother, you get Mrs. Bruce to give you Gracie's[32] address in Iowa— I have just got some nice copies of my Am. Institute piece from Boston,[33] & I will send her one—let Mr. or Mrs. Bruce write the address on a slip of paper and you enclose it in your next—The last time I saw Arthur Price here he invited me to come down to the Navy yard here to visit his vessel, the *Mahopac*—so Saturday, after I left work, I went down—but found myself a day after the fair—the vessel had gone about an hour before I got there—I believe she has gone to Norfol[k.][34]

Mother, on those envelopes you have you just cross out, draw a line over this way,[35] when you send them, & leave the rest, (like you did your last)—and they will come safe—I got your letter this morning—it is too bad the letter Mat sent Christmas was lost—that was a real nice present of a barrel of flour—Poor Mat,[36] I feel real blue to think of her condition— but perhaps she will come round yet—and may be live as long as any of us—

Well, mama dear, I will close for to-night & finish it to-morrow—

Wednesday afternoon | Jan. 24

Mother, I am feeling well to-day—I think my cold must have been a false alarm, or else I have got off very easy—The weather is bitter cold here to-day, but bright & clear—

What do you hear from George—I kind of hope he will not go to Milwaukee—should not wish to have him & Lou live so far away, unless the inducement is very great—

Nothing new in the office—I like this place just as well as the other—

32. Mrs. Haight (see 419) acknowledged the poem in her letter to Mrs. Whitman on February 7: "I missed much of it the day it was delivered" (LC).
33. "After All, Not to Create Only" was printed by Roberts Bros. of Boston; see 407.
34. WW wrote "Norfold."
35. WW drew a line through "Department of Justice."
36. Martha came to Brooklyn in late April or early May, evidently for consultation with New York doctors; see her daughter's letter of May 5 (LC). The diagnosis was cancer; see 455. Jeff either accompanied her or came for her; see Martha's letter to Louisa Whitman on May 27 (Missouri Historical Society).

I have not a room to myself, it is true—We are pretty well crowded—they are mostly young men, & a good deal of noise & moving about—but I don't mind it, as it is only from 9 to 3—& my work is much easier—Has Eddy got well of his cold?

I shall probably be on hand to eat some of Mat's cake—Good bye for to-day, mother dear—

Walt.

424. *To Thomas Jefferson Whitman*

DEPARTMENT OF JUSTICE,
OFFICE OF THE SOLICITOR OF THE TREASURY,[37]

Washington, D. C., Jan. 26, *1872.*

Dear brother Jeff,

I have just rec'd your letter, & glad indeed to hear directly from you all. I hear through mother, but have been expecting a letter from Mat now for some time—Mother's letters are almost always mentioning Matty with love & sympathy, & fretting when she dont hear from her—Dear Mat, we all love her so much, & think about her more than she knows—

I am now working in another branch of the Department—have it easier—whenever you write direct to me—*"Solicitor's Office, Treasury"* Washington, D. C.

I have just written a letter to Han—I write quite often, & send papers, &c—I shall write to mother this morning—Mother is quite alone there in the house, as the people down stairs[38] have moved out—(George turned 'em out for impudence to mother)—I write every other day, & send papers & stuff—My next piece is to appear in the *"Kansas Magazine"* for February[39]—will be out very shortly—It is a new magazine, same style as the Atlantic—intended *for Western thought* & reminiscences &c—

Dear Brother, & dear Sister Matty, I should like to come on, according to your invitation, & pay you a good visit, but it is doubtful this time— My bringing out a new book is only bringing out a new edition, from the stereotype plates, the same as the last—only in one Vol—as the edition printed a year ago is all exhausted—(But I stereotyped it, & have all the

37. WW underscored "Office of the Solicitor of the Treasury."
38. The Stantons; see 416.
39. "The Mystic Trumpeter," *The Kansas Magazine*, I (1872), 113–114. "Virginia —The West" appeared in the March issue, I (1872), 219; see *NEQ*, CLXXV (1938), 348– 349. In December the journal published Hinton's "Walt Whitman in Europe" (I [1872], 499–502), a review of European critical comment on WW since 1868. Probably Hinton, who was well known in Kansas (see 289), was responsible for the friendliness of the new magazine.

plates in New York.) But I should like to have a good long visit home, & be with mother—my getting leave does not work yet as I hoped—but I expect to fix it somehow, & go home before very long—I am very well this winter—My book is flourishing in foreign lands at a great rate—I get letters from all parts of Europe—I believe I told you Tennyson had written me twice and very hearty & friendly letters, inviting me to come & be his guest, &c—Then the professors in the Universities, Dublin & elsewhere in Great Britain deliver lectures on "Leaves of Grass"—&c—But *here* the enemy have the ground mostly to themselves—

I suppose you see we have a new Attorney General[40]—It doesn't seem to make much difference to me so far—

Jeff, did the photos I sent of mother & me come to you, December?

Dear sister Mat, & Hatty & California,[41] love to you all—I am writing this at my desk, toward noon, very bright & sunny, but cold enough—I often think of you all—Mat, when I go home I shall do my part at that *cake* you speak of in letter to mother—Wm. O'Connor & family have gone on a short trip to Cuba, to be back in three weeks—They are all well—

Mother told me the barrel of flour came safe—but it was too bad Mat's Christmas letter got lost—

Good bye to you for this time, Brother Jeff & Matty dear,

Walt.

Mat, you write to mother often as you can—

425. *To John Addington Symonds*

ENDORSED: "letter to J. A. Symonds, | went Jan 27, 1872." DRAFT LETTER.

sent in steamer | Jan 27, '72

J. A. Symonds,[42]

Not knowing whether it will reach you, I will however write a line to acknowledge the receipt of your beautiful & elevated "Love & Death,"

---

40. George H. Williams.   41. WW's niece, Jessie Louisa.

42. (1840–1893), author of *Renaissance in Italy* (1875–1886) and *Walt Whitman—A Study* (1893), translator of Michelangelo's sonnets, and a minor poet.

43. On the title page of *Love and Death* appeared: "To the Prophet Poet | Of Democracy Religion Love | This Verse | A Feeble Echo of His Song | Is Dedicated." Symonds noted in his letter that his poem "is of course implicit already in your Calamus, especially in 'Scented herbage of my breast'" (Feinberg; Traubel, II, 277). The printer's proof of the poem is in the Feinberg Collection. On December 8, 1872, Symonds wrote to Swinburne, somewhat abjectly, to implore his opinion of his poems: "I sent Walt Whitman the one called 'Love & Death,' & he graciously accepted it as a tribute to the author of Calamus. Yet no one on whose critical faculty I could rely has judged them" (Feinberg).

44. WW deleted: "I must apologize, & profoundly too, for not having written to

and of the friendly letter from you, of October 7th last.[43] I have read & re-read the poem, & consider it of the loftiest, strongest & tenderest.[44] Your letter was most welcome to me. I should like to know you better, & I wish you to send me word should this reach you—if the address is the right one. I wish to forward you a copy of my book—as I shall presently bring out a new edition.

I am, as usual, in good health, and continue to work here in Washington in a government office, finding it not unpleasant—finding, in it, indeed sufficient and free margin.

Pray dont think hard of me for not writing more promptly. I have thought of you more than once, & am deeply touched with your poem.[45]

426. *To William Michael Rossetti*

Washington, | January 30, 1872.

My dear Mr. Rossetti,

I send you my newest piece,[46] (in a magazine lately started away off in Kansas, fifteen or eighteen hundred miles inland)—And also improve the occasion to write you a too-long-delayed letter. Your letters of July 9 last, & Oct. 8, were welcomed—since which last nothing from you has reached me.

John Burroughs returned with glowing accounts of England, & heartiest satisfaction from his visits to you, & talks, &c.[47] I saw him day before yesterday. He is well & flourishing.

I still remain here as clerk in a government department—find it not unpleasant—find it allows quite a free margin—working hours from 9 to 3 —work at present easy—my pay $1600 a year (paper)—

Washington is a broad, magnificent place in its natural features—avenues, spaces, vistas, environing hills, rivers, &c. all so ample, plenteous —& then, as you go on, fine, hard wide roads, (made by military engineers, in the war) leading far away down dale & over hill, many & many a mile—Often of full-moonlight nights I have a habit of going on long

you before."

45. Encouraged by WW's reply, Symonds wrote on February 7, begging for clarification of "athletic friendship" (Feinberg; Traubel, I, 74–76). On February 25 he sent WW "Callicsates," a poem which, like Stoddard's sketches, has homosexual overtones. Perhaps because Symonds pressed too hard, as he was to do again later, for information about the Calamus poems, WW did not reply; see Symonds' letter of June 13, 1875 (Feinberg; Traubel, I, 203–204).

46. "The Mystic Trumpeter."

47. Burroughs had gone to London and Dublin in the fall of 1871; see 408. Writing to WW on October 30, Burroughs said: "Rossetti I am drawn toward, and though my first impression of him was that he was a high flown literary cockney, yet I soon saw that ، ، ، he was a genuine good fellow" (Syracuse).

jaunts with some companion six, eight miles away into Virginia or Maryland over these roads. It is wonderfully inspiriting, with such new presentations. We have spells here, night or day, of the finest weather & atmosphere in the world. The nights especially are at times miracles of clearness & purity—the air dry, exhilarating. In fact, night or day, this whole District affords an inexhaustible mine of explorations, walks— soothing, sane, open air hours. To these mostly my habits are adjusted. I have good sturdy health—am fortunate enough to almost always get out of bed in the morning with a light heart & a good appetite—I read or study very little—spend two or three hours every day on the streets, or in frequented public places—come sufficiently in contact with all sorts of people—go not at all in "society" so-called—have however the blessing of some first-rate women friends—My life, upon the whole, toned down, flowing calm enough, democratic, on a cheap scale, popular, suitable, occupied sufficiently, enjoying a good deal—flecked, of course, with some clouds & shadows. I still keep in good flesh & weight. The photos I sent you last fall are faithful physiognomical likenesses. (I still have yours, *carte*, among a little special cluster before me on my desk door.)

My poetry remains yet, in substance, quite unrecognized here in the land for which it was written. The best established magazines & literary authorities (eminencies) quite ignore me & it. It has to this day failed to find an American publisher (as you perhaps know, I have myself printed the successive editions). And though there is a small minority of approval & discipleship, the great majority result continues to bring sneers, contempt & official coolness. My dismissal from moderate employment in 1865 by the Secretary of the Interior, Mr. Harlan, avowedly for the sole reason of my being the author of *Leaves of Grass*, still affords an indication of the high conventional feeling. The journals are often inveterately spiteful. For example, in a letter in the correspondence of a leading New York paper (*Tribune*) from a lady tourist,[48] an authoress of repute, an allusion in the letter to mountain scenery was illustrated by an innocent quotation from, & passing complimentary allusion to me. The letter was all & conspicuously published, except that the editors carefully cut out the lines quoting from & alluding to me, mutilating the text & stultifying the authoress to her great vexation. This to give you a clearer notion—(and I distinctly wish my friends in England writing about my book for print, to describe this state of things here.)[49]

48. Perhaps Katharine Hillard; see 512.
49. Since, with the exception of the *Tribune* incident, all this material was familiar to Rossetti, WW was writing for his English friends. Rossetti, however, commented at length on this passage on March 31: "But certainly it does seem that in degree & duration the obduracy of Americans against your work is something abnormal & unworthy" (Feinberg; Traubel, III, 142).

Of general matters here, I will only say that the country seems to have entirely recuperated from the war. Except in a part of the Southern States, every thing is teeming & busy—more so than ever. Productiveness, wealth, population, improvements, material activity, success, results—beyond all measure, all precedent—& then spreading over such an area —three to four millions square miles—Great debits & offsets, of course—but how grand this oceanic plenitude & ceaselessness of domestic comfort—universal supplies of eating & drinking, houses to live in, farms to till, copious traveling, migratory habits, plenty of money, extravagance even—true there is something meteoric about it, and yet from an over-arching view it is Kosmic & real enough—It gives glow & enjoyment to me, being & moving amid the whirl & din, intensity, material success here —as I am myself sufficiently sluggish & ballasted to stand it—though the best is with reference to its foundation for & bearing on the future—(as you doubtless see in my book[50] how this thought prevails with me.)

But I will turn to more special, personal topics.

Prof. Dowden's Westminster Review article last fall made us all feel pleased & proud. He and I have since had some correspondence, & I have come to consider him (like yourself) fully as near to me in personal as literary relations. I have just written to him at some length.

I have received word direct from Mrs. Gilchrist.[51] Nothing in my life, nor result of my book, has brought me more comfort & support every way—nothing has more spiritually soothed me—than the warm appreciation & friendship of that true, full-grown woman—(for I still use the old Saxon word, for highest need.)

I have twice received letters from Tennyson—& most cordial & hearty letters. He sends me an invitation to visit him.

I deeply appreciate Swinburne's courtesy & approbation. I ought to have written him to acknowledge the very high compliment of his poem addressed to me in *Songs Before Sunrise*[52]—but I am just the most wretched & procrastinating letter-writer alive. I have sent him my last edition,[53] to care of Ellis & Green. If I should indeed come to England, I will call upon him among the first, & personally thank him.

I received, some while since, a generous, impulsive, affectionate letter from Joaquin Miller[54]—but have not yet met him personally. I hear he is now in far-off Oregon, amid the grand scenery there, studying & writing. I saw in a newspaper that he was writing a play.

50. *Democratic Vistas.*   51. See 405.
52. "To Walt Whitman in America" appeared in this volume.
53. This copy, now in the Houghton Library at Harvard, is inscribed: "To | *Alg.* *Chs. Swinburne* | from | Walt Whitman, | Washington, U. S. | November, 1871."
54. See 422.

Wm O'Connor, wife & daughter have just gone on a month's pleasure trip to Cuba.

I received some time since a most frank & kind letter, and brief printed poem, from John Addington Symonds, of Bristol, England. The poem *Love and Death* I read & re-read with admiration. I have just written to Mr. Symonds.

I received Roden Noel's "Study" in *Dark Blue*[55] for Oct. & Nov. last, & appreciate it—& also a letter from himself. I have sent him a copy of my last edition, & intend to write to him.

I proposed by letter to Mr. Ellis (Ellis & Green) of London to publish my poems complete, verbatim. Mr. Ellis has written me a good friendly letter, but declined the proposition.[56]

I shall be happy to receive a copy of your *Selections from American Poets*,[57] when ready—& always, always, glad, my friend, to hear from you—hope, indeed, you will not punish me for my own delay—but write me fully & freely.

Direct

> Walt Whitman
> Solicitor's office Treasury,
> Washington, D. C.
> U. S. America

P.S. Will send the magazine by next mail.

427. *To Cyril Flower*

ENDORSED: *"Feb. 3 '72* | to Cyril Flower."
DRAFT LETTER.

Feb. 2 '72

Dear Cyril Flower:[58]

You may think yourself neglected—perhaps forgotten—by your American friend—Not at all the latter, believe me—Twenty times during the last year I have promised myself to write you—

---

55. On September 13, 1871, Conway wrote that "the Hon Roden Noel (one of the Lord Byron blood, and author of a pleasing volume of Poems) submitted to me recently a very long and careful review of your work" (Feinberg; Traubel, III, 112). "A Study of Walt Whitman, The Poet of Modern Democracy" appeared in *Dark Blue*, I (1871), 241–253, 336–349; reprinted in *Essays on Poetry and Poets* (1886), 304–341. Burroughs, who did not "think the article amounts to shucks," sent it to WW on October 30 (Syracuse). On November 3 Noel (1834–1894) sent WW an inscribed copy of his essay: "The proclamation of comradeship seems to me the grandest & most tremendous fact in your work & I heartily thank you for it" (Feinberg; Traubel, I, 426). Symonds dedicated to Noel *Many Moods—A Volume of Verse* (1878). WW sent Noel a copy of the 1876 edition of *Leaves of Grass*; see Noel's *Essays*, 338n.

56. See 403.   57. See 401.

58. Flower was an English barrister and a friend of Tennyson; see Blodgett, 128–129. According to Flower's letter of April 23, 1871, he met WW in Washington in December, 1870. He had later delivered some of WW's books to Tennyson, who "was much

I am still here at Washington—every thing much the same as when you made your brief visit here. I continue well & hearty, in good spirits, spend much more of my leisure in the open air than reading or studying, or in-doors at all.

I am very soon going on to New York to bring out a new edition of my poems, (same as the copy you have, only in one volume)—shall remain there until about 7th of April—then to return here again, where my address will be Solicitor's[59]—Your two letters duly reached me at the time and were very welcome.

Tennyson has twice written to me—and friendly hearty letters. He invites me to visit him.

I shall mail you my latest piece[60] in a magazine, to be out presently.

And now, dear Cyril Flower, I send you my love, & hope you will not think hard of me for not writing before.

428. *To Rudolf Schmidt*

ENDORSED: "To Rudolf Schmidt." DRAFT LETTER.

Feb. 2, 1872

Dear Mr. Rudolf Schmidt,

Your note of Jan. 5, acknowledging receipt of "papers," & enclosing to me your photograph,[61] is just received. I like your photograph & thank you for it—& I like indeed the good frank way of sending such pictures, where interested & curious. I wish to know whether you have safely received the particular copy of the last edition of my poems, in One Vol., with some sheet photos. enclosed, which I sent you by Mr. Clausen. Mr. C. tells me that he put up the various matter I furnished in three parcels—if you have got the three it is all right.

I mailed you a letter of some length, Jan 16. I shall send you, probably by next mail, my latest piece, in a western magazine for February.[62] Also a second copy of my pamphlet "Democratic Vistas"—If the first copy

touched by your memory of him, and I told him of your deep regard for him" (Feinberg). On July 16 (Feinberg; Traubel, II, 373), Flower informed WW that Tennyson was sending a letter by the same mail (see 394). Flower wrote again on October 20: "When I read you or think of you . . . I feel that I hold in my hand clasped strong & tight & for security the great hand of a friend, a simple good fellow, a man who loves me & who is beautiful because he loves, & with the consciousness of that I feel never alone—never sad" (Feinberg; Traubel, II, 462).

59. WW's complete address was to have been inserted here.
60. "The Mystic Trumpeter."
61. The photograph, inscribed "To Walt Whitman | the poet of the american democracy," is in the Feinberg Collection; Schmidt's letter is in the Syracuse University Library.
62. "The Mystic Trumpeter."

reached you, send the second to Mr. Bjornson—if not, not. Yes, I am sure I should like your friend Bjornson much.

I am going next week to New York to stay there till April 10—my address there will be *107 north Portland av. Brooklyn, New York, U. S. America*—about April 10, I shall return here again, & my address will be[63]—

I am writing this at my desk—as above, Treasury Building, middle of afternoon—From my great south window I can see a far-stretching & noble view, many, many miles of open ground, the Potomac river, the hilly banks, the mountains of Virginia &c. We are having a severe cold spell. Every thing is white with snow, but the sun has been clear & dazzling all day—The hour of office-closing is nigh. And I too must close. I have much pleasure in writing to you, & expecting yours. Adieu.[64]

429. *To Anne Gilchrist*

DRAFT LETTER.

February 8, 1872.

Dear friend,

I send by same mail with this, my latest piece, copied in a newspaper[65]—& will write you just a line or two. I suppose you duly received my former letters (two)—I ought to have written something about your children (described to me in your letter of last summer, July 23d,[66] which I have just been reading again)—Dear boys & girls—how my heart goes out to them[67]—

Did I tell you that I had received letters from Tennyson, & that he cordially invites me to visit him? Sometimes I dream of journeying to Old England, on such visit—& then of seeing you & your children—but it is a dream only.

I am still living here in employment in a Government office—My health is good—Life is rather sluggish here—though not without the sunshine —(Your letters too were warm, bright rays of it)—

I am going on to New York soon to remain there a few weeks[68]—but my address will still be here—I wrote lately to Mr. Rossetti quite a long

---

63. WW's Washington address was to have been inserted here.

64. Schmidt on February 27 acknowledged receipt of the various books and articles (Feinberg).

65. "The Mystic Trumpeter" appeared in the Washington *Daily Morning Chronicle* on February 7.

66. WW must have meant Mrs. Gilchrist's letter of January 24 (LC; Harned, 72–74), in which she discussed the activities of her children, particularly of Percy, who was

letter[69]—My present address is *Solicitor's Office, Treasury, Washington, D. C. U. S. America.*

Best love & remembrance to you, dear friend, & to the young folk—

Walt Whitman

430. *To Peter Doyle*

ADDRESS: Peter Doyle | conductor, | [Of]fice Wash. & Georgetown City RR. | Washington, | D. C. POST-MARK: New York | Feb | 16 | (?)M.

Brooklyn, | 107 north Portland av. | Feb. 16, 1872.
Dear Pete, | Dear, dear son,

We are having a very cold spell here, the severest of the winter—freezes up the pipes through the house, & burst them yesterday, causing great trouble—I too have got a bad cold, my head all stopped—

I came through all right last Saturday,[70] on time—quite a pleasant trip—Mother is very well, full as well as usual—I am having quiet good times home here, with Mother—stay in the house more than usual, on account of the bitter cold, (but go out two or three hours during the day)—

I will only write this very short letter to you this time, but send you my love, my darling son—I think about you every day, dear son—will write more, soon—here is a kiss for you, dear loving son.

Walt

Pete, I am making out a poor scraggy letter to you this time—I feel pretty well, but don't seem to feel like writing—Good bye for to-day, my loving boy—

Your true Father & Comrade always

431. *To Peter Doyle*   *2.23.* [*1872*]

Brooklyn | Friday noon, Feb. 23.
Dear son,

Your letter, rec'd this morning, speaks of the mild weather there —but it has been & remains very cold here—so much so that I don't go

employed at a smelting works, and of Herbert, who was attending a drawing school. Mrs. Gilchrist's first letter to WW was written on September 3–6, 1871 (see 405).

67. In the draft of this letter WW deleted: "and how earnestly I wish them prosperity—well I feel that they must be noble children."

68. Note the misstatement concerning his intended stay in Brooklyn; see the preceding letter.

69. See 426.   70. February 10.

around half as much as I would like. My cold hangs on, though not so bad as at first. The state of the weather, & my cold, &c. have rather blocked me from having my usual enjoyment here, so far—but I expect to make up for it by and by.

Dear son, I see you are off[71]—I take it by your letter that you are feeling well in health, and having as good a time as the law allows—I wish we could be together there, some of these moonlight nights—but here it is too cold for comfort—(the water pipes here froze again last night, causing trouble)—I go out a couple of hours middle of the day, but keep in nights—

I have got the new edition of my book under way—& it will be satisfactory I think—It will be in one volume, & will make a better appearance than any of the former ones—Do you go up to the debates in the Senate—I see by the papers they are having high times—Senator Schurz appears to come out ahead of them all—he is a real good speaker—I enjoy the way he shakes them up, (very much like a first-class terrier in a pit, with a lot of rats)[72]—

Pete, I send you $10 enclosed, as you may need it—Should you want more, you write, as I have plenty—I am writing this up in my back room, home—have had a nice breakfast of hot potatoes & first-rate Oregon salmon—with the best coffee that's made—home-made bread, & sweet butter—every thing tip-top—get along well enough—you must try to do the same—so good bye for this time, my own loving boy—

Walt.

432. *To Peter Doyle*   3.4–[5. 1872]

Brooklyn, | Monday evening | March 4.

Dear son,

I am sitting here in my room home, alone—it is snowing hard & heavy outside, & cold & wintry as ever—there has not been one mild day here for the past three weeks—two thirds of the time spiteful and gusty wind & clouds of dust—& this with bitter cold—seems to me I have felt the cold more than for the last three winters—But I reckon I have said enough on this point—Pete, I cannot write anything interesting to you, as I do not go anywhere, nor see anything new. I have attended to the

71. Doyle was temporarily out of work.

72. Senator Carl Schurz (1829–1906), of Missouri, alleged that since the U. S. had violated its neutrality in the 1870 war by selling arms to French agents, Germany could bring claims for damages against the American government. Schurz's opponents charged that he had falsified documents. The New York *Times* on February 23 declared: "Schurz was the greatest toady any President ever had until he failed to get all the offices

bringing out the new edition of my book, but as the plates were all ready before, it is not much of a job—I am home every night (& half the days also)—

Tuesday noon

I am afraid this letter is not destined to be very cheering—I was attacked last night with sore throat, pretty bad—still I made out this morning to worry down a fair breakfast—The weather has been so infernal—last evening toward sundown, begun the spitefulest wind & cold I ever knew—great clouds suddenly come up, inky black, & all of a sudden snow fell so thick & fast, it was like a dense fog—so thick the hard wind didn't dissipate it in the least—This lasted about half an hour, & was about the highest old weather exhibition I ever witnessed—snow fell two inches thick in 15 minutes[73]—

Dear Pete, how are you getting along—how about Sailer[74] and the RR? —I suppose slow [&] aggravating enough—by what you said in your last. Dear Pete, I don't think I shall stay here as long as I originally intended—I shall be back by or before the end of this month—I am writing these lines home in the Kitchen—mother is sitting in the rocking chair sewing something—& Eddy is grinding some good coffee in a coffee mill —it smells good—(I have retreated to the Kitchen, for the hot fire—here now I am not like I am in Washington—you would laugh to see me hovering over the fire)—

My darling son, you must keep a good heart—dont get discouraged—love to you, baby—I enclose $10—& can send you whatever you want—

Walt—

433. *To Peter Doyle*   [*3.7. 1872*][75]

ADDRESS: Peter Doyle | Conductor | Office | Wash. & Georgetown City RR. | Washington, | D. C. POSTMARK: New York | Mar | 7 | 6 P.M.

Brooklyn, | Thursday forenoon.

Dear son,

Well I am still here, Pete, kept in pretty close quarters by the weather—but it seems to be something of a let up this morning. There is

he wanted, and then he turned round and became a 'patriot' and a 'reformer.' "

73. At this point WW pasted a brief clipping about the "Horrendous Blow" from the New York *Sun.*

74. Charles C. Sailer, superintendent of the Washington & Georgetown Railroad, of which Pete was an employee.

75. The date of this letter is established by the reference to the $10 sent on March 5.

nothing special to write about—but I thought I would send you a line this morning. I sent you a letter two days ago with $10—(the second 10 I have sent)—Write me whether you rec'd it all right. I hope you are not discouraged by the way things work on the road—It wont be very long, now before I shall be back with you—Give my love to Mr. & Mrs. Nash —tell Wash Milburne I wish him success in the "graduate of Pharmacy" line, & every thing else—give him my love—

Pete, I believe that is all this time, dear baby,

Walt—

with a kiss from your loving father—

434. *To John Burroughs* 3.15. [1872][76]

ADDRESS: John Burroughs, | Office Comptroller | of the Currency, | Washington, | D. C. POSTMARK: New York | Mar | 15 | (?)30 PM.

107 north Portland av. | Brooklyn, N. Y. | March 15.
Dear John Burroughs:

We have had cold & spiteful weather all the time of my visit here —over a month—& I have not had my usual outdoor enjoyment, loafing about &c—have been indoors most of the time—I also caught cold just on coming here, & it has bothered ever since.

How are you, dear friend? & how is 'Sula[77]—dear friend, too—Write me a few lines, John—let me know how Chauncey[78] is getting along—if he finds any difficulty—but I guess not—I guess he is getting along well— Is there any thing new among my friends there in Wash'n?

I have got out my new edition, from same plates as the last, only all bound in One Vol.—neatly done in green cloth, vellum—looks the best & most ship-shape of any edition yet—have not added any of my later pieces in this—leaving them to some future issue—

Rec'd a letter from Mrs. Gilchrist in England—she has been reading "Wake Robin" & takes to it greatly[79]—says Rossetti dined at her house not long since—(You know she is the authoress of the "Woman's Estimate," in the Radical)—

---

76. This letter, as the contents confirm, was written at the same time as the next one. Evidently one of the executors inserted " '71" after the date, and the date is retained in Nonesuch.

77. Burroughs' wife Ursula.

78. Chauncey B. Deyo, Burroughs' nephew, was substituting for WW while he was in Brooklyn; see Barrus, 88. See also 619.

79. In none of Mrs. Gilchrist's extant correspondence is there reference to Bur-

John, I think it likely I shall return about the 1st of April—Mother has had a bad spell for three days, but is about as usual again, yesterday & to-day—direct to me here—

Love to all,

Walt.

435. *To Peter Doyle* *3.15.* [*1872*]

ADDRESS: Peter Doyle, | Conductor, | Office | Wash. & Georgetown City RR. | Washington | D. C. POST- MARK: New York | Mar | 15 | 1:30 PM.

107 north Portland av. | Brooklyn, March 15

Dear son,

I will just write you a line, as you may be looking for word from me Saturday. The weather has let up a little, but it is cold enough yet—I have been to the Italian Opera twice, heard Nilsson both times—she is *very fine*—One night *Trovatore* & one, *Robert*, with Brignoli—both good[80]—

I expect to return in about two weeks—I am writing this here in the kitchen home—I have deserted my own room this visit, as it is so cold, even with a fire—Mother had a bad spell three days, commencing Sunday last—but is about as usual to-day & yesterday—We have splendid buckwheat cakes for breakfast—sometimes I fry them myself—I wish you could just be here & eat breakfast—I think my mammy makes the best coffee in the world, & buckwheats ditto—mince-pies ditto—

My new edition looks the best yet—it is from the same plates as the last, only in One Vol. bound handsomely in green cloth—my books are beginning to do pretty well—I send you the publisher's slip—

Well, Pete, I believe that is all this time—Remember me to any of the boys on the road that may inquire for me—also to Adrian Jones,[81] that works in the theatre—it is now after 10, Friday forenoon, clear, cold, & windy—& I am going over to N. Y. to have a lot of my books sent to England by to-morrow's steamer—Dear son, I send my best love, as always. We will soon be together again, dear son.

Walt

roughs' *Wake-Robin* (1871). It is surprising that not until this late date did WW inform his friend of Mrs. Gilchrist's authorship of the article in *The Radical*.

    80. Christine Nilsson (1843–1921), the Swedish soprano, appeared in *Il Trovatore* during the week of March 4 and in Meyerbeer's *Robert le Diable* on March 11, with Pasquale Brignoli (see 231). See Odell, IX, 190.

    81. Listed in the Directory of 1872 as a messenger.

436. *To Anne Gilchrist*

Brooklyn, N. Y. | March 20, 1872.

My dear friend,

Your letter is rec'd, having been sent on to me from Washington.[82] My address still remains Solicitor's office, Treasury there. I am moving about a good deal the past year, & shall be for the ensuing year—I am to start for northern New England, & remain awhile[83]—am also arranging for a trip afterward to California—a journey I have had in contemplation for several years, & which has been two or three times fixed, but postponed, during that time.

I have been stopping for two months, (Feb. & March,) home with my Mother, & am writing this home. Mother is towards eighty—has had an active domestic & maternal life—has had eight children—has brought them all up—has been healthy & strong, always worked hard—now shows the infirmities of age (indeed rapidly advancing) but looks finely, & is cheerful hearted—will probably soon give up her housekeeping & go to live with one of my brothers, who is married[84]—My father died seventeen years since.

Dear friend, I am quite sure that *every one* of your letters has safely reached me—sometimes after delays & circuits, (as you will now understand better) on account of my more & more frequent wanderings[85]—The letter with the photographs gave me great pleasure—& was acknowledged by a letter I sent you[86]—Have you not received it?

Walt Whitman

Dear friend, let me warn you somewhat about myself—& yourself also. You must not construct such an unauthorized & imaginary ideal Figure, & call it W. W. and so devotedly invest your loving nature in it. The actual W. W. is a very plain personage, & entirely unworthy such devotion.[87]

82. Evidently Mrs. Gilchrist's letter of January 24 or one now unknown.
83. A reference to his trip to Dartmouth College in June; see 451.
84. With George, who now lived in Camden, N. J.
85. This was a deliberate fib in order to explain his delays in replying to a woman whom he did not quite know how to handle.
86. Mrs. Gilchrist sent the photographs on January 24. Perhaps WW intended to acknowledge them in 429.
87. Mrs. Gilchrist on April 12 objected to this warning: "it hurts so, as seeming to distrust my love. . . . O, I could not live if I did not believe that sooner or later you will not be able to help stretching out your arms towards me & saying 'Come, my Darling' " (LC; Harned, 78). On June 3 Mrs. Gilchrist begged for a longer letter, "for I sorely need it." Though she declared that she would be satisfied with a gossipy letter about his affairs, she really wanted more: "And if you say 'Read my books, & be content—you have me in them'—I say, it is because I read them so that I am not content." Toward the conclusion of the letter she spoke of coming to America (LC; Harned, 79–81). On July 14

437. *To Peter Doyle*   *3.22.* [*1872*]

                              Brooklyn, | Friday forenoon, March | 22.
Dear Pete,

I rec'd your letter yesterday. Pete, you must be quite steady at
work, & no time to spare. Well, perhaps it is just as satisfactory, considering all things. The cold weather has just kept on here, as before—cold
enough all the time—and then a spell of *damned bitter, stinging cold*,
every now and then extra—not one single mild, warm day since I have
been home—six weeks—

I am middling well, go out some every day, but not much—Best thing
is my *eating & sleeping*—I fall back on them altogether—I sleep splendid,
have a good bed, plenty of cover—get up pretty early though & make the
fire, & set things a going, before mother comes out—she has had some
bad times with rheumatism, &c—one hand & arm quite disabled—still she
is very cheerful, looks well in the face, & does more work cooking &c.
than most young women—We have grand breakfasts, buckwheat cakes,
coffee, &c. eggs—just wish you could come in mornings & partake—We
two always breakfast together, & it is first rate—So you see I fall back on
sleeping & eating, (as I said)—Should be glad to see Parker Milburn—
hope he will call to-day—I send you a paper by mail—

Well, Pete, I believe that is all, this time. Good bye, my darling son—
So the *new shirts* turn out a success do they? I have a great mind to be
jealous—Give my love to Wash Milburn, Adrian Jones, & all the RR boys.
                                              Your loving old Walt

438. *To William J. Linton*   *3.22.* [*1872*]

                        107 North Portland av. | Brooklyn, March 22.
My dear Linton,[88]

Your kind letter came duly to hand. I have been delaying to write

she acknowledged his gift of *As a Strong Bird on Pinions Free*, and wrote again of the
effect of WW's poems on her: "Had I died the following year [1870], it would have been
the simple truth to say I died of joy" (LC; Harned, 83). Mrs. Gilchrist wrote again on
November 12—WW had been silent—"I must write not because I have anything to tell
you—but because I want so, by help of a few loving words, to come into your presence
as it were—into your remembrance" (LC; Harned, 85).

  88. Linton (1812–1897), British-born wood engraver, came to the U. S. in 1866
and settled near New Haven, Conn. He illustrated the works of Whittier, Longfellow,
Bryant, and others, wrote the "indispensable" *History of Wood-Engraving in America*
(1882), and edited *Poetry of America, 1776–1876* (London, 1878), in which appeared
eight of WW's poems as well as his picture. According to his *Threescore and Ten Years,
1820 to 1890—Recollections* (1894), 216–217, Linton met WW in Washington and later
visited him in Camden (see 554): "I liked the man much, a fine-natured, good-hearted,
big fellow, . . . a true poet who could not write poetry, much of wilfulness accounting
for his neglect of form."

you about the portrait[89] in answer—wanting *you* to do it—& wanting, if I could arrange it, to give you the full price—I will not have the job done by any second-rater, & have concluded to give it up for the present—unless it could be done by you for $50, which, I am fully aware, would not be your due engagement.

Walt Whitman

I return to Washington in ten or twelve days. Is there any chance of your coming on there?

439. *To Peter Doyle*   [*3.29. 1872*]

ENDORSED (by Doyle): "march 29."[90]
ADDRESS: Peter Doyle, | Conductor, | Office Wash &
Georgetown RR | Washington | D. C. POSTMARK:
New York | Mar | 29 | 6 P.M.

Brooklyn, | Friday afternoon

Dear boy Pete,

I have rec'd your letter, & the paper with acc't of Mr. Huntington's death[91]—it seems a sudden & sorrowful thing—

Pete, I shall continue here another week—I see you are working [it] appears quite steady—I continue pretty well—Mother is middling—

This last two days the weather has been real pleasant—I have been out most of the time—It is now between 4 and 5—I am writing this up in my room home—am going out, & over to New York this evening—nothing special to write about—

Pete, my darling boy, I have been writing some long letters on business &c[92]—& feel very little like writing—so I will just dry up for this occasion—here is a good buss to you, dear son, from your loving Father always—

440. *To Rudolf Schmidt*

Brooklyn, New York, | April 4, 1872.

Mr. Rudolf Schmidt, | Dear Sir & Friend,

Your magazine with the article on my book has safely reached me

---

89. Linton's engraving appeared in the 1876 edition of *Leaves of Grass*, in *Complete Poems & Prose* (1888–1889), and in *CW*, II, 156; it inspired the poem "Out from Behind This Mask." See Harold W. Blodgett, "Whitman and the Linton Portrait," *WWN*, IV (1958), 90–92.

90. The date is confirmed by the reference to Huntington at the beginning of the letter.

91. William S. Huntington (1841–1872) died on March 26. He entered the Treasury Department in 1861, and was selected in 1863 by Jay Cooke, the financier, to be cashier of the First National Bank in Washington.

92. This is the only known letter written on this date.

93. February 27 (Feinberg).

94. Petersen (1834–1918), for ten years the critic of the Danish magazine *Father-*

—& a second copy in sheets—also your last letter.[93] I only write now to make prompt, brief acknowledgment. I have gleaned a general knowledge of the article, & it pleases me very much. I have seen Clemens Petersen[94] in New York, & he ran over it for me. He has been very ill with erysipelas, but is now nearly well.

I am to return to Washington in two or three days. I will write to you thence more fully,[95] & hope to continue having letters from you—My address will be Solicitor's Office, Treasury.

Walt Whitman

441. *To Peter Doyle*   *4.5.* [*1872*]

Brooklyn, | Friday forenoon, | April 5.

Dear son,

I expect to be back in Washington next week—somewhere in the middle of the week. I am well—Mother is pretty well—I rec'd your letter three days since—Pete, things must be going on about the same as ever—

As I write, it is pleasant weather, & I am going out to get the good of it—Pete, take care of yourself till I see you, dear boy,

Walt.

442. *To Samuel Ward*[96]   *4.26.* [*1872*]

Washington | April 26.

Walt Whitman sends his heart-felt respects & thanks to Mr. Ward, for the prompt & generous contribution of $25. The money was conveyed by W. W. to the gentleman intended (Louis Fitzgerald Tasistro,)[97] at noon to-day, & will do him infinite good.

land, left Denmark in 1869 and stayed in the U. S. until 1904. See Schmidt's letter to WW on February 27 (Feinberg); *Orbis Litterarum*, VII (1949), 43*n.;* and LC #108. Also note 594.

95. See 445.

96. Samuel Ward (1814–1884), the brother of Julia Ward Howe, edited *An Elementary Treatise on Algebra* (1832), was the author of *Lyrical Recreations* (1865), and was a lobbyist for various financiers during the Johnson and Grant administrations.

97. Tasistro (1808–1875?) came to the U. S. from Ireland as a young man. He edited a newspaper in New York and later had a brief career on the stage. Subsequently he was a translator for the State Department and a lecturer. He was the author of *Travels in the Southern States: Random Shots and Southern Breezes* (1842) and translator of Paris' *History of the Civil War in America* (1875). On April 26 WW inserted in the

443. *To Alfred, Lord Tennyson*

TRANSCRIPT.

April 27, 1872.

My Dear Mr. Tennyson:

This morning's paper has a vague sort of an item about your coming to America, or wanting to come, to view the working of our institutions, etc. Is there anything in it? I hope so, for I want more and more to meet you and be with you. Then I should like to give my explanations and comments of America and her shows, affairs, persons, doings, off-hand, as you witness them, and become puzzled, perhaps, dismayed by them. America is at present a vast seething mass of varied material human and other, of the richest, best, worst, and plentiest kind. Wealthy inventive, no limit to food, land, money, work, opportunity, smart and industrious citizens, but (though real and permanently politically organized by birth and acceptance) without fusion or definite heroic identity in form and purpose or organization, which can only come by native schools of great ideas—religion, poets, literature[98]—and will surely come, even through the measureless crudity of the States in those fields so far, and to-day.

The lesson of Buckle's books[99] on civilization always seemed to me to be that the preceding main basis and continual *sine qua non* of civilization is the eligibility to, and certainty of boundless products for feeding, clothing, and sheltering everybody, infinite comfort, personal and intercommunication and plenty, with mental and ecclesiastical freedom, and that then all the rest, moral and esthetic, will take care of itself. Well, the United States have secured the requisite bases, and must now proceed to build upon them.[1]

I send you by same mail with this, a more neatly printed copy of my "Leaves"; also "Dem. Vistas."

Your letter of last fall[2] reached me at the time. Have you forgotten that you put a promise in it, to send me your picture when "you could lay hands on a good one?"[3]

Washington *Daily Morning Chronicle* an appeal for "pecuniary assistance for a man of genius," who was not named. On the following day the *Chronicle* noted "prompt contributions" from, among others, Samuel Ward.

In the Feinberg Collection there are three receipts written by WW and signed by Tasistro. On April 26 Tasistro acknowledged $70. On April 29 he accepted an additional $25, and on May 14 $10. On August 3, in his own hand, Tasistro signed a receipt for $17. On the verso WW noted the total of $122: "also $10 more handed by W. W. to Mr. Tasistro." On October 24, 1872, WW wrote: "also about $25 more in different sums since." See *WWR*, VII (1961), 14–16.

98. Here WW summarized one of his major points in *Democratic Vistas*.

I have been in Brooklyn and New York most of the past winter and current spring, visiting my aged dear mother, near eighty. Am now back here at work. Am well and hearty. I have received two letters from you, July 12 and September 22, of last year. This is the second letter[4] I have written to you. My address is: Solicitor's Office, Treasury, Washington, D. C., United States. Write soon, my friend. Don't forget the picture.

Walt Whitman.

444. *To James C. McGuire*

Washington, | May 2, 1872.

My dear Mr. McGuire,[5]

The money you gave me for Mr. Tasistro has been handed by me to him, and has substantially helped him. I have been out to see him several times since I met you—he is up & about & in much better spirits— has great thoughts of getting well, & going to work to earn his living himself.

He has had a very hard time during the winter—Can never again be strong & well—but has indomitable vitality.

Walt Whitman

445. *To Rudolf Schmidt*

Washington | May 28, 1872

My dear Rudolf Schmidt,

I have rec'd yours of April 25. Having an opportunity by Mr. Clausen, who is journeying home to Denmark, I send you some books— another copy of *Leaves of Grass*—and a copy for Björnsen—(though he may not read English, I have wished to send him something—& when he chances upon some one who reads English and Danish, I should be so glad to be communicated to him.)

Your article in the *Ide*[6] will soon be translated for me in full. It is

---

99. Henry Thomas Buckle (1821–1862), English historian and author of *The History of Civilization in England* (1857, 1861).

1. WW copied this paragraph almost verbatim from the preface to *As a Strong Bird on Pinions Free* (1872), which is dated May 31; see *CW*, v, 188–189.

2. The missing letter of September 22, 1871, referred to a few lines below.

3. Tennyson sent his picture in May. The envelope of this missing letter was endorsed by WW: "(from Tennyson with picture)." The postmark reads: Yarmouth | B | My 23 | (?)2 | (?) (Yale).

4. The first letter is lost; see 394.

5. A collector of Americana (1812–1888); see Gohdes and Silver, 75n.

6. Schmidt's review of WW appeared in *For Idé og Virkelighed* in March. WW included excerpts from it in an appendix to *As a Strong Bird on Pinions Free* (1872), 7–8. It was reprinted in entirety in *In Re*, 231–248.

pronounced magnificent by those who can read it. I shall have much to say about it in my next.

I send you two or three humorous American works.[7] The subject of American humor is very difficult to treat fully & satisfactorily, even for a native. In the books I send, the great difficulty will be the slang, the American local idioms, & the mis-spelling—all of which will certainly prove *chevaux-de-frise* making it impossible for any foreigner to penetrate the fun of them—Still I have thought it worth while to send them as (much more than the comic & pictorial papers) *idiomatic, native specimens,* (as minerals or insects)—

American humor is yet in its nebulous state—unformed—*struggling to be born.* Some traits already appear—it is very grim, loves exaggeration, & has a certain tartness & even fierceness—I will endeavor to gather something more for you on this business—& write you again—

I am going soon to a College about 500 miles from here to deliver a commencement poem[8]—it will be published, forming part of a little book—which I will send you—During June I shall be home with my mother in Brooklyn, N. Y.—then return again here—

Walt Whitman.

446. *To Rudolf Schmidt*

Washington | June 4, 1872.

My dear Rudolf Schmidt,

I have sent you some books by Mr. Clausen—All the real flavor of American fun resides in its *idioms,* which are untranslatable expressions of elements in the places, people, & *nativities* here—perceptible enough here, but in the nature of things invisible & inaudible to a foreigner—The extracts I enclose will illustrate[9]—

Mr. Clausen started for Denmark last Saturday, June 1st.

I am just having your criticism *fully* rendered into English—I am to obtain possession of it next Thursday[10]—From what I get of it, in advance, it is going to prove the grandest response & praise yet given any-

---

7. On April 25 Schmidt made a request: "Will you do me a service? I should like to write an article on 'American fancy' contrasting the grotesque humor that is scattered with no pretension in your newspapers with the humor of Luther and Shakespeare . . . Could you not find for me about a dozen jokes of this sort" (Feinberg; Traubel, I, 275). The titles of the books WW sent are not known.

8. "As a Strong Bird on Pinions Free" (later "Thou Mother with Thy Equal Brood") was recited on June 26. Evidently a student organization hoped to annoy the faculty by inviting WW to Dartmouth, a seat of New England sobriety and conservatism; see Perry, 203–205.

9. With this letter are three newspaper clippings: "American Slang in England,"

where to me & my poems. I rec'd the newspaper. I shall keep you advised of any printed use made of your criticism in this country—(The brief of the N. Y. *Commercial Advertiser*, has been copied in the papers somewhat.)

From the 10th of June to 10th of July I shall be home in Brooklyn, New York, & then return here again—

We are in the midst of the preparations & canvassing for one of our national elections—the election is next November—(for President for the term from March 4, 1873, to March 4, 1877)—There is nothing very radical or important in the political questions—it is mostly an excitement of personal piques, & for the *spoils*, as we call it, (i.e. the pay & perquisites of office)—

One of our great *nominating Conventions* is just now meeting, (at Philadelphia)[11]—You would enjoy the sight of such a spectacle greatly—there are many hundreds of *delegates*, and many thousands of active interested followers. (All *voluntary*—all perfectly good natured)—such talking, such gesticulation, such immense crowds by day & night—such manoevering by the different coteries, for their favorite men, (to get "the nomination")—&c. &c. &c.—It is all very salutary exercise for the bulk of the people. But the *spectacular* part of the scenes is the best, especially at night—many bands of music—

Walt Whitman

447. *To Peter Doyle*   *6.14.* [1872]

Brooklyn, | 107 north Portland av. | June 14.

Dear son,

I got home all right Saturday night—& have been having quite a good time. There is nothing very new—Mother is well as usual. I shall print my College Poem in a small book—it will be small—& is intended as the beginning of a larger one[12]—I am having it set up at the printing office—will send you one in ten or twelve days.

Pete, how are you getting along—I suppose on 14[13] the same as when

---

"Artemus Ward and the Press," and "Yankee Talk."

10. Emil Arctander, who was acting vice-consul for Denmark, translated Schmidt's article for WW. According to his letters of June 17 and 20 (Feinberg), he did not complete his self-styled "weak translation" until later in the month. The translation, with scores of corrections in WW's hand, is in the Feinberg Collection.

11. The Republican convention.

12. In the preface to this small pamphlet WW clearly states that he had completed *Leaves of Grass* and was about to start a new work—a clear indication, in Allen's words, that "he is not sure of his new literary intentions" (*Handbook*, 202).

13. The number of Pete's car.

I was there—I see by the papers that the head men have mostly migrated from Washington, & that it is said to be hot & dull enough there[14]—

Do you see any thing of Mr. Tasistro? I rec'd the letter he sent to the office for me—I am writing this in the house in Portland av—we are having a showery afternoon—

Good bye, my darling boy—& I will try to write again soon, (& a more interesting letter)—

Walt.

448.   *To John Burroughs*   6.18. [*1872*]

ADDRESS: John Burroughs, | Roxbury, | Delaware Co. | New York. POSTMARK: New York | Jun | 18 | 9(?).

Brooklyn, | June 18.

John Burroughs, | Dear friend,

I rec'd your letter this forenoon, & went over to New York to see about the trunks—finally found the man in charge of expressage on board the Mary Powell, who said that he took them up to Rondout on the Powell yesterday, & landed them, to be forwarded to you—So I take it that they have all reached you safely before you get this.

I am home here in Brooklyn, having the usual sort of a time—Mother is only middling this summer—My brother George & his wife, at Camden, N. J., are so strenuous for mother to break up housekeeping & go live with them, that I think she will go, next September—

I expect to be on hand at Hanover on Wednesday afternoon 26th—it is middle or latter part of the afternoon I am to be *on exhibition*—shall hope to see you, dear friend, on the great occasion[15]—

Walt Whitman

14.   On June 12 an article in the New York *Times* entitled "The Deserted Capital" noted the absence of the President and congressmen from Washington: "The transition is at once from scenes of busy excitement to dull times and hot weather."

15.   Burroughs was not able to attend the Dartmouth commencement; see Barrus, 73.

16.   The only evidence, which is hardly conclusive, that this note was sent to the Boston *Daily Advertiser* is the accession record in the Houghton Library at Harvard. "As a Strong Bird on Pinions Free" was not reprinted in this newspaper. However, on June 27 a correspondent may have used part of WW's blurb in his lengthy description of WW's appearance before the United Literary Society, where he followed Edward Everett Hale: "He stood up bravely, but did not fill the entire house with his voice. He appeared in his usual eccentric garb, and with a part of his brawny breast bared and his long, white, gray hair and tawny beard, set out by his Byronic collar, made his head and face a study.

"Mr. Whitman calls his poem the 'thread-voice' or 'the spine' of a new series of chants illustrating 'an aggregated, inseparable, unprecedented, vast, composite, electric, democratic nationality,' to be published on some far distant day in a book, and be a following of his 'Leaves of Grass,' which he calls 'the song of a great, complete democratic individual.'

449. *To Peter Doyle*   *6.18.* [*1872*]

Brooklyn | June 18.

Dear Pete,

I am having a better time here than I had my last visit. The weather is very pleasant—pretty hot during the middle of the day, but mornings & nights perfect—No moonlight walks out beyond Uniontown here—but I go on the river, & cross to & fro in the pilot house. Last night was beautiful—Saturday I spent at Coney Island—went in swimming— Mother is only middling—has some pretty bad spells with rheumatism— will break up here, & go with my brother George, to Camden, N. J., in September.

I suppose you got a letter from me last Saturday, as I wrote you the day before. Pete, dear son, if you should want any of your money, send me word. It is either $120 (or $130, I am not sure—but I have a memorandum in my desk at Washington)—I am feeling real well, & hope you are too, my loving boy.

Walt.

450. *To the Editor,* Boston Daily Advertiser (?)[16]

6.25. [*1872*]

New York | June 25.

Private[17] | My dear Sir:

I send herewith a proof of my poem, for convenience for use in your paper, should you think it desirable. As the piece is to be delivered on Wednesday, June 26, you are at liberty to print it, if you wish, in your paper of Thursday, [June][18] 27. Of course not before.

Very respectfully,

Walt Whitman

He seeks to demonstrate that America is to create a new literature, a new poetry, as well as new inventions and power, and to show that the poet of the age must sing vigorously of work, creation and development to be worthy of a hearing in this great epoch. I fear his hearers hardly comprehended his lines, or dreamed at what he was driving, and some in my immediate vicinity were so ungracious as to comment upon it severely, terming it 'words, words, meaningless,' while others characterized it, rather more roughly, 'stuff and nonsense.' But at the close of the reading the compliment of hearty applause was given it. The day must be considered an eventful one in the career of Walt Whitman, for it brought him for the first time within the walls of a college and before a college people." A dispatch to the New York *Times* on June 29 reported that WW "was cordially met by the venerable gentlemen sitting upon the platform. He then took his position at the desk and read, with clearness of enunciation, his poem, written for the occasion, 'As a Strong Bird on Pinions Free.' As Mr. Whitman himself said to the writer, 'There is no one expression that could stand as the subject of the poem.' " For another first-hand report of this recitation, see Perry, 203–205.
    17. Written in blue crayon. The note itself was written in ink.
    18. WW wrote "July."

451. *To Peter Doyle*   6.27. [*1872*]

ADDRESS: Peter Doyle, | conductor | Office | Wash. &
Georgetown City RR. | Washington, | D. C.
POSTMARK: Hanover N. H. | Jun | 27.

Hanover, N. H. | Thursday June 27.

Dear son,

I will write you just a line, to show you I am here away north, &
alive & kicking. I delivered my poem here before the College yesterday.
All went off very well. (It is rather provoking—after feeling unusually
well this whole summer, since Sunday last I have been about half sick &
am so yet, by spells.) I am to go to Vermont, for a couple of days, & then
back to Brooklyn—

Pete, I received your letter, that you had been taken off—write to me
Saturday 30th or Sunday—direct to usual address 107 Portland av.
Brooklyn. I will send you the little book with my poem, (& others) when
I get back to Brooklyn. Pete, did my poem appear in the Washington
papers—I suppose Thurs-day or Friday—*Chronicle* or *Patriot?*[19] If so,
send me one—(or one of each)—

It is a curious scene here, as I write, a beautiful old New England
village, 150 years old, large houses & gardens, great elms, plenty of
hills—every thing comfortable, but very Yankee—*not an African to be
seen all day*—not a grain of dust—not a car to be seen or heard—green
grass every where—no smell of *coal tar*—As I write a party are playing
base ball on a large green in front of the house—the weather suits me
first rate—cloudy but no rain. Your loving

Walt

452. *To Webster Elmes*

[July][20] 9th '72.

Webster Elmes, Chief Clerk. | Dear Sir:

I have been badly pulled by the heat—am sick—(home here with
my mother)—& would respectfully apply for two weeks further leave—
if it can be granted.

If so, I will try to make it up.

Yours, &c.

Walt Whitman
107 north Portland av.
Brooklyn, New York.

19. The poem did not appear in the Washington *Daily Morning Chronicle* or *The
Daily Patriot.* The Washington *Star*, however, printed WW's laudatory version of his
performance; see Holloway, *American Mercury*, XVIII (1929), 485.
20. By mistake WW wrote "June."
21. WW's letter was endorsed by Elmes: "Walt Whitman | Brooklyn | July 9,

I am due at office on the 11th, and would ask *two weeks* extension from that date.[21]

453. *To Peter Doyle*   *7.12.* [*1872*]

ENDORSED: "July 12."
ADDRESS: Peter Doyle, | Conductor, | Office | Wash.
& Georgetown City RR. | Washington, D. C.
POSTMARK: New York | (?).

Brooklyn, | July 12.

Dear son Pete,

I have been sick—but am feeling better now, & soon expect to be all right. Mother too is unwell. I expect to remain here ten or twelve days longer. Pete, I will only write a short letter this time. Love to you, dear son,

Walt.

454. *To Peter Doyle*   *7.19.* [*1872*]

New York, | Friday afternoon—July 19.

Dear boy Pete,

I rec'd your letter yesterday—nothing very new with me—am better than I was when I wrote you before—shall return to Washington next week somewhere about the middle of the week.

Pete, you must try to keep good heart—Perhaps this will find you at work again—if not, you must keep up a cheerful heart, all the same—I have just been spending a couple of hours with Joaquin Miller—I like him real well[22]—

Walt.

$10 enclosed—

455. *To Charles W. Eldridge*   *7.19.* [*1872*]

Broadway, N. Y. | Friday Afternoon—July 19.

Dear friend,

I rec'd your letter yesterday, and was particularly pleased to get it, bringing late intelligence about you all. It was a good letter. What you say about William, fagged with work & I suppose the weather—&

1872 | Applies for extension | of leave of absence | for two weeks | Office Solicitor of the | Treasury | July, 11/72 Extension | granted as requested | by direction of Asst. | Solicitor, & Mr Whitman | advised."
    22. See the following letter.

Nelly, half-sick, & Jeannie about the same (but she will soon spring up)—aroused my sympathies—Mother & I talked about them all—I send love to all. Nelly, I shall return next week, & then I shall surely come to the house, & see you & all.

Charley, I went leisurely up the Connecticut valley, by way of Springfield, through the best part (agriculturally, & other) of Massachusetts, Connecticut & New Hampshire, June 24th & 25th by day light—26th & 27th at Hanover, N. H.—28th & 29th slowly up the White River valley, a captivating wild region, by Vermont Central R. R. & so to Burlington, & about Lake Champlain where I spent a week, filling myself every day, (especially mornings & sunsets) with the grandest ensembles of the Adirondacks always on one side, and the Green Mountains on the other—sailed after that down Champlain by day—stopt at Albany over night, & down the Hudson by boat, 4th of July, through a succession of splendid & magnificent thunderstorms (10 or 12 of them) alternated by spells of clearest sunlight—Then home some five or six days—immediately following I was ill, real ill—I suppose the excessive heat, &c &c—but am now feeling all right.

Upon the whole, I have stood the unprecedented heat pretty well. Mother is not very well—has spells of weakness—has rheumatism—then good days again—will break up from Brooklyn in September, & go with George, at Camden—as they are vehement for it.

My sister Martha at St. Louis is better far than one would expect, after the alarm of two months ago[23]—she has since no trouble with the cancer, (or supposed cancer)—Jeff & the children well—My sister Hannah, (Mrs Heyde,) in Burlington, I found better than I had anticipated—*every thing much better*[24]—

Charley, who do you think I have been spending some three hours with to-day, from 12 to 3—(it is now 4½)—*Joaquin Miller*[25]—He saw me yesterday toward dusk at 5th av. on a stage, & rushed out of the house, & mounting the stage gave me his address, & made an appointment—he lives here 34th st. in furnished rooms—I am much pleased, (upon the whole) with him—*really pleased & satisfied—his presence, conversation, atmosphere*, are infinitely more satisfying than his poetry—he is, however, mopish, ennuyeed, a *California Hamlet*, unhappy every where—but a natural prince, may-be an illiterate one—but tender, sweet,

23. Martha had been East two months earlier for consultations with doctors in New York and Camden; see 423.
24. A veiled reference to the connubial relations of the neurotic Heydes.
25. In the MS "Interviews with Joaquin Miller," WW characterized him as "an ardent, pensive, gentle person—decidedly morbid & sensitive—(made a very favorable impression on me)" (Feinberg). See also 422.

& magnetic—Love to you, dear Charley, & to all—I will soon be with you again—

Walt

456.   *To Louisa Van Velsor Whitman*   *8.22–23.* [*1872*]

Thursday afternoon—Aug 22.

Mother, I suppose you got the letter last Wednesday, I sent—I have written a few words to Han. It continues very hot here, and is now dry again—nothing new with me—I am sitting in the office, writing this, Thursday afternoon—I keep quiet as possible—for if one stirs two steps, the sweat runs off him—It is 3 o'clock—there is a little air stirring to-day, but out doors it is like an oven—John Burroughs[26] has just been in to see me—he comes in most every day—Mother, I hope you will not get affected by the heat—By accounts it must be worse in New York than anywhere else—

Friday noon, Aug. 23.

Mother, I just rec'd your letter—I hope by the time you get this, you will get the things[27]—I want to come—perhaps about the 31st—(but if you all are not to rights I will put it off another week.)

When you write again tell me whether Ed has recovered his spirits—Mother, it is always disagreeable to make a great change, & especially for old folks, but a little time gets things working smoothly, & then one is glad of the change, & better off—

I am feeling quite well to-day—the weather is pleasanter—had a good sleep last night—

I think Grant stock is steadily going up, & Greeley[28] stock down, here & every where—

Love to you, mama dear, & to Lou & all,

Walt.

457.   *To Louisa Van Velsor Whitman*   *8.27.* [*1872*]

Washington | Tuesday afternoon | Aug. 27.

Dearest mother,

There is nothing particular for me to write about. I am well as usual, and getting along all right, except the hot weather. That continues

26. On August 16 Burroughs wrote to Dowden: "Walt Whitman is back again from his brief summer vacation but I am sorry to say is not as well as I should like to see him" (Barrus, 74).
27. Mrs. Whitman and Eddy had moved to Camden to live with George and Louisa.
28. Horace Greeley (1811–1872) ran against Grant for the Presidency in 1872.

here without much let up—Mother, I hope the things have arrived by this time, & that you have got your bed fixed. I have had a visitor to-day & yesterday, a young Hungarian gentleman, quite agreeable, talks English well, quite a traveler—went over to the White House with him yesterday, & went all through—the President & family are away, but Gen. Dent[29] conducted us through, & was very polite. Mrs. O'Connor[30] made me a call Saturday, & John Burroughs to-day—

Mother dear, as soon as I hear from you, I will write more particular about my coming to Camden for a day or two.[31] Mother, I shall probably send the order in my next.

Walt—

457.1 *To Alfred, Lord Tennyson*

Washington, | Sept. 2, 1872.

Dear Mr. Tennyson,

After a long absence in the mountains & lakes of Vermont & northern New York, I am now back again at work, & expect to remain here. Your letter of May 23d, also the one with the picture, safely reached me.[32] The picture is superb, & I consider myself in luck, possessing it. It brings you very near me. I have it now before me.

I send you, by same mail with this, in a little book, my piece lately delivered for Dartmouth College commencement, up north. Did *Democratic Vistas* reach you?[33]

We have had, in this country, a summer more fit for the infernal regions—but now the delicious Virginia September has set in, balmy-cool, & one dilates & feels like work again.

With best respects & love,

Walt Whitman

My address continues the same, *Solicitor's Office Treasury, Washington, D. C.*

---

29. Gen. Frederick T. Dent (1821–1891) was Grant's aide-de-camp during the Civil War and his military secretary during his administration.

30. It is a reasonable conjecture that the fracas between WW and O'Connor occurred about this time; see Introduction, Traubel, III, 75–78, and Barrus, 96–99.

31. WW visited Camden early in September; see 459.

32. Neither of these letters is known.

33. "As a Strong Bird on Pinions Free" ("Thou Mother with Thy Equal Brood") was printed as a pamphlet in 1872. WW had sent *Democratic Vistas* on April 27; see 443.

I am able to print this previously unknown letter through the courtesy of Lord Tennyson and Sir Charles Tennyson. Dr. Edgar F. Shannon, Jr., president of the University of Virginia, who is preparing an edition of Tennyson's letters, has graciously consented to

458. *To Thomas Carlyle*

ENDORSED: "To Carlyle | with Dem Vistas | & Am
Inst. poem." DRAFT LETTER.

Sept 3 '72.

Dear Sir:[34]

Following an impulse of the moment, I have just mailed to you
two little books of mine—writing this note to introduce them—and taking
permission to personally offer, as it were, from America true respects &
love.

459. *To Rudolf Schmidt*

Washington, | U. S. America. | September 15, 1872.
My dear Rudolf Schmidt,

Your letter of 17th August[35] has just reached me—also the *Dag-
bladet*, (four no's.) The feuilleton about me I have just had read in English by a Dane, Mr. Bendz.[36] I am deeply touched at being more and more
brought right among warm human hearts in Denmark, Norway, &c—&
so friendly entertained there. It comforts & nourishes me more than you
know. The former letters, & the papers you have sent, have all come
safely to hand—& I thank you.

I have just returned from a visit of some days to Philadelphia. It
is a great *materialistic city* full of the *middling classes*, (mechanics,
laborers, operatives in factories (both sexes), traders, &c)—in *extraordinary physical comfort*—700,000 people, & five-sixths of them well-off,
in plenty of the best food & clothing, & ample & respectable houses—
there are almost *no* very miserable & vagabond classes or quarters in the
city, vast & teeming as it is.

I am now back here at work for the fall & winter—My address is
permanently here—I get all your letters & papers safely. Clausen[37] has

my publication of the correspondence between the two poets. I wish also to thank the City
of Lincoln (England) Public Libraries, Museum, and Art Gallery for the photostat of
this letter.

34. Perhaps WW sent the poems to Carlyle, who was not one of his admirers, because of Burroughs' letter from London on October 30, 1871, written after his recent
visit to Carlyle: "I am sure you would like him & that he would like you" (Syracuse).

35. Since Schmidt's letter is not extant, it is not possible to clarify the next few lines.
The editor of the article in *Orbis Litterarum* did not find a reference to WW in the *Dag-
bladet*.

36. Waldemar E. Bendz was listed as a clerk.

37. Clausen had gone to Denmark in June; see 446.

not yet arrived. I have lately rec'd a paper from Pesth, Hungary, with a feuilleton about my poems.

Farewell, for this time.

Walt Whitman

460. *To William J. Linton*

October 4, 1872.

My dear Linton:[38]

How do you get on with the picture?

The time is approaching when I shall want to use it.

I am back here at work at my desk, for the fall & coming winter.

I have not heard from you for some months.

Yours as always,

Walt Whitman
Solicitor's Office Treasury
Washington, D. C.

461. *To Louisa Van Velsor Whitman*   *10.15.* [1872]

Washington | Tuesday afternoon | Oct. 15.[39]

Dearest mother,

There is nothing new with me—I am well—Mother, I feel as if I wanted to come on there & pay you a little visit—and as I can probably get off for a few days, I shouldn't wonder if I come soon. I think as I am likely to come quite a good deal, I would like in future to pay Sister Lou $1 a day for what time I stop there—I should feel better satisfied & come oftener.

It is quite cold here. I am wearing my overcoat—You see, mother, I am likely to prove a true prophet about Greeley—He is *not* expected here at the White House next March.

Mother dear, I hope this will find you feeling comfortable—I will send you a line before I come—which will probably be within a week—

Love to you, dearest mother, & to George and Lou—

Walt.

38. See 438.

39. The executors altered the date to August 13, 1872, because of the reference in 456 to a letter (now lost) sent on August 13. However, it is clear from WW's remarks in this letter and the following one that he was planning a second visit to Camden. He had gone to Camden early in September; see 459.

40. In this will, dated October 23, WW bequeathed to his mother, or in the event of her death, to George, as trustee for his brother Edward, all his personal property (over $1,000 in a Brooklyn bank), the amounts due from the sale of his books by Redfield, and the stereotype plates of his books in the possession of S. W. Green. Bucke's copy of this will is in the Trent Collection. A second will was drawn on May 16, 1873; see Barrus, 82.

462.   *To George Washington and Louisa Van Velsor Whitman*
10.23. [1872]

Washington | Oct. 23.

Dear brother George,

Dont be alarmed—& don't laugh either—at seeing the enclosed "will."[40] I wish you to put it away with your papers, where it will be kept safe—I just took a notion to-day that I would like to fix it so—

Dearest Mother,

I shan't come on till Monday next, 28th—but shall be with [you] then —think of coming in the 1 o'clock train from here—shall get to Camden by or before 8—I am well as usual—nothing new—

I have sent George my *will* to take charge of—I am writing this in the office, afternoon—we are having a dark rainy day here.

Love to you, dearest mother, & to Lou & all—

Walt.

463.   *To Louisa Van Velsor Whitman*   *11.14. [1872]*

Washington | Thursday afternoon Nov. 14.

Dearest mother,

I send you Jeff's letter[41] to me, just received.

Mat is better, it seems, & has put off journeying to Camden.

Jeff says it is doubtful whether she will come at all, unless she can have you go home with her to St. Louis.

Mother, just let the thing take its course, & not disturb your mind on the question of going or not going—It will be time enough to decide, when it comes to the point—

Mammy dear, I got your letter this morning—glad to hear you are as well as you are, & hope this will find you comfortable—All goes well as usual with me—Love to you, dear mother—& to all[42]—

Walt.

41. In his letter of November 10 Jeff suggested that Martha go to Camden and accompany Mrs. Whitman to St. Louis. Of Martha Jeff wrote: "Her chest and lungs both seem better now and if by [care?] I can get her in the way of taking some little food I have hopes she will get along yet" (Feinberg).

42. Mrs. Whitman was not entirely happy in Camden, for about December 3 she complained to WW: "lou and george are very clever but i think they are a very saving couple. what they want to save so much for i cant see as they have no young ones but maybe its all right. george is so changed in regard to being saving but i cant get used to being so ecomical" (LC). This from Mrs. Whitman, who was the very model of thriftiness!

Mother, just as I was closing this letter, who should come in to see me but Margaret Avery[43]—she has been down to Virginia, and is going through Baltimore & Philadelphia—When in Philadelphia, she will come over to Camden & make you a call—probably within a day or two—

464. *To James M. Edmunds*   *11.17.* [*1872?*]

DRAFT LETTER.

Nov. 17

J M Edmunds, P. M.[44] | Dear Sir:

Your letter, referring me the ruling of the P. O. Dept. [as] to what the term *"book manuscripts"* as used in Sec. 244. Postal Laws and Reg. includes, and what it excludes, makes me then respectfully request that, if convenient, that ruling shall be brought up before the proper officers of the Dept, to be reconsidered and reversed for the following briefly stated reasons:

1st the word "Book" as used in the statute is unquestionably the generic term "Book," comprehensive of all printed literary matter, (see Webster's Unabridged Dict. last ed. p. 151.) A pamphlet, monthly or weekly magazine, the "Living Age," the "Galaxy," or any literary composition, or printed issue, or any collection of sheets of paper, of literary character, or only two sheets, or one sheet—must, all & several, be included in the term.

2d. The intention of Congress [&] of its post office, & other legislation[45] to foster literature, education, authorship, general reading, publication, &c. & be liberal to the press: is well known to the Dept. I might claim therefore that the section must be construed generously. But I merely claim that it be construed according to the exact meaning & definition of its own terminology—See the Dictionaries[46]—Webster—Book—a general name of every printed literary composition—The quest. a generic term—The question also is, Is a magazine—(i.e. a pamphlet) —a book—See dictionary—*pamphlet* .... a small book—Worcester—*pamphlet*—a book consisting of only one or a few sheets stitched together, & not bound—

43. Margaret and William Avery, who lived in Brooklyn, were evidently cousins of Mrs. Whitman; see LC #108. They visited WW in Camden on October 19, 1876; see the *Commonplace Book* (Feinberg).

44. (1810–1879), postmaster in Washington, D. C., from 1869 to 1879.

45. The phraseology here is uncertain because of the interlineations.

46. The material from here to the end of the paragraph is actually a series of jottings which WW intended to clarify, and many of which he no doubt eliminated in the

I would respectfully apply a second time for a reconsideration & reversal of the ruling of the construction in your Dept. of that proviso of Sec. 244 of Postal Laws, which fixes the postage on "book Manuscripts and corrected proofs passing between authors & publishers," at the rate of ordinary printed matter, which ruling, as furnished me, is that MSS. and corrected proofs from or to *Magazines, pamphlets,* literary *periodicals,* &c. are *not* included in this proviso, but shall pay letter postage.

Against this I again offer as follows: The main question is, What is a book in fact, and in the meaning of the law?—I say, in both, it is[47]

In the ruling furnished me by the Department, stress is laid on the *distinction* Congress makes (in the postage rate) between *Books* and other printed matter, as pamphlets, magazines, & newspapers. So they do make such distinction, *invariably in order to decrease the rate of postage of the latter.*

The inference is a fair one then that if book MSS go for printed matter postage, the pamphlet and Magazine MSS should at least do so. The distinction is made for the purpose of *favoring* the periodical press. But it does not warrant any such inference as in the ruling furnished.

All *literary MSS.* are "book manuscripts," and when printed, they become "Books"—and the law covers *all* (literary matter)—To contend otherwise would be same as to confine the meaning of the word *man* as used by metaphysicians and statesmen (by Jefferson in the Declaration of Independence for instance,) to mean a full grown *male person only*—while, of course, it is an ensemble and generic term, for both sexes, and all ages.

465. *To I. N.(?) Burritt*   12.6. [*1872*]

TRANSCRIPT.

December 6.

My dear Burritt:[48]

This article *"Walt Whitman in Europe"* set close, would make *about two-thirds of a column*—it is *fresh,* speaks of me as here in Washington—& I think would be generally readable here. . . . [WW will call for the proofs on the following day.]

Walt Whitman

letter.
   47. WW left space for the insertion of the definition.
   48. Probably I. N. Burritt, assistant manager of the Evening Press Association in Washington. The Washington Directory listed him as a reporter for the New York *Tribune* in 1871, and as the editor and proprietor of the *Sunday Herald* in 1872. The article appeared in the latter on December 8; it was written by Hinton (see 289 and 424).

465.1 *To Albert B. Otis*

Dec. 16, '72.

My dear Mr. Otis,[49]

I mail you, same mail with this, two copies of the little Volume, *"As a Strong Bird"* &c.—the only form in which I have the Dartmouth College poem.

The price of the two is $1.50 cts.

"Democratic Vistas" is printed in a little book by itself, price 75 cts.

There is not (& probably will not be) any later or different edition of *"Leaves of Grass"* than the one I forwarded you last spring.

Walt Whitman
Solicitors Office Treasury
Washington | D. C.

---

49. On April 20, 1878, G. P. Lathrop wrote to WW: "I think you have corresponded with Albert Otis, a lawyer of Boston, whom I know" (Feinberg; Traubel, II, 316). Otis was also one of the subscribers to the 1887 fund; see Traubel, II, 299.

1873

466. *To Louisa Van Velsor Whitman* 1.17. [1873]¹

Friday noon, Jan 17.

Dearest mother,

Nothing new or particular²—I send you an "Appleton's Journal," with some good reading in it³—Well, mother, how are you all? Last night was a heavy rain here—I thought of your roof—the snow has all disappeared here—very pleasant yesterday indeed here—to-day the whole city looks all washed clean—

I went to a concert Tuesday night—very good—I heard a singer, Mario, I heard 30 years ago—an old man, now—yet he sings first-rate yet—then Patti, a lady—& others. It was in quite a fine hall here called Lincoln Hall⁴ —I go there once in a while—(an editor of a newspaper here sends me spare tickets some times—that's how I go, most of the time.)

I have got a letter from John Burroughs⁵—he is at Middletown, N. Y.—don't expect to return here permanently to live any more—but will return to pack up & move—his wife is still here—I was up there a couple of evenings since—Mrs. B. is alone—has lately been vaccinated, & is not very well—there has been a good deal of small pox here—all the clerks in the office have been vaccinated—Well, mamma dear, I believe I have scribbled down all the *small talk* I can think of to amuse you for this time—Love to you, mother dear,

Walt.

1873
    1. The executors dated this letter 1868. That this dating is erroneous is demonstrated in the notes.
    2. WW had made a New Year's visit to Camden, according to Hannah Heyde's letter to her mother on January 7–10 (LC); see also Mrs. Whitman's letter to Helen Price on January 6(?) (Morgan).
    3. The issue of January 18 (IX [1873], 106–108) contained Burroughs' "A Glimpse of France."
    4. A farewell concert for Giuseppe Mario (1810–1883), "The World-renowned Tenor," and Carlotta Patti (1835?–1889), "The Queen of the Concert Room," was presented at Lincoln Hall on January 14. The review in the *Daily Morning Chronicle* the next day gave greater praise to a young contralto, Annie Louise Cary, than to Patti or Mario, the latter of whom sang with "great effort." WW referred to Mario frequently in his prose writings (CW, IV, 26; VI, 186; VII, 56).
    5. On January 12 Burroughs wrote: "It cost me a pang to leave W[ashington]. I was so warm & snug & my nest was so well feathered; but I have really cut loose & do not expect to return again except briefly. I can make more money here, be much freer, be nearer home & have a new field of duties" (Feinberg; Traubel, III, 281). Burroughs became a bank inspector in New York State.

467. *To Louisa Van Velsor Whitman* [*1.26. 1873*]

Sunday afternoon

Dearest mother,

I have been not well for two or three days, but am better to-day. I have had a slight stroke of paralysis, on my left side, and especially the leg—occurred Thursday night last, & I have been laid up since—I am writing this in my room 535 15th st, as I am not able to get out at present—but the doctor gives me good hopes of being out and at my work in a few days—He says it is nothing but what I shall recover from in a few days—Mother, you must not feel uneasy—though I know you will—but I thought I would write & tell you the *exact truth—neither better nor worse—*

I have a first rate physician, Dr. Drinkard—I have some very attentive friends, (& if I have occasion can & will telegraph to you or George—but do not expect to have any need)—

I have had no word from St Louis or any where by letter for some days—The weather here is mostly stormy & cold the last week—I rec'd your last letter with Jeff's[6]—it is ½ past one—Lizzie the servant girl has just brought me up some dinner, oyster stew, toast, tea, &c, very good—I have eaten little for two days, but am to-day eating better—I wrote to Mat early last week—

Later—I have been sitting up eating my dinner—

Love to you, dearest mother, & to George & Lou—

Walt

I will write again middle of the week—

468. *To Louisa Van Velsor Whitman* [*1.27. 1873*]

Monday afternoon | ½ past 3

Dearest Mother,

Fearing you might worry about me I write to say I am doing very well indeed—(I understand the papers are making me out very sick in-

6. Jeff's letter of January 14 to his mother described Martha's illness: "her great trouble is her lungs—and I fear she is failing not fast but surely in this lately" (Feinberg).

7. See 391.

8. Despite the gravity of WW's condition, William O'Connor did not visit him: the breach between the two men was deep.

9. Mary Cole was listed in the Directories as a clerk in the Internal Revenue Department. Perhaps she was the sister of George D. Cole, a former conductor and a friend

deed—It is not so.) I wrote you Sunday which I suppose you rec'd—I may not write again for two or three days—

Walt

The doctor has just been here—says I am getting along first rate—will probably be out, and about as well as usual in a week—

It is a heavy snow storm here to-day—I have many callers, but they are not admitted—as I don't care to see them—I write this sitting on the side of the bed, after 4—Don't be frightened should you may-be see or hear of any thing in the papers—you know they killed me off once *before*[7]—it is just sunset—the sun is shining out bright at last—

469. *To Louisa Van Velsor Whitman*   *1.29.* [*1873*]

Wednesday afternoon | Jan 29

Dearest mother,

I am writing this lying in bed—the doctor wishes me to keep as much in bed as possible—but I *have* to keep in, as I cannot move yet without great difficulty, & I am liable to dizziness & nausea, at times, on trying to move, or even sitting up—But I am certainly over the worst of it, & *really*—though slowly—*improving*. The doctor says there is no doubt of it—

Yesterday afternoon I eat something like a meal for the first time—boiled chicken, & some soup with bread broken up in it—relished it well —I still have many callers—only a few particular ones are admitted to see me—Mrs. O'Connor[8] comes & a young woman named Mary Cole[9]—Mrs. Ashton has sent for me to be brought to her house, to be taken care of—of course I do not accept her offer—they live in grand style & I should be more bothered than benefitted by their refinements & luxuries, servants, &c[10]—

Mother, I want you to know truly, that I do not want for any thing—as to all the *little extra fixings* & superfluities, I never did care for them in health, & they only annoy me in sickness—I have a good bed—a fire—as much grub as I wish & whatever I wish—& two or three good friends here—So I want you to not feel at all uneasy—as I write, Peter Doyle[11]

of Doyle, who wrote to WW, probably in the early 1870's, after he had become a sailor (Yale). Barrus (72) mentions May Cole, a friend of Mrs. O'Connor, who later married Dr. Frank Baker of the Smithsonian Institute.

10. In June, however, WW consented to stay with the Ashtons for about ten days; see 510.

11. On January 30 Mrs. Whitman wrote: "i thought of peter. i knew if it was in his power to be with you he would and cherefully doo everything that he could for you" (Trent).

is sitting by the window reading—he & Charles Eldridge regularly come in & do whatever I want, & are both *very helpful* to me—one comes day time, & one evening—I had a good night's sleep last night—My mind is just as clear as ever—& has been all the time—(I have not been at all down hearted either)—(My January pay is due me, & as soon as I get up, I shall forward you your $20.)[12]

Dear sister Lou,[13]

Your letter came this morning & was very pleasant to get it—I shall be getting well soon—am on a fair way to it now—

latest ½ past 4

I have just set up & had my bed made by Pete—I am already beginning to feel something like myself—will write in 2 days—

470. *To Louisa Van Velsor Whitman*   1.31. *[1873]*

Friday—Jan 31 | noon

Dearest mother,

I write this lying in bed yet—but I sit up several times during the day now, for a few minutes at a time—am gradually gaining the use of my left arm & leg—(the right side has not been affected at all)—think I shall be able to move round a little by Sunday—The Doctor has just been—he says I am doing very well—

John Burroughs[14] is here temporarily—he comes in often—Eldridge and Peter Doyle are regular still, helping & lifting & nursing me—but I feel now that I shall soon be able to help myself—

I slept quite well last night—It has been very cold indeed here, they say—but I have not felt it—as I write, it looks pleasant & bright, the sun shining in real cheerful—I see by Sister Lou's letter that you had no news from St. Louis—poor, poor Mat, I think about her often, as I am lying here—I have not written to Han since I had the paralysis—Mother, you might send one of my letters to her, Han, when you next write—(this one, or any)—Say I sent my love, & will be up before long—

Well, mother dear, & Sister Lou & Brother George, I will close for the present, for this week—Will write Sunday—but I understand the mails are a little irregular this weather—

Walt.

12. WW paid for Ed's board, $15 a month, and sent additional money to his mother.
13. George's wife.

471. *To Louisa Van Velsor Whitman*   [2.2. 1873]

Sunday afternoon | ½ past 3

Dearest mother,

I am sitting up on the side of the bed writing this. Every thing is going on as well with me as I could expect. I rec'd your letter, dear mother—you may rest assured that I write the *exact facts* about my sickness—I am not gaining very fast, but it is *sure*—I am on the gain every day a little—I still have a good deal of distress in the head—the quieter I am left by general visitors the more comfortable I am—I slept fairly last night—& eat quite a nice breakfast this morning—(dinner I left mostly untasted)—I have all the attention I need, & food &c.

I will write toward the middle of the week—Write whether this & the money come safe.

Love to you, dear Mother, & George & Lou—& don't be uneasy about me. I have been up by the window looking out on the river & scenery—it is beautiful weather now—they have sent over & paid me my January pay— all are very kind—

Walt

472. *To Louisa Van Velsor Whitman*   [2.4. 1873]

Tuesday afternoon | 3 o'clock.

Dearest mother,

I wrote you Sunday enclosing the $20, which I suppose you rec'd all safe.

I am still anchored here in my bed—I am sitting up now on the side —Mrs. O'Connor has just been to see me—I was glad to see her—I am still improving, but slowly—the doctor did not come yesterday, which I suppose is a good sign—I expect him this afternoon or evening—he evidently thinks I am on the gain—Pete has just come in, & will take this to the p. o. for me—Love to you, dear mother, & to all—

Walt.

473. *To Louisa Van Velsor Whitman*   2.7. [1873]

Friday afternoon—Feb. 7 | ½ past 2

Dearest mother,

I am still anchored here—sit up some, but only for a short spell at a time—am feeble, and have distress in the head—these are the worst

14. Burroughs had returned to Washington to arrange for the sale of his house.

features—but am gradually regaining the use of my left limbs—very, very slowly, but *certainly gaining*—Doctor only comes now every other day—

As I write Mrs. O'Connor is sitting here in the room, mending some stockings &c for me—she has brought me some nice roast apple in a tumbler—It is a dark wet day to-day—not very favorable—

Mother dear, I rec'd your letter, acknowledging the money—I have written a short letter to Hannah, & also one to Jeff—which they must have rec'd by this time—

I keep up my spirits very well—do not need for any thing—Love to you, & all, dearest mother,

Walt.

I have tacked your picture up on the wall at the foot of the bed—the one I like—it looks as natural as can be—& is quite company for me—as I am alone a good deal, (& prefer to be)—

474. *To Thomas Jefferson Whitman*   2.8. [*1873*]

Washington | Feb. 8,—noon—
(sitting up on the side of my bed.)

Dear brother,

I have just rec'd your note of 5th.[15]

Dear, dear, dear sister Matty—O how I have been thinking of you, & shall all day—I have not now the use of my limbs to move from one room to the other—or else I should come on immediately to St. Louis—I can but send you my love, dear, dear sister—Your unhappy, sorrowful, loving brother—

Walt

475. *To Louisa Van Velsor Whitman*   2.9. [*1873*]

Sunday afternoon | Feb. 9.　4 o'clock

Dearest mother,

I suppose you have rec'd word from Jeff that poor Mat was sinking, & you might expect to hear of her death at any moment—that she was a very great sufferer when he wrote. I got his letter dated Feb. 5th yesterday—he said he was writing to you same time—He wrote very serious

15. Jeff's letter to WW is not extant, but in a letter written on the same day to Mrs. Whitman, Jeff expressed fears for Martha's recovery, and urged that WW come to St. Louis (Feinberg). When he wrote, Jeff was unaware of the seriousness of his brother's paralysis.

16. Jeff sent letters on February 7 to Mrs. Whitman and WW: there was no change in Martha's condition (Feinberg). Jeff informed his brother that he had learned about his

but calm—Mother, I will not write much to-day—I feel so bad about Mat
—I am still improving—but slowly though I realize some improvement
every day—my head is easier to-day—

Walt—

476. *To Louisa Van Velsor Whitman*   *2.10.* [*1873*]

Monday afternoon | Feb 10—3 o'clock

Dearest mother,

I send you Jeff's letter,[16] rec'd this morning, as it may possibly be
later than any you have—I had a very good day yesterday, & the best
night last night I have had for a week—Doctor Drinkard has just been
in—he says I am progressing the very best—In a day or two more I
think I shall get out—or to the front door, at any rate—

Dear sister Lou,

I rec'd your letter this morning—I will see how I feel, when I get
better—about coming on—Don't think of such a thing as George's coming
on here for me—You may be sure I shall be with you all, in as good health
as ever, yet—& before very long—to-day I have been sadly pestered with
visitors—every thing goes well with me, except the *slowness* of my improvement—

Walt

477. *To Louisa Van Velsor Whitman*
[*2.13*]–*14.* [*1873*]

Thursday night | 8 o'clock

Dearest mother,

It is a dismal winter snow storm outside, and as I write I am
sitting here by a good wood fire in the stove—have been alone all the
evening—I sit up as much as I can, especially evenings—as I sleep better
afterwards—I rec'd a letter from Jeff to-day,[17] Matty was as well as at
last accounts—about the same—no worse—I also rec'd a letter from
Heyde[18]—he said Han was well as usual—

I have been sitting up nearly all day—& have less distress in the head
than I have had—which is a great gain—I had a letter from Mrs. Price

illness in a newspaper.

17. Jeff wrote on February 11 both to WW and to his mother (Feinberg). Jeff still
hoped, since he did not appreciate the gravity of WW's illness, that his brother would be
able to visit Martha.

18. Heyde's letter to WW is not extant, but on February 6 he wrote to Mrs. Whitman most solicitously about WW's illness (Trent).

to-day—she invites me to come & stop awhile there, as soon as I can journey—

Mother, it is kind of *company* to write to you—it is very lonesome to sit here all the evening in my room—about 9 Charles Eldridge comes in & assists me to soak my feet in hot water, & then I turn in—(I have my trowsers on this evening, first time in 3 weeks)—

Friday noon | Feb. 14

Mother, I am sitting up again to-day—passed a comfortable night, & as soon as it is favorable weather I shall try to get *started* for outside— first, to get down stairs—& then perhaps across the street—

3 o'clock

I have just got a letter from Jeff, which I enclose as it is the latest— Mrs. O'Connor has just been to see me—brought a basket of nice things—

Mother dear, I hope you will have a pleasant Sunday—I send you Harper's & Frank Leslie's—I am having a very fair day to-day—it is moderate & pleasant here, but mostly cloudy—I have been quite occupied writing several letters about business[19]—have set up all day, with the exception of an hour—Love to you, dear mother,

Walt

478. *To Louisa Van Velsor Whitman*   2.17. [1873]

Monday afternoon—Feb. 17 | ½ past 3

Dearest mother,

I have been down stairs, & out on the street this afternoon—it is such fine weather, (after the bad storm of yesterday)—I got along very slowly, & didn't go far—but it was a great thing after being kept in for over three weeks—

I rec'd a short letter from Jeff again to-day, dated 13th[20]—nothing different with Mat—I rec'd your letter Saturday—I hope now to improve

19. These letters are not known; probably WW wrote to some of the dealers who handled his books.

20. Jeff's letter to WW is not extant, but on the same day he wrote to Mrs. Whitman: Martha "is cheerful and brave—nothing can make her despondent in the shape of personal suffering—and I do not allow her to suffer from any feeling that we feel mournful or despondent" (Feinberg).

21. Jeff's letter to WW is not known. Writing to his mother on February 15 and 16, he begged her to travel to St. Louis: "It seems to be the one desire of [Martha's] life to have you come and see her" (Feinberg).

22. On February 23 Jeff's daughter Mannahatta, almost thirteen years old, wrote to her grandmother about her mother's death: "when I got home from school the buggy was out side of the door and papa said he would take Mama out riding as it was such a pleasant day and Mama wanted to go so much. so papa lifted her out and put her in the buggy and then went to take the reins and while he [was] taking them Mama fell over in the buggy and when papa turned around he did not know what had happened so he lifted her

in walking—& then I shall begin to feel all right—(but am still very feeble & slow)—Peter Doyle & another friend accompanied me out—

Dear Mother, I hope this will find you feeling well—Love to all—

Walt.

479. *To Louisa Van Velsor Whitman*   [*2.19. 1873*]

535 Fifteenth st. | Wednesday afternoon | 3 o'clock.

Mother dear, I suppose you got a letter from me telling you that I had been down stairs & out on Monday—it was more exertion than I could bear, and I have not been so well since. I got two letters from Jeff to-day, the last one dated the 16th[21]—Matt had rested well the night before—poor, poor Mat, I am ready to hear of her departure any day—it seems terrible—

Things are going on as well as could be expected with me, but slowly —I overdid the matter day before yesterday, and am now waiting—I am sitting up by the stove alone writing this. Love [to] you, dearest Mother, and to all—

Walt.

480. *To Louisa Van Velsor Whitman*   *2.20.* [*1873*]

Thursday afternoon | Feb. 20.

Well, mother, it's over at last with dear Matty—I got a dispatch of her death on the evening of the 19th—I suppose you have too, of course —It must have been a relief from very great suffering, as Jeff's letters of late described it—poor dear sister, she has many *real mourners*—I have just written to Han about it—I am about the same—rather better[22]—

Walt.

in the house and just then I came home from school and found that Mama was dying but she seemed to know me though she could not speak. I felt so bad that I did not know what to do" (LC).

Jeff on the following day wrote of Martha's death to his mother: "The circumstances attending her death are quite impressive. Over two weeks before it the Dr told me that I might expect her death at any moment—that her lungs were in immediate liability to rupture and that each breath she drew was a risk, that I must not leave her alone a moment. On Tuesday she seemed to feel a little more like her old self—though suffering much pain from the fact that the right lung had been pierced by the gathering and the air in breathing would gather between the ports and remain—her right side and breast were very much enlarged from this cause—the pain was intense from the cancer and a few days before her death the old spinal trouble came back to her—yet with all this, dear Mother, did she keep up to the last—not a murmur escaped her—she was cheerful to a degree and at noon of the day she died sat up in her chair and directed how my lunch should be prepared" (Feinberg).

481. *To Louisa Van Velsor Whitman*   2.21. [1873]

Friday afternoon | Feb. 21.

Dearest mother,

I am about the same to-day, rather on the improve—have not tried to get out any more—feel pretty much depressed about Mat's death, (but it has been to her no doubt a relief from great pain)—Have just written a few lines to Jeff[23]—Wrote yesterday to Han—Mother, you must not get gloomy. Feel better as I write—I am sitting up by the stove.

Walt

482. *To Abby H. Price*   2.21. [1873]

ADDRESS: Abby H. Price | 331 East 55th street | New York City. POSTMARK: Washington | Feb | 21 | D. C.

Friday evening | Feb. 21.

Dear Friend Abby, | and all my friends, Helen & Emmy & Mr. Arnold,

I will write a line only—My paralysis still leaves me extremely feeble—& with great distress in the head—*but I shall certainly recover* —mind just as clear as ever. I have lost my dear, dear sister Martha, in St. Louis—I appreciate your kind letter, Abby dear, and it is possible when I get better it may be just the thing for me to come on a few days —but at present I can hardly move ten steps without feeling sick—I am sitting here now in the rocking chair in my room writing this—most of the time alone which suits me best—it is paralysis of left side—Love to all—

Walt

(My address is Solicitors Office Treasury)

483. *To Louisa Van Velsor Whitman*   [2.23. 1873]

Sunday afternoon | ½ past 2

Well, mother dear, here I sit again in the rocking chair by the stove—I have just eat some dinner, a little piece of fowl & some toast &

23. The letter is apparently lost.
24. Sixteen years later WW still considered Drinkard "the best Doctor that ever was": he "seemed to understand me well: he charged it to the emotional disturbances to which I was subjected at that time" (Traubel, IV, 472). Also note Dr. Grier's opinion in 531.
25. Around this remark Mrs. Whitman was to construct a dream-house: annoyed by George's economizing and, more important, loath to accept a (rightful) secondary position in her daughter-in-law's household, WW's mother despite her years hoped for a home of

tea—my appetite is good enough—& I have plenty brought to me—I have been sitting up all day—have some bad spells, but am decidedly gaining upon the whole—think I have fully recovered where I was a week ago, and even a little better—went down stairs yesterday and out for five minutes into the street—& shall do so again this afternoon—as I think it did me good yesterday—though I was very tired, on returning—as I have to go down & up 4 flights of stairs—The doctor comes every day—(I must tell you again I have a first-rate doctor—I think he understands my case exactly—I consider myself very lucky in having him)[24]—

Mother, yesterday was a very serious day with me here—I was not so very sick, but I kept thinking all the time it was the day of Matty's funeral —Every few minutes all day it would come up in my mind—I suppose it was the same with you—Mother, your letter came Friday afternoon—it was a very good letter, & after reading it twice, I enclosed it in one to Han—she must have got it Saturday night—

There are great preparations here for 4th of March—inauguration—if you & I had a house here,[25] we would have George & Lou come on & see the show, for I have no doubt it will be the finest ever seen here—(but I am in hopes to be able to get away for all that)—

½ past 4.

Mother, I have just been down & out doors—walked half a block—& have come back—*went all alone*—(got a little assistance at the steps)—this is the most successful raid yet—& I really begin to feel something like myself—

Hope this will find you all right, dearest Mother—

Walt.

484. *To Louisa Van Velsor Whitman*   2.26. [*1873*]

Wednesday noon | Feb. 26.

Dearest mother,

I am getting along real well, upon the whole—I went out and over to the office yesterday—went in & sat down at my desk a few minutes—It

her own. As early as October 9, 1872, hardly six weeks after she had moved to Camden, Mrs. Whitman complained to Helen Price: "i would rather have my own shanty and my good friends come to see me" (Morgan). Even more significant, she wrote to the same friend on April 18(?), 1873: "i wouldent mind living here if i had a place of my own but this living with and not being boss of your own shanty aint the cheese" (Morgan). WW himself referred to the possibility of purchasing a house in Washington; see 485, 491, and 494.

was my greatest effort yet, and I was afraid I had overshot the mark again, as I felt dizzy & tired last night—But to-day I feel getting along all right —I am going out a little to-day, but not much—I feel now over the worst of my bit of sickness, & comparatively comfortable—

Poor Martha—the thoughts of her still come up in my mind, as I sit here a great deal of the time alone—Poor Jeff, & poor children too—

I have received a letter from Lillie Townsend[26]—Aunt Sally[27] is still living and well as usual, & nothing very new—I have just got a second note from Mrs. Price[28]—

Mother, I shall try to get out, & get my Feb. pay, I have to get it from the old office, & then I will send you your $20. (I hope within a couple of days, or three at most)—

I expect Mrs. Burroughs[29] here probably to-day with a carriage to take me out riding—so you see I am beginning to sport around—

Every thing here now is *inauguration*—& will be till the 4th of March is over—for my part I want to get out of the way of it all—

Love to you, mammy dear, & to Georgey & Lou & all—

Walt.

485. *To Mannahatta Whitman*

Washington | Saturday afternoon | March 1, '73

Dear Hattie,

I have received your letter, & read it over & over again[30]—it is very, very good—so much about your dear mother, it brought the tears to my eyes, & I had to stop many times—my dear, dear Sister Martha, she must have suffered so much, & to keep up such fortitude & patience & even cheerfulness, while life lasted—

Hattie, I have just got a letter from your grandmother written Thursday afternoon, Feb. 27,[31] & she had not got your letter then—did you send her one a week ago, as you spoke of having written to her? She was very uneasy at not hearing from Jeff or any of you, since your mother's death. I wish you to write *immediately* to your grandmother, direct to her

26. Lillie Townsend was, like Priscilla Townsend (see 500), presumably a cousin of Mrs. Whitman.

27. Mrs. Whitman's aunt, Sally Mead (see 493).

28. See 477.

29. On March 2 Mrs. Burroughs reported to her husband how much WW had enjoyed the ride (Barrus, 81).

30. Mannahatta informed her grandmother on February 27 that she had written seven pages to WW—"the longest letter I have ever written" (LC). WW, obviously

                        care of Geo. W. Whitman
                        at Starr's foundry
                        Camden, N. Jersey

I have got just well enough to go out, in a carriage, but, dear Hattie, I am in a miserable condition, as to my power of moving—The doctor says I shall get well, but it is very, very slow and irksome—my mind is clear, but I have to sit in my room alone, by the fire, most of the time—visitors generally have been prohibited—but only a few come in—but now I have ventured out for a few minutes every fair day—It is now afternoon, very pleasant, & I shall just get out on the sidewalk & then back—

O how often I have thought of my dear sister Martha, as I have been alone here, both night & day—I think of your father too, & of you & California[32]—but here I am, unable to move—I hope Jeff will feel like writing to mother, & she will send it to me—As soon as I can travel I think of going on to Camden—

Dearest Hattie, if we had a house to invite you and California to, how much comfort it would be to your grandmother & me—But I have great thoughts—at any rate a great desire—to get one, here, when I get well, & have grandmother & Eddy here—& then you & California shall surely come—

        Love to you, dearest Hattie—& love to your dear father, & to California—If you can, dear niece, write me again, & dont wait very long, dear Hattie—Hattie dear, you must mind the address—(My letters from St. Louis are addressed wrong)—My right address is
                        Walt Whitman
                        Solicitor's office Treasury,
                        Washington, D. C.

486. *To Louisa Van Velsor Whitman*   [3].7. [1873]

            Friday afternoon [March][33] 7 | 2 o'clock.

Dear mother,

        I got your letter yesterday[34]—I was glad to hear all the things you wrote—every thing, however little, is interesting, when you are kept

pleased with the letter, sent it to Hannah, who on March 5 (LC) forwarded it to her mother.
   31. On February 27 Mrs. Whitman wrote about her uneasiness both to WW (Trent) and to Jeff (Northwestern University).
   32. Mannahatta's sister, Jessie Louisa.
   33. Mrs. Whitman struck out "Feb." and inserted "march."
   34. Mrs. Whitman's letter of March 4 dealt mostly with Jeff and his children (Trent).

in nearly all the time—I have rec'd a very good letter from Hannah this morning—she writes in good spirits, & wants you & me to come up there next Summer[35]—says Heyde thinks of going off then to the Adirondack, on a trip—

To-day is very pleasant indeed—the cold spell seems to be over for the present—I have been out (about noon) quite a while—Mrs. O'Connor came to visit me, & as I was all dressed, & it was so pleasant, I went out— she convoyed me—I didn't go far, but stopt in at one or two places, near by—have now returned, have just eat a bite of lunch, and am feeling quite comfortable—sit here now alone writing this—as I told you in my last, I am getting along well, but it is very, very slow—I cannot begin to apply my brain to regular work yet—though, for all that, I have written two or three little poems for the *Graphic*,[36] a N. Y. daily evening paper just commenced—(one of them was in the number for last Wednesday) —they pay me moderately—

I was glad you got a letter from Mary[37]—if you write tell her I am improving—

John Burroughs is just in to see me, having returned for a while to Washington—

Well, mother dear, I will bid you good bye for this week—Love to you & to Brother George & Sister Lou & all—

Walt.

487. *To Louisa Van Velsor Whitman*   [3.9. 1873][38]

Sunday afternoon | 5 o'clock.

Dearest mother,

I will not write much to-day, as I have just come in from being out over two hours, & I feel quite tired. I cannot walk any to speak of, but I have been out taking a ride in the cars, and sitting in the parks a little

35. Hannah, as WW observed, wrote "in good spirits" on March 4 to her mother and to her brother—no whining, no hypochondriacal wailing, and no reports about Heyde's behavior (Trent).

36. The New York *Daily Graphic* published a number of WW's poems and prose pieces in 1873 and 1874. In the former year the *Daily Graphic* printed the following works: "Nay, Tell Me Not To-day the Publish'd Shame" on March 5, "The Singing Thrush" (later entitled "Wandering at Morn") on March 15, "Spain" on March 24, "Sea Captains, Young or Old" (later called "Song for All Seas, All Ships") on April 4, "Warble for Lilac-Time" on May 12, "Halls of Gold and Lilac" on November 24, and "Silver and Salmon-Tint" on November 29.

David G. Croly (1829–1889) was editor of the *Graphic* until 1878. From 1862 to 1872 he had been managing editor of the New York *World*, a newspaper which had been sympathetic to WW; see 399. Croly, described in *DAB* as "an iconoclast and a reformer," was the author of *Miscegenation* (1864), which proposed the blending of the two races for the survival of civilization. See also Traubel, III, 560–561.

while. Peter Doyle has been with me. It is as pleasant and warm as summer here to-day. I have not rec'd any letters for the last two days—I suppose you got my letter Saturday—I have been out more to-day than any day yet, as it has been so warm & fine—Love to you, mama dear, & to all—

Walt.

Mother, write me what envelopes you would like to have me direct, & enclose you—I have not been over to the office yet, except that one time ten or twelve days ago.

488. *To Louisa Van Velsor Whitman*   [*3.13*]–*14*. [*1873*]

Thursday, | 2 o'clock p. m.

Dearest mother,

I wrote you a short & very hurried letter last night, only a few minutes before the mail closed—To-day Mrs. O'Connor has just paid me a pleasant visit—& I have been eating my lunch of a roast apple & biscuit—I am feeling about the same—I suppose you are most tired, and perhaps a little suspicious of hearing I am *"about the same"*—Well I am quite tired myself, & want much to get out, & go to work, & go about— But I just have to make the best of it, & console myself with realizing that disagreeable as it is, it might be a great deal worse—& that I am feeling free from pain & comparatively comforting, & that it cannot be *very long* before I shall have the good use of my limbs again—So I just try to keep patient & wait—& you must too, dearest mother—

I got a good letter from Hattie to-day, dated March 9[39]—she says she was writing to you—so I suppose you have one too—They seem to like it at Mr & Mrs. Buckley's.[40]

Mother, I got your letter of Monday and Lou's of Sunday[41]—it is an affection of the leg from the knee downward, partially helpless—but the principal trouble is yet in the head, & so easily getting fatigued—my

37. Mary Van Nostrand, WW's sister. On March 4 Mrs. Whitman expressed hope that she and WW could visit Mary during the summer: "i think it would doo us both good, so we must both get so we can walk without limping" (Trent).

38. One of the executors marked this letter "[9 March '73]," which seems a plausible assignment.

39. Mannahatta wrote to her grandmother on March 9 and on March 14 (LC); her letter to WW is evidently lost.

40. Mrs. Buckley, Jeff wrote on March 16, "was a particular friend of Mattie's" (Yale). After Martha died, the Buckleys immediately took charge of the funeral arrangements and provided for the children; see Jeff's letter to his mother on February 24 (Feinberg). When Mannahatta wrote to her grandmother on March 14, she appeared quite satisfied with her new home (LC).

41. In her letter of March 10 Mrs. Whitman complained of her loneliness (Trent). Louisa's letter is not known.

whole body feels heavy, & sometimes my hand—Still, I go out a little every day almost—accompanied by Peter, or some one—sometimes spend an hour out, but cannot walk, except a very little indeed, very slowly indeed—Mother, in *my looks* you would hardly know the least thing had been the matter with me—I am neither pale nor thin in the least—

Friday forenoon | March 14.

I am sitting here in my room—it is very pleasant out apparently—I generally go out a little between two & three, and shall probably get out a little this afternoon—

John Burroughs has been on here again—he is trying to sell or let his house, & does not succeed very satisfactorily—he left here again by the train last evening & returned north—his wife is here—Mother, I send the Harper's Weekly—that picture gives a very good idea of the Capitol, (what they call the east front)—in the Extra is a picture of the inauguration ball—very good, they say—you must look over them Sunday—

Well, mother dear, it is now after 12—I expect to get out a little from 2 to 3—Love to you & to Lou & George & all.

Walt.

489. *To Louisa Van Velsor Whitman*   3.17. [1873]

Monday afternoon | March 17—

Well, mother dear, I feel quite well to-day considering—in good spirits, & free from any pain—I suppose you got my letter Saturday last —The doctor has been here to-day, first time in three days—(so you see he don't think me a very critical case.)

We have had real March weather here for two or three days, strong & sudden winds, & dust—but it is pleasanter to-day—it is now about ½ past 1—I have had my lunch & Mrs. O'Connor has come in for a few moments—

I have a little piece in the N. Y. *Graphic* of Saturday afternoon, March 17[42]—it is a daily afternoon paper—I write for it, so far—they pay moderately.

Mother, I feel to-day as if I was getting well—(but my leg is *so clumsy*

42. WW meant to write March 15, when "The Singing Thrush" appeared.

43. WW summarized in the next few lines the contents of Jeff's letter of March 16 (Yale).

44. In her reply on March 21 to the missing letter of March 19, Mrs. Whitman complained of her lot: "i have many little things to put up with but we all have our annoyances, some one way and some another. george is good enough to me but he thinks

yet—& my head has to avoid much talking or being talked to)—I hope this will find you all right, dearest mother—I think about you much—

Walt.

Mrs. O'Connor wishes me to give her love to you.

490. *To Louisa Van Velsor Whitman*   3.21. [1873]

March 21, Friday noon.

Dearest mother,

I am still feeling on the gain to-day—I go out a little every day, & think I shall try to make a beginning at work in the office Monday or Tuesday—beginning by degrees—I got a letter from Jeff yesterday,[43] very good—they seem to like Mr. & Mrs. Buckley's—Jeff has some extra work, making plans for new water works for Kansas City, Mo.—it is all the better—Mother, I suppose you got the letters I wrote Monday & Wednesday,[44] this week—

It was dark and rainy here yesterday, but is pleasant to-day—I am going out a little this afternoon—I send you some more papers, to-day—mother, do you get the papers I send. Already you can see the grass looking green here, on the south side of buildings, & the willow trees are budding out slightly—Spring will soon be upon us—It is now noon, & I am sitting here in the room—Mrs. O'Connor has come in, first time in three days—Mammy dear, I hope you will have a pleasant Sunday—Love to you and Georgie & Lou & all.

491. *To Louisa Van Velsor Whitman*   [3.28. 1873][45]

Friday morning—9 o'clock

Dearest mother,

The sun shines out bright & cheerful this morning—& in my east window I have a fine healthy rose-bush—I see it has got two roses, in bloom, & one just budding out—(it was a present from Mrs. Channing[46] of Providence—she sent on here, and had it got for me, when I was first sick)—I think I am feeling better to-day, & more like myself—I have been in the habit of soaking my feet in hot water every night for two months now—& I think lately it has done me more harm than good—one thing is, it has probably made me catch a slight cold—so I have stopt it, & I have a

and its all right he should that every thing Lou does is all right. . . . george is a good man but i dont think i ever saw any one so changed. he used to be so generous and free but now he is very saving, never goes out any where. so we go walter dear" (Trent).

45. There is no reason to question the date assigned by the executors.

46. Mrs. O'Connor's sister.

notion I feel better from stopping it—I have just had my breakfast, & am sitting here alone by the stove, writing this—Charles Eldridge will be here in a few minutes, & bring the morning papers—he comes & sits a few minutes every morning before going to work—he has been very good indeed—he & Peter Doyle hold out through every thing—most of the rest have got tired & stopt coming—(which is just as well)—Mrs. O'Connor comes whenever she can, & generally brings a dish of roast apples, or something—

I go over to the office about 12 or 1 most every day—but only for a few minutes—have not resumed work there yet, but hope to, Monday—I find there is a great deal of paralysis around, and they say I have got along very well—but it [is] so slow, so aggravating, to be disabled, so feeble, cannot walk nor do any thing, when one's mind & will are just as clear as ever—Still *I feel* I shall get as well as usual yet, dearest mother— & then I shall *surely* get here or buy or build a little place here, rooms enough to live in for you & Ed and me[47]—I realize it more, far more now, than ever—even for my own comfort—this spring is better to buy here than usual—I think we could get along *very well* indeed—you could visit George & Lou as often as you liked (& George & Lou could come & pay us a visit in winter when Congress is in full blast)—

I miss John & Mrs. Burroughs—they are at a place called Waukill, N. Y. state—they have hired out their house furnished, 6 mo's, $50 a month. I have not heard any thing further from Jeff[48]—I hope to come on soon & pay you all a visit, but wait to see how things go in the office— & how I feel—(as I have been absent now nine weeks)—Every thing looks pleasant here to-day—quite spring like—Mother dear, I hope this will find you feeling well, & in good spirits, as that is the main thing. Mother, as I cannot get down to the p. o. I send the money once more enclosed—write me Sunday, if convenient—Chas. Eldridge has been in— it is now later, towards 12—I have washed & put on some clean clothes, & am going over to the office—

Walt.

47. Encouraged by WW's references to a home (see 483), Mrs. Whitman wrote on March 21: "i think walt when folks get old like you and me they ought to have a home of their own" (Trent). Mrs. Whitman also informed Jeff of her unhappiness at Camden, for on March 30 Jeff reported to WW that mother "is not quite as happy as when she kept her own house—what do you think about it" (Feinberg). About April 5(?) Mrs. Whitman wrote: "well walt i should never have made any complaint if you hadent have wrote to me. you should certainly get a place for you and edd and me. i hope you may succeed walter. i have not been very happy here but i thought you had trouble enough without hearing mine" (Trent). Meanwhile, George had begun to construct a house in Camden —much too elaborate for Mrs. Whitman's tastes. On April 8 she described the house she dreamed of: "if we ever build walt which i hope we shall, i dont think it will be quite so extensive. the cheapest house that you could build would be a 2 story house with 2 rooms be-

492.   *To Louisa Van Velsor Whitman*   *3.29–[30. 1873]*

Saturday afternoon March 29. | ¼ to 3.

Dear mother,

I have come over this afternoon to the office, & am now writing this at my desk. I did not succeed in working any—was not well enough the past week—although I have not gone behindhand—but as I sit here this afternoon, it appears to me I shall be able to make a commencement next Monday—for, though feeble, I feel just now more like work than any time yet—We have had real blowy March weather here to-day, sudden & fitful showers & heavy clouds & wind—& now it is quite clear and pleasant—I cannot walk around yet but feel in good spirits—am pleased to feel as well as I do, & get along as well as I do—Mother, I do not show my sickness in my looks, in flesh or face, except very little perhaps—

I will finish to-morrow or next day—

*Sunday night—8 o'clock—*I still feel as well as yesterday, & have been out twice to-day, riding in the cars, & walking a little—I get in the cars right at my door, & am brought back there again—It has been a beautiful day—I am now sitting in my room, by the stove, but there is hardly need of a fire—Peter Doyle is here for a couple of hours—he is reading—the doctor has been in to-day—he says I am getting along very well—

Monday afternoon | 1 o'clock

Mother, I am over at my desk in the office again, writing this. I have rec'd your letter that the money come safe. I have just written a letter to Jeff,[49] & enclosed Josephine's[50] & yours in it—I am feeling on the gain—but still very slowly. I am taking some medicine, to restore strength—yesterday was perhaps my best day—though I feel middling to-day—I have not sent the Graphics containing my pieces[51] as I have not had but one copy, & sometimes not that—I send papers to-day—Mother, you write me what envelopes you want directed to any of them, & I will send them—

low and 2 rooms above with a shed kichen with no fireplace in the house except in the kichen. . . . what do you think of my plan walt. we couldent have many visitors to stay all night" (Trent). The last sentence is especially interesting.

48. Jeff wrote to his mother on March 26 (Feinberg).

49. Since Jeff wrote to WW on March 30 (Feinberg), their letters obviously crossed. WW's letter is not known.

50. Josephine Barkeloo, a young Brooklyn friend of Mrs. Whitman, was the daughter of Tunis S., a clerk. Miss Barkeloo wrote three affectionate letters to WW's mother before she left for Europe in 1872 (LC). The letter which WW read was sent from Belgium, according to Mrs. Whitman's letter to Helen Price on March 31 (Morgan).

51. See 486.

It is gusty here but quite pleasant—I am feeling quite comfortable, & shall soon be walking around I feel confident—I want to come on to Camden, but wish to get a little more able to move around first—Love to you & all, Mother dear,

Walt.

493. *To Louisa Van Velsor Whitman*   [4.1]–2. [*1873*]

Tuesday afternoon, 2 o'clock.

Dearest mother,

I am writing this over at the office—I have made a sort of commencement of my work to-day—I have rec'd this note (enclosed) from Lillie Townsend—Mother, I believe I will write them a few lines, soon— (What is Aunt Sally's name—is it *Sarah Pintard*)[52]—when you next write tell me—I am feeling quite well—(only easily put out with my head)—I have been in the office nearly three hours to-day, & have got along comfortable—I can only move slowly yet—cannot walk any—at least any distance—

Wednesday, April 2.

Mother, I am over at the office—feel rather slim to-day—but the weather is so pleasant, I shall feel better I think—Your letter has just come, & I am glad as always to hear from you all—you say George's house is commenced, the cellar begun—I like to hear all about its progress—

I see in the papers this morning an awful shipwreck yesterday night[53]— seems to me the worst ever happened, a first-class, big steamship from England, went down almost instantly, 700 people lost, largely women & children, just as they got here, (towards Halifax)—what misery, to many thousand relatives & friends—Mother, I send you the Graphic—the pictures are amusing[54]—(I thought I would write a line to the Townsends, mostly on Aunt Sally's account, as it may humour her)—

Well, mother, I believe that is all to-day—I hope this will find

52. WW was understandably confused about the relationship. Sally Mead and Phebe Pintard were sisters (born Williams) and his maternal grandmother's sisters. Mrs. Mead was at the time over ninety years old, but Mrs. Pintard had been dead for several years. See Mrs. Whitman's letter to WW on April 3 (Trent), WW's jottings dated November 20, 1873 (Trent), and letter 565.

53. The first reports of the sinking of the steamship "Atlantic" spoke of the loss of 700 lives. On April 3 the New York *Times* noted that the number was 546. Later a board of inquiry attributed the disaster to dereliction of duty on the part of the captain.

54. The New York *Daily Graphic* took pride in its illustrations of topical happenings.

you feeling well & in good heart, dearest mother—Love to Brother George
& Sister Lou—

                                                                    Walt.

494. *To Louisa Van Velsor Whitman*   *4.4.* [*1873*]

                                              Friday afternoon, April 4.
Dearest mother,

I rec'd your letter to-day, and I also rec'd your letter of Tuesday,
(as I wrote Wednesday)—I will write a few lines to Lillie, (mostly for
Aunt Sally Mead)[55]—

I got a good letter from Jeff yesterday[56]—Mother, Jeff is evidently
feeling composed & well—of course he feels Matty's death very seriously,
but I think he has recovered from the shock, and attends to his business
as well as ever—They seem to be well situated at the Buckley's—Jeff
writes quite a good deal about you—he writes about Mat's death—about
her wishing to see us before she died—

I am writing this seated at my desk in the office—I come over to the
office about 12—I do not feel very well, most of the time, but have spells
when I feel much better, generally evening—I think the sun affects me—

Mother, we—I and the doctor—have talked much of the electric battery treatment[57]—but as long as the head is affected, (the brain & nerves)
they say it must not be applied, for it will do more harm than good, might
cause convulsions—My doctor, Dr. Drinkard, says he will use it as soon
as he feels it will do good—but the time has not come yet—I believe I told
you I am taking iron, strychnia & quinine to give strength—

I wrote to Jeff yesterday—I send you Harper's Weekly, to-day,
mother, it is quite interesting—I still hold my mind about getting a house
here & *shall certainly do so*—At present my great hope is to get well, to
get so I can walk, & have some use of my limbs—I can write, pretty well,
and my mind is clear, but I cannot walk a block, & have no power to do any
thing, in lifting or moving any thing in my room, or at my desk—Still I
keep good spirits, better far than I would have supposed myself, knowing

55. See the preceding letter.
56. Here WW summarized Jeff's letter of March 30 (Feinberg).
57. At the request of Mrs. O'Connor, his sister-in-law, Dr. Channing sent to WW on
March 19 a copy of his 1849 treatise on medical electricity, but warned against premature
use of electric shock: "In a word electricity must not be used while there is *existing lesion*
of the brain or nerve centres. . . . premature use of electricity . . . may induce conges-
tion, apoplexy or convulsions" (Feinberg).

that I shall get all right in time—I know *how much worse* things might be in my situation than they are, & feel thankful enough that they are as well as they are—Mother, I was glad to get your letter of Tuesday, April 1. I have been reading the wreck of the *Atlantic* April 1st—I think it the saddest thing I ever read—

Well, mama dear, I will close—I hope you will have a pleasant Sunday—Love to you, dear mother, & to all—it is now about ½ past 1 Friday afternoon—I wrote to you Wednesday 2d April, which I suppose you got.

Walt.

495. *To Louisa Van Velsor Whitman*   *[4.6]–7. [1873]*

Sunday evening—

Dearest mother,

I will commence a letter to you, though there is nothing particular to write about—but it is a pleasure even to write—as I am alone a great deal yet in my room. It is about ½ past 8, and I am sitting here alone—I have been out to-day twice, riding in the cars—it is a change—the weather here is very pleasant indeed—if I could only get around, I should be satisfied—

I expect Peter Doyle in yet this evening, to stay an hour or two—he works every night except Sunday night—

Monday noon | April 7.

Well, mother dear, I am now finishing my letter, over at the office seated at my desk—I do not feel very well. My head is still so feeble—I suppose I ought to be satisfied that I do not go behindhand—I send you quite a bundle of papers to-day—One of the Graphics with one of my pieces in[58]—the spring seems to be opening here, the grass is quite green, & the trees are beginning to bud out—it looks very pleasant—

Love to you, mama dear, & all[59]—

Walt.

496. *To Mr. French*   *[4.14. 1873?]*[60]

TRANSCRIPT.

To the Attorney Gen's Office, for Mr. French, Pardon Clerk.

58. "Sea Captains, Young or Old" appeared on April 4.
59. On April 8 Mrs. Whitman informed WW that Louisa was probably pregnant, and that everyone was carrying trays to her (Trent).
60. This appears to be a note written while WW was still in Washington; therefore, the year seems plausible, since before his illness WW would have gone for the books himself.
61. On April 12 Mrs. Whitman complained that George "has never given me 50 cts

Please unlock the case where my books & pamphlets are in Mr. French's room & send me by bearer 6 copies "Democratic Vistas."

497. *To Louisa Van Velsor Whitman*   *4.16.* [*1873*]

DEPARTMENT OF JUSTICE,

OFFICE OF THE SOLICITOR OF THE TREASURY,

Washington, D. C., Wednesday noon, April 16, *187* .

Dearest mother,

I have had one or two quite good spells—but am not feeling well just now—have got over to the office, & am now sitting at my desk—it is a rainy day here, not very cool—Mother, I have nothing particular to write to-day either—but thought I would send just a few lines, as you might like to get something—The season is quite advanced here—pleasant the past few days, I have been out in the cars every day. I have not written very lately either to Jeff or Hannah—

Well, Mammy dear, how are you getting along at Camden[61]—& how are Lou and George—I often wish you were here, mother dear, as it would be such a relief to me to have you where I could see you, & talk a while— I think there is no doubt that, take the time right through, I gain steadily, though very slowly indeed—but I get many tedious spells, both of head & limbs—there seems to be great deal of paralysis—I hear, or read of cases, every day—One man here to-day told me of his father, who had a very bad stroke at 70 years of age, but got over it after all, and lived 17 or 18 years after, by great care—So I hear of many cases, some good, some unfavorable—

As to myself, I do not lose faith for a moment, in my ultimate recovery —though, as I said, I have some bad hours—sometimes very bad—Well, mama dear, I have scribbled out this sheet nearly, such as it is—I sent you a letter last Monday[62]—I have changed the address on the envelopes to you, mother, as you see[63]—is it right?—I am feeling better—my head is some easier—Love to you, dear mama, & all—

Walt.

since i have been heere," and marveled that her son, who once did as he pleased, "gives the strictest account of every thing." Of Lou she wrote: "god forgive me if i judge wrongfully but i dont think there is much the matter" (Trent). Mrs. Whitman was correct: Louisa was not pregnant.

62. Unaccountably, WW deleted the following: "I hope you will have a pleasant Sunday."

63. On April 12 Mrs. Whitman advised her son not to send letters for her to George's office.

498.   *To Francis B. Felt*

ENDORSED: "letter to F. B. Felt | April 17, 1873."
DRAFT LETTER.

DEPARTMENT OF JUSTICE,
OFFICE OF THE SOLICITOR OF THE TREASURY,

Washington, D. C., | April 17, '73.

Dear Sir,[64]

Your letter of Feb. 8, '73, remitting my acc't, and sales up to 1st of June, '72, (with check of $12:60) was duly acknowledged at time. If convenient, could you advise me, or get Messrs. Lee, Shephard, & Dillingham[65] to advise me, of sales by them since that time, and to remit me the amount? Also how many books are now on hand.

Also please return me, if convenient, the printed slip I forwarded you of my last acc't. with you, marked in blue pencil "return this."

I would also like to inquire of Messrs. Lee, Shephard & Dillingham whether they would not take my books, (the new editions) & job them. Redfield sent me word that Mr. Dillingham declined, thinking there was no inducement, but I am in hopes he will still take them.

There is beginning to be a steady, though moderate demand for my books, & if there were a good & permanent place of publication, I should advertise sufficiently.

I am in a bad way at present from paralysis—and am sick, & unable to get to New York, or any where—but expect soon to be better.

499.   *To Louisa Van Velsor Whitman*   *4.19.* [*1873*]

TRANSCRIPT.

April 19, Saturday.

It is now about noon, & I have just come over to the office, and have put up the window for a few moments, to stand & get the fresh air, & then

---

64.   Frances B. Felt & Co., booksellers, were located at 91 Mercer Street, New York.

65.   Lee, Shepard, & Dillingham, publishers and booksellers, had offices at 47–49 Green Street, New York. In 1867 Trowbridge attempted to interest this firm in the fourth edition of *Leaves of Grass;* see Trowbridge's letter to O'Connor on March 24, 1867, reprinted in *AL,* XXIII (1951), 326.

66.   WW was mistaken. It was Colonel E. C. Mason, not his old friend Julius (see 152). The warfare with the Modocs lasted from November 29, 1872, to October 3, 1873; see Keith A. Murray, *The Modocs and Their War* (1959), 318–319.

67.   A cousin of Mrs. Whitman and apparently the granddaughter of Sally Mead. Her husband James H. was a clerk in the New York "Hall of Records." The letter referred to is apparently not extant. In February Priscilla wrote to Mrs. Whitman about WW's illness (LC).

put it down again. Right opposite the window—in the President's grounds a man in his shirt-sleeves is raking up the grass that has been already cut on a ¾ acre patch—so you can see spring has advanced here—the trees are quite green—

Mother, I have had the second application of electricity to-day, quite a good application by Dr. Drinkard—he rubs the handles over my leg & thigh, for perhaps twenty minutes—the shock is very perceptible—it is not painful at all, feels something like pressing a sore—I feel as I said before, that it will be beneficial to me, (though there are different opinions about it)—I feel better to-day than yesterday—I think, mother dear, there is no doubt at all that I progress surely though very slowly, (& with an occasional bad spell)—

Did you read in the morning papers to-day about the fight with the Modocs out in California—& Col. Mason—I think (but am not sure) it is Jule Mason[66]—it is quite interesting—I am going to work for a couple of hours now at my work in the office books—I am feeling quite comfortable this afternoon.

500. *To Louisa Van Velsor Whitman*   *4.21.* [*1873*]

TRANSCRIPT.

April 21st, Monday, 1 o'clock afternoon.

Mother, I am decidedly improving—feel more like myself the last three days—I walk very clumsily yet, & do not try to get around by walking—but I think I am stronger now, & my prospects are better than any time yet. The doctor has applied electricity again to-day, making the third application—So upon the whole I think I am doing real well—

I have rec'd a letter from Priscilla Townsend[67]—She speaks of you, says that Aunt Sally always wants to hear from you—She speaks of Sarah Avery's[68] calling there, & of Mrs. Tripp,[69] & all—nothing very new—

I am writing this over at the office—It is pleasant here, but cloudy & coolish—Mother, I suppose you got my letter Saturday last—How is Sister Lou getting along—when you write tell me about her[70]—George

68. Sarah Avery was another one of WW's cousins. On May 20 she suggested with trepidation and apologies—she was so overawed by WW's "knowledge and intellect"— that he should find a good wife for his old age (LC). Her husband John, a New York merchant, wrote to Mrs. Whitman twice in 1872 about interest due her from the estate of Elizabeth Maybee (LC).

69. Mrs. Maggy Tripp was Priscilla Townsend's sister, so Mrs. Whitman informed her son on April 3(?) (Trent).

70. Mrs. Whitman was not unduly concerned about Louisa's health; see notes to 497. On April 21 she bitterly bewailed Louisa's economy, and continued to look forward to keeping house in Washington: "walt if you think you cant get a house for us to live in dont worry about me. i shall live my allotted time. if you ever do get one i think one about the size of what i wrote about would do and wouldent cost very much" (Trent). See 491.

I suppose is full of business—Well I believe it is better for a man to have plenty to do, if he is well & active—Well, mamma dear, I have written you quite a rambling letter—Tell me when you want envelopes & I will send them—write whenever you can—I think I shall be able to soon give a good account of my improvement.

501. *To John Burroughs* 4.[29. 1873]

ADDRESS: John Burroughs, | Examiner Waukill Bank, | Middletown | New York. POSTMARK: Washington | A(?) | 29.

Washington, April [29].[71]

Dear John Burroughs,

I rec'd your letter, & was glad to hear from you—I am still in a pretty bad way—I am writing this over at the office, at my desk, but feel to-day more like laying down than sitting up—I do not walk any better, & my head has frequent distress—Still, for all that I slowly gain strength —very slowly—& *shall yet get well as ever*—

Every thing goes on about the same, in the sphere of my affairs, &c. as when I last saw you—Mother is at Camden—mopes & worries a good deal about me—I don't feel like leaving here, for visiting or any purpose, until I get so I can move about—The doctor is applying electricity, every other day—I have had it now five or six times—I anticipate benefit, in a while, but it makes no perceptible difference yet—How and where is 'Sula? I wish I was where I could come in & see her & you often—(those nice breakfasts were bright spots, & I shall not forget them)—if I could just get 'round and sit an hour or so for a change, & chat with 'Sula and you, two or three times a week, I believe it would do me good—but I must take it out in imagination—for it is impossible in reality—

I got a long letter from Dowden[72]—he mentions you—As I sit I look over from my office window on the President's grounds—the grass is green enough—they have already been over it once with the cutter, & Saturday there were men out there in their shirt-sleeves raking it up—I have a big bunch of lilacs in a pitcher in my room—Washington looks

71. WW dated this letter April 30, but, as the envelope indicates, he was in error. Note that in the following letter, also dated April 30, he wrote to his mother, "I have not gone over to the office to-day."

72. Dowden wrote on April 12 (Feinberg; Traubel, I, 441–443).

73. Burroughs replied on May 14 (Syracuse; Traubel, IV, 304–305): though he was not completely "weaned" from Washington, he was looking forward to settling in New

about the same—rather cool & cloudy to-day—but pleasant weather may-be by the time you receive this—best love to you & 'Sula[73]—

Walt Whitman

502. *To Louisa Van Velsor Whitman*   *4.30.* [1873]

Wednesday afternoon—April 30.

Mother dear, I suppose you got the letter Tuesday—I am about the same—I have not gone over to the office to-day, & am writing this in my room—mother, I send only $15 in this—will send the other 5 in my next—Write and send me word, soon as convenient after you get this—I have not been feeling so well this forenoon, but feel better now—As I said before I have ups and downs—but steadily advance, quite certain, though very slowly—I seem to have a bad cold in my head—I am going to try to go out in the car, as the day is so pleasant and bright—

Love to you & all, mother dear—

Walt

503. *To Louisa Van Velsor Whitman*   *5.7.* [1873]

Wednesday noon, May 7.

Dearest mother,

I have just rec'd your short letter of yesterday[74]—Mother, I feel so bad, you are not well, I don't know what to do—will not rest, and some food that suits, be good remedies? An old person wants the most favorable conditions, to get over any thing. Mother, I will come on about the 1st of next month—I am getting along favorably, they all say, but have frequent distress in my head, & my leg is clumsy as ever—I am writing this in the office at my desk—I send some papers to-day[75]—nothing particular in them—but I think the English paper, the *Sunderland Times*, good reading—Mother, write, if perfectly convenient, either Friday or Saturday, as I am anxious about you—

Good bye, dearest mother, & keep up a good heart—

Walt.

York State.
74. About the beginning of May Mrs. Whitman began to fail. On May 1 she complained of dyspepsia because of the poor food: "we have lived quite poor lately" (Trent).
75. In an undated letter, probably written about May 9, Mrs. Whitman said: "walter dont send any more papers as i cant read. my head gets confused" (Trent).

504. *To Edmund Yates*

Washington, D. C. | May 7, 1873.

My dear Edmund Yates,[76]

Pardon me for my forgetfulness about the pictures. I send you three, to make it up. I have been putting off every thing—forgetting every thing—till I feel well again—for I am still in a pretty bad way—but shall come round again by-and-by, with the blessing of God—And so, (as Mr. Philp's[77] messenger is waiting) I shake hands across—& abruptly bid you good bye, for this time.

Walt Whitman

My address here is *Solicitor's Office, Treasury*, and shall always be happy to hear from you.

505. *To Louisa Van Velsor Whitman*   *5.11. [1873]*

Sunday forenoon | May 11

Dearest mother,

Well, mother dear, I am certainly getting well again—I have made a great improvement the last three days, & my head feels clear & good nearly all the time—& that, the doctor says, will bring my leg all right in a little while—Yesterday was a beautiful day, & I was out a good deal—walked some, a couple of blocks, for the first time—Peter Doyle convoyed me—This morning I have had my breakfast, and have been sitting by my open window looking out—it is very pleasant & warm, but cloudy—we have heavy showers here nights—too much rain indeed—still spring is very fine here, & it looks beautiful from my windows—I am writing this in my room—

I am feeling just now well as usual in my general health—part of the time, just as well as ever—but of course I expect a few set-backs before I get well entirely, & supple in my limbs—It is remarkable how much

76. Edmund Yates (1831–1894) was the drama critic of the London *Daily News*, a novelist, and the author of several farces. On a lecture tour of the United States in 1872 and 1873, he met WW in Washington in March; see Yates, *Memoirs of a Man of the World* (1885), 402, and Doyle's comments on Yates's meetings with WW, in *CW*, VIII, 13–14. In 1868 Yates had reviewed the London edition of WW's poem in the *Leader;* see 289.

77. A messenger of Philp & Solomon, Washington booksellers.

78. The body of Salmon P. Chase, chief justice of the Supreme Court, was sent from New York to Washington on May 11 for funeral services.

79. Theodore Tilton (1835–1907), a protégé of Henry Ward Beecher, accused his mentor on December 30, 1870, of improper relations with his wife. The accusation was suppressed by all parties until a sensational account of Beecher's relations with Tilton's family appeared on November 2, 1872, in *Woodhill and Claffin's Weekly*. Strangely,

paralysis there is—cases occur here, every few days—& in other cities—
There is quite a time here about the burial of Mr. Chase,[78] his body is at
the Capitol to-day, & he is buried to-morrow—mother, the paper I send
you has a picture of a railroad depot they are building here—it is for the
road Peter Doyle works on—You will see a piece in that paper about the
Beecher and Tilton scandal[79]—it is very coarse—I think Beecher a great
humbug, but I don't believe there is any truth in that piece—(but of
course don't know)—

I am still having electricity applied—the doctor applied it yesterday—
I am certainly getting along better the last few days—feel better—feel
more like myself—I shall come & pay you a visit the first part of next
month—shall write before I come, the time, &c—Mother, I hope this will
find you feeling better—I shall be anxious to hear—write a line or two,
Tuesday—As I sit by the window this forenoon looking out, I wish you
could take a look at the prospect, it is so fine, the trees & grass so green,
and the river & hills in the distance—it does one good to look at it—

Mother, I shall feel anxious until I hear from you—

Walt.

506. *To Louisa Van Velsor Whitman* 5.13. [1873]

Tuesday afternoon | May 13.

Dearest mother,

I suppose you got my letter Monday 12th (written Sunday.) I am
still improving—(I don't feel quite as well to-day as for some days past—
but it is a great advance on what I have been)—& am in good spirits—

Dear mother, I feel very anxious about you[80]—it is very distressing to
have the nervous system affected, it always makes one feel so discouraged,
that is the worst of it—Mother, I am afraid you are more unwell than you
say—I think about it night & day—the enclosed letter came to me yesterday—Jeff sent it to me, by mistake (may-be one for me has gone to you)—
I got another letter from Jeff to-day[81]—all are well—Jeff too is anxious

Beecher did not make a public denial until June 30, 1873. After Tilton published in the
following June a statement concerning Beecher's alleged misconduct, a committee from
the minister's church examined the allegations and exonerated Beecher. On August 20,
1874, Tilton accused Beecher of adultery and asked $100,000 in damages. The trial lasted
for six months and ended in a split verdict. In 1875 a committee of the Congregational
churches found Beecher innocent.

80.   About May 12 Mrs. Whitman explained that her "nervous system is very much
out of order . . . my head feels bad . . . i have such trembling spels" (Trent). She
thought that she would improve if she got away from Camden. Louisa, unknown to her
mother-in-law, also wrote to WW about the same time (LC).

81.   Writing on May 9, Jeff was concerned about the situation in Camden, Louisa's
stinginess, George's failure "to make things good and happy" for his mother, and the
possibility of having her go to Washington (Feinberg).

about you—Mother, try to write a line soon after you get this—I am writing this in the office—Mother, I shall come on—

Walt.

507. *To Louisa Van Velsor Whitman*   5.16. [1873]

Friday forenoon—May 16.

Dearest Mother,

I am sitting in my room waiting for the doctor—Mother, you are in my mind most of the time—I do hope as I write this you are feeling better—dear mother, do not get discouraged—there is so much in keeping good heart, (if one only can)—I think that is what has kept me up, & is bringing me through—I think I am still on the gain, though it is very slow—my breakfast is brought up yet, has been this morning—I don't go out till about noon—then I *hitch* over to the office, & stay there for a couple of hours—then I hitch out & get in the cars & take quite a long ride, (sometimes jolting pretty lively, as the track is bad—but I don't mind it much)— I don't eat any dinner, only a light lunch, as I find it is much better for me—I certainly don't get behindhand any, that's pretty clear, & I count on time bringing me all right—the only thing I think of now is you, dear mother, & about your getting well and strong as usual—

I got your letter yesterday (Thursday)—I suppose you got mine yesterday—I sent Hattie a late "Graphic,"[82] & one to Han also—(the same as the last one I sent to you)—

It is singular how much nervous disease there is—and many cases of paralysis & apoplexy—I think there is something in the air, for a year past, last summer, especially—Fortunately, it seems as if most people got over it—

Friday afternoon—1 oclock

I am over at the office—Have got a letter from Sister Lou written Thursday morning,[83] which gives me great relief, as it says that Sunday

---

82. "Warble for Lilac-Time" was printed in the *Graphic* on May 12. It had originally appeared in *The Galaxy;* see 356.

83. In a postscript to this letter WW's mother added: "dont come till you can walk good and without injury to your getting fully recovered" (Hanley; Allen, 452).

84. Burroughs wrote on May 14 (Syracuse; Traubel, IV, 304–305).

85. About May 17 the mother wrote: "my dearly beloved walter thank god i feel better this morning" (Trent). But this was a false recovery. WW went to Camden on May 20, and three days later his mother died. Her "last lines" reveal her affection for her favorite son: "farewell my beloved sons farewell. i have lived beyond all comfort in this world. dont mourn for me my beloved sons and daughters. farewell my dear beloved walter" (Trent).

In the New York *Evening Post* on May 31, 1919, Helen E. Price recalled that at Mrs.

was your worst day, & that you have got relief now—Dear, dear mother, I hope you are still getting better—you must try to feel good courage—I shall come on soon, probably about the 1st of June—

I have got a letter from John Burroughs this morning[84]—he & wife are both a little homesick, for Washington—they had got a nice home here—but he is going to sell it—& settle up there—he does better there—but he was doing well enough here, & was very comfortable—My head troubles me to-day, but I am over here at my desk, at office—Mother, if convenient write me a line Sunday, so I will get it Monday—

Walt.

Lou writes a very good, feeling, letter, about you—was very unhappy Sunday[85]—

508. *To Louisa Van Velsor Whitman*   *[Before 5.23. 1873]*[86]

FRAGMENT.

Mother, I will write only a short letter this time, as I have a good deal of work to do to-day in the office. Every thing goes on with me just the same as usual—I hope you are feeling well, dear mother, & the rest too.

Walt

509. *To Peter Doyle*   *5.31. [1873]*

ADDRESS: Peter Doyle | M Street South | bet 4½ and 6th | Washington, | D. C. POSTMARKS: Camden | May | 31 | N.J.; Carrier | Jun | 1 | 8 AM.

Camden, | May 31.

I expect to return Monday, June 2, bet. ½ past 5 & 6, but probably too late to see you that evening. Come up Tuesday. I am about the same as to my sickness—no worse.[87]

Walt.

Whitman's funeral about thirty persons had been present. "On taking my seat among them, I noticed a curious thumping at intervals that made the floor vibrate beneath my feet. I was so absorbed in my own grief that at first I was hardly conscious of it. I finally left my chair, and going to the back of the room where we were sitting, I noticed a half-opened door leading to another room. Glancing in, I saw the poet all alone by the side of his mother's coffin. He was bent over his cane, both hands clasped upon it, and from time to time he would lift it and bring it down with a heavy thud on the floor. His sister-in-law told me that he had sat there all through the previous night."

86.   Because it is impossible to date this fragment, it has been inserted at this point.

87.   WW evidently returned to Washington on June 2, as planned. Unwell and depressed, he finally went to the home of the Ashtons, where he at least did not have to climb to the fourth floor. About June 16 he returned to Camden.

510. *To Peter Doyle*   *[6.9(?). 1873]*[88]

Dear Pete,

I have been very unwell—but am better again—at least at the present moment.

I am stopping at Mr. Ashton's, 1202 K st. next door to the southwest cor. of K and 12th—Come up & see me. I wrote you a line two days ago, to Milburn's[89]—Did you not get it?[90]

Walt.

511. *To Peter Doyle*   *6.18–20. [1873]*

ADDRESS: Peter Doyle | M street south, | bet 4½ and 6th | Washington, D. C. POSTMARK: Camden N.J. | 20.

322 Stevens st. Camden, N. J. | Wednesday forenoon | June 18. Dear Pete,

It has been a good move of me coming here, as I am pleasantly situated, have two rooms on 2d floor, with north & south windows, so I can have the breeze through—I can have what I wish in the grub line—have plenty of good strawberries—& my brother & sister are very kind—It is very quiet, & I feel like going in for getting well—There is not much change so far—but I feel comparatively comfortable since I have been here—& better satisfied[91]—

My brother is full of work (inspecting pipe, manufactured here at the foundries for Water Works, & Sewers, northern cities)—he is in splendid health—a great stout fellow—weighs more than I do—he is building a handsome new house here, to be done latter part of August—

Thursday, 19th

Nothing very new—I have had some bad feeling in the head yesterday afternoon & this morning—but it will pass over, no doubt—It is warm weather here, days, but pleasant nights so far—Pete, when you get the

88. Dated 1873 in *CW*. The executors had trouble dating this note because they were convinced that WW did not return to Washington immediately after his mother's death; see *CW*, VIII, 89*n*.

89. Milburn's drug store. Doyle was evidently not informed of WW's move.

90. Eldridge wrote to Burroughs on June 26 about WW's health: "Walt returned here about a week after the funeral in a very depressed condition and complaining more in regard to himself than I have ever heard him do since he got sick. . . . I begin to

Star save it & send to me—you can send two in a wrapper with a one cent stamp, (I enclose some, for fear you havn't any)—

Friday, 20th

Pretty hot weather here & needs rain badly—I am about the same—feel pretty well for a while, & then have a bad spell—have distress in the head at times, but keep up a good heart—or at any rate try to—Give my respects to all inquiring friends—tell them I expect to return to Washington in about a couple of months—tell me who you meet, & every little thing, & who asks about me, &c. as it will interest me—

I have made a raise of some new summer clothes, real nice—thin black pants & vest, a blue flannel suit, & some white vests—Love to Wash Milburn—let him read this letter if he wishes—Write how you are getting along—good bye, dear son,

Walt

512. *To Charles W. Eldridge*   6.23. [*1873*]

322 Stevens st.   Camden, N. J. | Monday afternoon June 23d
Dear Charley,

I have now been a week here, & am about the same—well enough to keep up and around, but with bad spells most every day, & sometimes very bad ones. My head does not get right, that being still the trouble—the feeling now being as if it were in the centre of the head, heavy & painful & quite pervading—locomotion about the same—no better. I keep pretty good spirits, however, & still make my calculations on getting well.

I am pleasantly situated here—have two nice rooms, second floor, with windows north & south, if there is any air. They are the rooms in which my mother died, with all the accustomed furniture, I have long been so used to see. I am quite satisfied here, so far—Sleep good, & appetite sufficient. It has been warm weather here, but I have stood it fairly. I hear by your letter & the papers it has been very oppressively hot in Washington. To-day, as I write, it is cloudy & cooler here. I have not felt well enough yet to strike out for Atlantic City.

Charley, I rec'd your letter Saturday, with the one enclosed. (It was a

doubt whether Walt is going to recover, and I am very apprehensive of another attack. . . . He is a mere physical wreck to what he was. . . . His mental powers seem to be as vigorous as ever, which is the brightest part of his case, but to be stricken with such physical weakness that he cannot walk a block without resting—it is very pitiful" (Barrus, 83).

91. WW's description of life in George's home is in sharp contrast with the querulous letters of his mother in the six months preceding her death.

very kind sympathetic note from Kate Hillard.)[92] I have written to Harry Douglas, my fellow clerk in the office, asking him to send me my letters here under frank from the office, till July 1st—I am glad to hear Nelly is feeling better—I hope quite well—I send my best love to her—please hand her this letter to read—Nelly, I still feel that I shall pull through, but O it is a weary, weary pull—& when I have these spells in the head that still afflict me, it requires all my phlegm. My lift at the Ashton's was a great help to me—the change from the 15th st. rooms, & then the weather being so favorable—the change here is so far good, too—As soon as I get a little stronger, & free from head-distress, I shall go down to Atlantic City —Remember me to Dr. Drinkard if you see him, & if you have a good chance, read to him what I have said of my case—if he has any suggestions, write me—

Charley, I have amused myself with *Kenelm Chillingly*—read it all— like it well—Bulwer is *such a snob* as almost redeems snobdom—the story is good, & the style a master's—Like Cervantes, Bulwer's old-age-produc- tions are incomparably his best. Send me a Chronicle occasionally.

Walt.

513. *To Peter Doyle*   *6.26.* [*1873*]

Thursday evening, June 26.

Dear Pete,

I rec'd your note to-day. I send you a note I have written to Mr. Edmunds[93]—first take it to Mr. Noyes,[94] (to whom it is enveloped,) and get an additional line I have requested from him—& then, if you conclude to try for the Carrier's place, go up & take it yourself to Mr. Edmunds.

I must tell you another thing. I have written (wrote yesterday) a short note to Mr. Dubarry, your Superintendent, asking him if you couldn't be better placed, when the changes of the Baltimore connection are made. It may not amount to any thing, but I took a notion to write it.

Pete, I am not having a very good time—My head troubles me—yes- terday was as bad as ever—as far from well as ever—to-day I am a little

---

92. Writing to WW on September 13, 1871, Conway quoted from a letter sent to him by Katharine Hillard (1839?–1915): "I have made a discovery since I have been here [in the Adirondacks], and that is, that I never half appreciated Walt Whitman's poetry till now, much as I fancied I enjoyed it. To me he is the only poet fit to be read in the mountains, the only one who can reach and level their lift, to use his own words, to pass and continue beyond" (Feinberg; Traubel, III, 112). The first meeting of the poetess with WW took place on February 29, 1876 (*LC* #108); see also WW's letter of this date. A Brooklyn resident, she was a friend of Mrs. Price (see 533); in fact, according to Mrs.

easier, & have been out a few steps. But I keep up a good heart, dear son— & you must too.

Walt.

If you conclude not to try for the Carrier's berth, let the letters go.

514. *To John and Ursula Burroughs*   *6.29.* [*1873*]

Camden, N. J. | 322 Stevens st. | June 29.

My dear friends John and 'Sula Burroughs,

I am here again in Camden, stopping awhile, with the intention, as soon as I can move with comfort, of getting to the sea-side—probably Atlantic City[95]—about an hour & three quarters from here, by rail—I am not much different from when I saw you last—have been a good deal worse, (by spells, several of them)—but have now brought round again to where I was six or eight weeks ago.

Mother died here on the 23d of May—I stood it all better than I would have expected. I returned to Washington about nine days afterwards— but I was very restless & dissatisfied there—staid about a couple of weeks —obtained two months leave of absence, & (after almost making up my mind to go into quarters at a Hospital, as boarder, but was persuaded out of it)—here I am & have been for about two weeks—(I think comparatively better the last two days)—occupying the rooms in which my mother died—waiting for time to restore my health, which I still think it will— but I feel that the blank in life & heart left by the death of my mother is what will never to me be filled—

I am comfortably fixed here, have great kindness—I try to compose myself to writing at some of my themes, already outlined, but it don't amount to much yet. 'Sula, O how I wish you was near-by keeping house —I should consider it such a privilege to hobble there for an hour or two every day, while I am in this condition—The last nine or ten days in Washington, I left my den on 15th, & visited the Ashton's on K st. & lived there.

John, I don't think I have any news either of Washington, or of literary affairs or persons, to tell you, nor have I heard any thing since from

---

Whitman's letter to Helen Price on November 26, 1872, the Prices expected that Arthur and Miss Hillard would marry (Morgan). She was also the translator of Dante's *Banquet* (1889) and the editor of *An Abridgement . . . of The Secret Doctrine . . . by Helena Petrovna Blavatsky* (1907).

93. Postmaster of the District of Columbia (see 464).
94. The editor of the Washington *Star.*
95. According to her letter of June 5(?), Louisa inquired of one of her friends about rooms in Atlantic City (LC). WW was too ill in 1873 to undertake the trip.

abroad. Love to you & 'Sula. I hope you will write me soon, and spread yourself about gossip, about self & 'Sula, and the place & every thing—a letter written when you are in the mood, & let your pen run—I depend much on letters, as I am tied up here, & it is pretty lonesome.[96]

Walt

515. *To Charles W. Eldridge*   7.7. [1873]

322 Stevens st. | Camden, N. J. | Monday forenoon July 7.
Dear Charley,

Your letter came last week, enclosing one from the office. I have just written to the Postmaster at Washington,[97] asking him to forward my letters here, as I suppose that can be done. How is it? Can it be done—do you know? So you are to leave Washington on Thursday next—& Nelly and Jeannie are also—for a New England visit—May it be a pleasant & healthful & happy one for all of you.

In my case there is no notable amendment—& not much change—I have irregular spells of serious distress, pain &c. in the head, full as bad as ever, sometimes lasting all day, & sometimes part of the day or night only, with intervals in which, (while I remain still,) I feel comparatively easy—but my locomotion is about as bad as it was—last evening I thought it worse than usual—(to-day it is not)—I am not taking any medicine, nor have I talked with any doctor since I left W[ashington]—nights & sleep are quite good—appetite middling—&c &c.—I still stay here, afraid to go to Atlantic City, or any where, while I am liable every day to these depressing spells—& incapacitated from walking—

We have the weather in *streaks* of hot & cool here—last evening it turned coldish & remains so this forenoon, very bright & pleasant—but we had it very hot here too, some days—

By what I see in the *Phil. Ledger* and N. Y. Herald[98] Wash[ington] items to-day, I infer that William has rec'd the appointment of C[hief] C[lerk] at which I am *truly pleased*—Nelly, as I suppose you will see this letter, I will send you my love in it, and you must take this letter the same as if written to you—I wont ask you to write from W. at present in the midst of your preparations—but write me from Newport, after you get well rested & settled—did you see Dr. Drinkard? & did he say any thing new about my sickness or symptoms?

96. Burroughs on April 11 and again on June 2 urged WW to visit them (Feinberg).
97. See also 517.
98. On July 7 the New York *Herald* noted: "The Chief Clerkship of the Lighthouse

I have rec'd a letter from John Burroughs to-day—he & wife are evidently having real good healthy country times away there in the cool uplands of Delaware county—he is home—

I am feeling comparatively comfortable to-day, & still hope for the best—*but*—Charley, go in to my office a moment, before you go & see if any letters—tell me if William is definitely appointed—write very soon from Boston, if not before.

Walt.

516. *To Peter Doyle*   *[7].7. [1873]*

322 Stevens st. | Camden, N. J. | Monday [July] 7.[99]

Dear son,

I am only able to write the same old story—since I last wrote, I have had some pretty bad spells—suffered at intervals all last week, & yesterday, with the strange & painful distress in the head, I have had so much of—But I feel better to-day—Every time I feel better, I find myself much encouraged—I still stick here, as I dont dare to trust myself in a strange place, if I can help it.

I rec'd your letter telling me you was too late to get any chance for the letter carrier's position—& about Mr. Noyes' friendliness—Are things just the same, as far as you and your crew are concerned? I think about you every night—I reproach myself, that I did not fly around when I was well, & in Washington, to find some better employment for you—now I am here, crippled, laid up for God knows how long, unable to help myself, or my dear boy—I do not miss any thing of Washington here, but *your visits*—if I could only have a daily visit here, just as I had there—

I go out very little here—there is not much convenience here, for me to go out—one car line, passing about two squares off, consists of 4 cars, running semi-occasionally—and another line, about 3½ squares the other way, has I believe 6 or 7 cars—I get out & take a ride in them sometimes —my best jaunt is going in them to the ferry, & crossing on the boat to Philadelphia, to & fro, several times—But a great portion of the time I do not feel able to go out alone—fortunately I do not have any dizzy spells, nor any symptoms of them, so far—so I am not worried about that, when I *am* out—As I write this, it is a very pleasant cool afternoon, & I am sitting here by the window in a big easy chair—

Board, now vacant, will, it is said, be filled by the appointment of William D. O'Connor, who has for some years past been the corresponding clerk of that office and is thoroughly familiar with its details." O'Connor's tenure was brief; see 593.

99. WW wrote "June" by mistake.

Pete, I hope this will find you feeling well, & in good spirits—Write me a good long letter, & tell me every thing—it will do you good—how does the new time go on the road, since Baltimore tunnel connection?—how about Washington—Tasistro—everybody?—get a good sheet of paper, & sit down in the park, with your lead pencil—I send you an envelope— also some one cent stamps—

Love to you, dear boy—Keep up a good heart—I do yet—though it is a long & hard pull sometimes with me lately.

Walt.

517. *To The Postmaster, Washington, D. C.*   [*7.15. 1873*]

[*WW gave instructions to have all his mail sent to Camden.*]

518. *To Peter Doyle*   *7.15–[16. 1873]*

Camden, | Tuesday afternoon | July 15.

Dear Pete,

There is nothing new or different with me—I am no better in any respect—don't know what is going to come out of it all—We are having pretty hot weather here just now, but it does not affect me much—it is not near as oppressive here as the Washington heat—I rec'd your letter, my dear son—with the paper—I will write more to-morrow—

Wednesday | afternoon.

Pete, I have little to write to you about, as I remain anchored here in the house nearly all the time. As I write I am sitting in my mother's former room, in her old arm chair—Spend a great deal of my time here, as I haven't felt like going out lately—half a block tires me. Pete, my darling son, I still think I shall weather it, but time only can show—

Mother's death is on my mind yet—time does not lift the cloud from me at all—

I want much to get to the sea-shore, either Long Island or the Jersey coast, & shall make a start if I get strong enough—It is not so hot here to-day.

So long, my darling boy.

Walt.

519. *To Peter Doyle*   *7.24–25.* [*1873*]

Camden | Thursday noon | July 24.

Dear son Pete,

It is still the same old story with me—the best I can say is that I dont seem to get worse, even if I don't get better. Your letter came—and the Star, with the item about Tasistro. It must be very hot there in Washington, but you stand it better than most any one I know. I too never used to think any thing of heat or cold, from 20 to 50—but last summer I felt the heat severely, for the first time.

Pete, as I have told you several times, I still think I shall get over this, & we will be together again & have some good times—but for all that it is best for you to be prepared for something different—my strength cant stand the pull forever, & if continued must sooner or later give out— Now, Pete, don't begin to worry, boy, or cry about me, for you havn't lost me yet, & I really don't think it is likely yet—but I thought it best to give a word of caution, if such a thing should be—

I am quite comfortable here & have every thing I want—I went out at ½ past 5 yesterday afternoon, & rode in the cars here to the ferry, & crossed the Delaware from Camden to Philadelphia four or five times— very pleasant. To-day is burning hot, but I am feeling as well as usual.

Friday 25th—4 o'clock—Pretty hot again to-day here, but not so oppressive to bear as in Washington—I am feeling about as usual to-day— shall try to get out a few steps, after I send this—Good bye for this time, dear loving son.

Walt.

520. *To Ellen M. O'Connor*   *7.26.* [*1873*]

ENDORSED: "Ans'd." ADDRESS: Mrs. E. M. O'Connor, | Care of Dr. W. F. Channing, | Newport, | R. I. POSTMARK: [*indecipherable*].

322 Stevens st. | Camden, N. J. Saturday after- | noon, July 26. Dear friend,

Your welcome letter reached me to-day. Yours from Washington of over two weeks since, also came safe. Since my letter of about three weeks since to Charles Eldridge—in which I wrote to you also[1]—I have

1. See 515.

not improved any—the distress in my head has not abated—some spells are very bad indeed—(but it fluctuates, some days, or parts of days, leaving me comparatively comfortable.) Nor can I walk any better—some of the time, not so well—My saving points are pretty good nights' rest, and a fair appetite, digestion, &c. Still I can see I am gradually being pulled, and, though I have not at all given up hope of eventual recovery, I do not shut my eyes to the other termination—

I am very comfortable here, as I believe I told you, occupying mother's former rooms, (a north & south one, second floor,) and with all her nice & homely furniture & bed & chairs—& living day & night in her memory & atmosphere.

We are having the hottest sort of weather here—in New York and Washington it must be terrible—but here I find I stand it quite well. I rec'd a note from John Burroughs telling me of his flitting visit to Newport & call on you. I have been waiting till I felt stronger, to go to Atlantic City (Jersey sea shore) or Long Island, but in my present condition feel it best to stay here—(Nelly, I don't feel as well as when you used to come there to White's)²—I shall be glad indeed to have Charles Eldridge come here & see me—& it will be a *real disappointment* if he does not—but I count on his coming *without fail*—I hope to get a letter from him soon.

I still manage to get out a little, towards evening—not always, but nearly every day—get to the ferry boat, & sail to & fro across the Delaware, occasionally—I had seen in the newspapers of William's appointment, & was truly pleased—I hear from Peter Doyle quite regularly—he is well, & working at his dangerous post on the Baltimore & Potomac RR—I miss him much—& I miss you too, Nelly—I am very lonesome here, (& yet I keep up very good heart)—

If Charles Eldridge is there, I send him my love, & the same to all—to your daughter Jeannie, (whom you do not mention) & to your sister & the Doctor,³ & all who in good will enquire for me—It is now between 3 and 4 Saturday afternoon—I am sitting here in mother's great arm chair —we have had a hot day—but a breeze is springing up—it is a shady quiet spot here—I shall try to hobble out soon though I am quite feeble.

Walt.

2. WW stayed at the Whites' from March 1, 1871, until he left Washington. He had paid $236 in rent through June 10, 1873 (LC #73). On November 28 Dr. George A. White, a chiropodist, acknowledged for his wife receipt of $28 "on account . . . for rent of room etc from May 1st/73" (Feinberg). WW gave up one room at the Whites' on June 10: "Kept the other at $2.50 a month" (LC #68). See also 630.

521. *To Peter Doyle*   *8.1.* [*1873*]

Camden, Friday afternoon | Aug. 1.

Dear son,

Your letter is rec'd to-day, and enclosed I send you $20—I want you to write soon—as I shall want to know if it reached you safe.

I am feeling relieved of the worst distress in the head, now for the last two days—had it straight along bad enough the first three days in the week—but yesterday & to-day it has mostly let up—have been out to-day, & over to Philadelphia—it is hard work, especially as I have no one to go with me—but I put a bold face on, *& my best foot foremost*—Is Wash Milburn there in the store? or has he gone on his vacation in the country? —answer me in your next—I think of writing a few lines to him—Hot weather here, but I don't suffer much from it—though I think it is bad for me, & I hope much more from the cool season, if I get through this—

Pete, I too see quite a good deal of *Railroad*, & hear more—some 70 rods off is the great depot of the Camden & Amboy, bells & whistles & trains rumbling continually, night & day, & lots of RR men living near, around here—if I only felt just a little better, I should get acquainted with many of the men, which I could very easily do if I would—I should like much to go on the trips so handy & cheap, right as you might say from my door, to Cape May, or to Long Branch, &c. to say nothing of the numerous fine jaunts from Philadelphia by RR. or up or down the Delaware by steamboat—

If you was only here to convoy me—but I suppose no one is to have *every thing* wanting—(Pete, dear son, there was $89 coming to you, of the money you put in my charge, & now there will be $69 yet due you from me—your own soap)—As I write, it is 4½ o'clock Friday afternoon— I am sitting here alone, in the 2d story front room—every thing quiet here —I rec'd the other letter, & Sunday Chronicle—when you write, tell me who you see, & every thing—I like such letters far better than the formal ones some send me—I had a visit from a good, kind-hearted, rather queer old fellow named Ingram,[4] from Philadelphia—he said he see in the Phil. paper I was laid up very sick in Camden—so he came over, & hunted for hours through the hot sun, found me at last—he evidently had thought I was keeled up, & hard up, & he came to offer help—he has been a great

3. Mrs. O'Connor's sister was Dr. William F. Channing's wife.
4. William Ingram kept a tea store in Philadelphia. To Traubel WW observed: "He is a man of the Thomas Paine stripe—full of benevolent impulses, of radicalism, of the desire to alleviate the sufferings of the world—especially the sufferings of prisoners in jails, who are his protégés" (Traubel, I, 185).

traveler, is English by birth—I found him good company, & was glad to see him—he has been twice—so you see there are good souls left—

Pete, when you see Judge Fisher[5] tell him I shall yet be back all right one of these days, & in the mean time tell him I send him my love—also my love to Mr. & Mrs. Nash the next time you go there—so good by for the present, my darling son, & you must keep good heart, for I do, though it is pretty glum around & over me sometimes—

Walt.

Pete, you must read this over Sunday, as a ten minutes' talk like, about all sorts of odds & ends—

522. *To Webster Elmes*   *8.14. [1873]*

322 Stevens st. | Camden, N. J. | August 14.

Mr. Elmes,[6] | Dear Sir,

I respectfully ask to substitute the services of the bearer *Walter Godey*, in the office, for the present, instead of my own—having made an arrangement with him to that effect, if permitted by you. He writes a good hand, and I think would soon get broke in, and prove efficient. I would ask you to put him at my desk and give him a trial—on some letters first, before giving him the books—(or any other work or arrangement thought best.)

I have had a tedious time but I seem to be now decidedly though slowly recovering and hope to be in Washington before long.[7]

Walt Whitman

523. *To Peter Doyle*   *[8.14—15(?). 1873]*[8]

Camden | Thursday evening

Pete, dear son, I am not sinking nor getting worse—I have had some *very* bad times, & have some pretty bad ones yet, mostly with my head—& my leg is about as useless as ever—still I am decidedly no worse, & I think now I am even *getting better*—it is slow & with great alternations —but I have the feeling of getting more strength, & easier in the head,

---

5. George P. Fisher (1817–1899) served in the House of Representatives from 1860 to 1862, and was appointed by Lincoln in 1863 to the Supreme Court of the District of Columbia. He presided at the trial of John H. Surratt, which WW described in 240. Fisher left the bench in 1870 to become District Attorney of the District of Columbia.

6. Webster Elmes was the chief clerk in the Attorney General's office.

7. George H. Williams, the Attorney General, wrote on the verso of this letter: "If the pay of Mr Whitman goes on I see no objection to this personal arrangement if the bearer is a suitable person of which you must judge."

8. One of the executors, probably Dr. Bucke, dated this letter "Aug 28, 1873." However, the reference to Eldridge in this letter would seem to be earlier than that in the following letter. The probabilities are also that WW would have referred to the "Wawas-

more like myself—something like what I was before mother's death—I cannot be reconciled to that yet—it is the great cloud of my life—nothing that ever happened before has had such an effect on me—but I shall get well, yet, dear son, probably, (of course not certainly) and be back in Washington this fall, & we will be together again. I think I am now about as I was the day you came down to Baltimore depot with me, 20th May I think—

Friday | after dinner

I have thought of you the nights of this week, the heaviest rains here almost ever known—great trouble & loss to railroads—was you in any tight spot?—that described in your last made me feel a little nervous— That was a fearful disaster of the Wawasset[9]—sad beyond description—

So Tasistro is around yet—The Chronicle came—Mr. Eldridge has returned to Washington from his month's leave—he stopt here and paid me a 3 or 4 hours visit—John Burroughs has an article in the Sept. number of Scribner's Magazine,[10] just out, in which I am extracted from— Pete, it is now towards 3, and I am going to try to get down to the ferry boat, & cross to Philadelphia—so you see I am not altogether disabled— but it is awful tough work—when the weather is cooler, (which will be soon) I shall be better off in Washington, as it is very lonesome to me here, & no one to convoy me—I shall return there—I want to get a couple of unfurnished rooms, or top floor, somewhere on or near the car route— Pete, if you see Charley Toner[11] give him my love, & ask him to give you his address to send me—He works in the Printing Bureau (M'Cartee's)[12] Treasury.

Good bye, my dear loving boy.

Walt.

set" disaster shortly after it occurred on August 8, though the investigation lasted from August 18 to 23.

9. The "Wawasset" was a river steamer which caught fire on August 8 on the Potomac River near Aquia Creek, with a frightful loss of life. The official investigation attributed the tragedy to dereliction of duty.

10. "The Birds of the Poet," Scribner's Monthly, VI (1873), 565–574, in which Burroughs quoted at length from "Out of the Cradle Endlessly Rocking."

11. Towner (as WW meant to write) was a clerk in the Treasury Department; see 534. At one time WW wanted to lodge with the Towners.

12. George B. McCartee, general superintendent of the Treasury building.

524. *To Anne Gilchrist*

ADDRESS: Mrs. Anne Gilchrist | 50 Marquis road |
Camden Sq. N. W. | London, | England.
POSTMARKS: Camden | Aug | 18 | N.J.; London,
N.W. | ZX | SP 1 | 73.

Camden, New Jersey, August 17, 1873.

I must write you a few lines, dear loving friend, once more at any
rate. Since I last wrote clouds have darkened over me, & still remain. On
the night of 23d of January last I was paralyzed, left side, & have remained
so since. February 19th I lost a dear sister, who died in St. Louis, leaving
two young daughters. May 23d my inexpressibly beloved mother died in
Camden. I was just able to get from Washington to her dying bed, & sit
there. I thought I was bearing all stoutly, but I find it affecting the progress of my recovery since, & now. The doctor says my disease is really
cerebral anaemia, resulting in paralysis. I am still feeble, palsied, & have
spells of great distress in the head—But there are favorable points—I am
up & dressed every day, sleep & eat middling well, & do not change much
yet in flesh & face, only look very old, (though that is nothing new.)
Though I move slowly very short distances, I walk with difficulty, & have
to remain in or near the house. I think the probabilities are quite strong
yet that I shall get well, (though I may not.)

Many times during the past year, especially during the past six months,
have I thought of you & your children—Many times indeed have I been
going to write, but did not. I have just been reading over again several of
this & last year's letters from you, & looking at the pictures sent in the
one of January 24, '72. The letters of Jan 24, June 3, & July 11, of '72,[13]
& of Jan 31 & May 20, this year[14]—with certainly one other, & may-be two
—all came safe. Do not think hard of me for not writing oftener, especially the last seven months—If you could look into my spirit & emotions
you would be entirely satisfied & at peace.

13. Mrs. Gilchrist in 1872 wrote on January 24, April 12, June 3, July 14 (not 11),
and November 12. These letters are summarized in the notes to 436.

14. On January 31 Mrs. Gilchrist complained of WW's ten-month silence, and
begged him to write: "& do not fear that I shall take it to mean anything it doesn't mean."
But, she assured WW, she was willing to serve "a long long noviitate" (LC; Harned,
86–87). On May 20 she sent birthday greetings: "What can I tell you but the same old
story of a heart fast-anchored—of a soul to whom your soul is as the Sun & the fresh
sweet air, and the nourishing sustaining earth wherein the other one breathes free & feeds
& expands & delights itself. There is no occupation of the day however homely that is not
coloured, elevated, made more cheerful to me by thought of you & by thoughts you have
given me blent in & suffusing all" (LC; Harned, 88–89). Writing at almost the same time
as WW, on August 12, Mrs. Gilchrist, moved by newspaper reports of his continued illness, addressed him as "My Darling" (LC; Harned, 91–93). Fearful that WW would not
receive this twelve-page letter, she sent one to Washington and another to Camden.

I am at present temporarily here at Camden, on the Delaware river, immediately opposite Philadelphia, at the house of my brother. I am occupying the rooms where my mother died—every object of furniture &c. is familiar & has an emotional history. You must not be unhappy about me, for I am as comfortably situated as can be—And many things—indeed every thing—in my case might be so much worse. Though my plans depend on yet uncertain results, my intention, as far as any thing, is, on getting stronger, & after the hot season passes, to get back to Washington for the fall & winter. My post office address continues there, (Solicitor's Office Treasury.) I send my love to Percy, & all your dear children. The enclosed ring I have just taken from my finger & send you with my love.[15]

Walt Whitman

525. *To Peter Doyle*   8.22. [1873]

ADDRESS: Peter Doyle, | M street south | bet 4½ & 6th sts. | Washington, | D. C. POSTMARK: Camden N.J. | Aug | 22.

Camden, August 22.

Dear son,

I rec'd your letter of last Saturday & Sunday—& was interested in reading all the particulars you wrote about the RR. &c, and the young man, your friend the fireman[16]—poor fellow, it was indeed a sad fate— There has been great washing away & trouble with RR. tracks hereabout too—for myself I never remember an August with so much rain—Write to me whether your road has repaired damages, & is running through again—also every thing you think of & see about people & Washington &c. that would interest me—as I live a very quiet life here.

I am still about the same as when I last wrote—am no worse, & not much better—though I perceive my general strength is at least as good as any time since I have been sick—My head still troubles me with pain &

15. Ecstatically Mrs. Gilchrist replied on September 4: "O the precious letter, bearing to me the living touch of your hand, vibrating through & through me as I feel the pressure of the ring that pressed your flesh & now will press mine so long as I draw breath" (LC; Harned, 96). Although WW did not write again until 1875, he sent Mrs. Gilchrist newspapers and magazines. On November 3 (LC; Harned, 98–101) she wrote about her children; and on December 18 she said of his health: "Perhaps if my hand were in yours, dear Walt, you would get along faster. Dearer and sweeter that lot than even to have been your bride in the full flush & strength and glory of your youth. I turn my face to the westward sky and before I lie down to sleep, deep & steadfast within me the silent aspiration that every year, every month & week may help something to prepare and make fitter me and mine to be your comfort and joy" (LC; Harned, 103).

16. According to the Washington *Daily Morning Chronicle* of August 14, George Allen, a fireman on the Baltimore and Potomac Railroad, had had his leg crushed in an accident near Baltimore, and had died on the previous day.

distress a good deal of the time—I hobble out a little every day when not prevented by the rain—& console myself with thinking that *every thing* with me might be a great deal worse—I can put up with all but the death of my mother—that is my great sorrow that sticks—affects me just as much now, or more, than at the time.

Have you seen Mr. Eldridge since his return to Washington? Have you seen any thing of Mr. O'Connor? (You know he is now Chief Clerk of the Light House Board)—You must have had a sweet time with Dr. Duncan and Dr. Blake,[17] (though I must confess I rather like the latter—I suspect he has some real good points)—Sometimes, when one has plenty of time, I think it very good, for a change, to let such fellows buzz you to their heart's content, when you fall in with them—think of them as acting a part for your amusement—how well they do it—if they could only do it on the stage, it would make their fortune—So Mr. Tasistro still lives—he deserves credit for his perseverance & vitality—I hope he will come to the top of the heap yet—

I cut out the piece below from a Philadelphia paper,[18] thinking it might interest you—As is, I sit here in my arm chair, finishing this, it is 3 o'clock Friday afternoon, it clouds up again as if for rain—we had a shower last night—it was quite cool, but has been pretty warm here for two days, & is now—I am feeling as if I would & should come out all right yet—had a nice dinner—Pete, dear son, send me the Sunday Herald Aug 24—dont forget—So long, dear son.

Walt.

526. *To Peter Doyle*   8.29. [1873?][19]

Camden, | Aug. 29.

My dear son,

Your letter came all right last Monday, & the papers. Send me the *Herald* to-morrow, (with one blue stamp on)—you needn't mind the other Sunday papers—I send you Harper's magazine for September—I am still holding my own—gain a little strength, & am certainly improving though very slowly—both head & leg are bad enough, but *general feeling* is much better, most of the time—

17. Dr. J. M. Duncan and Dr. E. Tucker Blake.

18. The clipping reported "probably the narrowest escape in the history of railroading from a total wreck."

19. Though, admittedly, there is little concrete information in this letter to aid in establishing the year, the executors' assignment of this letter to 1875 seems questionable for the following reasons: in the preceding letter WW also asked for a copy of the Sunday *Herald;* he expected this letter to arrive in Washington on Saturday, August 30—

I have sent Philadelphia papers once or twice & may again—there is nothing in them, but I thought you would know I was still around—The weather here is pleasant, & cool enough, favorable to me—I get out a little every day—am going out when I finish this—Cannot write much to-day—am having a bad head ache all day—still I feel in good heart. So long, Pete, dear boy,

                                                        Walt

527. *To Charles W. Eldridge*   *8.29.* [*1873?*][20]

         TRANSCRIPT.

                                                        Camden, | Aug. 29.
Dear Charley,
       All continues to go well with my health &c. The Union now promises to reconstruct—(after a violent and somewhat doubtful struggle.) My leg is not much different, & I still have an occasional spell with the head—but I am *much better.*
       Please go down & hand Godey his money to-day.
       Write me a line.
                                                        Walt.

       Yours of a week since rec'd.

528. *To John Burroughs*   *9.2.* [*1873*]

         TRANSCRIPT.

       . . . There is his old Brooklyn partner . . . who is also a natural builder and carpenter (practically and in effect) architect. . . . My brother thinks (and I think so, too) that if you have not committed yourself, you could not do better than to get Smith[21] to plan and supervise and practically work with you . . . an honest, conscientious, old-fashioned man, a man of family . . . youngish-middle-aged—you would like him—I do— . . . If you need him, & he will go, he is your man.
       John, I think 'The Birds of the Poets' your best article, in many respects—it has a jaunty air, *in a perfectly natural way*—flits and hops and soars

"Send me the *Herald* to-morrow"; and in 1875 he invariably gave his Camden street address in the headings of his letters.
       20. Again the contents are of slight help in dating the letter, but Barrus' conjecture (85) that it was written in 1873 seems plausible.
       21. When George was building homes in Brooklyn after the Civil War, Smith was associated with him in his speculations.

and sings around in a birdish way itself[22] . . . I shall remain here for the present.[23]

529. *To Byron Sutherland*

Sept. 2. 1873.

Dear soldier boy,[24]

I have been very sick for many months—& am still unable to work or go round—But think I shall recover yet. I send you a paper same mail with this, containing a little piece that describes my case. I rec'd your letter of last June—have not only been sick, but in much trouble & affliction all summer—& I now write at a venture to see whether you are in Warren— & if so you must write to me at once. I have not forgotten you, my loving soldier boy, & never shall.

Walt Whitman
322 Stevens st.
Camden,
N. Jersey

530. *To Peter Doyle*   9.5. [1873]

ADDRESS: Peter Doyle, | M street south, | bet. 4½ & 6th sts. | Washington, | D. C. POSTMARK: Camden N. J. | Sep | 5.

Camden, | Friday noon, | Sept. 5.

Dear boy Pete,

Your letter, with cheering wishes & prophecies, came last Tuesday —God bless you, boy—for all such things help much—I had a bad spell this morning—have something of the kind pretty often—Still it seems certain I am improving, generally—& that my general strength is better— I am not near as bad as I was five weeks ago—have some hours in which I feel quite like myself again—Keep up good heart nearly all the time—& you must too, dear son.

So I see Beau Hickman[25] has died of a stroke of paralysis—in the paper this morning I see a piece about his body being resurrected from potter's field—

---

22. In the essay in *Scribner's Monthly* Burroughs quoted passages pertaining to birds in various poems.

23. The last sentence is taken from the text in the catalog of the American Art Association, November 5–6, 1923.

24. See 359.

25. On September 1 the Washington *Daily Morning Chronicle* noted that Robert S. Hickman, about 49 years old, was close to death. Evidently Hickman had squandered a fortune of $40,000, had been disowned by his family, and was now impoverished. On the same day the New York *Herald* observed that Hickman "is known throughout the country

Pete, I see a collision of some trains on the B[altimore] & P[otomac] road reported in the tunnel at Baltimore yesterday morning early in which a brakeman named Hankinson[26] was instantly killed—

I was over to Philadelphia yesterday—there is a large reading room, the Mercantile Library, 10th st. where I go occasionally—it is quite handy —they have all the papers from every where—have the Wash. Chronicle, Capital, &c.—Then I took a ride in the Market st. cars, & was caught in a violent rain at ½ past 7 coming home—the moment I got home, it stopt, & cleared off a beautiful moonlit night. It is clear and pretty hot here to-day—I am sitting here in the front room in the same big old mahogany chair I gave mother 20 years ago, by the open window writing this —I am feeling better since breakfast.

Pete, the papers you sent came last Monday all right—I have rec'd a letter from Chas Eldridge—& another from Walter Godey, the young man who is working for me as my substitute in the office—all was going on well in the office—I send a couple of papers to-day—nothing particular—send the *Herald*—

Did I tell you that a doctor[27] I have talked with here says my real disease is *the brain not being properly furnished and nourished with blood*—(it is a disease the doctors call *cerebral anâemia*)—the doctor says it has been long a-coming, & will be long a-going—says I will get over it though—says the *paralysis* comes from that, & that it (the paralysis) is not very 'formidable'—I am following Dr. Drinkard's advice, taking no medicine, living very carefully—

Walt.

531. *To Ellen M. O'Connor*   *9.5.* [*1873*]

ENDORSED: "Ans'd." ADDRESS: Mrs. E. M. O'Connor | care of Dr. W. F. Channing | Newport, R. I. POSTMARK: [*indecipherable*].

Camden, | Friday afternoon, Sept. 5.

Dear friend,

I still remain here in Camden, & in a condition not much different—alternating constantly between the bad spells, & then hours, & some-

by reputation and familiar to visitors to Washington for many years." He was interred in the potter's field on September 2. On the following day, after a subscription was raised among Washington businessmen to rebury the body in the Congressional Cemetery, it was discovered that the remains had been desecrated. On September 4 the headlines in the *Chronicle* read: "Ghouls. | Graveyard Hyenas. | Beau Hickman's Body Exhumed. | Horrible and Revolting Details." For WW's opinion of Hickman, see 534.

26. The New York *Tribune* reported this accident on the Baltimore and Potomac Railroad, in which C. J. Hawkinson (not Hankinson) was crushed to death.

27. Dr. Matthew J. Grier; see the following letter.

times days, not so bad. I suppose you rec'd the little Philadelphia paper I sent a week since—Dr. Grier here is confident my principal trouble is cerebral anæmia (blood not properly going to the brain to nourish it) — says it arises from a long continued excessive emotional action generally[28] —& thinks it so has arisen in my case—does not think writing, or study, or ordinary brain action has been the cause—it has been long a-coming & will probably be long a-going—thinks I will get well however.

He thinks it has been coming on for many years, says I need rest, rest for a long time & social exhilaration—(The paralysis, according to him, is only an incident, or result, & not the cause-disease)—Since I have been here I have followed Dr. Drinkard's advice—taken no medicine, & lived very prudently—(I still quite thoroughly believe in Dr. Drinkard)—

Charles Eldridge called upon me on his way back—his visit was a great treat, & was only too short—I rec'd a letter from him a few days since—all goes on as usual in Washington matters we are interested in— I have a substitute[29] working for me at my desk, and he seems to give satisfaction—When I shall be able to go to work again, if ever, is as indefinite now as it has been for over seven months—

I have rec'd a letter from John Burroughs. He has bought some land at Esopus, on the Hudson, west bank, some 80 miles from New York, & is going to build him a house & home there forthwith.

I get out some—went over to Philadelphia yesterday—go sometimes to the Mercantile Library Reading Room, as it is very pleasant there for a change—or rather for a place to go to & rest—though the atmosphere of a *reading room* soon weighs on me, & I feel like retreating—Yesterday took a ride up in the Market st. cars to West Philadelphia—& was caught in a violent shower coming home in the evening, & nicely soaked—Soon as I got home it stopt, and we had a splendid moonlight evening—It is bright & clear to-day, & rather hot—It is socially here an utter blank to me— my cynical dread of being bored by any one is now completely gratified with a vengeance—I look long & long at my mother's miniature, & at my sister Mat's—I have very good one's of each—& O the wish if I could only be with them—

Nelly, this has grown to be a perturbed sort of letter—& had better be torn up—but I will let it go.

                                                                Walt.

28. Is it perhaps significant that WW omitted this part of Grier's diagnosis in the preceding letter to Pete Doyle?

532. *To John Burroughs*   *9.9.* [*1873*]

Camden Sept. 9.

Dear John Burroughs,

Your letter of 6th came duly—with the plans & photo., which I return herewith—John, the questions you ask cannot judiciously be answered, except as they involve *the whole* house, ground, purposes, mate-
rials, &c. &c. And in reference to, & connection with, twenty different
matters besides themselves. My brother & I are pleased with your plan,
in general—my brother favors the ground story of *stone*—but the 1½
superstructure of *wood*, (says it is healthier & drier)—But I have no
doubt at all that *you will cipher out the sum yourself*, & the result will be
something cosy & natural.

I am not very well to-day—but am up & have been out—am generally
about the same as noted in my last.

Walt Whitman

533. *To Abby H. Price*   *9.9.* [*1873*]

ADDRESS: Abby H. Price | 331 East 55th street | New
York City. POSTMARK: Camden N. J. | Sep | 9.

Camden, | Sept. 9.

Abby, your letter has come, & is welcome. Dear Abby, & dear
friends all, the doctors say I will get well, & I say so too—but which ever
way it goes, it will be all right—the little Philadelphia paper piece was
about the right statement of my case from a favorable point of view—I
shall remain here for the present—I get around middling well—the worst
is bad spells in the head which persistently return—if I get a little better I
may like to come on & pay you a visit—upstairs will do just as well for me,
as I get up & down better than you would think. I will write to you before-
hand should I come.

My brother Jeff has come on from St. Louis for a while—stopt here
yesterday though only a few hours—has gone on to N. Y. to a good sailing
excursion, a week on a yacht voyage—I told him to call on you, if possible—& he will if he can work it—My brother & sister here are well as
usual—Eddy the same—

Helen, if you see Miss Hillard tell her I rec'd her letter & thank her for
it—I have not felt to write to her, or any one but my sisters, about mother's

29. Walter Godey.

death—the great dark cloud of my life—the only staggering, staying blow & trouble I have had—but *unspeakable*—my physical sickness, bad as it is, is nothing to it—

534. *To Peter Doyle*   9.12. [1873]

ADDRESS: Peter Doyle, | M street south, | bet. 4½ and 6th | Washington | D. C. POSTMARKS: Camden | Sep | 12(?) | (?); Carrier | Sep | 13 | (?).

Camden, | Friday afternoon, Sept. 12.

Dear boy Pete,

It is a very fine September day here—it must be delightful down in Virginia—the sun shines just warm enough & there is a slight haze, which makes it just right—I have been out just a little, but was glad to get back —I am feeling tolerable, but my leg still gives out, in a few minutes' walk—I have had two or three quite *good spells* this week—sufficient to arouse my hopes—but am in a pretty bad way yet—however I am not without some pretty steady *small* expectations, if not great ones. I am enough better to be perceptible, & to make me in hopes of getting better still— (but I have so many times got a little better, only to fall back again as bad as ever, or worse)—I have just had my dinner, nice beef steak, potatos, &c. My appetite still holds out—& my sister cooks very nice, gets me what I want—

Pete, your letter of Sept. 8. came safe—also the Herald & Republican— I send you Phil. papers.

My brother Jeff has been on here this week, from St. Louis—got in a car in St. Louis, 6 Saturday evening, week ago, took off his boots for easy shoes, and, (sleeping, he says, very well & sound in his bed on the car,) had his meals regular—got in here at Philadelphia about 9 o'clock Monday morning, in the same car, (which went on to New York)—He is now out on a good yacht excursion from N. Y., out in the sound & sea, for a week— quite a voyage—He only stopt here 3 or 4 hours—but is to return last of the month—both my brothers are stout & hearty, & full of business, & interested in it thoroughly—& doing well.

I hear quite often from John Burroughs—he has bought a spot of land, right on the Hudson river, about 80 miles from N. Y. & is building

30.   The hand points to a pasted newspaper clipping which described a car-coupler invented by William A. Boyden of Harrisburg, Pa.
31.   WW had trouble with the spelling of Hawkinson's name; see also 530.

himself a house there, right on a steep bank, with the road on one side, & the river on the other, a 2½ story stone house—(but sufficient space between)—

I have heard from Charley Towner—I got a very nice letter from him Thursday—he said you met him Tuesday & told him—A long while ago, I wanted to get a house in conjunction with Charley & his family, where I could have a couple of rooms, & they could see to them—& that was one thing I wanted to write to him about, to see if we could do it now—but he tells me his wife is quite sick—I quite pricked up my ears to read the short interview between Mr. Dubarry & you, & what he said about the *schedule* &c—I see you are a little *nervous*, Pete—& I dont wonder, nor blame you—Still the true point to attain is (like a good soldier, or officer,) to keep on the alert, to do one's duty fully, without fail—& leave the rest to God almighty—

I was reading the paper here this morning, & I see a list of some new inventions said to work first rate, among the rest this[30] ☞ for car-coupling—I wonder if there is any thing in it—It is awful, the way men are slaughtered of late years on the trains—there must be three or four hundred every year, take the country through—& the papers put 'em in in items of three or four lines, down somewhere out of the way—such a thing as the killing of that young man Harkinson,[31] in the Baltimore tunnel, a grand magnificent young *man*, no doubt—(while half the papers in the land have had long obituaries & notices of the death of that rotten old apple, Beau Hickman)—

Well, son, I have made out quite a letter for you this time—My brother & I have been talking about the Balloon splurge[32] in New York—my brother is quite a balloonist, in his belief—believes that something will yet come of it—I see they advertise to go yet, perhaps this afternoon—but it is a wild undertaking—(perhaps an advertising humbug) anyhow—

I shall still remain here for the present—every thing seems to be going on smooth in the office at my desk, from what I hear from my substitute[33] —He writes me now & then—does my work very well, & more work besides—Dear Pete, I am much in hopes I shall be able to send some news before long about my improvement for good—& something definite about my coming back to Washington—So long, dear son—you must try to keep up a gay heart & let the world wag on as it may.

                                                                Walt.

---

32. A Prof. Wise was attempting to launch a balloon named "Graphic" after its sponsor, the New York *Daily Graphic*. Wise expected to gather scientific information.
33. Walter Godey.

535. *To Thomas O'Kane*

ENDORSED: "letter sent to | Thos. O'Kane, | 130
Nassau st. | Sept. 13, '73." DRAFT LETTER.

Sept. 13, 1873

Tho's O'Kane,[34] | Dear Sir,

I have rec'd your letter of the 12th. I agree to allow you better than
half off, namely you to acc't to me at $1.40 cts a copy on the bound *Leaves
of Grass* (which retails at $3)—and at 30 cts each for *As a strong bird*,
(which retails at 75 cts.)[35]

I will be very happy to see you, at any time. I am stopping at 322
Stevens st. Camden, (cross by Phil. ferry from foot of Market st.—or
Camden depot from N. Y.)[36]

If you are willing to go into selling my books, I think you ought to
have some of the little 30 cts brochure *"After All not to Create Only"*
published by Roberts Bros. Boston.

I do not of course expect the sale could any how be a rushing one—
but[37]

536. *To Peter Doyle*   9.19. [1873]

Camden, | Friday afternoon, Sept. 19.

Dear boy Pete,

Your letter came all right last Tuesday. I still keep the same—no
worse, & no better. It is the same old story. I have a great deal of pain in
my head yet—no let up. Dear son, I would like to write you a good long
amusing letter—but I cannot to-day. We have had a rainy night and
forenoon—but as I write the sun is shining out again—& I must get out &
drag myself around a little for a change. Farewell, my loving son, till
next time.

Walt.

I send a small bundle of papers.

34. WW's relations with his book agents were complicated and troubling during
these years. O'Kane, a New York book dealer, took over the books still in the possession
of Doolady (see 256.1 and 605). On December 29 WW withdrew his books from O'Kane,
and also dismissed Piper, the Boston outlet. At the same time he entrusted the whole matter to Asa K. Butts & Co., which went into bankruptcy in the following year. Though
WW wrote cordially to O'Kane on April 22, 1874, he later became hostile. Citing only the
initials, Bucke, in his "official" biography (46), averred that O'Kane and Somerby, Butts's
successor, "took advantage of [WW's] helplessness to embezzle the amounts due—(they
calculated that death would soon settle the score and rub it out.)" This sounds like an in-
terpolation composed by the poet himself; note also 698. In an address book (LC #108)

Washington Dec. 3, 1867

My Dear Mr. Rossetti:

I have just received
& have considered, your letter of Nov. 17
In order that there be the frankest understanding
with respect to my position, I hasten to write
you that the Authorization in my letter of
Nov. 1st to Mr. Conway, for you, to make verbal
alterations, substitute words, &c. was meant to
be construed as an answer to the case presented
in Mr. Conway's letter of Oct. 12. Mr. Conway
stated the case of a volume of selections, in
which it had been decided that the poems reprinted in London should appear verbatim, &
asking my authority to change certain words
in the preface to first edition of poems, &c.
I will be candid with you, & say I had not
the slightest idea of applying my authorization
to a reprint of the full volume of my poems.
As such a volume was not proposed, & as your
courteous & honorable course & attitude called &
call for no niggardly or hesitating response
from me, I penned that authorization, & did not
feel to set limits to it. But abstractly, &
standing alone, & not read in connection with

Mr. C's. letter of Oct. 12, I see now it is far
too loose, & needs distinct guarding. I cannot
& will not consent, of my own volition, to
countenance an expurgated edition of my
pieces. I have steadily refused to do so here
in my own country, even under seductive offers,
& must not do so in another country.
— I feel it due to myself to write you
explicitly thus, my dear Mr. Rossetti, though
it may seem harsh, & perhaps ungenerous.
Yet I rely upon you to absolve me, sooner
or later. Could you see Mr. Conway's letter
of Oct. 12, you would, I think, more fully
comprehend the integrity of my explanation.

I have to add that the points made
in that letter, in relation to the proposed reprint,
as originally designed, exactly correspond with
those, on the same subject, in your late
letter. — that the kind & appreciative tone of
both letters is in the highest degree gratifying,
to me & is most cordially & affectionately re-
sponded to by me — & that the fault of
sending the loose authorization has surely
been, to a large degree, my own.

And now, my friend, having set
myself right on that matter, I proceed to say,
on the other hand, for you & for Mr. Hotten

that if, before the arrival of this letter, you have practically invested in & accomplished, or partially accomplished, any plan, even contrary to this letter, I do not expect you to abandon it, at loss of outlay. but shall, bona fide consider you blameless if you let it go on & be carried out as you may have arranged. It is the question of the authorization of an expurgated edition proceeding from me, that deepest engages me. The facts of the different ways, one way or another way, in which the book may appear in England, out of influences not under the shelter of my umbrage, are of much less importance to me:-

After making the foregoing explanation, I shall, I think, accept kindly whatever happens. For I feel, indeed know, that I am in the hands of a friend, & that my pieces will receive that truest brightest, of light & perception coming from love. In that, all other & lesser requisites become pale.

It would be better, in any introduction to make no allusion to me as authorizing, or not prohibiting, &c.

The whole affair is somewhat mixed, & I write off-hand to catch to-morrow's New York steamer — but I guess you will pick out my meaning. Probably indeed Mr. Hotten has preferred to go on after the original plan — which, if so, saves all trouble.

4

I have to add that I only wish you could know how deeply the beautiful personal tone & passages of your letter of Nov. 17. have penetrated & touched me. It is such things that go to our hearts, & reward us, & make up for all else, for years. Permit me to offer you my friendship.

I sent you hence, Nov. 23, a letter through Mr. Conway. Also a copy of Mr. Burroughs's _Notes_, Mr. O'Connor's pamphlet, & some papers containing criticisms on _Leaves of Grass_. Also, later, a prose article of mine, named _Democracy_, in a magazine.

Let me know how the work goes on, what shape it takes, &c. Finally, I charge you to construe all I have written through my declared & fervid realization of your goodness to me, nobleness of intention, &, I am fain to hope, personal, as, surely, literary & moral sympathy & attachment. And so, for the present, farewell.

Walt Whitman

Washington D.C. 1865 — Walt Whitman & his
rebel soldier friend Pete Doyle

Brooklyn,
September 3, 1869.

Dear Pete, I thought I
would write you a letter
to-day, as you would be
anxious to hear. I rec'd
your letter of Aug. 24.
& it was a great comfort
to me. I have read it
several times since —
Dear Pete, I hope every
thing is going on favorably
with you. I think about
you every day & every night.
I do hope you are in good
spirits & health. I want
to hear about the face.
I suppose you are working
on the road.

There is nothing
new or special in my affairs

or doings. The weather is
pleasant here - it is pretty
cool & dry. My folks all
continue well - mother first
rate, & brothers ditto. I do
not have such good luck.
I have felt unwell most
every day - some days not so
bad. Besides I have those
spells again, worse, last longer,
sick enough, come sudden,
dizzy, & sudden sweat -
It is hard to tell exactly
what is the matter or what to do.
The doctor says it is all from
that hospital malaria, hospital
poison absorbed in the system
years ago - he thinks it better
for me in Washington than here.
        About one third of the time
I feel pretty well. I have taken
three or four of my favorite rides
on Broadway. I believe I
described them to you in my
letters a year ago. I find many
of my old friends, & new ones too.

& am received with the same
warm friendship & love as ever.
Broadway is more crowded
& gay than ever, & the women
look finer & the shops richer
— then there are many new
& splendid buildings, of
marble or iron — they seem
to almost reach the clouds,
they are so tall — some of
them cost millions of dollars,
— Staging in N. Y. has been
very poor this summer — 9 or
$10, even on the big Broadway lines
— Railroading has also been slim.
— New York is all cut up with
railroads — Brooklyn also —
— I have seen Jimmy Foy —
he was over to Brooklyn,
looking for work on a road.
He was well & hearty, &
wished to be remembered to you.
They pay $2½ on many of the
roads here, & 2¼ on the rest.
The work is pretty hard, but the
hours not so long as in Washington

There is all kinds of
fun & sport here, by day
& night — & lots of Theatres
& amusements in full blast.
I have not been to any of them
— have not been to see any
of my particular women friends
— though sent for, (the papers here
have noticed my arrival) — have
not been down to the sea-shore
as I intended — In fact my jaunt
this time has been a failure —
Better luck next time. —
— Now Pete, dear, loving boy,
I don't want you to worry about
me — I shall come along all right.
— As it is, I have a good square
appetite most of the time yet,
good nights' sleep — & look about
the same as usual, (which is,
of course lovely & fascinating
beyond description.) Tell Johnny
Lee I send him my love, & hope he
is well & hearty. I think of him
daily. I sent him a letter sometime
ago, which I suppose he rec'd about
Aug. 26 & showed you — but I have
not had a word from him. Send him
this letter to read, as he will wish to
hear about me.   God bless you
dear Pete — dear loving comrade &
Farewell till next time, my darling boy.
                                          Walt

1872

Attorney General's Office.
Washington, Sept 28, 1869.

Dear William O'Connor:

As you were interested in Mr. Parton's money-borrowing item about me, I enclose you the receipts signed & given me by his Attorney at the time, (June 1857.) — The sum borrowed by me of Mr. Parton was Two hundred dollars. He had, just before, kindly volunteered the loan himself, without the least request or hint from me. I then declined, but afterward borrowed the money, & gave a short-time Note. —— I felt ~~then~~ & feel now, that it was a great impropriety

on my part, & it has caused me
much compunction & real unhappiness since. Any how when the
time for paying the note came,
I had no money. Mr. Parton then
put the matter in the hands of
his Attorney, Mr. Oliver Dyer,
who sued. My recollection is that
I confessed judgment, & proposed to
Mr. Dyer that he should receive
payment in goods. He came by
appointment to my room in Classon
avenue, Brooklyn, June 17. 1857
talked over the matter, behaved
very kindly, – positively accepted
there & then, & conveyed away, goods
to the amount of One hundred
and eighty one dollars, and receipted

for them, on account. He also, for
the balance, conditionally accepted
other goods, (which he also conveyed
away with him,) on the agreement
between us that if they, when more
deliberately examined, proved acceptable, they would requite the balance
& the debt would be considered paid,
— Otherwise they would be returned, &
the balance would still stand against
me. These goods he retained, and
subsequently told me that they had
proved acceptable, and consented
to give me a receipt in full, &
satisfaction paper — but, (I think,)
said the latter would require the
signature of Mr. Parton. This was
a meeting either in the street, or on

the Brooklyn ferry. On meeting him afterwards in a similar way, once or twice, I mentioned the matter of a receipt in full, but never pressed it — never procured such receipt, nor the original note either.

I consider the debt <u>paid</u> — (though if I had wealth, to-day, I should certainly pay it over again, in cash,) Among the goods rendered I remember an oil painting, an original, of marked beauty & value by 'Jesse Talbot,' illustrating a scene from Pilgrim's Progress, worth from four to five hundred dollars. This I put, if I remember right at one hundred dollars. I presume Mr. Dyer or Mr. Parton has it yet.

The enclosed receipt marked 1, was, on turning over the goods, written by me & signed by Mr. Dyer, who then remarked that he would also give me one in more technical form, and wrote, signed & handed me the receipt marked 2 — I presume (but do not know for certain) that Mr. Dyer considers the debt fully paid.

(The balance of thirty five dollars mentioned, besides the one hundred & eighty five includes ~~sixteen~~ ~~twenty~~ dollars as Mr. Dyer's fee, over & above the original two hundred.)

Walt Whitman

J. A. Symonds,　　　　　sent in steamer
　　　　　　　　　　　　　　Jan 27, '72

　　Not knowing whether it will
reach you, I will however yet write
a line to acknowledge the receipt
of your beautiful & elevated "Love
& Death," and of the friendly
letter from you, of October 7th last.
I have read & re-read the poem, & consider it
one of the loftiest, strongest & tenderest.
I must ~~see~~ apologise, & profoundly
too, for not having written to you
before. Your letter was most welcome to me.
I should like to know you
better, & I wish you to send me
word should this reach you, & if
the address is the right one. I wish
to forward you a copy of my
I shall presently print out a new edition
book. I am, as usual, in good
health, and & continue to work here as
government clerk in Washington
in a government office, finding it
not unpleasant, and the best — finding, in it,
indeed sufficient and free margin to me.
　　Pray dont think bad of me for not
writing more promptly. I have thought
of you more than once, & am deeply impressed
　　　with your poem.

1873

537. *To Peter Doyle*   9.26. [*1873*]

Camden, | Friday noon, 26th Sept.

Dear son Pete,

Your letter of yesterday came this forenoon—that was a rather serious runaway of cars in the tunnel a week ago—& mighty lucky to get off as you all did—Pete, I got a few lines from Parker Milburn—he told me you had a very bad sore on a finger of right hand—they are plaguey bad things—I am in hopes yours will partly make up in giving you a little resting spell. I sent you "The Children of the Abbey,"[38] an old novel that used to be all the rage—did you get it? To-day here is a great turn out & dedication of the *Masonic Temple* in Philadelphia—it is truly a handsome & noble building. A rain last night here, & to-day is really perfect. The Camden free masons marched by here this morning, about 250, the finest collection of men I thought I ever saw, but poor music, all brass, a lot of fat young Dutchmen, blowing as if they would burst, & making a hell of a hullabaloo—

Pete, I am about the same—may-be a little improved in general strength —had bad spells a good deal all the earlier part of the week—some very bad—but feel better yesterday & to-day—I am making some calculations of the cool weather—think it may be favorable to me—did not go out any yesterday—shall try to get out this afternoon a couple of hours— I don't know a soul here—am entirely alone—sometimes sit alone & think, for two hours on a stretch—have not formed a single acquaintance here, any ways intimate—My sister-in-law is very kind in all housekeeping things, cooks what I want, has first-rate coffee for me & something nice in the morning, & keeps me a good bed & room—All of which is very acceptable—(then, for a fellow of my size, the *friendly presence* & *magnetism needed*, somehow, is not here—I do not run foul of any)—Still I generally keep up very good heart—still think I shall get well—When I have my bad spells, I wait for them to fade out—I have got a letter from Charley Towner—I am finishing this by the open window—still in the rooms

WW scrawled on a piece of O'Kane's stationery, "rascal." For other letters dealing with the distribution of WW's books, see 564, 577, 579, and 605.

35. The next paragraph was stricken: "I send herewith adv't, which I wish (would like) to have inserted twice forthwith, in *Tribune*, as that seen."

36. Because the directions for reaching Camden were repeatedly corrected, the reading at this point is somewhat conjectural.

37. The draft is incomplete.

38. *The Children of the Abbey*, by the Irish novelist Regina Marie Roche (1764?–1845), was published in 1798 in four volumes.

where my mother died, with all the old familiar things—but all drawing to a close, as the new house is done, & I shall move on Monday.

Walt.

538. *To Daniel G. Gillette*   9.26. *[1873]*

TRANSCRIPT.

Camden, N. J. | September 26.

Dear Sir,[39]
I am delighted to please you in so trifling a matter as signing the pictures for your—and my—English friends—(substituting portraits I like better, instead of those you sent, which I don't like—though they are fine bits of work.) . . .

Walt Whitman

539. *To Charles W. Eldridge*   9.29. *[1873]*

431 Stevens st. | cor. West st. | Camden, N. J. | Sept. 29.
Dear Charley,
I enclose the money for Walter Godey. Please go down & see how things are going on—& pay him. Please write me at once, as I shall want to hear if the money comes safe.
Don't be alarmed—but I am worse to-day—having a bad spell—a succession of those *blurs* I used to complain of, only far more intense & persistent—it is now ½ past 3, & I have had a succession of them all day—still I am not dismayed—still think I shall get well—We are moving into the new house to-day.[40]

Walt Whitman

540. *To Richard J. Hinton*   10.2. *[1873?]*

[*WW discussed his health and noted an article in the New York Daily Graphic which had pleased him.*]

39. According to the New York Directory of 1874–1875, Gillette, which WW spelled Gilette (see 553), was a clerk in the county courthouse. An undated entry in one of WW's address books (LC #108) indicates that Gillette was at one time employed in the postmaster's office in New York.
40. 431 Stevens Street, WW's home until 1884.
41. See the following letter.
42. The New York *Tribune* printed the entire address of Dr. William Adams. The Evangelical Alliance, an international meeting of Protestants who sought unity among all Christians, met in New York from October 3 to 10. It convened to answer the ques-

541. *To Charles W. Eldridge*   10.3. [1873]

TRANSCRIPT.

The bad spells in my head continued at short intervals all through
Tuesday, Wednesday and Thursday. Today there is a sulking sort of lull
—have not had any actual blurs, but all the while ready to have them,
and pretty sick and sore and bad, especially in head, confusing me, and
affecting my eyes. I have rewritten my Will, with some slight changes and
additions, and placed it in the pocket of my trunk here.[41]. . . Ate my
breakfast like a man this morning. I don't go out any.

Have been reading Dr. Adam's speech before the Evangelical Alliance
in today's "Tribune."[42] My eyes gave out before through.

. . . Charley, I think I fully appreciate my situation and the possibilities and contingencies—and honestly think yet I shall come round—that
this is a pretty bad flurry, but one which will pass over. . . .

. . . We like the new house.

542. *To Peter Doyle*   10.3–[4. 1873]

                                    Camden, | Friday afternoon | Oct. 3.

Dear Pete, Dear son,

        I rec'd your letter the first of the week, & was interested in your
acc't of your week of laying off, & of the playing of the band under
Schneider and Petrola[43]—also about City RR. men—I send my love & best
respects to all of them—

I have had a bad spell again this week—for three days I have had a
succession of those *blurs* again—only very much worse than ever before—
last night I slept pretty well, & havn't had any of them yet to-day, but my
head feels sore & ready to have them, almost if I move across the room—I
am sitting here, feeling pretty bad, my head unsettled and dizzy—I
don't go out any more—but am up & dressed—

Still, Pete, I do not get discouraged but think it will pass over, & I shall
feel better, & strong enough to come back to Washington—Still I don't

tions raised by the new Catholic doctrines of papal infallibility and the immaculate con-
ception of the Virgin, as well as the threats posed to Christianity by science and material-
ism. The *Tribune*, with unconcealed Protestant zeal, reprinted verbatim virtually all the
speeches of the delegates.

    43. WW was fond of Salvador Petrola, a cornetist in the Marine Band; see Hans
Nathan, "Walt Whitman and the Marine Band," *The Bulletin of the Boston Public Library*, XVIII (1943), 51, 53. Petrola became the assistant to Louis Schneider, who was appointed conductor in September, 1873. See also *CW*, VIII, 9.

know—I think it best to face my situation—it is pretty serious. I send you a card—& if I should get bad, I will certainly send you word, or telegraph —I will write Monday or Tuesday next—We have moved into my brother's new house—I am up in the 3d story room, fronting south—the sun is shining in bright—it is beautiful October weather here—My brother had a large room, very handsome, on 2d floor, with large bay window fronting west built for me, but I moved up here instead, it is much more retired, & has the sun—I am very comfortable here indeed, but my *heart* is blank & lonesome utterly—

11 o'clock a. m.—sitting by the window—1st floor
I have just been talking with a young married RR man Thomas Osler, I fell in with—he has a bad bone-gathering on his left hand, a sort of felon, suffered greatly with it 5 days & nights—had it lanced yesterday, & is better—he stood by the open window, 1st floor, & talked with me, while I sat in an arm-chair inside—he is a regular RR. man—you could tell by the cut of his jib, low collar, cap, clean shirt (for holiday), dark complexion, & hard dark hands. I took quite a fancy to him & *of course*, I suppose he did to me—I believe he works on the locomotive—Pete, you must tell me how you put in the past week—I like such a letter as your last one—written two or three different times—It gave me a good idea of what you are doing—& also of how things look in Washington. I have written a line to Col. Hinton & shall write a line to Eldridge—

3 o'clock p. m.—My head is feeling very sore & touchy & sensitive—I dont go out—I have re-written my will[44]—What little I have to leave I have left mainly to my lame brother Ed, poor man—Pete, I have left you $200 & my gold watch—(but it will be much better for us to spend the money together, & I have no doubt we shall do so). This house is quite pleasant—it is on the corner—fronts south—side to west—plenty of light and air—and view—

This afternoon I am quite in hopes I am getting better of my spells to-day—as I have not yet had any actual *spells*, though I have felt pretty sick all day. But I have been up all day, & eat quite a breakfast, and quite a bite for dinner—

Pete, I have written plainly, because I want you to be prepared, if any thing should happen to me—but I tell you *honest*, I still think I shall pull through—& that I shall be able to write better news early next week —don't you be alarmed yet—

Walt.

44. For a previous will, see 462. According to Barrus (82) WW also made a will on May 16, in which he bequeathed a silver watch to Doyle.
45. The postmark of this post card furnishes evidence for the date: October 8

543. *To Peter Doyle*   [*10.8. 1873*]⁴⁵

ADDRESS: Peter Doyle | M street south, bet 4½ &
6th | Washington, D. C. POSTMARKS: Camden |
O(?) | 8 | N.J.; Carrier | 9 | Oct | 8(?).

Wednesday afternoon | ½ past 3

Am still about the same, pretty feeble, but no worse—no decidedly bad spells the last three days—Consider myself much relieved—
do not go out any—expect to be around next week—shall write Friday—

W W

544. *To Peter Doyle*   *10.9–[10. 1873]*

431 Stevens st. | cor West. | Camden, N. J. | Thursday noon Oct. 9.
Dear son,

Your letter of 8th came this morning—You did perfectly right⁴⁶
—I believe you are the greatest comfort I have & if I get well, our love &
attachment will be closer than ever. As I write it is about noon, & I am
sitting up in my room, with a window open & the bright sun streaming in.
I have confused spells of the head, & have just had one, lasting about 20
minutes—they are not so bad & prostrating as those of last week—I
have to just sit still & wait till they pass over. I eat my breakfast with
relish this morning, salmon, Graham bread, coffee, &c. But did not rest
well last night. John Burroughs has been to see me—staid a day & night
—he has settled up & sold out in Washington, & left—He is building a
home on the Hudson river, 75 miles from N. Y.—has 10 acres of land on
west side of river. I am feeling quite bad to-day about a 13 year old boy,
Rob Evans, I know here, next door but one—he has had his eye very badly
hurt, I fear it is put out, the doctor has given it up—by an arrow yesterday, the boys playing—I thought quite a good deal of him, he would do
any thing for me—his father was French, & is dead—the boy suffers very
much—& the misfortune is a very, very sad one—

It is now ¼ after 12—& every thing looks so sunny & inviting out, I am
going to try to get out on the walk for a few minutes—but I don't navigate
as well as I did before I left W[ashingto]n.

Friday afternoon ½ past 2.

Another beautiful day—I enjoy it, but cannot go around in it—I went
out yesterday, not far, but was badly overcome before I got back. At

was on Wednesday in 1873.
    46. Since Doyle's correspondence during this period is not extant, it is impossible to
explain WW's comment.

present my head cannot stand any thing. Still, to-day I am feeling rather better than usual. I have eat my dinner—beef steak & potatos, with pumpkin pie & a cup of tea—I eat very moderately, but with quite a relish. Dear Pete, serious as these spells are, (& seems as if they *will* continue to come on,) I still have abiding hopes & trust of my recovery yet—though I don't want to be too confident, & wanted you to be prepared for whatever might happen. I shall write a line to-day to Charles Eldridge—I am glad you have got some acquainted with him—I know him thoroughly—he is a thoroughly good & true man—has some ways & notions of his own, but the main things are *as solid* as the hills—Hinton too is a real good, kind man—

Now, dear son, dont worry about me—I think in all probability we shall yet be together—& that I shall come round to be wholly or partially better—but whichever way it goes with me, it will be all right—your latest two letters have *been first rate*—I read the one before the last, many times, it is very dear to me.

Walt.

545. *To Charles W. Eldridge*   [*10.10. 1873*][47]

431 Stevens st. | cor West. | Camden, N. J. | Friday 3 p. m.
Dear friend,

I suppose you got my postal card. I am still about the same as then —or, if any different, it is on the side of relief & improvement—I have the feeling to go out & try to get around—have better spirits than I could expect—but on trial, the least exertion confuses my head, & overcomes me. But I am sitting here at present in my room, comparatively comfortable—& feel every hope that I shall be able to give better account of myself next week. I am still clear of the pronounced bad spells of seven or eight days ago—a great gain & let-up. The weather here is fine.

Walt Whitman

Isn't that Evangelical Alliance a pretty kettle of fish? I read the Tribune through every day.

546. *To Charles W. Eldridge*   *10.13.* [*1873*]

Camden, Oct. 13. | ½ past 1, p. m.

My dear friend,[48]

I am having quite a good spell to-day, (if it only lasts)—I wish you, in conjunction with Peter Doyle, would go over to my room at Dr.

---

47. The date of this letter is determined by the reference to it in the preceding letter and by the allusion to the Evangelical Alliance (see 541).

White's, & unlock the big trunk, (the one that is strapped) and take out

My gray suit, coat, vest, & I think there are two pairs of pants, both alike.

My *black overcoat*, quite heavy—it is the one in the trunk—

Black felt hat, (there are two black hats, this is the lightest, most flexible one—*not* the big fellow.)

The pair of *old buckskin gloves*, with sheepskin cuffs and do them up in a bundle—I think you can get three or four large sheets of *very strong brown paper* for wrapper, *tied securely* with very strong cord—direct plainly to me, 431 Stevens st. cor. West, here—put duplicate directions on—& send by Adams express—I write to-day to Peter Doyle, same request as this, and asking him to meet you at Milburn's[49] bet 3½ and 4, this afternoon—if not to-day, to-morrow, (or next day, or next still) will do just as well, as I am in no particular hurry. Pete put the things in the trunk for me, & will know about them. Then lock & strap the trunk again, & return key to me. There are two locks, both of which this key unlocks.

I rec'd your good letter yesterday. I will write promptly if there is any marked change in my condition. I rec'd a letter from Walter Godey, Saturday, & wrote to him yesterday.

Walt Whitman

After the bundle is dispatched to express office, write me a line—(As I have said, I am in no particular hurry—use your convenience)—

547. *To Peter Doyle*   10.13. [*1873*]

431 Stevens st. | cor West. | Camden, N. J. | Oct. 13.

Dear Pete,

I want some things taken out of my trunk, & put in a bundle & sent here by express. I have written to-day to Mr. Eldridge & sent him the key. I have asked him to go into Milburn's between 3½ and 4 this afternoon, & meet you—or if not convenient for you, *this* afternoon, *to-morrow*, or *next* will do just as well, as I am in no hurry—

You both go up in my room & get them—I want

My *old gray suit*, coat vest &c, (I think there are two pair of pants)

My old *black overcoat* that is laid away in the trunk

Black felt hat—(the smallest lightest one)

The *old buckskin* gloves

48. This letter and the following one indicate that WW had abandoned his plans to return to Washington in the near future.

49. A drug store run by WW's friends.

I think some big sheets of very stout wrapping paper, & stout cord will do—the directions must be very plain, & in two places—If not convenient to go to-day, go *to-morrow afternoon, or next.*

I *don't* want the freight paid, as I will pay it on delivery here. I enclose a dollar as there may be some expense—(some little fixings.) Pete, I rec'd your letter this morning, & it was very welcome, as always. I rec'd the Sunday Herald too.

I am having a *good spell* so far to-day—(if it would only continue)—The bundle will come well enough, as it is a short straight route, if you only do it up so they wont get loose, & put on *plain directions.*

Walt.

548. *To Peter Doyle*   *10.16–[17. 1873]*

ADDRESS: Peter Doyle | M street south | bet 4½ & 6th | Washington | D. C. POSTMARK: Camden | Oct | 17 | (?).

431 Stevens st. | cor West | Camden, Oct. 16. | 2 p.m.

Dear son,

I sent you a postal card yesterday that the bundle had come all right, with the right things I wanted. My condition is still what may be called favorable—that is I still keep up without having any of those decidedly bad spells—*blurs* as I call them—of a while ago—& in general I feel as well & as strong (such as it all was) as before I was taken with those spells. I go out again a little.

Pete, I told you about a young railroad man, Tom Osler, 26 years old, that I met occasionally & talked with, that had a felon on his hand—I took quite a fancy to him, & he to me—Well, he is dead, killed instantly—(I have marked the piece in the paper already sent)—I went around yesterday to where he lived, it is near here, he was married, leaves a young widow, & a nice little 2 year old boy—I saw them—his body, broken & scalded, lay in the front room—Whenever you have the *Star* or *Republican,* once in a while you can send them (you can send 2 for a 1 ct stamp) I dont mind their being a little old—I see the *Chronicle* and *Capital* at the reading room—I am feeling full as well as usual to-day, & think of going out & across the ferry—it is so pleasant this afternoon—

Friday afternoon—I went out yesterday afternoon—across to Philadelphia, & up to the Mercantile Library Reading Room, I have spoken of. Yesterday, & yesterday evening, I felt better than usual—but am not so well to-day—the worst of my case is these *fall backs*—But I have been out

50. Rob Evans; see 544.

a little to-day. My walking does not improve any at all. (Then to make things more *cheerful*, there are many deaths hereabout from paralysis) —

I quite miss poor Tom Osler. I am in the habit of sitting of the forenoon by the first-floor window, reading the papers, & Tom would often stop a few minutes & talk to me at the window, on his way to & from the depot—He would never come in the house, but seemed to like to stop & talk that way with me. My boy[50] that had his eye hurt is doing rather badly too. About myself, my *general strength* not only holds out, but I think rather improves, which helps a good deal. Your postal card came— also a letter from Eldridge, enclosing the key. Good bye for this time, my loving boy.

Walt

549. *To Peter Doyle*   *10.21.* [*1873*]

ADDRESS: Peter Doyle | M street South | bet 4½ &
6th | Washington, D. C. POSTMARKS: Camden | Oct |
21 | N.J.; Carrier | 22 | Oct | 8 AM.

431 Stevens st. | cor West. | Camden, N. J. | Oct. 21.[51]

Am getting along favorably now—strength more enduring—am still very lame, but decidedly *doing well generally*—

W. W.

550. *To Peter Doyle*   *10.24.* [*1873*]

431 Stevens st. | cor West. | Camden, N. J. Oct. 24
Friday afternoon.

Dear son Pete,

I am still doing as well as when I last wrote—I have many alternations, but upon the whole have no reason to complain of the last ten days. My head has some bad spells, & a touch or more nearly every day, & my locomotion is still as clumsy as ever—but for all that I am happy in not having any of those spasms of three weeks since, & indeed I have *glimpses* again of my *real self*—have had two or three such, of an hour or two each—which I felt very encouraging. Your letter came Tuesday, & I wrote you a few lines on a postal card, which I suppose you rec'd next day. I went to Tommy Osler's, the young RR man's funeral last Sunday—it was near here—poor fellow, he used always to stop a minute at the window, & talk off hand & cheerful—Pete, he often made me think of you, dear son—he was your age & size—he was an only son—I go out now about

51. This is the post card referred to in the following letter as written on Tuesday.

every day, my strength is certainly improving—shall go out this afternoon—

About an hour ago the big Adams express wagon drove up to the door, with a box for me—it was 2 doz 2 lb cans of fresh Oregon salmon from St. Louis, from my brother Jeff—I am very fond of it for breakfast, can eat it every day—(My appetite is pretty fair, but I must have just the things I want, cant eat any others)—Pete, your description of the old Evangelical Alliance fellows, as if they had just walked out of Noah's Ark, made me laugh heartily—you just hit it—

I have just got a long letter from Mrs. O'Connor—she is in Massachusetts—returns to Washington in November—How are Mr. & Mrs. Nash, & Ed, & all—give them my love—tell Ed I shall yet want him to build me *that small house*—I send my love to Wash Milburn—I am writing this up in my room, 3 o'clock, pleasant weather, sun shining, window open—I am feeling quite fair to-day. Good bye for this time, my loving boy.

Walt.

551. *To Peter Doyle*   10.31. [1873]

ADDRESS: Peter Doyle, | M street South | bet 4½ & 6th | Washington | D. C. POSTMARK: Camden | Oct | 31 | N.J.

431 Stevens st. | cor West. | Camden, N. J.
Friday afternoon, Oct. 31.

Dear boy Pete,

My condition remains about the same—I don't get ahead any to notice—but I hold my own, as favorable as I have stated in my late letters, & am free yet from the very confused spells of the head & spasms of three weeks ago. Besides I think upon the whole, my general strength is the best it has been yet—for an interval every now & then it certainly is. All very encouraging—(But my disease seems to have such ups & downs I have learned to fear to make calculations, almost.) The weather here is fine—cool mornings & nights, indeed quite cold at times—but the bulk of the day perfect—I think the cool weather season is beneficial to me. I am sitting here writing this with one of the windows wide open, & the afternoon sun streaming in. I got a letter this morning from Mr. Eldridge that he had paid Godey, my substitute, the money I sent on for his October pay.

Washington must be looking pleasant this fall. Write me how you are

52. Since Alden's acceptance of this poem is unmistakably dated November 1 (Barrett), either the date of this letter (which may be a draft) or of Alden's is incorrect. The poem appeared in *Harper's New Monthly Magazine* in the following February, XLVIII

fixed, and I like to hear all the particulars about your work, on the RR. Good bye for this time, my loving boy.

Walt.

It is now a little after 2—I have had my dinner, beefsteak & potatos—pumpkin pie & a cup of tea—Don't you think that is doing very well?—It is a glorious afternoon & I am going down to take a trip once or twice across the Delaware in the ferry boat. It makes a pleasant little trip as the river here is most as wide as the Potomac from 7th st. wharf—has two little islands in the middle, which sometimes we steer between, & sometimes go round—Then *these nights*, Pete—last night I was out, came home about 8—the moon shining bright as silver—I thought of our old walks, dear son.

552. *To Henry M. Alden*

431 Stevens st. | cor West | Camden, N. Jersey. | Nov. 2, 1873.[52] Editor Harper's Magazine, | Dear Sir,

I offer the *"Song of the Redwood Tree,"* herewith, for your consideration for the Magazine. The price is $100. If accepted send me a proof here when put in type. If not available would you do me the favor to return the MS. by mail without delay?

Walt Whitman.

I reserve the right to print the piece in future book.

553. *To Daniel G. Gillette*

431 Stevens st. | cor West. | Camden, N. Jersey. | Nov. 4, 1873. My dear Dan Gilette,[53]

Your kind letter—with that of your English friend Chrissie Deschamps, (so full of kindness & affectionate sympathy, plainly enough from the heart, & not conventional merely)—have reached me to-day. I am getting along pretty well. It seems to be a fluctuating & pretty stout struggle between my general physique & constitution, & my special cerebral ailment—in which I think the physique will yet carry the day.

My best regards & love to you, my friend, & to my English friends the same.

Walt Whitman

Dan, it is very lonesome to me here, I go out hobbling a little, but to no satisfaction, although I am very comfortably fixed in domestic matters.

(1874), 366–367. Alden (1836–1919) was managing editor of *Harper's Weekly* from 1863 to 1869 and editor of *Harper's New Monthly Magazine* from 1869 until his death.
    53. See 538. WW consistently dropped an *l* in Gillette.

Write to me when you can, send me any stray printed thing you are sure might interest me, or if you come Philadelphiaward come & see me.

---

554. *To Peter Doyle*   *11.9.* [*1873*]

ADDRESS: Peter Doyle, | M street South, | bet. 4½ &
6th sts. | Washington, | D. C. POSTMARK: Camden |
Nov | 9(?) | N.J.

431 Stevens st. | cor West. | Camden, N. Jersey.
Sunday afternoon, Nov. 9.

Dear son Pete,

By accident your usual letter was not sent to P. O. so that you could get it Saturday—which may have made you some uneasy—but you need not be, as I still continue to hold my own, full as good as at previous advices—I still remain clear of any of those real bad spells of the head—I cannot walk any better yet—but otherwise am getting along *very favorably*—I rec'd your postal card acknowledging the 10. I get out every fair day—shall go out about 4 to visit a family here, Col. Johnston,[54] the jolliest man I ever met, an artist, a great talker, but real, natural, first-rate, off-hand cheerfulness & *comical-sensible* talk—a man of good information too, travelled in Europe—an hour or two does me real good—he has a wife, daughter & son, all good—I go Sunday evenings to tea—Pete, I send you a paper with a piece in about Richmond affairs, manufactures, &c I thought you might like to look over[55]—Here there is great talk of the proposed Centennial Exposition[56]—I will send you pictures of the buildings soon—

I am sitting here in my room, 3d story—We have had quite a storm—but at present the sun shines out, by spells—I am feeling quite comfortable—I would almost think of coming back to Washington—but have learned not to make calculations *too soon* or *too sanguine*—so I shall remain here for the present—If you see Col. Hinton tell him I am getting along favorably—tell him Mr. Linton,[57] the artist, has lately called upon me—tell Hinton to be sure & come and call on me, should he come to Philadelphia—Tell Wash Milburn, & Parker also, I send them my love, & that I shall be back to Washington this winter—tell Parker I was sorry to hear of his illness—

As I write, the wind is crooning and whistling around the house at a great rate—it is a music though I like to hear—

54. See 654. That evening WW gave Mrs. Johnston an inscribed copy of *Drum-Taps* (Trent).
55. An article in the New York *Times* of this date entitled "Attractions of Virginia" discussed the natural resources and industrial development of Richmond. Doyle came from Virginia.
56. The Exposition was held in 1876.

That is a bad business, the shooting of Ryan, and the three good fellows, in Cuba[58]—the Spaniards will probably just keep on at their bloody tricks till the U. S. (& perhaps England) steps in & kicks them out of Cuba—which in my opinion ought to be done without delay—I suppose you knew Ryan by sight, he was around Washington so much—Well, good bye for this time, dear loving boy—

Walt

555. To Peter Doyle   *11.14. [1873]*

431 Stevens st. | cor West. | Camden, | Friday afternoon   Nov. 14.
Dear Pete, dear son,

I am sitting here in my room again writing to you—there is no particular change in the situation—we are having some pretty cold weather here—I go out a little every day, but my walking does not improve any —I had a partially bad spell yesterday afternoon, & did not go out, but it passed over, & to-day I feel as well as I usually have lately—I shall get out this afternoon, & over to the Reading room in Philadelphia—(Looking over the papers, I see occasionally very interesting *news*, about myself— a paper in Salt Lake, Utah, had me dead—& the Philadelphia *Item*, about the same time, had me at a public dinner, in Phil. making a speech.) I rec'd your last. I suppose you got mine last Tuesday—

I have just had my dinner, bean soup, boiled beef, & pumpkin-pie, all good—so you see I might be doing worse—it is now just after 2, & I am feeling quite comfortable—& hope this will find you all right, my loving boy—

Walt.

556. To Peter Doyle   *11.21. [1873]*

431 Stevens st. | cor West. | Camden, N. J. | Nov. 21.
Dear Son Pete,

Nothing very new with me—I continue about the same—my general strength the best it has been yet—I go out a little most every day, but it is very cold weather here—I was quite non-plus'd at that affair in Bergazzi's with Frank Rives[59]—who is he? Is he some one I know? Was he drunk or loony? tell me more of it—what he said—the exact words— It seems unaccountable to me—from what I gather from your letter you did exactly right. If I hadn't met with some queer characters myself—&

---

57. See 438.
58. The New York *Times* on November 9 reported that General Washington Ryan and three Cuban "patriot generals" had been shot by the Spaniards as traitors. An account of Ryan's career with the Cuban insurgents had appeared on the preceding day.
59. Probably Franklin Rives, of F. & J. Rives and George A. Bailey, publishers in Washington. The nature of the barroom brawl (see 557) is not ascertainable.

been the subject of such strange & unaccountable remarks—I should hardly think any thing of the sort possible—

I have occupied myself lately writing—have sent a letter to the Graphic, describing the Capitol, which they have accepted, and may publish Saturday or Monday.[60] Have also written a poem which I have sold[61]—will send you one when it appears. As I write this, holding the paper on my lap, I am sitting here in the parlor, by the heater—have had my dinner—drank quite a goblet of wine, which I believe has flown into my head. (My brother west, & another friend here, have both sent me presents of good wine—& I drink it occasionally, half water—but this time I have taken a little extra)—

Pete, I thought I would send you a couple of shirts—so I have ordered them made here, got as near the measure as I could—they will be done in some ten days, perhaps less, & then I will send them. I like mine so well, I have had yours made like them, with collars on. I have had no new togs made this winter. I wear my old gray suit, & the old black overcoat—& when very cold, or stormy, my gray shawl—If you should see me now leaning against Milburn's counter, you wouldn't *see any difference from last winter*—(but my heart tells a different story)—

I have been in all day, & must get out a little—the evenings are the most tedious with me—I can manage to put in *the days*, but these long *cold evenings*, I think if I only had the right quarters in Washington, *my own quarters & a good wood fire, & you with me* as often as possible, I should be comparatively happy—

Walt—

557. *To Peter Doyle* [11].28. [1873]

431 Stevens st | cor West. | Camden, N. J. | Friday, 28th—2 p. m.
Dear Son Pete,

Here I sit again by the heater in the parlor, writing my weekly letter—I have just had my dinner, some cold turkey & glass of Missouri wine &c.—had been out to the P. O. some five or six squares distant—but have to take my time—Am still getting along very satisfactorily (for I

---

60. "Halls of Gold and Lilac" appeared in the New York *Daily Graphic* on November 24; reprinted in *UPP*, II, 42–49. Editorially the newspaper commented: "Walt Whitman's prose is as remarkable in its way, as is his poetry, and is characterized by the same curious rhythm and same wealth of color. . . . The public will be glad to learn that Mr. Whitman has in a great degree recovered from his recent illness—an illness which had its origin in the exposures undergone by Mr. Whitman in the army, and which at one time threatened his life. Though not yet as strong as he hitherto has been, he is still well enough to resume in a measure his duties at Washington and to wield his pen with as much effectiveness as ever."
61. "Song of the Redwood-Tree"; see 552.
62. The picture and "Matador's" review (excerpted by Bucke, 209–210) occupied

am now satisfied with things not being *very* bad with me)—& my *strength* is undoubtedly better, which, I hope, will in time bring improvement in my walking, & in my head, &c &c—

The letter you spoke of about Penn. av. in the paper was not by me— In the Graphic of Tuesday last, Nov. 25, they print a portrait of my beautiful phiz. & a criticism on my books, one of the best & friendliest I have seen yet[62]—if you can get one in Wash. you will like it—if not you may see it at Graphic office, in Wash—I have not rec'd any. Also Monday's, Nov. 24, *Graphic* prints my letter about the Capitol[63]—Your letter came Tuesday—As I said before, you seem to have done what was unavoidable in the Rives muss—but I have a horror of bar room fracases & fights—& I know you have too—As a general thing, I don't think it necessary to resent the insults of drunkards or fools, (unless there is something unavoidable in the case)—Did you get the *Scottish Chiefs*[64] I sent? Good bye, my dear, loving boy—I am doing quite well—I hope this will find you feeling well in health & jolly in spirits.

Walt

Pete, I will probably send the shirts early next week by express—

558. *To Henry M. Alden*   [11(?). (?). 1873]

DRAFT LETTER.

Please find herewith another poem[65] I have written, the "*Prayer of Columbus*," which I offer for the magazine. If accepted send me word here, & a proof when ready—otherwise, please return me the MS. My price is $60—same reservation as before & same obligation on my part[66]—

559. *To Peter Doyle*   12.5. [1873]

431 Stevens st | cor West | Camden, | Dec. 5—after 12 M

Dear Pete,

I am still holding on about the same—it is pretty certain I don't get behindhand, & that's about the best I can say—continue to get out a little

---

an entire page in the New York *Daily Graphic;* an editorial in the same issue added biographical details, probably supplied by WW, and announced the forthcoming publication of the sixth edition of *Leaves of Grass.*

63. "Halls of Gold and Lilac."

64. *The Scottish Chiefs; A Romance* by the English novelist Jane Porter (1776–1850) was published in 1810; it relates the fortunes of the Scottish patriot William Wallace.

65. WW had submitted "Song of the Redwood-Tree" on November 2; see 552.

66. Alden accepted the poem for *Harper's New Monthly Magazine* on December 1 (Feinberg); it appeared in March, XLVIII (1874), 524–525.

every day when the weather will permit—but my walking power is still very bad indeed—

Pete, I sent the shirts[67] this morning by Adams express—they are enveloped in a flat paper box about 2 feet long by 1 wide—I hope they will get there Saturday—(but possibly may not reach you till Monday)— (You must pay the freight there)—I hope they will fit—the blue one (it wasn't done till last night) is to wear over—I got the stuff, it is first rate Middlesex flannel, cost $5, (same as my summer suits are made of,) is not intended to be washed often—but can be when necessary—must then be washed by some one experienced in washing nice flannels—I sent Graphic with my portrait[68]—(as they sent me some)—also my Capitol letter[69]—I rec'd your good letter last Tuesday—

Dear son, I send you $10 for your Christmas present—perhaps you will need a pair of winter boots, (or some good cotton flannel for under-clothes—or something)—I rec'd a good letter from Mr. Eldridge— Mrs. O'Connor was to come home last Tuesday—I sent a paper to Parker Milburn with my portrait—also to Charley Towner—I hope you carried yours up to Mr. Nash, as I know it would interest & amuse him & Mrs. Nash—give them both my love—(I see just a line in the paper that Mr. Nash had given some reminiscences at a meeting of the Oldest In-habitants)[70]—I see the B & P. RR.[71] had a bad freight car accident last Wednesday night at Patapsco, but no injury to human life or limb—

I have not been quite so well in the head yesterday & to-day—but am around as usual, as it is nothing very heavy—We are having a mild spell here, this is the third day, with partial rain & fog—It is now just after 1— I am sitting here writing this in the parlor by the heater—my dinner is about ready, & I am going—Every thing is very complete & correct here—but O I need your dear loving face & hand & voice—Your old
Walt

560. *To Peter Doyle*   *12.12.* [*1873*]

431 Stevens st. | cor West. | Camden, N. J. | Dec. 12.
Dear boy Pete,

I felt bad enough to hear of the death of Bill Barnes[72]—& in such a sudden, cruel way—poor young man—he has had a reckless unsatis-

---

67. See 556.   68. See 557.

69. "Silver and Salmon-Tint," like "Halls of Gold and Lilac" a description of the Capitol, was published on November 29; it is reprinted in *UPP*, II, 49–53.

70. On December 4 the Washington *Daily Morning Chronicle* noted Nash's speech before the Oldest Inhabitants' Association.

factory life—many deficiencies & very shiftless—all of which I understood perfectly well—but I had an affection for him after all—Have I not heard that he had a wife & child? which, (if so,) he has left—but was parted from quite a while ago—

Pete, so your shirts came all safe, & they fit you, do they? Good—The blue shirt (did I write?) is to wear *over*, loose—it is made large for that purpose—I like the looks of them, the blue shirt collar turned down low with a nice black silk neck-handkerchief, tied loose—over a clean white shirt without necktie—I think they are very becoming to young workingmen—I sent 3 Graphics to Mr. & Mrs. Nash—when you hear, tell me if they came safe. I send you some papers to-day—

There is nothing new with me, or my condition—My principal malady is about the same, (no worse)—but I have had for three or four days a wretched cold in the head, sore throat, most lost my voice for two days—every thing bad enough—am better rather to-day, begin to speak so I can be understood—shall be all right soon—

As I write, it is now between 11 and 12 a. m. Friday—it is very mild, sunshiny forenoon—I am sitting here in the parlor—looks south, looks down a pleasant street, West street, full view, makes quite a nice view for me to sit & look out—the letter carrier comes around in about an hour from now, & takes my letters to p. o.—I have become sort of acquainted with most of the carriers, ferry men, car conductors & drivers, &c. &c.—they are very good indeed—help me on & off the cars, here & in Philadelphia—they are nearly all young fellows—it all help[s] along—Well, Pete, dear loving boy, I will bid you good bye for this week.

Walt.

561. *To Peter Doyle*   *12.19. [1873]*

ADDRESS: Peter Doyle | M street south, | bet. 4½ & 6th | Washington, | D. C. POSTMARK: Camden | Dec | 19 | N.J.

431 Stevens st. | cor West. | Camden, N. J.
12 M Friday   Dec. 19.

Dear boy Pete,

Well, I am sitting here in the parlor again writing my weekly letter —as I write, the rain is pouring & it is a thick & dark day enough—I am

---

71. Baltimore and Potomac Railroad.

72. On December 8 the Washington *Daily Morning Chronicle* reported the death of Barnes in an accident on the Baltimore and Potomac Railroad four days earlier.

feeling pretty bad, but it seems to be mostly from a severe cold in the head
—anyhow I am having one of my bad spells, of which I have gone
through so many—had a bad night last night—but have eat my breakfast
this morning, & have no doubt I shall feel better before many days. Pete,
I rec'd your letter & the Herald last Monday all right. Did Mr & Mrs.
Nash get the 3 Graphics I sent them?

I have been out most every day the past week, & been across the river
to Philadelphia—it has been a very pleasant week, & I have enjoyed sailing
across the Delaware, & the splendid sunsets most every evening—it is my
greatest enjoyment—

Pete, all you write about folks & things in Washington is interesting to
me—it will be read, every thing you scratch down, as I sit here a great
deal of the time, (& time is dull & lonesome, at the best)—

My pieces I have written (I believe I mentioned about it,) have not yet
appeared in the Magazine[73]—but the money has been paid me for them,
& they are in type, & I have read the proofs—I will either send them to
you, when printed, or send you word, so you can get them yourself—Did
I send you *both* my letters about the Capitol in the *Graphic?*[74] I believe
I did, but if not I can yet—I send you to-day's Phil. *Press*—nothing special in it—Well, good bye for this time, dear loving boy,

Walt.

Pete, how about running on here to see me for a day or two? Couldn't
you come, convenient, say latter part of next week? If you can, I will fix
the time—

562. *To Peter Doyle*[75]   *12.26.* [*1873*]

431 Stevens st. | cor West | Camden | N. J. | Dec. 26—Noon.
Dear boy Pete,

I have been looking for you the last two days & nights—but I have
about given you up now. I have been kept in pretty close, as we have
had real winter here, snow & bad weather, & bad walking—I have been
quite alone, as my brother & sister went off to Delaware on Wednesday on
a Christmas visit, to return to-morrow, Saturday—I am about the same—
My strength still keeps quite encouraging—I think is better than any

73. "Song of the Redwood-Tree" and "Prayer of Columbus."
74. "Halls of Gold and Lilac" and "Silver and Salmon-Tint."
75. The year is confirmed by the reference to George's visit to Delaware, also mentioned in 565.
76. This letter is apparently lost.
77. The London agents for his books. On April 13, 1874, in a letter not presently
available, WW acknowledged receipt of $41.54 from Trübner & Company.
78. A New York bookseller at 39 Dey Street. WW was having difficulties—real or
imaginary, as his mother might have said—with booksellers. When WW wrote this let-

time yet—my walking no better, & still a good deal of distress in the head—but, as I said in my letter of Monday last,[76] (did you get it Tuesday?)—I somehow feel a little more like myself than any time since I was taken down—your last letter was quite a treat—so much about Washington, & folks, one thing & another—As I write I sit here in the parlor—we have had an awful time from the fire going out in the heater, & making it up again—there is so much complicated machinery about one of these heaters with all the late improvements—give me my old stove & wood fire yet—It is snowing by fits here this morning.

Walt

563. *To Messrs. Trübner & Company*

DRAFT LETTER.

431 Stevens st. | Camden, New Jersey. | U. S. America. Messrs. Trübner & Company,[77] | Dear Sirs,

Please make out acc't of sales of my books, *Leaves of Grass* &c. for the closing year, & remit me am't due, by mail here, by draft payable to my order.

Respectfully, &c.

Walt Whitman

Dec. 27, | 1873.

564. *To Asa K. Butts & Company*

DRAFT LETTER.

431 Stevens st. | cor West. | Camden, [N. J.] | Dec. 29, '73. A. K. Butts,[78] | Dear Sir,

Yours of 26th rec'd. It looks like something beginning to be done. About Piper's[79] bill you can wait till you go personally to Boston.

I have written to O'Kane[80] to-day, & I hope you will have no further difficulty in getting the books—I have requested him to send word to you to come & get them. If we get started in the way we talked of, (& I have no doubt we shall,) & satisfaction is felt on both sides, it is certainly my

ter, he had decided to let Butts, as he said, "have actual & complete control of the sales." Commenting on one of the letters to Butts, WW observed to Traubel in 1889: "What a sweat I used to be in all the time . . . over getting my damned books published! When I look back at it I wonder I didn't somewhere or other on the road chuck the whole business into oblivion" (III, 561). Butts went bankrupt in 1874.

79. The Boston agents for WW's books; see 413. Evidently Piper settled the bill in February; see 581.

80. See 535. The letter to O'Kane is not known.

intention that you shall have actual & complete control of the sales—& all supplies.

565. *To Charles W. Eldridge*   *12.29. [1873]*
TRANSCRIPT.

431 Stevens St. | cor. West. | Camden, N. J. | Dec. 29.

Dear Charley,

I am getting along favorably—looking on the sunny side of the case, I am probably better now than at any time since I was paralyzed—(though bad enough yet.) My improvement is not much in the head troubles, & hardly any in my left leg, but very perceptible in my strength & vim generally—& in my confidence (still unaffected in the main, by all the tediousness of hope deferred again & again) that, for all I am in the woods yet, *I shall emerge* & see light again. It was *to Harpers* I sold at handsome prices my pieces—(I sent a second one which, like the first, they took, at my own price at once & sent me the money)—They are in type, and I have read the proofs. So they are off my mind. One is called "Song of the Redwood tree," (California) & one the "Prayer of Columbus"—When they will appear I don't know, but suppose soon—take this to Nelly.

Nelly, my dear, I received your welcome letter last evening. I am waiting for the photos of my St. Louis Nieces to be returned from an old grandaunt of mine (92 years old),[81] mother's mother's sister, who wanted to see them in N. Y., & then I will send them to you. I spent Christmas alone here, as my brother and sister had gone down for three days on a visit to Delaware—I am in good heart. We shall yet meet, Nelly dear.

Walt

I send a P. O. Order for $30. for Godey—I sent him $20 on the 23rd.

566. *To Abby H. Price*   *[1873?]*[82]
DRAFT LETTER.

Mrs. A. H. Price | 331 East 55th st. N. Y. City

I have had a very bad spell, but am now about as before. Recovery yet probable, & a visit to you.

W. W.

431 Stevens st.
Camden, N. J.

81. Sally Mead; see 493.
82. Written on the verso of "A Word for Dead Soldiers," this draft letter is a rephrased version of an item intended for a newspaper.

1874

567. *To Peter Doyle*[1]   *1.2.* [*1874*]

431 Stevens st. | cor West. | Camden, N. J. | Jan 2—12 M.
Dear boy,

I am about the same—consider myself improving, if any thing, though slowly enough—Pete, I will get you the Dictionary, I will see about it soon. You spoke about the post of baggage master on the through New York train—& the appointment being in Philadelphia. Who appoints them? Tell me more fully about it in your next. I got your last letter, & several papers. To-day I have rec'd a letter from Charles Eldridge—We have had a long rainy & dark time here, but mild—no snow on the ground now—I go out—as I write, the trains are going by about 400 feet off, ringing & smoking—there are 20 a day in full view from here.

Walt.

I send you a picture for your New Years.

568. *To Peter Doyle*   *1.9.* [*1874*]

431 Stevens st. | cor West | Camden, | Jan 9.

Well, Pete, my dear loving boy, I have just come in from a 15 minutes walk outside, with my little dog—it is now ½ past 1 Friday afternoon—the bright sun shining, & the air & every thing as pleasant as one could wish—(after most a week of rainy, dark, & disagreeable but warmish weather)—I have the same old story to tell—& thankful enough to have nothing worse to communicate—it is probable I am really slowly gaining—though I have occasional bad spells yet.

Your letter was received—I was thinking whether something could not be done about getting the position of through baggage master—& feel inclined to try for you—(You know there is nothing of that sort done without trying)—Did you get the story "Rolling Stone,"[2] I sent by p. o.? I have had a visitor from New York this forenoon—an old acquaintance, a

---

1874

    1. I have accepted the dates assigned by WW's executors to the correspondence addressed to Doyle in January: all except one of the letters were written on Fridays, and most of them referred to Doyle's search for another position on the railroad.

    2. George Sand's *A Rolling Stone* was translated by Carroll Owen and published in 1871.

printer & foreman, I knew 20 years ago, very sickly & expecting to die, at that time—*now* quite lively & well, really jolly & magnetic, & good company & a good fellow, (like Parker Milburn)—I have an occasional visitor, but not many—Pete, if you see any body coming to Phil. you think I would like to see, give 'em my address—I am glad to see most any one for a change—

Your old Walt

569. *To Abby H. and Helen Price*   [*1.11(?). 1874*][3]

ADDRESS: Miss Helen Price | 331 East 55th street, | New York City. POSTMARK: Camden | Jan | (?) | N.J.

431 Stevens st. | cor West, | Camden, N. Jersey,
Sunday afternoon—4½

Dear Abby, & Dear Helen, not forgetting Emmy, & all

As I am sitting here alone in the parlor, the sun near setting pleasantly & brightly, (though cold to-day,) I just think that I ought to write you, even if but a line—that I am neglecting you—that perhaps you will be glad enough to hear from me. Well, I am still here—still alive, after quite a many pretty hard pulls & pressures—maintain pretty good spirits—which *would* be, quite *first-rate & good*—but every day & every night comes the thought of my mother—I am not despondent or blue, nor disposed to be any more *ennuyeed* than ever—but that thought remains to temper the rest of my life.

I am probably improving, though very slowly—go out a little most every day—go over to Philadelphia—get along pretty well in the cars & crossing the ferry. (The car fellows & ferrymen are very kind & helpful—almost all know me, I suppose instinctively)—appetite fair—rest at night tolerable—general strength better than at any time—(it is now just a year since I was paralyzed.) Can't use my left leg yet with any freedom —bad spells in the head too frequent yet—then, with all those, I am certainly encouraged to believe I am on the gain. (But I am not out of the woods yet.) I write some—(must occupy my mind.) I am writing some pieces in the *Weekly Graphic*—my reminiscences of war times—first num-

3. On the basis of the reference to his illness and the appearance of articles in the New York *Weekly Graphic*, January 11, a Sunday, appears to be a plausible date; January 18, however, cannot be ruled out.
4. "'Tis But Ten Years Since" appeared in the New York *Weekly Graphic* from January 24 to March 7. For a discussion of these articles, see Thomas O. Mabbott and Rollo G. Silver, AL, xv (1943), 51–62. Later these articles appeared in *Memoranda During the War*.
5. The word was underscored twice.
6. The executors assigned this date, which is confirmed by the description of his health and his newspaper series.

ber appears in *Weekly Graphic* of Jan. 24[4]—three or four others to follow—

We are in the new house my brother has built—very nice. I find myself *very*[5] *lonesome* here, for all social & emotional consolation—(Man cannot live on *bread alone*—can he?)—I want to come & see you—*must* do so before long—want to pay a moderate board, (same as I do here,) if convenient for you to have me—*Shall not come on any other condition*—Well, Abby, I have just *skurried* rapidly over the sheet, & will send it to you just as it is, with love.

Walt Whitman

570. *To Peter Doyle*   [*1.16. 1874*][6]

431 Stevens st | cor West. | Camden, N. J.
Friday forenoon 11½

Well, son, how do you make out this cold weather?—for I suppose you are having it there as we are here—we had quite a snow storm here three or four nights ago, & since then it has cleared off bitter cold—(thermometer at 10 above, an hour ago, at our west door.) Still I go out some, though very stiff—& lately some spells in my head rather bad & queer. What I have said in former letters about my general strength still holds good—otherwise I am in a bad way yet, & dont consider myself out of the woods, have not been so well as usual the last week—

If you come across the *Weekly Graphic* just out get it, as I have commenced a series of pieces about things just before & during the war.[7] The series is to continue through four or five numbers. Get one for Mr. & Mrs. Nash—Pete, I rec'd the "Golden Grain"[8]—also the letter, Herald, & *Repub*[*lican*]—send me one of *the latter*, occasionally—I had rather have it than any—(but you needn't put yourself out to get it)—As I write the sun is shining bright & clear as can be—the ground is white with snow in all directions, it is not melting anywhere—as I crossed the river yesterday toward dusk, the old fellow, the chargè of the ferry house, told me that between 12 & 2 o'clock the previous night over 30 persons crowded in there, poor houseless creatures, to keep from freezing to death—he

---

7. " 'Tis But Ten Years Since."
8. Timothy Shay Arthur's *Golden Grains from Life's Harvest Field* (1853) is a collection of awesomely sentimental anecdotes in awesome prose, the type of tritely "moral" work likely to appeal to Doyle: "Golden Grains from Life's Harvest Field, what are they but good and true principles, pure affections and human sympathies, gathered by the mind as it passes through its fields of labor? . . . A handful or two have we shaken from the full ears, and now present them to our readers. May the offering bear with it strength to the weak and the tempted, comfort to those who are in affliction, and good impulses to all."

keeps a great stove red-hot all night—some were young, some old, some evidently real respectable people—the orders are to not allow it, but he hadn't the heart to turn 'em out—God help the homeless & moneyless this weather—

Walt

571. *To Ellen M. O'Connor*   [*1.16.1874*][9]

ENDORSED: "Ans'd." ADDRESS: Mrs. E. M. O'Connor, | 1015 O street, n. w. | Washington, | D. C. POSTMARKS: Philadelphia | Jan | 1(?) | 1CR(?) | Pa.; Carrier | 17 | Jan | 6 AM.

431 Stevens st. | cor West. | Camden, N. Jersey,
7½ Friday evening.

Dear Nelly,

Your letter came with the sad news of good Mr. Dille's[10] death—I had seen it in the paper—I have thought much of it, through the interesting account you gave—Indeed death has been much in my quiet thoughts & musings now for many months.

Nelly, there is nothing very new to write you—I have not been so well the past week—but feel better this evening. I still have spells of great distress in the head—though they pass over—Walking no better—but *general strength* seems to steadily though very slowly improve—

I am writing some war memoranda in the *Weekly N. Y. Graphic* first number just out—ask Charley to get it for you—In my next—anent of Bull Run—I mention Mrs. Johnson[11] & her sister, (though not by name) —will be out next Thursday—

Nelly, I am scratching this off at the Mercantile Library in 10th st. Philadelphia (though I date home in Camden) & will have to close to get it in the box in time for the carrier.

Love to you, dear, dear Nelly—

Walt.

572. *To Peter Doyle*   *1.19.* [*1874*]

431 Stevens st | cor West. | Camden, N. Jersey | Jan. 19.
Monday noon

Dear loving Son,

I rec'd your letter this forenoon. Pete, I thought I would send you a little change enclosed—all I have by me to-day—(but I have plenty at my

---

9. The envelope and the contents confirm the date.
10. Israel Dille, clerk in the Internal Revenue Bureau.
11. Probably Mrs. Nancy M. Johnson, a widow; see February 24, 1876.
12. The date is established by his allusion in the final paragraph to his paralysis.

command)—It is wet & foggy to-day, and a glaze of ice everywhere—so I am compelled to remain in. I am feeling decidedly better the last 24 hours—Am surely getting through the winter very well—guess I shall come out with the frogs & lilacs in the spring—I keep a bully good heart, take it altogether—& you must too, my darling boy.

Walt

573. *To Peter Doyle* [1.23. 1874][12]

431 Stevens st. | Cor West. | Camden, | N. Jersey, | Friday, 1½ p. m.
Dear Boy Pete,

Your letter came Wednesday—You must try to cultivate & keep up a gay & cheerful heart, & shed off botherations, & the impositions of employers, &c. as a duck sheds water in a rain storm—that's the best capital a fellow can have through his whole life, I find.

I am only so-so—had a very bad night last night—it's a tough pull, Pete—still I think I shall come out of it—We are having it very mild here now—after snow & cold the first of the week—too mild, like April to-day, cloudy & some rain. I keep myself some busy writing—have a piece in Harpers' Monthly just out (February)—shall have another in the March number[13]—

Can't seem to do, without occupying my mind through the day—nights are worst for me—I cant rest well—have been so now for a month—But I must not fill my letter with my complaints—

To-day is just a Year, since I was paralyzed, (23d Jan. '73)—What a year it has been to me—Good bye, my loving boy—write me all the news & gossip.

Walt

574. *To Rudolf Schmidt*

Jan. 25, '74

My dear Rudolf Schmidt,

Your letter of Jan. 2[14] has just reached me here. I am always glad to get word from you. Write oftener. I have been very ill—now just a year—from paralysis & *cerebral anæmia*. I have been at death's door myself—& during the year have lost my dear mother & a dear sister by death.

---

13. "Song of the Redwood-Tree" and "Prayer of Columbus."
14. Schmidt reported that the first part of his translation of *Democratic Vistas* had gone to the printers: "It is a devilish hard task to translate your prose, and our ordinary translators most surely would break the neck in trying it" (Feinberg; Traubel, III, 361).

I sent you a newspaper, with account, five months since, but as you do not allude to it I suppose you did not receive it. I send another by this mail. (I have sent you several papers & magazines the past year.) I am not in bed but up & dressed, & go out a little every day, & shall probably get well again—But I remain paralyzed yet—walk with difficulty & very little—have bad spells in my head—& ameliorate very slowly—Still I write & publish a little—Mental faculties not affected.

I have at present no thought of visiting England.[15] In a letter two years since Tennyson kindly invited me to come to his house[16]—which aroused some thought & wish for a time—but it has passed away.

What have I heard about some great German University, proposing for one of its prizes, for some annual or bi-annual literary *fête*, the question, *Has America really produced any real poet?* Have you heard any thing of such a discussion?

What about Bjornson? Is he coming to America? If so, give him my address, & tell him to come & see me. (It is almost a part of Philadelphia, where I now live—on the opposite side of the Delaware river.)

When you write, or send me (the Danish) Democratic Vistas, direct here. Write me from Germany,

Walt Whitman
431 Stevens street,
Camden, N. Jersey.
U. S. America.

(I have not given up my place in the Solicitor's office, Washington—but keep up communication—& if I get well, expect to go back there)—I want to hear all about Bjornson—

575. *To Peter Doyle*   *1.30.* [*1874*]

ADDRESS: Pete Doyle, | M street south, | bet 4½ &
6th | Washington, | D. C. POSTMARK: Philadelphia |
Jan | 30 | 10 PM | Pa.

431 Stevens st. | cor West. | Camden, N. Jersey
Friday afternoon   Jan 30,   2 o'clock
Dear Pete,

I am having another of my bad spells to-day—but it will pass over—I have had a pretty good time most of the week till last night—thought I was getting decidedly better—(& guess I am yet, & that this will pass over.)

Every thing goes on the same with me here. As I write this, I am sitting

15. Schmidt had been told by "an American gentleman" that WW was going to England.

here alone as usual in the parlor by the heater—I have just been out, but it was so chilly & raw, I didn't venture off the block, but came back in 5 or 6 minutes—the air feels like snow.

The trains of the Camden & Amboy are going by on the track about 50 or 60 rods from here, puffing & blowing—often train after train, following each other—& locomotives singly, whisking & squealing, up the track & then down again—I often sit here & watch them long—& think of you.

I think I shall try again to get out, evening—sometimes it makes me feel better, after I get out in the open air, & move around a little—

7:15 evening—Friday—

I am writing this over in the Mercantile Library, 10th st. Phila.— I have felt better since 4 o'clock & have come out & crossed the river, & taken quite a ride up Market st. 2 miles in the Market st. cars. The cars are very nice, old style, cushioned, fare 7 cents—if you get a transfer you have to pay extra—the working hours are from 16½ to 18—they have the new alarm punch, every fare or ticket, rings a little bell every time you punch—I suppose you have seen it—they say it is quite a success, & they are introducing them in other cities—but it will get played out—

Pete, write how you are getting along—& all about the folks, every one I know—I am feeling as well as usual, as I finish this letter— Good bye for this time, my loving son—

Walt—

Dont you get discouraged at work—or on the road—I feel that we shall yet be together, & have good times just being with each other, no matter how poor—

576. *To Ellen M. O'Connor* 2.3. *[1874]*

ENDORSED: "Ans'd." ADDRESS: Mrs. E. M. O'Connor, | 1015 O street | near 11th N. W. | Washington, | D. C. POSTMARK: Camden | Feb | 3 | N.J.

431 Stevens st. | cor West. | Camden, N. Jersey,
Tuesday noon, Feb. 3.

Dear Nelly,

I sent you the Weekly Graphic No. 2 yesterday—wish you to take an opportunity, when convenient, & loan it to those two dear ladies, Mrs.

16. See 394.

Johnson & her sister mentioned in my article[17]—& please give them my best remembrances. Dear Nelly, how are you getting along, this winter? —We have just had a snow storm here—cold & white, as I look out, and the sleigh-bells occasionally jingling by—I am sitting here alone in the parlor by the heater, as I write. I am alone most of the time, (to all intents & purposes.)

I feel that I am better, in the main—yet still have daily & nightly bad spells in the head, & my leg most of the time disabled as ever. In fact not much different from the same old story—(yet certainly a good streak, or vein, of encouragement, & feeling of encouragement—maintaining it-self—accumulating—never more than temporarily leaving me.) I even begin to think about coming back to Washington & trying it again.

Nelly, I sent a P. O. check for $50 to Charley last Friday to pay my young man[18]—havn't rec'd any word from Charley yet, up to this present writing[19]—hope it came safe—may hear from him, this afternoon or to-morrow. Charley is always so prompt in responding. I hear regularly from Peter Doyle—he is well & hearty, works hard for poor pay, on the Balt & Potomac RR., works nights a great deal. He writes me regularly every week. I have been waiting ever since I wrote,[20] to get the photos. of my nieces, (my dear sister Mat's girls,) returned from New York, & send them to you—but have not yet got them. Shall write for them. My "song of *the redwood tree*," in last Harpers is copied a little, & abused & sneered at in the newspaper criticisms, a good deal, (from what I glean)—*of course*, that last makes me feel *very bad*—I expect to have another piece in February[21] Harpers—(but am not certain)—"prayer of Columbus"—as I see it now I shouldn't wonder if I have unconsciously put a sort of auto-biographical dash in it—Nelly dear, write oftener—put in all the gossip & items that will be next best to seeing you—do you see Dr. Drinkard—I sent Garaphelia Howard[22] a paper, the Graphic[23] that has my picture—how is she? Is she married? Give her my love—Poor, good Mr. Dille—yet amid all its sombreness & terror how blessed to die "by touch ethereal," painless, instantaneous—Nelly, death has become to me a familiar thing —Yet, as I sit here writing, I do not feel a particle less of life in me, than ever.

God bless you, dear, dear Nelly.

Walt

17. See 571.   18. Walter Godey, WW's substitute.
19. Eldridge wrote later in the week; see 578.
20. See 565.
21. WW meant the March issue, in which "Prayer of Columbus" appeared.
22. Probably the "Miss Howard" mentioned in 149.
23. The New York *Daily Graphic* of November 25, 1873.

577. *To Asa K. Butts & Company*

ENDORSED: "To | A. K. Butts | 36 Dey st | N. Y."
DRAFT LETTER.

Camden, Feb. 4 '74

Beyond O'Kane's copies of Leaves of Grass (200 or about), and the copies (27 was it?) of the '67 edition you got of Shephard,[24] four or five weeks ago—with the remaining copies (if any) of the 25 sent by my order two months since to Piper & Co.—*there are, positively, no other copies in existence, & of course none in the market.* There are no other copies in N. Y.—none in Boston—none in Washington—whatever you were "told" —none *anywhere* in America. A hundred copies were sent by me to England about a year & a half ago.[25] But these have certainly been mostly sold. I made & exclusively own the plates, & of course [*indecipherable*].

What I told you in our interview, upon that subject, you must remember, & can fully depend on & act on. I have somewhere between 300 & 350 of my little book of later poems, "As a Strong Bird on Pinions free," bound & ready, I should like to furnish you with—

Should be willing—guaranteeing the just mentioned—to make over the whole of the copies L of G. and every thing to you on liberal terms, one half cash down, the remainder in three months—with a guarantee that no new edition of L of G. or any of these books shall be put out for at least six months. If you care to have the *sole & exclusive* command of all my books in existence, take this offer. I am sick & paralyzed—a tedious prospect still before me—& should be glad to have the books off my hands.

About Piper's debt, take *this* note & collect it when you go to Boston. The one I furnished you with, is for a wrong am't. Destroy it.

Please get the books from O'Kane, soon as convenient, & send me receipt specifying number—also receipt for those of ed. '67.

Order on Piper enclosed.

A. K. Butts & co. 36 Day st. N. Y. have had, & have to acc't to me for,

27.	Leaves of Grass ⎫	Mr. Butts got from Lee, Shepherd & Dill
	ed. 1867— ⎬	49 Greene st. as per letter Dec. 26 '73,
9	Drum Taps ⎭	from Mr. Butts.

24. Lee, Shepard, & Dillingham; see also 498.

25. Redfield sent *Democratic Vistas* and *Leaves of Grass* to Sampson, Low & Co., London booksellers. According to a statement dated December 31, 1872, the firm had on hand at that time 48 copies of the prose tract and 41 copies of the poetry (Feinberg). According to a notation in the *Commonplace Book*, the account was closed in 1876, when the firm sent $9 to WW through Rossetti (Feinberg). Trübner also had copies: see 563.

got from O'Kane Feb. 3, '74

168   Leaves of Grass

86   Democratic Vistas

?94   As a Strong Bird

42   Notes on W. W. as Poet & Person

18   Passage to India

2   After All not to Create Only[26]

see his letter Feb. 4 '74

578. *To Peter Doyle*   2.6. *[1874]*

431 Stevens st. | cor West. | Camden, N. Jersey,
Friday noon—Feb. 6.

Dear boy Pete,

Both your letters came this week—also one from my friend Eldridge, he too speaks of meeting & talking with you. It is real winter here, the ground all covered with snow, as I look out—not the least thaw to-day, as it is cloudy—I rise pretty late mornings—had my breakfast a little while ago, mutton-chop, coffee, nice brown bread & sweet butter, very nice—eat with very fair appetite—I enjoy my breakfast better than any other meal—(eat a light dinner pretty late, & no supper)—Feel generally about the same as before described—no worse, no better, (nothing to brag of anyhow)—

I have mentioned about my crossing the ferry—from our house, the cars run by the next corner, (200 feet, or less,) a half mile or so to the ferry—the Delaware here is full three quarters of a mile wide—it is a noble river, not so wide as the Potomac, nor with the fine banks like Arlington, but grander, & with more style, & with powerful, rushing tides, now great processions of broken ice, many little & some great big cakes—the boats are very fine & strong, go crashing right ahead, with a loud noise, breaking the cakes often a foot thick & more—I enjoy crossing these days—it does me good—the ferrymen are all very kind & respectful—

I have been reading a book *"Merrie England in the Olden Time,"*[27]

26. In 1875 Charles P. Somerby (see April 23, 1876), bookseller and publisher, assumed the liabilities of Butts & Co. According to a statement dated May 12, 1876, WW received credit on January 5, 1874, for merchandise valued at $46.58, and on February 3, 1874, at $314.82 (Feinberg). In 698 WW declared that his three New York agents (O'Kane, Butts, and Somerby) "had embezzled the proceeds."

27. By George Daniel (1789–1864), published in 1842, with illustrations by John Leech and Robert Cruikshank. The book contains familiar lore about old England related with gusto and sentimentality by a Dickensian character named Uncle Timothy.

28. See also 605.

a London book, with pictures, full of fun & humor—I have enjoyed it much—There is an awful amount of want & suffering, from no work, hereabout—a young man was here yesterday—had seen me in Wash-[ington]—wanted help—I gave him a little—I see the cars & locomotive skurrying by as I close.

Walt

579. *To Asa K. Butts & Company*

ENDORSED: "To A. K. Butts." DRAFT LETTER.

Camden | Feb. 8, '74.

O'Kane has undoubtedly sent you *all* the copies of my books remaining in his possession—he received originally (April 28 '73 from Doolady,)[28]

239 Leaves of Grass,
100 As a strong Bird,[29]
 92 Democratic Vistas,
 45 Notes by John Burroughs, &c.

And since then he has delivered about 30 Leaves of Grass to my order—leaving only 30 or 40 more to be accounted for as sales &c. so that, as just said, he has unquestionably *retained none* in his possession. As said in my note, you now, (with the exception of about 350 copies of *As A Strong Bird*, which are at my printer's[30] in N. Y., & which I can send you an order for,) you now have *all* my books in the market. (The edition you have, L. of G., only consisted of 500 copies, when issued, over a year & a half ago.)

Will write you again early this week, anent of your yesterday's letter, offer, &c.[31]

580. *To Ellen M. O'Connor*   2.11. [1874][32]

ENDORSED: "Ans'd." ADDRESS: Mrs. E. M. O'Connor, | 1015 O st—near 11th N. W. | Washington, | D. C. POSTMARK: Philadelphia | Feb | 11 | 11 PM | Pa.

29. According to a receipt in the Feinberg Collection, Doolady received 100 copies of *As a Strong Bird on Pinions Free* from S. W. Green on February 25, 1873.

30. S. W. Green, according to a receipt in the Feinberg Collection, had 572 copies of the poem on July 12, 1872. At that time WW owed Green $175, evidently for printing this poem as well as other works, the names of which are indecipherable. On the verso of the receipt Green noted that WW had paid $100 on July 20, 1872, and in a letter on August 9 he acknowledged payment of $50 (Feinberg).

31. Butts's letter is lost.

32. The allusion to Townsend's death establishes the year.

431 Stevens st. | cor West. | Camden, N. Jersey,
Feb. 11, 4 p. m.

Dear Nelly,

Your letter of yesterday came this morning. Yours of 5th came safe—Sunday night late, (on returning from spending the evening, so you see I gad about *some*—)[33] I found it waiting for me, & read it all through. Both letters are welcome. Thank you particularly for the slip from the *Nation*,[34] which I had not seen nor heard of. Nelly, I looked some five or six weeks ago for Mrs. Banfield's letter—& now day before yesterday a second hunt—but cannot find it, & fear it has been destroyed or lost—I am distressed that I cannot find & return it, as I know you think so much of your friend's letters—(Besides moving in this house from the former one—I have twice hurriedly destroyed a large mass of letters & MSS.—to be ready for what might happen)[35]—

I am indeed interested in what you write about Mrs. Huntington[36]—it does not surprise me that she meets emergencies, &c. so splendidly & expands to greater womanly beauty & development—I always thought it in her to do so—Nelly, when you next see her give her my love—I return Willie's[37] picture—dear child—it has pleased me much—I held it a long time in my hand & thought of H street—

Nelly, I think very highly everyway of little Harold's[38] picture—it is, to begin with, one of the best photos ever taken, & it seems so beautiful, & a real *man-child*—I liked it much, & have always kept it where I could see it. (Nelly, did you wish me to return it? I have overlooked—or forgotten—any request to that effect in the letter sending it)—

I send my love to Mrs. Brownell—also to Garry Howard[39] when you see her—(what you say of her in your letter I fully endorse as my mature conviction—she is a good, tender girl—true as steel.) Nelly dear, I am guiltless of the cologne present—(don't know any thing about Peter Doyle, in this case)—

Dear Nelly, I feel that you are—or have been—under the depressing influences of Mr Dilles's and Mr. Townsend's[40] deaths—If it were eligible you should come frequently & spend the days with *me*, to cheer you up—meantime take early opportunities to get a change of scene of surroundings—& often—

---

33. WW visited the Johnstons on Sunday; see 654. Once again his life fell into a pattern; in Washington he had visited the O'Connors on Sunday.

34. See 582.

35. WW's statement explains why letters from Eldridge, Doyle, Mrs. O'Connor, and others are not extant.

36. Perhaps the widow of William S. Huntington (see 439), or the widow of Joshua, a clerk in the Third Auditor's office.

37. Probably Mrs. Huntington's son.

It is very fine here, to-day—I have been hobbling out—plenty of snow on the ground—but air, sun & sky delightful—

Walt

nearly 5— It is near sundown, very fine, & I am going out—as I like to be on the river, (on those strong boats crashing through the ice now plentiful on the Delaware)—I shall probably cross to Phil—& mail this letter thence.

581. *To Peter Doyle*   *2.13.* [*1874*]

431 Stevens st. | cor West. | Camden, | N. Jersey,
Feb. 13, 2½ p. m.

Dear Pete,

Here I am yet, in my big chair in the parlor—I am up & around, but not very well—I am having a return, (though not so severe,) of those old *blurs* that used to trouble me—have had a succession of them all day to-day so far—begun yesterday—but I have no doubt they will pass over. It is cloudy & sulky here to-day, partially thawing—& is raining now— I have been out, managed to walk round the block, but had to return— did not feel well. Pete, there is nothing new—I got your last letter—have rec'd letters from Mrs. O'Connor—I have no doubt I shall feel better— my sickness comes & goes—& my relief spells the same—I shall probably have to stay in the rest of the day & evening—which is very dull & stupid for me—in fact quite dismal—But I must not write what will make you blue—would rather cheer you up—I am still continuing the pieces in the Weekly Graphic[41]—(will be ended with one or two more)—expect to have a piece[42] in next Harper, (March) but am not certain—

Just as I close, the carrier has tapped at the window—he brings me a letter from Boston,[43] & in it a check paying a debt due me a long time, & which I had quite given up—which puts me in better spirits—good bye for present, my dear loving son—

Your Walt

38. Not identified.   39. See 576.
40. Henry Townsend, an employee in the First Auditor's office, died on February 7; he lived at 1013 O Street, next door to Mrs. O'Connor.
41. " 'Tis But Ten Years Since."   42. "Prayer of Columbus."
43. Probably a payment from William H. Piper, Boston bookseller, a debt which WW had authorized Butts to collect; see 577.

582. *To John Burroughs*   *2.[14. 1874]*

ADDRESS: John Burroughs, | Wallkill Bank |
Middletown | New York. POSTMARK: Camden |
Feb | 14 | N.J.

431 Stevens st. | cor West. | Camden, N. J. | Feb.
Dear John Burroughs,
     I enclose you an article from the *Nation* of Jan. 29. How will the
MS. article I have scratched off, do, in the main, as an answer to it? (to
help keep the pot a-boiling.) Do you feel like making up an article out of
said MS—adding or excising what you see fit—signing your name to it
—& sending to Mr. Nation man?⁴⁴—

583. *To Peter Doyle*   *[2.20. 1874]*⁴⁵

ADDRESS: Pete Doyle, | M street South, | bet 4½ &
6th, | Washington, | D. C. POSTMARK: Camden |
Feb | 20 | N.J.

431 Stevens st. | cor West. | Camden, | N. Jersey,
Friday afternoon—2½
Dear boy Pete,
     Well, Pete, dear son, I have just had my dinner (stewed chicken
& onions—good,) & here I sit again in the same old chair, in the parlor,
writing my weekly screed to you—Nothing to brag of, this week—have
passed a disagreeable week—mainly, I suppose, from a bad, bad cold in
the head—have suffered badly from it, every way—but keep up and
around—& shall get through with it, when the time comes—
     Have not written any for publication the past fortnight—have not felt
at all like writing—My *Weekly Graphic* pieces are about concluded—
(the next week's, the 6th number, ends them—I am just reading the last
proof to-day)—I have a poem⁴⁶ in the March *Harper* as I believe I
mentioned in my last. (I am told that I have colored it with thoughts of
myself—very likely)—
     Pete, I rec'd your letter last Monday—& *Herald*—I have not sent you
any papers or books lately—but will, again—As I sit here, concluding

44. In a review of Joaquin Miller's *Songs of the Sunlands* in *The Nation* on
January 29, an anonymous writer sharply criticized WW's catalogs, mystic raptures, and
lack of restraint. WW sent a manuscript entitled "Is Walt Whitman's Poetry Poetical?"
to Burroughs, who was to send it to the editor of the magazine. If Burroughs submitted
the essay, it was not published. It is reprinted by Barrus, 107–110.

this, I am feeling quite comfortable. Take care of yourself, my darling boy—

Your old

Walt,

as always.

Pete, as I am a little in extra funds to-day, I enclose you $5—thinking (like Mrs. Toodles' *coffin*) it "might perhaps come in use, somehow"—

584. *To Ellen M. O'Connor*   *2.23. [1874]*[47]

ENDORSED: "Ans'd." ADDRESS: Mrs. E. M.
O'Connor, | 1015 O street, | near 11th N. W. |
Washington | D. C. POSTMARK: Camden | Feb |
2(?) | N.J.

431 Stevens st. | cor West. | Camden, | N. Jersey, | Monday,
Feb. 23—2½ p. m.

Dear Nelly,

I write mostly to send the pictures—you needn't hurry at all about returning them—not that I have any thing special to write about. It has not been well with me now for some ten days—not even as well as usual—Still I am up & around every day. I suffer much with my head, & locomotion is more clumsy & paralyzed even than usual—But my *inward feeling* & faith are not seriously demoralized yet. We are having it warm & bright & spring like here at present—very attractive out, but my head prevents me going out with any good enjoyment of it. My nieces are well—the one with the hair a la Chinois is California, (Jessie,) the younger—the other is Mannahatta—Jeff is still at St. Louis, full of work —both my brothers have plenty of noble, manly work, & very remunerative. I have just heard from John Burroughs—he is full of house—

Walt

45. The allusions to his published works, in addition to the envelope, confirm the date assigned by the executors.
46. "Prayer of Columbus."
47. The year is established by WW's reference to the pictures of his nieces; see 576.

585. *To Peter Doyle*   2.27. [1874]

431 Stevens st. | cor. West. | Camden, | N. Jersey | Feb. 27.
Dear son,

Nothing very different or new with me—I have had rather a hard week, (continued from the former one)—but still I dont get *flat*—am often thankful to be as well as I am—I rec'd your letter & paper—

We too have had the same snow-storm I see you have had in Washington—it is bright & sunny to-day here, though middling cool—I am sitting here in the parlor alone—it is about 10—I have had my breakfast—I amuse myself by seeing the locomotives, & trains go by—I see them very plainly out of the back window—they are only 7 or 800 feet off—they go by constantly—often one right after another—I have got used to them & like them—

Did you see my last pieces in the *Weekly Graphic?*[48]—(the sixth paper, just out, is the last)—I sent you a couple of Phil[adelphia] papers yesterday—I was glad you wrote me about Wash Peddrick[49]—I have not heard from him in a long time—(he did me a good turn once in the office, just out of good will, & I shall never forget it)—Pete, write whoever you see, & about any thing in Washington—I met a young man here from Washington last night, Wm Colein,[50] an engineer in the fire room Treasury—Love to Mrs. & Mr. Nash—& to Parker & Wash Milburn—& in short to all my friends—

Your old Walt

586. *To Ulysses S. Grant*   [2.27(?). 1874][51]

DRAFT LETTER.

. . . to give [you a] moment's diversion from the weighty stream of official and political cares, I take the liberty of sending (same mail with this) some reminiscences I have written about the war, in Nos. of the N. Y. Weekly Graphic, & thinking you of all men can best return to them, in the vein in which they are composed. I am not sure whether you will remember me—or my occasional salute to you in Washington.

48. " 'Tis But Ten Years Since."
49. W. F. Peddrick, a clerk in the Attorney General's office.
50. Mentioned in an address book (LC #108): "(took me around through the vaults, &c)."
51. This fragment was written on the verso of some notes describing his illness. The date is approximately correct, since Grant's secretary, Leon P. Luckey, on March 6, replied that the President "wishes me to assure you of his appreciation of the polite atten-

I am laid up here with tedious paralysis, but think I shall get well & return to Washington.

587. *To Ellen M. O'Connor*   3.3. [*1874*][52]

ADDRESS: Mrs. E. M. O'Connor, | 1015 O st. near 11th N. W. | Washington, D. C. POSTMARK: Camden | (?) | 3 | N.J.

Camden, N. J. March 3.

Yours just rec'd—welcomed, late bad spell seems to have mainly passed over—am better to-day—

W W

588. *To Abby H. Price*   3.3. [*1874*][53]

ADDRESS: Mrs. Abby H. Price | 331 East 55th street | New York City. POSTMARK: [*indecipherable*].

431 Stevens st. | cor West. | Camden | N. Jersey, | March 3. Dear friend Abby, | (& Dear friends all)

The letter of the 28th reached me yesterday after going wrong and was truly welcome. (I suppose you rec'd my postal card[54] acknowledging your previous one, briefly, & saying I should prefer the upper room.) Since then I have had another bad spell—has lasted some fifteen days—head, legs, gastric region, *all* bad—but am to-day feeling decidedly better. I shall *quite certainly* come on—cannot now [pla]n the time, but will write before—& take up my quarters a while with you, as it seems to be agreeable, & the moderate sum you mention I should pay thankfully— Though badly disabled, I am perfectly able to take care of myself, & my sister says I am no trouble—I am sure we would all get along well together—

I have just rec'd a letter from Mrs. O'Connor, from Washington, to-day. Her daughter, (just 16,) is not well, has had a form of measles, a second attack, quite severe, & is otherwise ailing, but I think will probably come out of it all, & grow stronger. I was glad to hear about your dear grandchildren—and about our friends Mrs. Davis[55] & Mrs. Rein[56]—I am

tion, and his best wishes for your speedy recovery" (Feinberg).
   52. This post card was apparently written at the same time as the following letter, since both allude to the "bad spell" of February. Note that in 588 WW referred to the receipt of a letter from Mrs. O'Connor.
   53. See the preceding post card.   54. This post card is not known.
   55. See 149.   56. See 306.

alone, in the house to-day, (except Eddy)—as my sister has gone out to spend the day, & my brother has gone to Easton, about his work. My brother Jeff, at St. Louis, is well—his girls are growing finely.

I am sitting here in the parlor—it is about 11½—the sun has just come out, after a cloudy half-rainy morning—is mild & warm—I go out for about an hour generally about noon, with my cane, (& accompanied by my little yellow & white dog, a most faithful affectionate companion)—frequently take a ride in the cars, or across in the boat—the men quite all know me, & are very kind.

Walt Whitman

Abby—mind the address—your last letter went wrong—had the wrong state—

589. To Rudolf Schmidt

431 Stevens st. | cor West. | Camden, New Jersey,
March 4, 1874.

Dear Rudolf Schmidt,

The Danish edition *Demokratiske Fremblik,* of my Democratic Vistas, has reached me to-day, (one copy, complete, paper-bound, and two instalments of loose sheets)—makes a handsome little book, very neatly & appropriately printed & bound—It is a great, deep, joy to me to be thus in communion with thoughtful & democratic men & women in the Scandinavian countries—I think much, much of it—& of you as the medium of it.

I suppose you rec'd my letter from here of Jan. 25—about my illness, paralysis—(& the papers I sent giving some details of it.) I am still unwell —Cannot work any—To-day I send you *Harper's Magazine* for February, with a piece[57] I have written to idealize our great Pacific half of America, (the future *better half*)—also a N. Y. *Tribune,* with a poem, (my latest,) *Prayer of Columbus.*[58] So you will see I cannot desist from writing, sick or well.

Clemens Petersen I see his pieces occasionally in the magazines—I have sent you one or two, formerly—I only met him that time, over two years ago, I mentioned[59]—have not seen any thing of his lately in print.

57. "Song of the Redwood-Tree."

58. In reprinting the poem on February 24 the *Tribune* commented that it "shows the brawny vigor, but not the reckless audacity, by which the name of that wild poet has become best known to the public."

59. See 440. Schmidt pressed WW for his opinion of Petersen, as in his letter of February 28: "I have asked you at least two times how you did like Clemens Petersen; you have not replied and most probably you wont speak of this matter. If that is the case, I shall repeat the question no more" (Feinberg).

You speak of a jaunt or tour in Germany—O how I should like to be with you & go around with you, in some of those quaint old cities & spots —the motherhood, (or rather grandmotherhood) of so much in this New World. Don't fail, my dear friend, to write me at least as soon as you return. Mention whether you have rec'd the paper, (N. Y. *Graphic*) with acc't of my illness[60]—also February *Harper's*, and the *Tribune*, by this mail—I like to hear specifically whether the papers and letters I send, reach you all right—address me here, Camden, N. Jersey, until further notice. (On papers, printed matter, &c. don't write any thing on wrappers, but only address, as our post office law strictly prohibits it.)

As I am laid up here, very lonesome, your letters will be doubly welcome. I am saving up for you some pieces on *American humor*, which I will send, when ready. About *Demokratiske Fremblik* I shall next time have something further to say. I enclose in Harper's, two copies, proof of my portrait—wood engraving,[61] rough but good, lately made—looks quite like me—(for all my sickness, which is pretty serious, I keep much the same in flesh & face.) It is mild & pleasant here to-day as I write, middle of the day—I am sitting here with open doors, the bright sun shining—Don't fail to write me—try to take some time of an hour's leisure—I like to hear about your people there—about the lady[62] you spoke of who was interested in *Democratic Vistas*—& the Professor[63] you once wrote of also—about Bjornsen also.

Walt Whitman

590. *To Peter Doyle*   3.6. [*1874*]

ADDRESS: Pete Doyle, | M street South | bet 4½ & 6th | Washington | D. C. POSTMARKS: Camden | Mar | 6 | N.J.; Carrier | 7 | Mar | 8 AM.

431 Stevens st. | cor West. | Camden, N. Jersey, | March 6. Dear boy Pete,

I was quite shocked to hear of Parker Milburn's death[64]—he was never very rugged, but he kept up so well, & always had some cheerful, lively thought or saying—I was far from anticipating this—I think he

60. WW referred to an article in the *Daily Graphic* on January 23, in which C. F. presented "A Biographical Sketch—An American Poet Graduating from a Printer's 'Case.'"

61. Linton's engraving appeared in the 1876 edition of *Leaves of Grass*.

62. Roos suggests the reference is perhaps to Nathalie Zahle, a reformer of Danish female schools; see *Orbis Litterarum*, VII (1949), 49n.

63. Roos proposes two possibilities—Falbe Hansen and Rasmus Nielsen.

64. J. Parker Milburn, age 38, died of pneumonia on March 1.

had very noble traits, & both you & I liked him thoroughly—Pete, I hope he is better off—I will try to write a few words to Wash[65]—

Pete, I have rec'd both your letters—I go out often in the Market st. cars past the West Philadelphia depot you speak of, but never get out or go in there, as it is a great depot, full of hurrying people, and hacks & drivers, & trains coming & going continually, & people rushing & crowding—too much excitement for me—So you saw Colein, in the Treasury— I saw him only a few minutes in a street car, but he could give you some report of me from his own eyes,[66] & that I know satisfied you better—I am feeling quite an improvement, or let up, the last two days & nights on the bad spell I spoke of in my last letters—have slept better the last two nights.

To-day as I write here, it is cloudy, & feels a little like snow coming— it has been very mild here too—Pete, go up some time when you start out early in the afternoon & see Mrs. O'Connor, 1015 O Street near 11th—she will be very glad to see you. I hope you won't fail to go.

I am feeling quite comfortable to-day, as I write. Pete, I sometimes think if I was fixed so that I had you with me every day, I should get well—good bye for this week, my loving son—from your old

Walt

591. *To Ellen M. O'Connor* [3.8. 1874][67]

ENDORSED: "Ans'd." ADDRESS: Mrs. E. M. O'Connor, 1015 O street, near 11th N. W. | Washington, | D. C. POSTMARK: Camden | (?) | 8 | N.J

431 Stevens st. | cor West. | Camden, | N. Jersey. | Sunday, noon. Dear Nelly,

I must first tell you what will please you best, namely that I [am] feeling *decidedly better than usual* this morning—I have spent an hour in the bath room, (quite my regular test,) & come out not only without any diminution of strength or elasticity—but an increase—& with a visit or descending upon me like of a long-absent feeling of physical ease & *unconsciousness*, which I will welcome as a precursor, even if [it] soon passes over (as it doubtless will)—but hope for return. For I suppose you know that my condition is very tantalizing in its fluctuations—Like to-day as I write—*now* the sun is out bright enough—& fifteen minutes since,

65. Parker Milburn's brother.
66. See 585.
67. For dating this letter the reference to Ada Clare is conclusive. March 8 was on Sunday in 1874.
68. The clipping from the March 6 issue of the New York *Herald* is with the letter. Headed "A Sad Case of Hydrophobia," it recorded the death of the actress and author,

I noticed from the window quite a flurry of snow—& cloudy—At any rate I am feeling again to-day one of the glimpses I had or was beginning to have last May, before mother died—am under its influence & benefit to-day—& you shall have the good of it, Nelly dear—as far as this note can give.

Poor, poor, Ada Clare—I have been inexpressibly shocked by the horrible & sudden close of her gay, easy, sunny free, loose, but *not ungood* life—I suppose you have seen about it, but I cut the enclosed from the *Herald* in case you have not[68]—

Nelly, I rec'd your letter—I send *W. Graphics* of 21st & 28th as you request—The W. G. of 7th March is my last no.[69]—did you get it?—I rec'd Charley's letter—Love to you & all—I feel to-day as though we shall yet be together again & have better times than ever, Nelly dear.

Walt

592. *To Ellen M. O'Connor*   *3.9.* [*1874*][70]

ADDRESS: Mrs. E. M. O'Connor |
1015 O street, near 11th N. W. | Washington, D. C.
POSTMARK: Camden | (?) | N.J.

Camden, | March 9. 5 p. m.

Yours rec'd last night. The let up & somewhat favorable condition mentioned in my letter of Sunday still continues. Have not the slightest idea of hastening to W[ashington]—Shan't come till I get good & ready. Continue to write often. Wish Ch.[71] to write me all news, & oftener.

W.

593. *To Peter Doyle*   [*3.12*]–13. [*1874*]

431 Stevens st. | cor West. | Camden, | N. Jersey,
Thursday, 5½ p. m.

Dear boy Pete,

I have been in all day—I don't think I ever knew such long continued gales of wind—this is now the fourth or fifth day—night & day—& as I write it is howling & whirling just as bad as ever—I havn't been out any to speak of for three days—the gales are too much for me. My spell of

Ada Clare (see 247), now Mrs. Ada Noyes, on March 4 as a result of a rabies infection she had received five weeks earlier.
69. The last three parts of " 'Tis But Ten Years Since."
70. This post card apparently refers to the preceding letter.
71. Charles Eldridge.

let up & feeling somewhat more comfortable continues, with some inter-
ruptions—night before last, & for some time yesterday, I was in a bad
way again—but had a good night's rest last night, & am comfortable to-
day—I think I am decidedly more improving than going behindhand—

I have thought frequently of Parker Milburn—all his ways, & his
good points, come up in my mind—& now the news comes of the sudden
death of Mr. Sumner[72]—Your letter came Monday, & the *Herald*—

Friday, March 13—12 M

Not very well to-day—To add to my troubles, a very bad cold in the
head & all over me, again—this is the third attack this winter—but enough
of grunting—The papers are filled with Sumner's death, funeral, life, &c.
The cold, dry gale continues here. I get letters from Mrs O'Connor.
Don't fail to go up & make her a call, when convenient.

You remember Arnold Johnson[73] that used to live over on the hill by
the Insane Asylum—well he has come back to Washington, & is Chief
Clerk again Light House Board, & Wm O'Connor has changed to a
clerkship in the Library, Treasury.[74] I am sitting here alone in the same
old seat in the parlor writing.

Good bye for this time, dear boy—

Walt

594. *To Rudolf Schmidt*

431 Stevens st. Camden, N. Jersey, | U. S. America
March 19, 1874.

My dear Rudolf Schmidt,

My lonesomeness & sickness here, (for I am still sick, & here,)
have been much rejoiced to-day by my getting your good & copious letter
of 28th February, on your return to Kopenhagen. I rec'd with it the
Fatherland with Mr. Rosenberg's criticism[75]—which (perhaps luckily
for me) I cannot now read—but will one of these days have translated &
read to me. I keep it very carefully—as I do all you send me—& shall yet
read and commune with, & dwell upon & absorb *all* thoroughly & at leisure—(especially your own review in the *Ide*.) I think probably *all*—certainly *most*—papers, sheets, &c. you have sent me to Washington, have

---

72. Charles Sumner died of a heart attack on March 11.
73. See 138.   74. See 515.
75. According to Schmidt's letter on February 28, an eight-column review of WW's
works appeared in the *Fatherland* (*Fædrelandet*): "The author of the criticism Rosenberg
is a silly little fellow, who understands nothing between heaven and earth, and least of all,
you" (Feinberg). Roos identifies Carl Rosenberg as a friend of Schmidt; see *Orbis Lit-*

reached me here—the post office forwards them here—I rec'd two complete copies *Demokratiske Fremblik*, & one copy in sheets—also three
copies picture paper *Folkeblad*, with my portrait,[76] which is most excellent—(and the notice I will have read to me)—I rec'd at the time, a year
ago, the translation of Swedish and Norwegian poems, you sent me,
acknowledged it, but the letter seems to have missed you, & have read it
& had much pleasure, & am to read it more—I also rec'd from Clausen
your picture, which I have with me—& prize. A friend lately looking at
it said, "Why, he looks like a born Yankee—& of the best."

I wrote you March 4th, acknowledging *Demokratiske Fremblik*, &
sent you (one in *Harper's Magazine*, & one extracted in the N. Y. *Tribune*)
my two latest pieces *Song of the Redwood Tree*, (California,) and *Prayer
of Columbus*, which I suppose you have rec'd all—For the last ten weeks
I have not felt inclined to write—have suffered in the head—walk hardly
any, (from the paralysis,) but maintain good spirits, keep up in body &
face, (my brother & sister said at dinner yesterday that portrait in the
Folkeblad looks greatly like me now, & has caught the true *expression*
better than any of them.) In body I have always been, & still remain,
stout, in the American sense, (i. e. *not* corpulent)—

In my letter of March 4 I wrote a few lines about Clemens Petersen[77]—
my only interview with him was about 40 minutes, one very rainy Sunday,
nearly two years since in New York—he was just recovering from an
attack of erysipelas which had left large red blotches on his face—two
other visitors were just leaving—C. P. received me very kindly & talked
well—all was agreeable, but under the circumstances I could not say
much nor stay long—received a pleasing but passing, & not very pronounced impression—which is the reason, my dear friend, that I have not
written more fully—Partly too I have been waiting expecting that
perhaps somehow C. P. and I would meet again, & talk more & get better
acquainted, & I could write you further—but I have not seen any thing
of him since—& only seen some of his pieces casually in the magazines.
I have not heard him or them mentioned here in America—certainly no
essay in the *Atlantic* magazine nor any thing of his elsewhere in English
that I have seen has attracted any special attention nor deserves it—shows
nothing of the *forte* or heartiness of which I have no doubt he is capable—
(I think your letter & opinion of C. P.'s essay, of last summer, have missed

terarum, VII (1949), 49n.
   76. WW's portrait, with an extract from Schmidt's essay, appeared in the *Illus-
treted Folkeblad* on February 22, according to Roos.
   77. See 589.

me.)—I cannot understand your allusions to Bjornson[78]—as you will be doubtless aware yourself.

The same *hardness*, crudeness, worldliness—absence of the spiritual, the purely moral, esthetik, &c—are in Democracy here too—(though there are signs & awakenings here very plain to me)—probably in Great Britain, & in Europe & everywhere—*Here*, it is much counterbalanced & made up by an immense & general basis of the eligibility to manly & loving comradeship, very marked in American young men—but generally, I am the more disposed to be satisfied with the case as it is because I see that the only foundations & *sine qua non* of popular improvement & Democracy are *worldly & material success established first*, spreading & intertwining everywhere—*then* only, but then surely for the masses, will come spiritual cultivation & art—they will then firmly assert themselves—

Thank you for the graphic line-sketch you write of Bismark, in your letter. My own opinion is, that we can well afford—I will say, *such as you & I*, can well afford, to let those little & great *chunks of brawn*—Attilas, Napoleons, Bismarks—prepare the way, & cut the roads through, for *us.*[79]

Write me *here*, till further notice—let me hear what is said about *Vistas* or my poems—let me hear always of yourself fully.

Walt Whitman

595. *To Peter Doyle*   3.20. [1874][80]

ADDRESS: Peter Doyle | M street south | bet 4½ & 6th | Washington, | D. C. POSTMARK: Camden | Mar | 20 | N.J.

431 Stevens st. Camden, | March 20. | 4½ P. M.

Dear boy Pete,

Nothing particular or new in my condition—I have been to the Doctor's to-day—had quite a long interview—no great satisfaction—I still have pretty uncomfortable times—& yet I keep up good heart in the

78. Schmidt wrote at some length on February 28 of Björnson: "His poetry comes from the source, that is throbbing in the people's own heart. He has been the spoiled darling of the whole Danish public. But he is a living test of the hideous and venomous serpent, that hides his ugly head among the flowers of the *pantheistic* poetry. You have in your 'vistas' spoken proud words of the flame of conscience, the moral force as the greatest lack of the present democracy. You have, without knowing it, named the lack of Björnson at the same time! Björnson owes Denmark *gratitude*. He has shown it in the form of deep and bloody offences, that make every honest Danish heart burn with rage and indignation" (Feinberg).

79. On February 28 Schmidt reported that he had seen Bismarck in Berlin: "It is

main. I will make out only a short letter this time, I see. Good bye, my loving son, I will try to do better next week.

                                                                Walt

596. *To Ellen M. O'Connor*   3.22. [*1874*]

ENDORSED: "Ans'd." ADDRESS: Mrs. E. M.
O'Connor, | 1015 O st. near 11th N. W. |
Washington, | D. C. POSTMARK: Camden | Mar | 22 |
N.J.

                431 Stevens st. | cor West. | Camden, | N. Jersey,
                          Sunday, March 22, | after 4, p. m.

Dearest Nelly,

I will just write you a word (for I feel to.) I am feeling well enough to be hopeful—Whether it is because I *am* hopeful—or whether the precursor of health yet, after all—tedious as it is a-coming—this deponent cannot swear—but we will think it the latter. I have had a bad week since I wrote you—feel more comfortable to-day. Saw the doctor (Grier) day before yesterday—he made a careful auscultation of my heart—pronounced it all right there—(I have been suffering considerable pain & oppression on left side)—He still thinks I will recover —says he is not disposed to recommend galvanism, (though the electric business is his specialty)—says he is sure the main trouble is the *cerebral* anæmia—cure, great care, good surroundings, time & hygiene—arrives, in fact, at the same conclusions as Dr. Drinkard[81]—(though an entirely different man from Dr. D., a great talker, & very demonstrative)—

Nelly, you needn't send the photos of my nieces back yet. Keep them a while yet.

Nelly, your last letter is very blue, mainly about political & public degradation—Sumner's death & inferior men &c. being rampant &c—I look on all such states of things exactly as I look on a cloudy & evil state of weather, or a fog, or long sulk meteorological—it is a natural result of things, a growth of something deeper, has its uses, & will hasten to exhaust itself, & yield to something better—

                                                                Walt.

Thanks for your letter of 20th—give my love to Mrs. Brownell—

worth the travel to get a glance on this so very powerfull and so excessively beastly face. Attila called himself 'God's scourge,' Napoleon did not call himself so, but he was it. But Attila was imposing in the splendour of his barbaric greatness; of Napoleon the German H: Heine has said 'every inch a God.' A scourge like this Brandenburgider fox hunter mankind never has known. Perhaps mankind never has been so deeply fallen!" (Feinberg).

    80. The year is established by the discussion of Dr. Grier's diagnosis in the next letter, which can be positively assigned to 1874.

    81. See also 530.

597. *To Peter Doyle*   3.23. [1874][82]

ADDRESS: Pete Doyle, | M street South, bet 4½ & 6th |
Washington, D. C. POSTMARKS: Camden | Mar(?) |
23 | N.J.; Carrier | 24 | Mar | 8 AM.

Camden, Noon—March 23.

It will be very easy to come here—get out at West Philadelphia &
come down in Market st. horse cars to ferry, foot of Market st—cross to
Camden, it is only ⅓d of a mile from ferry. Send me word a day ahead &
I will meet you at West Philadelphia. We have plenty of room. Come
whenever convenient. You will find me *much better*—to-day I feel like
getting well, (& confidently expect to)—wish you were here to-day—
'twould be most like old times—

W W

Your letter & paper just rec'd—

598. *To J. C. Mann*

ENDORSED: "sent at date." DRAFT LETTER.

Camden, March 25 '74

To: J. C. Mann[83]
Tuft's College | Box 55   College Hill, Mass.

Your letter of the 20th (for committee) has reached me here. I accept with pleasure the invitation to deliver a poem to your college & visitors
next June. Without any thing very definite at this moment, my idea is of
a poem, fitting in not unappropriately to such an occasion, the recital of
which would not occupy more than 30 minutes. All the pay I would want
would be enough to pay my expenses, transportation &c., probably between 30 and $40, certainly not more than the latter sum. Please ac-
knowledge this & please write me more particulars about your college,
where it is, specialties, if any &c. I am stopping here, not entirely well,
but able to get around, recovering from an attack of paralysis of over a
year ago.

W. W.

82. This is the post card referred to in 599.
83. On March 20 Mann invited WW to deliver on June 17 a poem before the
Mathematician Society of Tufts College, a society "of young men of the Col. desiring to
become more proficient in the art of speaking, writing and debate." Mann replied to

599. *To Peter Doyle*   [*3.26*]–*27.* [*1874*]

ADDRESS: Pete Doyle, | M street South | bet 4½ &
6th | Washington | D. C. POSTMARK: Camden | (?) |
27 | N.J.

431 Stevens st. | cor West. | Camden, N. Jersey.
Thursday afternoon 2½

I have just had my dinner—roast beef, lima beans, graham-bread
& sweet butter, with a cup of tea, & some stewed cranberries—eat quite a
good dinner, & enjoyed it all. I still consider myself getting along very
well. O if *this* only holds out, & keeps on favorably, even if ever so moderate & slow—But I seem to have so many of these gleams that delude me
into thinking I am on the way to recovery, but soon cloud over again, &
let me back as bad as ever—But every time I feel pretty easy, I still keep
thinking, *now* I am *certainly* going to get much better *this time*—

Pete, your short letter came to-day, written on the cars—dear son, come
whenever you can—As I said on my postal card, if you were here this
week, you would find me more like myself, (with the exception of walking) than I have been for fourteen months—whether it will continue or
not, God only knows—but we will hope for the best. As I sit here writing
to you to-day, it appears to me every way hopeful, & likely that we shall
yet have good times. Every thing is quiet—rather lonesome. My little dog
is stretched out on the rug at full length, snoozing. He hardly lets me go a
step without being close at my heels—follows me in my slow walks, &
stops or turns just as I do. We have had a most windy blustering March,
but it is pleasanter & milder yesterday & to-day—(I saw the new moon
over my right shoulder a week ago—*of course* a *sure* sign of good luck)—
Will finish the letter & send it to-morrow.

Friday—March 27—noon.

Pleasant & bright weather—have been out on the side walk in front,
once or twice, with my shawl around me—walk slow & quite feeble—have
some spells of bad head-ache—Went by the West Philadelphia depot
yesterday afternoon, in the Market st. horse-cars—saw plenty of RR men
& conductors, about the place, lounging & waiting their time—thought
if I could only see *you* among them—As I sit here writing I can see the
trains of the Camden & Amboy, in full view, some 40 or 50 rods off—
makes it quite lively—As I write I am feeling pretty comfortable, & am

WW's queries on April 2. WW composed "Song of the Universal" for the occasion, but,
unable to deliver the poem in person, sent it to Mann on June 11. I am grateful to Mr.
Oscar Lion for permission to quote from this correspondence.

going out awhile after I finish this—but had a bad night last night. Hope this will find you all right—good bye for this time, dear son.

Walt

600. *To Peter Doyle* 4.10. [1874][84]

ADDRESS: Pete Doyle, | M street South, | bet 4½ & 6th | Washington | D. C. POSTMARK: Camden | Apr | 10 | N.J.

431 Stevens st. | cor West. | Camden, | N. Jersey.
April 10, 12 M

Dear Pete,

Nothing very new or different in my condition, or any thing else—have hardly been doing as well since I last wrote, as before—but still hope to pull up. Rec'd your letter last Monday, & the *Herald*.

Not much of a letter this time, my loving boy—as I dont seem to be able to write much—though, as I sit here, I am not feeling any worse than usual. Ashton has lost his little child, died last Thursday.[85] I have just rec'd two letters from Mrs. O'Connor. How does all go with you? Pete, darling, shan't I send you a little money?

Walt

601. *To Ellen M. O'Connor* 4.10. [1874][86]

ADDRESS: Mrs. E. M. O'Connor, | 1015 O street, near 11th, N. W. | Washington, D. C. POSTMARKS: Camden | Apr | 10 | N.J.; Carrier | 11 | Apr | 8 AM.

431 Stevens Camden, N. Jersey. | April 10. 12 M.

Both letters just received. I will try to write to the A[shton]s. I deeply sympathize.

Last week has not been so encouraging with me—but am about as usual as I write to-day.

W.

84. That this post card and the next one were written in 1874 is demonstrated in the following note.

85. Kitty Ashton, who was nineteen months old, died on April 8. The child mentioned in 299 must also have died.

86. See the preceding post card.

87. The date of this letter is confirmed by the account of Burroughs' visit in the

602. *To Peter Doyle*   4.16. [1874][87]

ADDRESS: Pete Doyle, | M street | South | bet 4½ &
6th | Washington | D. C. POSTMARK: Camden |
Apr | 16 | N.J.

431 Stevens st. | cor West. | Camden, | N. Jersey.
April 16—1 p. m.

Dear son,

I send you my letter a day ahead this week[88]—Nothing new with
me—rec'd the letter of last Sunday—also the *Capital*, and the *Herald*—
I had a day or two's visit (very acceptable) from John Burroughs last
Saturday & Sunday—he has built a house on the Hudson river about
80 miles from N. Y.—has a little farm there, 9 or 10 acres, very nice—
As I write I am feeling comfortable, (but every day & every night seems
to bring its bad spell, or several of them.) Somehow I still feel that I shall
come round, & that we shall be together & have some good times again—
but don't know.

Your Walt

603. *To Ellen M. O'Connor*   4.17. [1874][89]

ADDRESS: Mrs. E. M. O'Connor, | 1015 O street, near
11th N. W. | Washington, D. C. POSTMARKS:
Camden | Apr | 17(?) | N.J.; Carrier | 18 | (?) |
8 AM.

431 Stevens st. | cor West. | Camden, N. Jersey. | April 17.
Condition still hopeful, & (though tedious as ever, & with relapses
& bad spells,) still seem *decidedly* to gain more than lose—I have written
to the A[shton]s. Am quite comfortable to-day. J[ohn] B[urroughs] was
here Saturday & Sunday.

W W

604. *To Peter Doyle*   4.21. [1874][90]

ADDRESS: Pete Doyle, | M street South, bet 4½ &
6th | Washington, D. C. POSTMARKS: Camden |
Apr | 21 | N.J.; Carrier | 22 | Apr(?) | (?).

431 Stevens st. Camden, April 21. | 11 a. m.
Friday's letter rec'd—also that of Sunday—also papers—Graphic
this morning—I feel pretty fair to-day considering—Keep on about same

dated letter to Schmidt (607).
    88. WW ordinarily wrote on Friday; April 16 was on Thursday in 1874.
    89. The year is verified by the reference to Burroughs' visit mentioned in the pre-
ceding letter and in 607.
    90. The reference to the new express train here and in 608 permits assignment of
this post card to 1874.

—(cloudy & sunshine)—Rain here too past four days, but I go out—clear to-day—I get or see N. Y. and Phil. papers nearly all, & the Wash. Chronicle & the Capital—Write me how new train makes out—Do you go through to Balt[imore] only—or further? Am glad Buck is your conductor—

W

605. *To Thomas O'Kane*

ENDORSED: "sent Thos. O'Kane"; "Letter to O'Kane | April 22 | '74." DRAFT LETTER.

April 22, '74

I am anxious to have our acc't settled up.[91] Comparing your rec't of my books from Doolady, April 28, '73 (239 Leaves of Grass, &c. &c)—with the acc't of books handed over by you to Butts (168 Leaves of Grass, &c &c)—see my last letter to you, Feb. 16[92]—there are to be acc't'd for to me, 71 copies, *L of G*. Deduct 25 copies sent to Boston by my order, & 3 copies to *Graphic*, leaves 43 copies (@ $1.40) to be acc't'd for to me at $60.20. Deduct from this the adv. 2 times in *Tribune* and *Graphic* (4 times)—(?7, or 8 or 9$) leaving over $50 due me—May I not hope for the settlem't of this acc't without delay—& remittance to me of am't due.

W W

I still remain here partially paralyzed. I have not charged the copies of other books besides L. of G. as the sales were slight.

606. *To Peter Doyle*   *4.24. [1874]*[93]

ADDRESS: Pete Doyle, | M street South—bet 4½ & 6th | Washington, D. C. POSTMARK: Camden | Apr | 24 | N.J.

431 Stevens st. | cor West. | Camden, N. J. | April 24—12 noon
Yours of 23d just rec'd—Nothing new or different with me. Come —When you once find the way you'll discover its very easy—A bright pleasant forenoon here at last. Am going out now.

W W

91. See 535 and 577.   92. Apparently lost.
93. Since WW wrote about Doyle's first visit to Camden in 597, 599, and 615, this post card can be dated 1874.
94. This picture, now in the Feinberg Collection, appears in Traubel, II, 84.
95. On April 4 Schmidt described a critical article composed by a young Norwegian named Kristian Elster, who had expressed "a great fear that the editor (in Christiania) would not print it. In the war, on the roaring sea the Norwegians are a people of heroes; but in their civil and literary life they are a race of cowards" (Feinberg). According to

607. *To Rudolf Schmidt*

431 Stevens st.   Camden, | N. Jersey, | U. S. America.
April 25, 1874.

Rudolf Schmidt | Dear friend—

Yours of April 4 has come to hand—with picture, which I prize[94] —you speak of Mr. Elster's[95] criticism—when it comes I shall have it carefully translated to me—if you communicate with him, please give him my serious thanks & good will—

All your *papers*, copies of *D. Fremblik* & your *letters* have reached me safely in the past—(also the large *photo.* by poor Clausen.) Did you receive *Redwood Tree* in Harper's Magazine—& *Prayer of Columbus*— sent some weeks (March 4) since? *This piece* of C. Petersen is in the May *Galaxy*,[96] a New York Monthly. I will make inquiry about Petersen, & if I see him or find out I will duly write you. I am not well yet—far from it —but live in hopes—

Walt Whitman

John Burroughs visited me for two days lately[97]—He is well, is married, (36 years old), has left Washington, & has settled on a little farm with horse, cows, & fowls on the banks of the Hudson river, 60 miles from New York, his native state & mine. I am to go there the coming summer. J. B. is a most natural, homely, good man—(like an *apple-tree*, or *pine*, or a good *field* of *wheat*—yet thoroughly *human*)[98]—has a nice wife, kind & good to me, like a sister.

To-day is dark & rainy here—spring very backward here—I sit here in the room alone, writing this—I am much alone—

W. W.

608. *To Peter Doyle*   5.1. [1874][99]

ADDRESS: Pete Doyle, | M street South, | bet 4½ &
6th | Washington | D. C. POSTMARK: Camden |
May | 1 | N.J.

431 Stevens st.   Camden, | N. Jersey, | May 1—2 p. m.

Dear Pete,

I have been out halting around for a walk, as it is quite pleasant to-day—But I believe I have overdone the matter, as I have a pretty bad

Roos, Elster (1841–1881) was a friend of Björnson; see *Orbis Litterarum*, VII (1949), 51*n.*

96. "Scandinavia" appeared in two parts in the May and June issues; see *The Galaxy*, XVII (1874), 610–618, 770–778.

97. See 602.

98. This description of Burroughs was inserted in answer to Schmidt's request.

99. This and the following letter were obviously written on the same day. The allusion to the Ashtons, who had recently lost a child (see 600), conclusively establishes the year.

feeling the last hour or two both in the head & left side—& as I sit here writing—So your *limited express* seems to be a real success—if it keeps up as well as it has begun I have no doubt it will increase, & be patronised, & become a permanent institution—(I had got the idea, somehow, at first, that the same crew went *through* from Wash[ington] to New York, & so was some in hopes of seeing you in Philadelphia)—

No change in my condition or prospects—the young man, Walter Godey, still works as my substitute in the Solicitor's office—I havn't had any word from Eldridge in two months, nor from Mrs. O'Connor in some time—(have you been up there?) Do you see Hinton or Tasistro?— My sister has just called me to my dinner—so I will close for this time.

Your old Walt

609. *To Ellen M. O'Connor*   5.1. [1874]

ENDORSED: "Ans'd." ADDRESS: Mrs. E. M. O'Connor | 1015 O st. near 11th N. W. | Washington | D. C. POSTMARK: Camden | May | 1 | N.J.

431 Stevens st. | cor West. | Camden, | N. Jersey. | May 1. 3 p. m.
Dear Nelly,

I will write you just a line—it is still the same with me—the same strange alternations—not perhaps quite as well, of late, (the last ten or twelve days)—& yet I dont abandon my anchorage of heart & hope—dont *feel to*, which is a main thing with me—I have a good deal of pain, more or less steady, in my left side—in addition to the bad spells in the head —To-day has been pleasant, & I was out hobbling around from 10 to 12— probably overdid matters—as I came back sick & have been so since— (though not enough to prevent me from eating some nice stewed oysters in moderation for my dinner, a half hour since)—

So dont be needlessly apprehensive, Nelly dear—for I shall get better, & we will meet yet—

When you write tell me about my dear Mr & Mrs. Ashton—I wrote them a line off-hand, which I suppose they rec'd. Tell me all the news—tell me about Charles Eldridge—& all my other friends. With love—

Walt

1. This and the following post card to Doyle can be assigned to 1874 because of the particularized descriptions of WW's physical symptoms, which are elaborated upon in 609 and 612, both of which can definitely be assigned to 1874.

610. *To Ellen M. O'Connor*   *5.6–7.* [*1874*][1]

ADDRESS: Mrs. E. M. O'Connor | 1015 O st—near
11th N. W. | Washington, D. C. POSTMARK:
Camden | (?) | 7(?) | N.J.

431 Stevens st.   Camden, N. J. | May 6.

Yours rec'd, & welcomed. Have been to the doctor's to-day[2]—
troubles of breast & left side getting steadier & more severe—in fact in
addition to other troubles ugly gastric & catarrhal ones—Am still out &
around some, however, & shan't give up yet—

May 7—2 p. m. Nothing new or different—have had a long good
call from a friend from Minnesota this forenoon—& a letter & papers from
Denmark[3]—

W. W.

611. *To Peter Doyle*   *5.8.* [*1874*]

ADDRESS: Pete Doyle, | M st. South, bet 4½ & 6th |
Washington, D. C. POSTMARKS: Camden | May | 8 |
N.J.; Carrier | 9 | May | 8 AM.

431 Stevens st. | Camden, N. Jersey. May 8—noon—

Every thing pretty much the same. Rather a bad week with me—
no improvement—great distress in head & left side, at intervals—cannot
write much to-day—Will do better next time—

W W

Your letter & paper came.

612. *To Peter Doyle*   *5.15.* [*1874*]

ADDRESS: Pete Doyle, | M street South, bet 4½ &
6th | Washington, D. C. POSTMARKS: Camden |
May | 15 | N.J.; Carrier | 16 | May | 8 AM.

431 Stevens st.   Camden, | N. Jersey. | Friday, May 15.

Yours of last Sunday rec'd—paper also—Pretty bad spells of
last week have let-up this morning—feel more comfortable than usual
to-day—I don't get discouraged—& you mustn't either—

W W

2. See notes to 619.
3. Probably a lost letter from Schmidt.

613. *To Ellen M. O'Connor*   5.15. *[1874]*

ENDORSED: "Ans'd." ADDRESS: Mrs. E. M.
O'Connor | 1015 O street | near 11th N. W. |
Washington, | D. C. POSTMARK: Camden | May |
15 | N.J.

431 Stevens st. | cor West | Camden, | N. Jersey. | Friday,
May 15.

Dear Nelly,

I have had a succession of bad spells, (& pretty close together)
since I wrote the encouraging lines, some two or three weeks ago[4]—indeed
for a month now, in addition to other troubles, a pronounced pain & distress in left side, growing intenser & quite extended—often coming on at
night, waking me up, & keeping me from sleep all night afterward—But
this morning as I write, (9 o'clock after breakfast—fish, Graham bread,
tea, my appetite, though modified, by no means lost)—I feel quite *peert*,
in good spirits, free from any marked distress—& if you were to come in
this minute, (than which, dear Nelly, I can think of no blesseder God-
send,) you would say I appear in face, flesh, color, expression, &c. *just the
same Walt as of yore*—Will this good turn & let-up of today (yesterday
morning at this time I felt like death—& thought of it—) be followed by
other relapses? Probably—for so it has been now for nearly a year. And
yet each time I cannot help fancying that *now* I am going to recuperate—

As I write, sitting here in the parlor alone by the window, it is very
pleasant—soothing—it is a sweet balmy, not hot morning—my sister's
sister,[5] from Norwich, Conn. is here on a visit, with her little 8 months old
babe-boy—She is walking in the other room, singing it to sleep, in her
arms—she has a fine contralto voice, & is singing beautifully, unconsciously—it does me good too—

Walt

614. *To William Stansberry*

DRAFT LETTER.

May 20, '74

Dear Wm. Stansberry,[6]

I will just write you a few lines off-hand. Your letter of May 14[7]
has come to hand to-day, reminding me of your being in Armory Square

---

4. Actually WW was not "encouraging" in 609.
5. A sister of George's wife Louisa.
6. "After the lapse of over 8. years," William Stansberry, a former soldier whom
WW had met in Armory Square Hospital, wrote on December 9, 1873, from Howard
Lake, Minn., and recalled "the Blackbery [Jam?] you gave me & all the kindness which
you shown." After WW replied on April 27, 1874 (lost), Stansberry wrote again on
May 12 about the hospital visits. On June 28 he thanked WW for his letter and "22 News
Pappers." On July 15 his wife informed WW of her husband's failing health and poverty

Hospital & of my visits there, & meeting you, in '65. Your writing, or something it has started, strangely, deeply touches me. It takes me back to the scenes of ten years ago, in the war, the hospitals of Washington, the many wounded bro't up after the battles, and the never-to-be told sights of suffering & death. To think that the little gift & word of kindness, should be remembered by you so long—& that the kiss I gave you amid those scenes, should be treasured up, & as it were sent back to me after many years! Dear Comrade—you do me good,[8] by your loving wishes & feelings to me in your letters.

I send you my love, & to your dear children & wife the same. As I write, you seem very dear to me too, like some young brother, who has been lost, but now found. Whether we shall ever meet each other is doubtful—probably we never will—but I feel that we should both be happy, if we could be together—(I find there are some that it is just comfort enough to be together, almost without any thing else)—

I remain about the same in my sickness. I sleep & eat pretty well—go about same, look stout & red, (though looking now *very* old & gray, but that is nothing new)—weigh 185 now—am badly lamed in my left leg, & have bad spells, occasionally days, of feebleness, distress in head, &c. I think I shall get well yet, but may not. Have been laid up here a year doing nothing, except a little writing. As far as room, food, care, &c. are concerned, I am well situated here—but *very lonesome*—have no near friends, (in the deepest sense) here at hand—my mother died here a year ago—a sorrow from which I have never entirely recovered, & likely never shall—she was an unusually noble, cheerful woman—very proud-spirited & generous—am poor, (yet with a little income, & means, just enough to pay my way, with strict economy, to be independent of want)—

614.1 *To John Burroughs*   *5.21. [1874]*

ADDRESS: John Burroughs, | Esopus, | Ulster co. | New York. POSTMARK: Camden | May | 21 | N.J.

431 Stevens st. | Cor West, | Camden, | N. Jersey, | May 21. John & Ursula Burroughs, | Dear friends,

and inquired about the possibility of a pension. Evidently in reply to another lost letter from WW, Stansberry asked on July 21, 1875, for "the Lone of 65$" in order to return to West Virginia, where he expected to find witnesses to support his application for a pension. This was evidently the last letter in the correspondence. These letters are in the Trent Collection. See also *CW*, IV, 134.

7. Stansberry's letter was written on May 12.

8. Originally WW wrote: "Dear, dear comrade—for so I must call you—you have done me good, much good."

Thank you for the kind reminder that *room & breakfast plate are ready*—I shall be coming along—will send you word when—

I have hardly any thing to tell about my improvement in health—it is certain I do not get really worse—& yet lameness & pretty bad head-spells—added to which lately a great deal of pain & oppression in left side—keep me back. John, I sympathise with you in that jolly bother among the bees & the ground, & birds, nag, &c. Such homely ties—& to come in real contact—& have to do with them—

The piece I thought might amuse you in the Galaxy is "Our Neighborhood" by Lady Blanche Murphy.[8.1]

John, I enclose a slip about Carlyle, the latest news—seems to be authentic—

So long, dear friends,

Walt Whitman

615. *To Peter Doyle*   5.22. [*1874*][9]

ADDRESS: Pete Doyle | M street South | bet 4½ &
6th | Washington | D. C. POSTMARK: Philadelphia |
May | 22 | Pa.

431 Stevens st. | cor West. | Camden, | N. Jersey.
May 22—3¼ | p. m.

Dear Pete,

I hope you will be able to come, as you said in your last—If I knew when & where you would arrive in Philadelphia, I would try to meet you—As I wrote you before[10] you must come to Market st. ferry Philadelphia, a mile and half, or 2 miles from RR depot, & cross over by boat to Federal st. Camden—(The Phil. horse cars run Sundays—run down to foot of Market st—but the Camden ones do *not*—but it is not very far from the ferry in Camden.)

I am very much the same—My being disabled & want of exercise for 16 months, (and many others wants too,) have saddled me with serious dyspepsia & what the doctor calls gastric catarrh, very obstinate, causing me really more suffering & pain than my paralysis—but though I have bad spells enough, thank God I also have middling good ones—& as I write this have just had my dinner, nice salt oysters, raw, fresh, & am feeling quite comfortable—Dear son, I shall look for you—

Walt

8.1 Lady Blanche's account of English social life appeared in the May issue of *The Galaxy* (679–688).

9. The year is verified by the references to his catarrh, to "want of exercise for 16 months," and to Doyle's impending visit, which evidently took place a few days later (see 617).

616. *To Alfred, Lord Tennyson*

ENDORSED: "To Tennyson, May 24 '74." DRAFT
LETTER.

May 24 '74 Camden

Dear Mr. Tennyson,

It is a long time since my last to you.[11] I have, however, mailed you once or twice pieces of mine in print, which I suppose you rec'd. Jan. '73 I was taken down with illness—some three months afterward, was recovering at Washington, when called here by the death of my mother—& from that time, becoming worse, I have given up work & remained here since. I had paralysis, from cerebral anæmia.[12]

I rec'd your last letter, & the good, good photograph—which I have looked at many times, & sometimes almost fancied it *you* in person silently sitting nigh.

To-day, a cloudy & drizzly Sunday, I have taken it in my head, sitting here alone, to follow the inner mood & write—(a tinge of Quaker blood & breed in me)—though really without any thing to say, only just to write to you.

It is pleasant here, right on the banks of the noble Delaware, opposite Philadelphia. The doctors say I shall yet come round, & I think so too. I do not fail in flesh, color, spirits—appetite & sleep pretty good—am up & dressed every day, & go out a little—but very lame yet.

truly your friend—

W W

617. *To Peter Doyle*   *5.29. [1874]*[13]

ADDRESS: Peter Doyle, | M st. South, bet 4½ & 6th | Washington, D. C. POSTMARK: Camden | May | 29 | N.J.

431 Stevens st.   Camden, | N. Jersey. | May 29.

Much the same with me since you left. Had an easier day yesterday—but down again to-day.

WW

10. See 597.   11. See 457.1.
12. At this point WW deleted the following: "sixteen tedious months now, & still laying me up—but it might be much worse—& I shall come round yet."
13. Doyle's visit to WW makes the date certain.

618. *To Ellen M. O'Connor*   *5.29.* [*1874*][14]

ADDRESS: Mrs. E. M. O'Connor, | 1015 O st near
11th N. W. | Washington, D. C. POSTMARKS:
Camden | May | 29(?) | N.J.; Carrier | 30 | May |
8 AM.

431 Stevens st.   Camden, | N. Jersey, | May 29

Rec'd your welcome letter this morning. Much the same with me
as when I last wrote—far from well, with frequent alternations—but up
& around every day.

W

619. *To John Burroughs*   *6.5.* [*1874*]

431 Stevens St.   Camden, | N. Jersey. | June 5.

Dear friend,

Your second letter, with sad news—following the sad, sad, inexpressibly sad news of the first—has just reached me.

I will not write any of the usual condolences. Chancy's[15] malady &
death seem to be of those events sometimes mocking with unaccountable
sudden tragedies & cross-purposes, all of us, & all our affairs.

I have again had some pretty bad spells, (gastric & brain)[16]—but am
decidedly better as I write, & for a day or two past—Shall come—Will
write again soon—

Walt—

620. *To Peter Doyle*   *6.5.* [*1874*][17]

ADDRESS: Peter Doyle, | M street South—bet 4½ &
6th | Washington, D. C. POSTMARKS: Camden |
(?) | 5 | N.J.; Carrier | 6 | Jun | 8 AM.

431 Stevens st. | Camden, | N. Jersey. | June 5.

Am getting along somewhat better last two days—As I write this,

14. Note the reference to 613 and the similar phrasing of this post card and the
preceding one.

15. Burroughs' nephew, Chauncey B. Deyo, visited WW in March and wrote to
his uncle on March 29: "It seemed hard to see the great man afflicted, bowed down, and I
could not suppress my tears, and cannot suppress them now. . . . His death would be a
heavy, heavy blow to me. Oh, Uncle John, I can't think of it without crying, as I do now"
(Barrus, 89). See 622.

16. In some manuscript jottings, WW described a visit to Dr. Grier on June 2: "He
reiterated his theory that my sufferings, (later ones) come nearly altogether from gastric,
stomachic, intestinal, non-excretory, &c. causes, causing flatulence, a very great distension
of the colon, of passages, weight on valves, crowding & pressing on organs (heart, lungs,
&c) and the very great distress & pain I have been under in breast & left side, & pit of

(3 p. m.) have had my dinner—& shall probably go out an hour or two toward sundown—

WW

---

621. *To Peter Doyle*   6.10. [*1874*][18]

ADDRESS: Pete Doyle | M st. South, bet 4½ & 6th |
Washington, D. C. POSTMARKS: Philadelphia | Jun |
10 | 10 PM | (?); Carrier | 11 | Jun(?) | (?)AM.

431 Stevens st.   Camden, | N. Jersey. | June 10.

Your letter & paper came to-day. Am standing the extreme hot weather very well indeed so far—am about as usual, (& better than when you saw me)—

W W

---

622. *To Ellen M. O'Connor*   6.10. [*1874*]

ENDORSED: "Ans'd." ADDRESS: Mrs. E. M.
O'Connor, | 1015 O street, N. W. | Washington, |
D. C. POSTMARKS: Camden | Jun(?) | 10 | N.J.;
(?) | 11(?) | Jun | 8 AM.

431 Stevens st. | cor West. | Camden, N. Jersey.
June 10—11 a. m.

Dear Nelly,

Your letter has reached me this morning—&, as always, is welcome—I shall *not go on* to Boston—am not well enough (& the hot spell besides)—but shall send the piece I have composed for the occasion—a ten or fifteen minute piece I call the "Song of the Universal"—to be read by proxy in its place in the programme, just the same as though I were there. I will next week send it you in print[19]—

I am only reconciled to Charles Eldridge's *not* coming to see me Decoration Day, by taking it for granted that he will consequently feel bound to visit me without fail before long—Come, Charley, by all means —It will do me good—

stomach, & thence to my head, the last month. Advised me by all means to begin the use of an injection syringe, (Fountain No. 2. tepid water for clysters)—was favorable to my using whiskey—advised assa[feti]da pills, 2 ? kneading the bowel[s] . . ." (Trent).

17. Observe the similarities between this post card and the preceding letter.

18. Doyle's visit to WW establishes the year.

19. "Song of the Universal" appeared in the New York *Daily Graphic* and *Evening Post* on June 17, in the Springfield *Republican* on June 18, in the New York *World* on June 19, and in the Camden *New Republic* on June 20. According to the Springfield *Republican*, the poem was read by Prof. Brown "probably better than the poet himself would have rendered it . . . The poem . . . is very Whitmany, being one of the most grotesque in expression and one of the richest and subtlest in thought which he has put out for a long time."

Nelly, John Burroughs has had a terrible & sudden sorrow befall him—the sudden insanity & death of his young nephew, his dead sister's son, (he visited me here during the past winter) Chancy Burroughs,[20] at Brooklyn two weeks since—Abruptly, mysteriously, from *apparent* health & strength he became a raging maniac & died in three days—& J. B. took up the poor young man's corpse & buried him by his mother's side, there in the mountains of Delaware County—

If I remember right the picture in the gilt frame is the one with the hand up at the right side of the head—so? If so, I have some of them, & will give Mrs. Johnson one with the greatest pleasure—(it is one of Brady's photos)—I wish you to give my best respects & love to Mrs. J. and sister—Also to Garry Howard, Mrs. Huntington, Mrs. Brownell & in fact to "all inquiring friends"—

I still maintain the "great expectations" I have before mentioned—the severe gastric affection, trouble in side & breast, &c still assert themselves at times—dyspepsia, from 17 months inaction—but upon the whole not so severely—& I think very decidedly gradually growing less—The worst is my singular alternations, fluctuations. The heat here too is & has been extreme—but I am standing it well, so far—to-day as I sit here writing, a fair breeze blowing in—

Peter Doyle has ten days since paid me a short visit of a couple of days[21]—the dear, dear boy—& what good it did me!—(Unfortunately it was, however, at a time when I was feeling almost at my worst.) Yesterday George Bacon came, bringing a friend—& we had a capital good hour & a half—*talked Spiritualism*—I enjoyed it though—

Love to you, Nelly dear.

                                                            Walt Whitman

623. *To Rudolf Schmidt*

431 Stevens st.   Camden, | N. Jersey, | U. S. America
June 11, '74.

My dear Rudolf Schmidt,

As you have rec'd my letter of April 25, you know that the copies of *Demokratisk-Fremblik* and of some six newspapers with criticisms, safely reached me here—& one or two more since—& now, yesterday, *Dags*

---

20. Chauncey B. Deyo.
21. The visit took place about May 25; see 617.
22. Roos notes that the conservative *Dags Telegrafen* criticized *Democratic Vistas* on May 20; see *Orbis Litterarum*, VII (1949), 53n.
23. In acknowledging receipt of the poems and other items sent to him, Schmidt

Telegrafen[22]—all of which I treasure, & am to have carefully read to me.

I am still unwell enough to make me remain here, quite idle, but am encouraged to still keep up the expectation of getting quite well—& indeed am improving, though slowly—I enclose a piece of mine just written for Commencement Poem to a College near Boston city—the College is the headquarters of the Universalists—my piece is to be read by proxy—

I enclose you some pieces more on *American humor*, as you are interested in that subject—& a very amusing & 'cute letter by a lady about the darkeys down South—American humor, (like the old Greek, and now the best Italian, Spanish, French humor) is, in a sense *the other side or opposite radiation of pensiveness, & even mystery & hypochondria*—I think it more idiosyncratic & untranslatable than any I have mentioned, Greek, Italian, &c—It is *entirely different* from the English, or English-German[23]—

We have been having one of our American hot-weather spells—real hell-blasts—here lately—four, five, six days. But I have stood them very well indeed. To-day as I sit here writing by the open window, there is a sufficiently cool breeze, & it is very agreeable & moderate, though just past noon. When you write mention whether you rec'd *Redwood Tree* and also *Prayer of Columbus*, both sent March 4. (The *address* on the last papers & letters to me is exactly right, & is sure to reach me.) I intend to send Kristian Elster a copy of my poems, & my photograph—how shall I address him? John Burroughs has been to visit me here—he is settled on a little farm of his own on the Hudson river, 60 miles north of New York city. Your photo. sent in the letter of April 4 is before me as I write.

Walt Whitman

624. *To Peter Doyle*   6.12. [1874][24]

ADDRESS: Peter Doyle, | M st. South—bet 4½ & 6th | Washington, D. C. POSTMARKS: Philadelphia | Jun | (?); Carrier | 13 | Jun(?) | 8 AM.

431 Stevens st. | cor West. | Camden, | N. Jersey.
June 12—5½ p. m.

All about the same—I am standing the hot weather well—shall not go on to Boston, to the College.

W. W.

commented on June 26: "But your humorists of the day I don't like. Mark Twain has been translated into Danish this year. He is a detestable fool" (Syracuse; Traubel, IV, 464).

24. The reference to Tufts College verifies the year.

625. *To Ulysses S. Grant*

431 Stevens st. | Camden, | N. Jersey. | June 22, 1874.

Would it be convenient to the President to personally request of the Attorney General that in any changes in the Solicitor Treasury's office, I be not disturbed in my position as clerk in that office—all my duties to the government being & having been thoroughly & regularly performed there, by a substitute,[25] during my illness.

I shall probably get well before long.[26]

Very respectfully,

Walt Whitman

625.1 *To John Swinton*   *6.24.* [*1874*][26.1]

ADDRESS: John Swinton | 134 E. 38th st. | New York City. POSTMARK: Camden | Jun | 24 | N.J.

431 Stevens st. | cor West. | Camden, | N. Jersey. | June 24.

Your good letter rec'd this morning. Come & see me whenever you can. It is very easy—6 or 8 trains fro & to N. Y. every day & night. Come either by boat to Amboy, & so directly here to Camden depot, (only 60 rods from this house,) or from Jersey City to West Philadelphia depot, & so down Market st. by horse cars to Camden ferry at foot of it. I am about the same. Jeff is here with me (from St. Louis) for a couple of days.

W. W.

626. *To Peter Doyle*   *6.26.* [*1874?*][27]

ADDRESS: Pete Doyle | M st. South bet 4½ & 6th | Washington D C. POSTMARKS: Philadelphia | Ju(?) | 26 | 9 PM | Pa; Carrier | 27 | J(?) | (?).

431 Stevens st.   Camden | N. Jersey | June 26.

Have been quite sick all the week—but as I write (5½ p m) somewhat easier.

W.

25. Walter Godey.

26. WW was evidently aware that a bill approved by Congress on June 20 required a reduction of personnel in the Department of Justice. WW's letter was sent by Grant's secretary to the Attorney General on July 26. It was accompanied by a clipping from the Camden *New Republic* of June 20, which included "Song of the Universal" and WW's (anonymous) comments on his illness. Wechter conjectures that WW had the article printed "with the hope that it might catch Grant's eye more effectually than would a letter"; see *PMLA*, LVIII (1943), 1108.

26.1 This post card was written in reply to Swinton's letter of June 23, in which he spoke of "going toward social radicalism of late years," and promised to visit WW "within a few weeks" (Feinberg; Traubel, I, 24–25 [misdated January 23, 1884]).

27. Since WW wrote to Doyle on Fridays, and since the account of his illness here

627. *To George H. Williams*

431 Stevens st. | Cor West. | Camden, | N. Jersey, | July 1, '74
Hon. Geo H. Williams,[28] | Attorney General. | Sir:

Yours of June 30, informing me of the necessity of terminating my services in the Solicitor's office, Treasury, is respectfully acknowledged.

I see that the dismissed clerks in the Treasury, &c. are to have two months extra pay, (July & August.) Can this allowance be made to me?

Very respectfully,

Walt Whitman

628. *To Peter Doyle*   7.3. *[1874]*[29]

ADDRESS: Pete Doyle | M st. South—bet 4½ & 6th | Washington, D. C. POSTMARKS: Camden | Jul | 3 | N.J.; Carrier | 4 | J(?) | (?).

431 Stevens st.   Camden, | N. J. | July 3—noon

Past week nearly same as heretofore with me—much distress in head & side—rec'd card last Monday—will write more fully next time—

W

629. *Alfred, Lord Tennyson to WW*   *[7.8. 1874]*[30]

TRANSCRIPT.

Dear Mr. Walt Whitman:

I am grieved to hear[31] that you have been so unwell and can only trust that your physician is a true prophet, and that you will recover and be as well as ever. I have myself known a case of cerebral anæmia in a young lady living near me. She lost her mind and no one who saw her believed she could live; but under the superintendence of a good doctor she has perfectly recovered and looks plumper and fresher than ever she did before.

does not contradict that in 622, this post card can be plausibly assigned to 1874.

28. On June 30 Bluford Wilson, Solicitor of the Treasury, informed Williams that "Walt Whitman is the clerk of this class who can be discharged with least detriment to the national service" (National Archives). On the same day Williams informed the poet of his dismissal (Yale). On July 6 (copy in the National Archives) Williams replied that WW was entitled to two months salary.

29. The symptoms mentioned here are fully discussed in 630, in which WW also referred to a post card that Doyle should have received on July 4.

30. According to Donaldson, who reprinted this letter (227–228), the postmark read: "Haslemere, July 8, 1874."

31. See 616.

This is the first letter I have written for weeks, and I am afraid I write rather obscurely, for my hand and arm have been crippled with rheumatism (I hope it is not gout), and I am not yet perfectly recovered.

I was beholden to you for your Democratic Vistas,[32] and if I did not answer and acknowledge them I regret to have done so; but if you knew how great the mass of my correspondence is, and how much I dislike letter-writing, I doubt not, you would forgive me easily.

When I next hear of or from you may the news be that you are fully re-established in your old vigor and body: Meanwhile believe me
Yours ever

A Tennyson

630. *To Peter Doyle*   *7.10.* [*1874*]

431 Stevens st. | cor West. | Camden, | N. Jersey. | July 10.
Dear, dear son,
I am still here—still suffering pretty badly—have great distress in my head, & an almost steady pain in left side—but my worst troubles let up on me part of the time—the evenings are my best times—& somehow I still keep up in spirit, &, (the same old story,) *expect* to get better.

I have been discharged from my clerkship in the Solicitor's office, Treasury, by the new Solicitor, Mr. Wilson.

I think of laying up here in Camden. I have bought a cheap lot—& think of putting up a little two or three room house for myself.[33] My darling son, you must not be unhappy about me—I hope & trust things may work so that we can yet be with each other, at least from time to time —& meanwhile we must adapt ourselves to circumstances. You keep on, & try to do right, & live the same square life you always have, & maintain as cheerful a heart as possible—& as for the way things finally turn out, leave that to the Almighty—

Pete, I shall want you or Mr. Eldridge to see to the sending on here of my boxes at Dr. Whites.[34] I will write further about it—I have not heard any thing from Eldridge, or Mrs. O'Connor, or any of the Washington folk for quite a long time. Have you been up to see Mrs. O'C. Pete, didn't you get my *last Saturday's* postal card? I wrote you one. I got yours last Monday—Did you get the Camden paper with my College piece in?[35] I sent one.

32. WW sent *Democratic Vistas* in 1872; see 443.
33. On May 26 Thomas A. Wilson had offered WW a lot on Royden Street for $450 (Feinberg).
34. According to a letter dated July 29, Mrs. Isabella A. White, WW's landlady (see 546), had written, evidently early in July, about the rent due for his room. His reply is not extant. On the 29th Mrs. White offered to purchase WW's bedstead and certain other effects. WW had not settled his account when Mrs. White wrote again on October 6, and offered him a credit of $10 for his furnishings against a balance of $38. These

Very hot here yesterday & to-day. I don't fret at all about being discharged—it is just as well—I wonder it didnt come before—How are your folks at home—your dear mother & all—write about all, & about Mr. & Mrs. Nash, Wash Milburn, & the RR boys—

Your old Walt

631. *To Peter Doyle*   *7.17. [1874]*

> ADDRESS: Peter Doyle, | M st. South, bet 4½ & 6th |
> Washington, D. C. POSTMARKS: Camden | Jul | 17 |
> N.J.; Carrier | 18 | Jul | 8 AM.

431 Stevens st. | cor West. | Camden, N. J. | Friday noon
July 17.

Your last rec'd. As I write am quite comfortable—but have been pretty sick the past week, by spells.

W W

632. *To Rudolf Schmidt*   *7.28–8.28. 1874*

July 28, 1874.

Yours of June 26[36] duly arrived some days since.

1) I have sent a paper to Kr. Elster at Throudhjem, containing my last, (the College poem) & a piece in about my sickness. I sent you a copy same paper.

2) The letter you speak of, (March 20,) duly reached me. I have no doubt, dear friend, that all the letters, papers, sheets, &c. during the last three years sent me by your loving kindness & attention have every one reached me. (The post office here is among the best things of the New World—is sure, quick, cheap, & every way admirable. If letters addressed to me go to other cities, as they sometimes do, they are pretty sure eventually to come *here*—the post office men, even the carriers, are wonderfully bright & intuitive.)

3) I will be on the look out for John Burroughs's photograph—he is well at last accounts.

4) I myself have *pleased myself* more fully with *Redwood Tree* than any of my pieces of late years.[37] But it is generally thought wild & cloudy

letters are in the Feinberg Collection.
>   35. "Song of the Universal" appeared in the Camden *New Republic* on June 20.
>   36. WW's letter is a point-by-point reply to Schmidt's (Syracuse; Traubel, IV, 464–465).
>   37. Of "Song of the Redwood-Tree" Schmidt observed: "It is your old great theme in a simple and powerful stile, embracing the holy and original nation of the far West" (Syracuse; Traubel, IV, 464).

here—(the *Columbus* is more popular far)—I suppose it is hardly necessary to tell you that I have *pitched* and *keyed* my pieces more with reference to fifty years hence, & how they will stand mellowed and toned *then*—than to pleasing & tickling the immediate impressions of the present hour.

6)[37.1] I have not heard any thing more of C. Petersen lately—but if I meet with any thing of his printed, I will send you.

7) All the criticisms, Danish papers, & those from Norway, duly rec'd—to be carefully translated & read to me—*I prize them all, very much*—but I am yet feeble, & read, write &c. as little as possible. 8) One or two little items have been in the papers here about the *Fremblik* translation. I get along with your English very well indeed—

W. W.

431 Stevens st. Camden, | N. Jersey. | U. S. America | Aug. 28, '74
Rudolf Schmidt | My dear friend,

Your letter of July 28, from Gaûsdal,[38] in "old Norway" reached me to-day. Quite curiously, on the very same day, I was writing to you—as per sheet accompanying, written at date (a month ago) but not sent until I could add further. I am glad to get your letter from Norway—am still laid up sick & lonesome here—do not seem to get any thing like well, & at times the prospect is very uncertain—yet maintain a steady heart. I was dismissed from my clerkship under Government at Washington about two months ago. I write this by my open window—the majestic & beautiful Delaware flows near, in sight—we have had a fine summer in America—& now a spell of rich, golden, mellow weather—far & near wonderful crops of every thing—now beginning to be gathered.

Walt Whitman

633. *To Peter Doyle*   *7.31.* [*1874?*][39]

ADDRESS: Pete Doyle, | M street South bet 4½ &
6th | Washington, D. C. POSTMARKS: Philadelphia |
Jul | 31(?) | 12 M | Pa.; Carrier | Aug | 1 | 8 AM.

431 Stevens st. | Camden, | N. Jersey | July 31.
Though some bad spells still, things *decidedly more favorable* in my condition. I shall get up yet.

W

37.1. WW's numbering is inaccurate.
38. This letter is in the Feinberg Collection.
39. The dating of this post card as well as the notes and letters to Doyle on August 7, 14, 21, and 28, depends in part on WW's habit of writing on Fridays. However, as evidenced in 634 and 637, both of which were conclusively written in 1874, WW's "alternations" were especially marked during the summer of this year, and despite his

634. *To Ellen M. O'Connor*   8.5. [*1874*][40]

ENDORSED: "Ans'd." ADDRESS: Mrs. E. M.
O'Connor, | 1015 O street, near 11th N. W. |
Washington | D. C. POSTMARKS: Camden | Aug |
5 | N.(?); Carrier | 6 | Aug | 8 AM.

431 Stevens st. | cor West. | Camden, | N. Jersey. | Aug 5.
Dear Nelly,
      Your good letter came all right—it is pretty much "the same sub-
ject continued"—with my health & feelings—very grave depressions,
alternated with more favorable spells—
      To-day, as I write, I am in good spirits & comparatively comfortable—
after a painful attack last night—So it goes—What will be the finale remains to be seen.
      I await your further letters with some curiosity—(for strange as it may
seem, *men* have that weakness as well as *your sect*)—I have to-day dispatched dear Mrs. Johnson's picture by mail—(It is intended to be put in
a *square gray or white mat with oval top*, & then in a plain black walnut
rustic square frame, with thin strip of gilt inside, & good plate glass)—I
shall look for Charles Eldridge—
      My sister is spending a few weeks at Atlantic City—I am *here*, (de-
clining several invitations) muchly but pleasantly, *alone*—We have a
fine old Irish woman, (an old maid, not so very old either) who cooks
nicely & runs the domestic machinery, for brothers George & Eddy, &
self—She little knows how much good she does me with her great splendid
coarse face & stout figure & warm-blooded & quaint & simple & affectionate
ways—Write soon, Nelly dear—
                                                           Walt.

635. *To Peter Doyle*   8.7. [*1874*][41]

ADDRESS: Pete Doyle, | M street South, bet 4½ & 6th |
Washington, D. C. POSTMARKS: Camden | Aug |
7 | N.J.; Carrier | 8 | Aug | 8 AM.

431 Stevens st. Camden, N. J. | Aug. 7.
      All about the same—write to me about *Tasistro* in your next—Am
here partially alone—folks gone to Atlantic city—I prefer staying here—

"natural buoyancy" he was frequently depressed by the inability of his once healthy body
to triumph over his ailments.
      40. The date is corroborated by the allusion to Mrs. Johnson in the third para-
graph; see 622.
      41. The visit of George and Louisa to Atlantic City was mentioned in the preceding
letter. See also 633.

wish you was here with me—head aching badly to-day—in good spirits though—

W. W.

636. *To Peter Doyle* 8.14. *[1874]*[42]

ADDRESS: Peter Doyle, | M street south | bet 4½ and 6th streets, | Washington, | D. C. POSTMARK: Camden | Aug | 15 | N.J.

431 Stevens st. | cor West. | Camden, | N. Jersey. | Aug 14. Dear Son,

I am not feeling very bright to-day—hardly capable of writing a cheerful letter—& I dont want to send you a *blue* one—Will feel better by next time,

Your Walt

637. *To John and Ursula Burroughs* 8.18. *[1874]*[43]

431 Stevens st. | cor West. | Camden, | N. Jersey. | Aug. 18. Dear John & 'Sula Burroughs,

The interval of some weeks, (or is it months?) since I last wrote you[44] has passed on, bringing no decided change in my condition—in my bad spells, (& I have them often enough) I 'most think the end is not far off—but I get over them & my natural buoyancy reässerts itself—(& in the main keeps control of the helm)—though to a man of my *lazy-activity* this whole condition & sickness of mine is very wearing—

To-day I am feeling very comfortable, sitting here in the front room by the open window writing this—eat this morning quite a respectable breakfast, beefsteak, bread, & tea—& at about 3 shall make a light, moderate bite of dinner—no supper—I find I get along best with *one pretty fair meal only*, & that I make breakfast—The gastric & dyspeptic trouble has been serious, & is perhaps so yet—pains in left side, distress in head, &c— the old story—

John Swinton came down from N. Y. & spent Sunday with me—told me lots of N. Y. newspaper news, &c.—it was a very welcome visit to me.

42. See 633.
43. The reference to his dismissal from his government post establishes the year.
44. See 619. 45. See 629.

I was discharged from my clerkship on the last of June, by B. Wilson, the new Solicitor of the Treasury—(it is all right)—All questions of *what I shall do* are to me so subordinate to the question of whether I shall soon or ever get well, (or partially well,) that I hardly entertain them seriously —I enclose you Tennyson's latest letter to me[45]—also a slip Swinton gave me—Send them both back in your next letter—Eldridge is in Boston on his vacation—I expect a visit from him in about 12 days, on his way back —Best love to you both, & I shall be with you yet, I have no doubt.

Walt.

638. *To Peter Doyle*   8.21. [1874][46]

ADDRESS: Pete Doyle, | M street South, bet 4½ & 6th | Washington, D. C. POSTMARKS: Camden | Aug | 21 | N.J.; Carrier | 22 | Aug | (?).

431 Stevens st | Camden, | N. Jersey. | Aug 21.
Your last, & paper, rec'd—have had a tolerably good week but nothing to brag of—middling comfortable to-day—very hot here to-day— tell your RR. chum if he sees me in Phil. he must make himself known to me.

W. W.

639. *To Peter Doyle*   8.28. [1874][47]

ADDRESS: Pete Doyle, | M street South | bet. 4½ & 6th | Washington, D. C. POSTMARK: Camden | Aug | 28(?) | N.J.

431 Stevens st. Camden, | Aug 28.
Dear Pete,
Nothing very new with me—rather a mixed week—some suffering —Pete, if you have a decided wish to go on the Pulman car, & are pretty clear that it would be a good move, I will let you have $100.
Good bye for this time, dear son—Your

Walt

46. See 633. According to the preceding letter WW was enjoying a slight respite from pain.
47. See 633.

640. *To Peter Doyle*   *11.3. [1874]*[48]

ADDRESS: Peter Doyle | M street south | bet 4½ &
6th | Washington | D. C. POSTMARK: Camden |
Nov | 3(?) | N.J.

Camden, Nov. 3.

Dear boy,

I have rec'd your letter, & enclose the $10 for you. I am still the
same—am all alone in the house to-day, as my brother has gone to New
York & my sister has gone somewhere visiting to spend the day. How I
wish you were here to-day—

Walt.

641. *To Ellen M. O'Connor*   *11.23. [1874]*[49]

ADDRESS: Mrs. E. M. O'Connor, | 1015 O street, n.
11th n. w. | Washington, | D. C. POSTMARK:
Camden | No(?) | 23 | (?).

431 Stevens st. | cor West. | Camden, | N. Jersey.
Nov. 23—2 p. m.

Dear Nelly,

Your late letter reached me, enclosing the piece from the *Academy*.[50]

I have been worse than usual for a week—very pronounced swimming spells & dizziness in the head, with sometimes deathly faintness &
great prostration—(twice I thought serious)—am sitting up to-day &
yesterday—havn't been out—now this is the ninth day—continuous
qualmishness & headache—doctor thinks however it is all substantially a
stomach & liver business—he comes every day—does not seem to be
alarmed—I am taking mild powders of mercury for the liver—& drops
composed of bromides of potash & ammonia—

There is death all around me here—Two yesterday of persons I know
—I send you a piece by me from the paper here[51]—the young man alluded
to was much like one of my most cherished soldier cases in the Hospitals

48. This letter cannot have been written in 1875, as the executors suggested:
Louisa had a baby on November 4, 1875, and WW at that time was preparing to leave
for Washington.
    Since WW for fifteen months had written a weekly letter or post card to Doyle, it is
strange that there is no correspondence which can be assigned with certainty to this
period of over two months.
    49. The year is confirmed by the succeeding notes.
    50. *The Academy* of October 10 (VI, 398–400) contained George Saintsbury's
favorable review of *Leaves of Grass*.

ten years since. He lived on the next block, & I was with him a great deal— & at death.

Nelly, I just send you, (although one or two items confidential, sort o') Mrs. Price's last letter to me, two days since—read it, & destroy it—I also send Mrs. Davis's, she (Mrs. P) sent me, as you are interested in her—

I shall get better, & shall come on to Washington yet—on a brief visit—Tell Charles Eldridge I shall write to him this week—My brother & sister & Eddy here are well—My sister at Burlington, Vt. was as usual at last acc'ts—also Jeff & his girls at St. Louis—As I write I am sitting here in my big chair alone (*alone muchly,*) in the parlor by the window— It is a rainy darkish day here—the wind south & mild—

Walt

If Pete Doyle comes up to see you, read him this letter—also give him the printed slip to read—

642. *To Charles W. Eldridge*   *12.2.* [*1874*]

431 Stevens st. | cor West. | Camden, | N. Jersey, | Dec. 2—p. m.
Dear friend,

The address I want you to send the Tax & Revenue books, reports, documents, or whatever to is

To Paul Liptay[52]

Care of Otto Behrens[53]

140 Eighth avenue

New York City

& write me a line as soon as you have sent them, naming what you have sent.

I wrote to Nelly about a week ago, stating my condition, & what a plight I have been in—& am partially yet—though slowly coming round to what I was just previous—

The doctor still comes every day—rather a curious fellow—a great bully, vehement, loud words & plenty of them (the very reverse of my valued Dr Drinkard)—& yet I value what *he* says & does for me—He is inclined to think the seat of all my woe has been (what no one ever whis-

51. "Death of a Fireman," a tribute to a Camden fireman named William Alcott, appeared in the Camden *New Republic* on November 14, 1874. Harry Bonsall, the editor of this newspaper, was one of WW's Camden friends; see Allen, 461.

52. According to a calling card pasted in the *Commonplace Book* (Feinberg), Lipstay (not Liptay) was a correspondent for "Hungarian Journals." He visited WW on August 26, 1876. He was also listed in one of WW's address books (LC #108).

53. Listed as a carver in the New York Directory of 1874-1875 and as an engraver in the following year.

pered before,) the *liver*, acted upon largely also, perhaps almost primarily, thro[ugh] the emotional nature—at any rate he is decided that the present botherations are absolutely *liver* troubles, & their radiations—

Charley, I have had a sick, sick three weeks since you were here—havn't been out, except just in front of the house in the sun, & only three times that—but don't be alarmed, my dear friend—the probabilities are, (in my opinion any how,) that I shall get partially well yet—

Walt.

643. *To Peter Doyle*   *12.3.* [*1874*][54]

431 Stevens st. | cor West. | Camden, | N. Jersey, | Dec. 3—noon
Dear Pete, Dear son,

I am getting over my late bad spell—I have been very sick indeed, the feeling of death & dizziness, my head swimming a great deal of the time—turning like a wheel—with much distress in left side, keeps me awake some nights all night—the doctor says, however, these troubles, in his opinion, are from a very serious & obstinate *liver affection—not* from head, lungs, heart, he still thinks there is nothing but what I will get the better of—(& we will trust he is a true prophet)—

I wrote about like the foregoing to Mrs. O'Connor,[55] but was too sick to repeat it to you—& that was one reason I asked you to go up there—I havn't been out for three weeks, but ventured out yesterday for an hour, & got along better than I expected—& shall go out, or try to, to-day, as it is very pleasant—You must not be needlessly alarmed, my darling boy, for I still think I shall get, at any rate, partially well & strong enough—The doctor is quite encouraging—comes every day—& I feel a good heart yet—My young fireman friend Alcott[56] (I think I mentioned his sickness,) is dead & buried, poor fellow—I send you a bit of piece of mine about him from the paper—I have some spurts of visits, & company—but very little that goes to the right spot, with me—my brother George has got a horse &

54. The year assigned by the executors, 1875, is erroneous, as the notes below confirm.

55. See 641.   56. William Alcott; see 641.

57. The letter is dated "[1874]," evidently by Reid.

58. Reid (1837–1912) was the editor of the New York *Tribune* from 1872 to 1905. He met WW in the hospitals during the Civil War. Of his relations with the poet Reid later observed: "No one could fail then [during the War] to admire his zeal and devotion, and I am afraid that at first my regard was for his character rather than his poetry. It was not till long after 'The Leaves of Grass' period that his great verses on the death of Lincoln conquered me completely"; see Charles N. Elliot, *Walt Whitman as Man, Poet and Friend* (1915), 213, and *SB*, VIII (1956), 242–249.

59. Reid apparently did not publish this unidentified article.

60. Seemingly in a lost letter to Reid, WW had protested what he considered a slurring reference to his health in a news item in the *Tribune*. In apologizing on December 22, Reid promised to "have a paragraph within a day or two, which will I think relieve

light wagon, & takes me out now & then—I enjoy it much—but I have been too feeble lately—altogether pretty lonesome here, but might be much worse—Love to Mrs. & Mr. Nash, & to all inquiring friends—

Your old Walt

644. *To Whitelaw Reid*   12.5. *[1874]*

431 Stevens st. | cor West. | Camden, | N. Jersey, | Dec 5.[57]

My dear Reid,[58]

Hasn't this got vim enough—from your point of view, even as editor of the paper—to make you print it in the *Tribune?*[59]

I am still tediously invalided here—but have not at all given up the hope of getting out of the woods, & doing some work yet.

When you come to Philadelphia, try to come over & see me.[60]

Walt Whitman

645. *To John Burroughs*   12.11. *[1874]*[61]

431 Stevens st. | cor West. | Camden, | N. Jersey.
Dec. 11—p. m.

Dear John Burroughs,

I have had another severe spell the last five weeks—head troubles, & stomach troubles, & *liver* troubles—the doctor thinks the latter the seat & basis this time of all, or nearly all—head-swimming, faintness, vomiting, &c—but for three or four days past have been easier—am up—didn't go out for three to four weeks, but am venturing out a little now—hope & quite expect to get at least as well as I was before this spell—

Eldridge has made me a call of two or three hours, (on his return from Boston to Wash'n)—Seems to be nothing very new among our friends at Wash'n—Marvin[62] has written me twice—he has been reading your "Notes," & is quite possessed with them—also "Dem. Vistas"—

you of the idea that we had any such intention" (Feinberg; Traubel, I, 463). A complimentary notice appeared in the issue of December 26; see 651.

61. The executors dated this letter 1873. However, that 1874 is the correct year is evidenced by the following notes.

62. Joseph B. Marvin had been co-editor of *The Radical* in 1866–1867; see Mott, III, 78n. Later he was employed in the Treasury Department in Washington. On December 15, 1874, Marvin wrote to WW: "I read and re-read your poems, and the 'Vistas,' and more and more see that I had but a faint comprehension of them before. They surpass everything. All other books seem to me weak and unworthy my attention. I read, Sunday, to my wife, Longfellow's verses on Sumner, in the last Atlantic, and then I read your poem on the Death of Lincoln. It was like listening to a weak-voiced girl singing with piano accompanyment, and then to an oratorio by the whole Handel Society, with accompanyment by the Music Hall organ" (LC). His veneration of WW is also transparent in an article in *The Radical Review*, I (1877), 224–259.

I am writing very little—have a piece, a *melange*, prose & verse, in the "*Christmas Graphic*"[63]—(comes out in a week or so,) in which I say a brief word about Emerson—

To eke out my letter I send a scrap from paper about death of a young friend of mine[64]—also another scrap—also another from London *Academy*,[65] (which latter only please return when you write)—

Best love to 'Sula—*Merry Christmas*—do you get in the new house? Write me a good long letter—I wish I was with you—

Walt.

646. *To the Editor of the New York* Daily Graphic
12.16. [*1874*]

TRANSCRIPT.

Camden, N. J., December 16.

Your notes[66] inviting me to write about Spiritualism reached me during a late severe spell of illness, which will account for their not being answered at the time. I thank you for your courtesy, but I am neither disposed nor able to write anything about this so-called Spiritualism. (It seems to me nearly altogether a poor, cheap, crude humbug.)

Walt Whitman

647. *To Bethuel Smith* [*12. (?). 1874*]

DRAFT LETTER.

My dear friend,[67]

Your letter has reached me here, & it is a real comfort to hear from Bethuel once more. Years have passed away but I find there is something in the friendship formed amid sickness, or with the wounded in hospital that comes up again fresh and living as ever and remains as if it cannot pass away. Bethuel, dear comrade, I must write a few [lines] how I should like to see you. I want to hear all about you, & how you are getting

---

63. "A Christmas Garland" consisted of miscellaneous observations on various subjects and occasional poems; it is reprinted in *UPP*, II, 53–58.

64. "Death of a Fireman"; see 641.

65. George Saintsbury's review of *Leaves of Grass*.

66. When this letter was printed on December 19, the newspaper item stated that WW had been sent a circular and an "accompanying letter." The *Daily Graphic* had printed in other issues comments (mostly sympathetic) on the subject. This letter was discovered by Professor Harold W. Blodgett.

67. See 79.

68. Bethuel, who replied on March 12, 1875, had four children, hauled wood for a paper mill near Queensbury, N. Y., and had grave financial problems: ". . . this spring I

along—all the particulars will be interesting—when I think of those old times in the hospital & our being together, you seem to me like my own son.[68]

I worked in Washington after the war—had a stroke of paralysis now two years since, was getting better, then some serious troubles happened to me, & I fell back again—I have left Brooklyn & Washington for good —& am now laid up here—I am neither well enough to do any work, nor sick enough to give up—go out some though lame, & keep a pretty good heart, hoping for better times. Bethuel, I enclose an envelope for you— dear boy, I want you to write me a good long letter—my best best love to you, & a happy new year—

Mrs. Smith, I thank you for writing to me,[69] it has done me good— I send my best respects & love to you—& my love to the youngest son living with you. I will send some papers.

648. *To Peter Doyle*   [*1874?*][70]

431 Stevens st. | cor West. | Camden, | N. Jersey.
Friday—2 p. m.

Dear Pete,

Nothing special to write you, about myself, or any thing else, this week. Your letter & the Herald came last Monday. The time goes very tedious with me—& yet I think I am getting better, (but don't know for sure.) Still have frequent bad spells.

I stopt at the W. Philadelphia depot, Market street, two or three evenings ago, in the general passengers' room, to rest, about 10 minutes. Then took the car for Market st. ferry, (a mile and a half, or three quarters) & over to Camden, home—I get desperate at staying in, not a *human* soul for cheer, or sociability or fun—& this continued week after week & month after month—

So you met Johnny Saunders, in Baltimore, & he is flourishing. If you see him again, tell him to write to me—he is a young man I always loved.

am owing some debts that I dont no whether I can pay them or not" (Feinberg).

69. Mrs. Smith wrote about her family on December 10. WW's draft was written on the verso of her letter. In reply to WW's letter and later ones, she wrote again on February 1 and March 14, 1875 (Feinberg). In the latter she said: "it awlways seemed to me that god sent you to save the life of our son that he might Come home and see his parents once more."

70. The only clue to the date is the reference to the dictionary, which WW mentioned in 567. April 3, 1874, is a possibility since it is the only Friday in the early part of the year for which there is no extant letter or card. There is an envelope in the Feinberg Collection with the following postmarks: Camden | Apr | 3 | N.J.; Carrier | 4 | Ap(?) | 8 AM.

½ *past* 2—I have just had a nice oyster stew for my dinner—it is blustering weather, partly clear, partly cloudy, & one or two little flirts of snow to-day. I send you a paper or two, but nothing in them. I will try to stop in Philadelphia & find that little dictionary I promised you—

So long, my loving son,

Your old Walt

649. *To Peter Doyle*   [*1874?*][71]
Camden, | Friday afternoon.

Dear Pete,

I still remain about the same, & with nothing to write about in the way of my improvement, or any thing else—but I thought you would want to have a word. Your letter of last Sunday came all right. The paper has also come. I am no worse—& continue to live on *hope*—fortunately I have been stocked with a good plentiful share of it. It is pleasant weather here, though hot—we have frequent rains—We have had one to-day, about an hour ago, but now it is very bright and pleasant—I am going to try to get out a little

So good bye for this time, dear son—I hope to write more of a letter next time.

Walt.

71. The date given to this letter by the executors, August 29, is incorrect, since it fell on Saturday in 1874. The letter could have been written at any time during the warm months.

1875

650. *To A. C. Floyd*   *1.7. [1875?]*

431 Stevens st | cor West. | Camden, | N. Jersey. | Jan 7.
A. C. Floyd,[1] | Dear Sir,

As far as I can tell by my impression—which is a very vague one—
for I have never seen the book—"the White Rose & Red," was reprinted
from the foreign copy by the publishers, Roberts Bro. of Boston, a year or
two ago—(perhaps more.) Seems to me it was attributed to Robert Buchanan the English poet.[2]

I am still unwell from my cerebral trouble—but still looking for better
times, & counting on them.

Walt Whitman

651. *To Ellen M. O'Connor*   *1.7. [1875][3]*

ADDRESS: Mrs. E. M. O'Connor | 1015 O street, near
11th N. W. | Washington D. C. POSTMARKS:
Camden | Jan | 8 | N.J.; Carrier | 9 | Jan | 8 AM.

431 Stevens st. | cor West. | Camden, N. Jersey, | Jan. 7.

Am feeling better than during Nov. and first part of Dec—
strength better than for a long time—rec'd the *Springfield Rep[ublican]*[4]
this morning—(is it from you or Ch[arley]?)[5]—That ¶ in the T[ribune][6]
was the most flourishing puff yet given me—& from *them!*—A leaden,

---

1875
1. Unidentified. The year, of course, is conjectural.
2. *White Rose and Red. A Love Story* was published by Osgood & Co. in 1873.
The name of the author, Robert Buchanan, did not appear on the title page, but there
was the following inscription: "To Walt Whitman and Alexander Gardiner, with all
friends in Washington, I dedicate this book."
3. In light of the references to the two newspapers, discussed in the notes below,
the year seems reasonably certain.
4. Perhaps the issue of December 29, in which a correspondent expressed surprise
that WW was not included in Emerson's *Parnassus*, and noted the New York *Tribune's*
change in attitude; see notes to 644.
5. Charles Eldridge.
6. Probably a reference to a paragraph in the New York *Tribune* on December 26,
which commented on WW's services during the Civil War, and concluded: ". . . we
need not share or contest the opinion of his poetry held by Mr. Tennyson and Mr. Emerson, to hope that he may soon recover and that he may enjoy the peaceful age he has
earned." In the judgment of WW and his friends, the *Tribune* had been hostile chiefly
because of the influence of Bayard Taylor.

heavy day here, with sulky rain & some snow & sleet—I have to stay in, but am feeling comfortable.

WW

652. *To Ellen M. O'Connor* 1.11. [1875?][7]

ADDRESS: Mrs. E. M. O'Connor | 1015 O st. near 11th N. W. | Washington, D. C. POSTMARKS: Camden | Jan | 11 | N.J.; Carrier | 12 | Jan | 3(?) PM.

431 Stevens st. | cor West. | Camden, | N. Jersey | Jan. 11.
Card came this morning. Letter you speak of must have been destroyed, as I have rec'd none—Rec'd letter from P[eter] D[oyle] this morning. Am still getting along favorably considering all things—Heard from J[ohn] B[urroughs] last week—all well. Had a letter from Dr. Drinkard—

WW

653. *To Peter Doyle* 2.5. [1875][8]

ADDRESS: Pete Doyle, | M st South—bet 4½ & 6th | Washington, D. C. POSTMARKS: Camden | Feb | 5(?) | N.J.; Carrier | 6 | Feb | 8 AM.

431 Stevens st. | cor West. | Camden, | N. Jersey. | Feb. 5.
About the same as at last writing—ups & downs. I want to come on to Wash'n yet—& shall do so, soon as able—Did you get a Camden paper? Yours came, & card, last Tuesday.

W W

654. *To John R. and Rebecca B. Johnston*

431 Stevens St. | Cor. West. | Camden | N. Jersey. | Feb. 9, 1875.
My dear friends, John R. & Rebecca B. Johnston,[9]
This then is the 28th anniversary of your marriage day.
God bless you both.

Walt Whitman.

7. Since Mrs. O'Connor's letters to WW during this period are not extant, the year must remain conjectural. Certain facts point to 1875: the post card WW used was discontinued early in 1876, and Burroughs visited WW at Camden about the middle of January in 1876.
8. The four brief post cards to Doyle in February were written on Fridays, and the discussion of his ailments is confirmed in 660, which can be positively assigned to this year. Obviously this post card was written before WW's visit to Washington in November, 1875.
9. Among early friends at Camden was John R. Johnston, "the jolliest man I ever

I wonder if you either of you have any idea how the otherwise monotony of my Camden existence has been pleasantly rippled—how warm & bright those gleams to me—from the unvarying hospitality and sweet friendship of both of you—God bless you.

W.W.

655. *To Peter Doyle*   2.12. [1875][10]

ADDRESS: Pete Doyle, | M st South, bet 4½ & 6th | Washington, D. C. POSTMARKS: Camden | Feb | 12 | N.J.; Carrier | 13 | Feb | (?) AM.

431 Stevens st. | cor West. | Camden, | N. Jersey. | Feb. 12.
All about as usual. Yours rec'd. The past week here the stormiest of winter—have kept in—

W W

656. *To Peter Doyle*   2.19. [1875][11]

ADDRESS: Peter Doyle, | M st South—bet 4½ & 6th | Washington, D. C. POSTMARK: Camden | Feb. | 19 | N.J.

431 Stevens st. | cor West. | Camden, | N. Jersey. | Feb. 19.
Had another par[alytic] stroke Tuesday last—but not severe. This time, *right side*—Am now about as usual—Snow storm as I write, but I am going out, but not far—

WW

657. *To William J. Linton*

ENDORSED: "to W. J. Linton | Feb 24 '75." DRAFT LETTER.

Camden, | Feb. 24 '75.

My dear Linton;
I want you to have printed very nicely for me 1000 impressions of the cut, my head, to go in book.[12] Herewith I send the size of sheet. If convenient I should like to see a proof, facsimile, first.

met, an artist, a great talker," WW wrote in 554. Johnston was a portrait and landscape painter who for years maintained a studio in Philadelphia and lived at 434 Penn Street in Camden. See *The New-York Historical Society Dictionary of Artists in America, 1564–1860* (1957). On the verso of Anne Gilchrist's letter of February 21, 1875, WW scrawled some trial lines for an inscription: "written in memory of the good times Sunday evening's in Penn street, 1875—'4 & '3." The poet was fond of Johnston's children, Ida and Jack (John Jr.).

10. See 653.   11. See 653.
12. Appeared in the 1876 edition of *Leaves of Grass*.

I am still holding out here—don't get well yet—& don't go under yet. Love to you—Write immediately on receiving this.

This sized sheet—print *dark* in color as you think they will stand, (I dont like them too weak in color).

658. *To Peter Doyle*   2.26. [1875][13]

ADDRESS: Pete Doyle, | M st. South—bet 4½ & 6th | Washington, D. C. POSTMARK: Camden | Feb | 26 | N.J.

431 Stevens st. | cor West. | Camden, | N. Jersey. | Feb. 26.
A bright day again here, after some ugly weather. Pete, a bad month past, with me, but might have been worse—Bad spells frequent—strength, however, pretty fair—Out a little every day or so. Spirits good. Comfortable now as I write—Wish you was here—paper & card came all right—

W. W.

659. *To John Swinton*   2.26. [1875][14]

ADDRESS: John Swinton | 134 East 38th st. | New York City. POSTMARK: Camden | Feb | 26 | N.J.

431 Stevens st. | cor West. | Camden, | N. Jersey, | Feb. 26.
Will write you just a line to-day—Have had a perverse two months, past—frequent bad spells, (some very bad)—general strength, however, pretty fair—get outdoors a little most every day. Spirits good. Write soon, or come personally—

W W

13. See 653.
14. WW's description of his health establishes the year. Note also the following letter.
15. That this letter was written in 1875 is confirmed by the succeeding notes. In addition, as indicated in 657, WW had begun plans for a new edition of his works.
16. On February 16; see 656.
17. Conway arrived in America in September; see 689.
18. At the time WW wrote to Burroughs he had received, as he said, six letters from the colorful and eccentric John Newton Johnson, a self-styled philosopher from rural Alabama. There are about thirty letters from Johnson in the Feinberg Collection, but unfortunately there are no replies extant, although WW wrote frequently for a period of approximately fifteen years. When Johnson wrote for the first time on September 13, 1874, he was forty-two, "gray as a rat," a former Rebel soldier with an income between $300 and $400 annually, though before the war he had been "a youthful 'patriarch.'" He informed WW that during the past summer he had bought *Leaves of Grass* and after a

660. *To John and Ursula Burroughs*   3.2. [*1875*][15]

431 Stevens st. | cor West. | Camden | N. Jersey. | March 2.
Dear John, & 'Sula,

This will show you that "the lamp still holds out to burn"—though I have had a bad two months past—I have had another paralytic stroke,[16] but it passed over, without any thing serious, (it is probable I have had several slight strokes)—but I am feeling, as I write, about the same as is now usual for me—still entertain expectations—

If practicable I shall bring out a Vol. the coming summer—I hope to pay you *the visit* yet—Did you get the paper I sent with a report of Emerson's late lecture on *Eloquence*—of course interesting, from him, but nothing very stunning, it seemed to me—I see that Conway is coming to America next autumn certain, to see things, travel, lecture, &c[17]—

John, [I] send you the last letter from a quondam correspondent & unseen rebel friend of mine, away down in Alabama[18]—He seems to me a good affectionate fellow, a sort of uncut gem—I have had five or six letters from him, all primitive but good—What are *you* about?—& how are you & 'Sula getting along?

Walt Whitman

My brother & sister well—brother full of business—

661. *To John Swinton*   3.12. [*1875?*][19]

ADDRESS: John Swinton | 134 E. 38th Street | New York City. POSTMARK: Camden | (?) | 12 | N.J.

431 Stevens st. | cor West. | Camden, | N. Jersey. | March 12.
Yours rec'd—Come by all means—nothing very new—bad spells continued, & then a let up—(pretty much the same old story)—Telegraph to me about coming—

WW

momentary suspicion that the bookseller should be "*hung for swindling,*" he discovered the mystery of WW's verse, and "I assure you I was soon 'cavorting' round and asserting that the $3 book was worth $50 if it could not be replaced. (Now Laugh)." He offered either to sell WW's poetry and turn over to him all profits or to lend him money. In the letter he enclosed a gold dollar: "So much grand poetry nearly kills me with the pain of delight." Characteristically, he concluded his letter with an unexpected question: "Walt! Are you Orthodox or Universalist? I am Materialist of late." On October 7, after describing Guntersville, Ala., he commented: "*Orthodoxy* flourishes with the usual *lack* of *flowers* or *fruit.*" His amusingly detailed description of his face on November 7, 1875, WW marked in red crayon. Thus Johnson became a self-designated philosophical jester to amuse WW. See also Elliot, *Walt Whitman as Man, Poet and Friend* (1915), 125–130.

19. This post card can be plausibly assigned to 1875, since Swinton visited WW within a few weeks; see 665.

662. *To Peter Doyle*   *3.19. [1875?]*[20]

ADDRESS: Pete Doyle, | M st South, bet 4½ & 6th, |
Washington, D. C. POSTMARK: Camden | (?) |
19 | N.J.

431 Stevens st. | cor West. | Camden, | N. Jersey. | March 19.
Think I am getting round to my former state—(Still some bad
spells)—go out when the weather permits—hope confidently for better
times when the spring opens—card & paper came—

WW

663. *To Peter Doyle*   *3.26. [1875?]*[21]

ADDRESS: Pete Doyle, | M st. South, bet 4½ & 6th |
Washington, D. C. POSTMARKS: Camden | Mar | 26 |
(?); Carrier | 27 | Mar | 8 AM.

431 Stevens st. | cor West. | Camden, | N. Jersey. | March 26.
Still around, much the same—ups & downs, (plenty of the latter)—
Ah, Pete, if you [could] only come on to Phil. & lay over, instead of
Balt[imore]. Remembrances to Mr. & Mrs. N[ash] & Mrs. C.—card &
papers came—

WW

664. *To William J. Linton*   *3.28. [1875]*

431 Stevens st. | Cor West. | Camden, | N. Jersey. | Sunday,
March 28.

Dear Linton,
My note of yesterday, (or day before,) *asking for the bill* was written in the midst of a splitting headache—& without fully reading yours.
To-day, better, I have just taken up yours to read a second time, (as I
generally do with my friends' letters,) & see your kind & friendly gift to
me of the prints[22]—which I accept with thanks & pleasure.
Two days now of fine weather—which I fancy is telling on me, as well
as on the frozen ground & sap in the trees—
Love to you—

Walt Whitman

20. This and the following post card were written on Fridays, if the year is correct.
In both notes WW seems to refer to the serious relapse in February. The latter card
alludes to Doyle's new, but temporary, position in Baltimore; see 680.
21. See 662.
22. WW ordered 1,000 impressions of the engraving in 657.
23. Burroughs published "A Word or Two on Emerson" and "A Final Word on
Emerson" in *The Galaxy* in February and April, 1876; the essays were reprinted in *Birds
and Poets* (1877), 185–210. For WW's final verdict on the articles, see June 17, 1876.

665. *To John Burroughs*   4.1. [1875]

431 Stevens st. | cor West. | Camden | N. Jersey. | April 1.

Dear John,

I have look'd over the Emerson notes[23]—read them all over once—
am precluded from any thing more or giving any very deep or elaborate
analysis of them, in connection with the Emerson question, (as my brain is
in a state not allowing thought, argument or study)—but still I will give
you my first impressions of your pages:

In their totality, they produce a not agreeable notion of being written
by one who has been largely grown & ripened & gristled by Emerson, but
has at last become dissatisfied & finnicky about him, & would pitch into
him, but cannot—perhaps dare not—and so keeps running around in a sort
of circle of praises & half praises, like a horse tied by a tether.

Your Notes also seem to me (to be plain) a good deal too diffuse, & too
Emersony in themselves—I should select *about one third of the MS. as
first rate*, (including the opening part)—My opinion is that you had perhaps better work it all over, & leave out at least half—

About the allusions to me, my off-hand thought is that my name might
be brought in, in one or two places, as foil or suggestive comparison—but
my name only, without any praises or comments, (only the silently in-
ferred ones)—to my friends, & circle, who know the relations & history
between me & Emerson, the mere mention of the name itself, in that way,
will be significant—(& it might give pungency to the sentence)[24]—

I have had a bad time the last two weeks—head & belly—& I almost
wonder I stand it so well—for I *do* stand it—I go out most every day, a
little—John Swinton, from N. Y. has been to see me—

Love to you & 'Sula—

WW

666. *To William Michael Rossetti*   [4(?). (?). 1875][25]

TRANSCRIPT.

Still unwell and paralysed, but up and around. Post-office address
at Camden, New Jersey, U. S. A.; shall probably remain there. Design

24. Deferring to WW's wishes, Burroughs deleted a paragraph expressing "wonder" that Emerson had ever accepted WW. The passage was restored in *Birds and Poets*.
See Barrus, 135–136.
25. On April 14 (Feinberg) Rossetti wrote to WW that he would include in *The
Academy* "the substance of your last note," probably a post card. The text given here
appeared on April 17. Rossetti also observed that he had quoted from WW's estimate of
Robert Burns in *The Academy*, VII (February 27, 1875), 214–215.

to bring out a volume, *mélange* of prose and verse, partly fresh matter, this summer.

667. *To Peter Doyle*   4.16. [1875][26]

ADDRESS: Pete Doyle, | M street South—bet 4½ & M. | Washington, D. C. POSTMARKS: Camden | Apr | 16 | N.J.; Carrier | 17 | Apr | 8(?) AM.

431 Stevens st. | cor West. | Camden, | N. Jersey | April 16.
Condition tolerable—I keep good heart yet—have no doubt I shall be able to come to Wash[ington]—but *when*, don't know now—John Bur[roughs] was here last night to see me, on his way to Wash[ington] —hope you are all right—do you like the berth?—papers, card, &c. rec'd— Can't you come on, & get back to Balt[imore] in time?

WW

668. *To Reuben Farwell*   4.21. [1875][27]

TRANSCRIPT.

All goes on about the same—still unwell, but up—yours of March 5 rec'd and welcomed—O how I should like to see you, *every day*, dear Mitch—my own dear boy and *comrade of the war*—the hospital—I have to sit here alone much of the time, and think of those old times—very cold here, yet—this is the 21st April, and the ground is frozen here—I keep cheerful spirits, and still hope to get around—Love to you, and to the wife and little girl—Write soon—Address, Camden, N. Jersey.

669. *To Peter Doyle*   4.23. [1875?][28]

ADDRESS: Pete Doyle, | M street South, bet 4½ & 6th | Washington, D. C. POSTMARK: Camden | Apr | 23(?) | (?).

431 Stevens st | cor West. | Camden, | N. Jersey. | April 23.
Here yet, & no particular change—Was out yesterday & over to

26. The correspondence (again chiefly post cards) with Doyle in April and May was sent on Fridays, according to WW's habit. At this time Doyle was working out of Baltimore; note 670 and 680. This post card can be positively dated on the basis of Burroughs' visit; see his letter to Dowden on May 4, quoted by Barrus, 94.

27. "Little Mitch," or Reuben Farwell, served with the Michigan Cavalry during the War and met WW in Armory Square Hospital early in 1864, and upon his release from the hospital he corresponded with WW. After Farwell received his discharge on August 24, 1864, he returned to his home in Plymouth, Mich. Evidently the correspondence was renewed when WW sent a post card on February 5, 1875. On March 5 Farwell, who owned a farm in Michigan, wrote: "Walt my dear old Friend how I would like to grasp your hand and give you a kiss as I did in the days of yore. what a satisfaction it

Phil. by cars & ferry—but bad, very bad spell all night—Eat my breakfast this morning, & here I am ab't the same as usual—So things go—
WW

670. *To Peter Doyle*   *4.30.* [*1875*][29]

ADDRESS: Pete Doyle, | M street South, | bet 4½ &
6th | Washington, | D. C. POSTMARK: Camden |
Apr | 30(?) | N.J.

431 Stevens st | cor West. | Camden, | N. Jersey. | April 30,
noon.

Dearest Son,

I saw the RR. smash the first thing in the paper in the morning, &
run my eyes over the account with fear & trembling—& only on reading it
over a second time, was I satisfied that you were not in it—poor souls! for
I suppose every one that *was* in it, had some who heard or read the news
with pain & terror—some parent, wife, friend, or child—poor Buchanan—
but I hope, from accounts, that he will get up again, before long, without
serious damage—The papers here publish full, & I guess very good accounts of the whole affair—I liked what the *Star* said so plainly—that
the cause below all others, of such accidents, is because they run such a
route, *over a single track*—you may remember my warning on the same
point three years ago, in a talk with you—

Pete, this spring finds me pretty much in the same tedious & half-way
condition I have been lingering in now over two years—up & around every
day, look not much different, & eat pretty well—but not a day passes
without some bad spells, sometimes *very bad*—& never a real good night's
sleep—yet still I have a sort of feeling not to give it up yet—Keep real
good spirits—don't get blue, even at my worst spells—

I am sitting here to-day as usual alone in the front room, by the window—feel pretty comfortable—the weather is bright & pleasant here to-
day, but cool for the season, & the most backward I have ever known—
My sister is going away for some 10 days to-morrow or next day, & I shall

would be to me." In Farwell's last letter, on August 16, 1875, he said that he was planning
to leave shortly for California. Eleven letters from Farwell are in the Trent Collection. He
is mentioned in "Memoranda During the War"; see *cw*, IV, 134.

The year is confirmed by the reference to Farwell's letter of March 5, 1875 (Trent).
When Bucke wrote to Farwell after WW's death, apparently only this one note, written
"on the back of a circular," was extant.

28. See 667.

29. The railroad accident described in the opening paragraph establishes the year.
Two trains of the Baltimore and Potomac Railroad collided in a tunnel outside of Washington on April 26. Captain "Tim" Buchanan, a conductor on one of the trains, was hos-
pitalized.

be quite alone in the house—wish you could come on & pay me a visit—
Would you like to have me direct any letters or papers to the American
Hotel, Balt[imore] or shall I just direct to you at Wash. as usual?—
love to my darling son—

Walt

671. *To William Michael Rossetti* (?)   [5(?). (?). 1875][30]

TRANSCRIPT.

Yes, I shall, unless prevented, bring out a volume this summer,
partly as my contribution to our National Centennial. It is to be called
Two Rivulets (*i.e.*, two flowing chains of prose and verse, emanating the
real and ideal), it will embody much that I had previously written. . . .
but about one-third, as I guess, that is fresh. *Leaves of Grass*, proper, will
remain as it is identically. The new volume will have nearly or quite as
much matter as *L. of G.* (It is a sort of omnibus in which I have packed
all the belated ones since the outset of the *Leaves.*)

672. *To Edward Dowden*

TRANSCRIPT.

431 Stevens St | Camden, New Jersey | May 2, 1875
Edward Dowden, | Dear friend,
Your kind letter of April 16[31] reach'd me yesterday—I find it full
of animation & cheer, with items of news &c interesting to me, & only hope

30.   This excerpt appeared on May 29 in *The Academy*, to which Rossetti
contributed; see 666. The article began: "Walt Whitman writes to a correspondent. . . ."
However, Perry (217*n.*) quotes an identical description of *Two Rivulets* in a letter to
Edward Dowden on May 2 which was excised from the transcription now in the Berg
Collection. WW probably used similar phraseology in two letters, one written on May 2 to
Dowden and another written about the same time to Rossetti.
31.   WW sent this (lost) letter to Burroughs; see 673.
32.   At this point Bliss Perry, to whom Dowden had sent the transcription, cut out
part of the letter for inclusion in his biography. Evidently WW referred to the two works
which he was preparing for publication, and explained that *Two Rivulets* symbolized
"two flowing chains of prose & verse, emanating the real & ideal," a passage quoted by
Perry (217*n.*). See note 30 above.
33.   Dowden commented on this letter to his future (second) wife, Elizabeth D.
West: "He writes very simply and affectionately and manfully." Dowden also had received
about the same time a letter from Burroughs: "A deep alarm possesses Burroughs about
Whitman's state of health (he says W. is so inexpressibly dear to him, the earth would
seem hardly inhabitable without him.)" See *Fragments from Old Letters, E. D. to*

to get letters from you oftener. In my condition they are trebly welcomed. My tedious prostration continues—primarily & mainly [*text lacking*][32] . . . reward, art and part with me, in my pages, (for I have come to solace & perhaps flatter myself that it is *they* indeed in them, as much as *I*, every bit.)

My condition physically is pretty much the same—no worse, at least not decidedly. I get out nearly every day, but not far, & cannot walk from lameness—make much of the river here, the broad Delaware, crossing a great deal on the ferry, full of life & fun to me—get down there by our horse cars, which run along near my door—get infinite kindness, care, and assistance from the employees on these boats & cars—My friend, next time you write, say more about yourself, family, & Mrs Dowden, to whom with yourself best love & regards[33]—

Walt Whitman

673. *To John Burroughs*   5.2. [*1875*]

TRANSCRIPT.

431 Stevens St. | cor. West, | Camden, | N. Jersey | May 2.
Dear John Burroughs,

I send you a letter, &c. I rec'd from Dowden, as you are alluded to. I have written to Dowden, today, & sent it off—so I suppose he will send you the books alluded to. Mine have arrived—Dowden advances, expands, or rather *penetrates*—the first two Chapters of his Shakespere, which I have read thoroughly, are very fine—(I have underlined passages on every page)[34]—the Victor Hugo I have not yet read[35]—

. . . I am pretty strong yet, & go out—but head, stomach & liver, all in a bad way, & seems as if nothing could bring them round.

E. D. W., 1869–1892 (1914), 130.

34. The presentation copy of Dowden's *Shakspere: A Critical Study of His Mind and Art* (1875), now in the Feinberg Collection, is marked on every page for the first eighty pages but only sporadically after that, although there are underlined passages throughout the entire volume. The underscoring in various kinds of pencils and comments dated in the 1880's indicate that WW examined Dowden's study several times.

In his reply to WW on July 27, Burroughs was not impressed with Dowden's book: "It does not differ very much from the rest of the critical literature of that subject, I do not yet see that it throws any new light. His Victor Hugo article strikes me as much more masterly" (Feinberg).

35. Dowden referred to his article on Hugo in a letter on April 12, 1873: "There is much in common between Victor Hugo & you, but if I had to choose between 'Leaves of Grass' & 'La Légende des Siècles' I should have not a moment's hesitation in throwing away 'La Légende' " (Feinberg; Traubel, I, 442). To Burroughs on June 9, 1875, Dowden admitted that "my article on Victor Hugo is only partially satisfactory" (Feinberg; Traubel, III, 216). In a postscript he inquired about WW's physical comforts because a Camden newspaper which he had seen had described the poet as "ill and *indigent*."

Have rec'd a long & good letter from Rossetti[36] which I will show you when you come. How are you getting along? How is 'Sula? . . .

Walt

674. *To Robert Carter*

TRANSCRIPT.

431 Stevens st. | cor West. | Camden, | N. Jersey. | May 7, '75
Robert Carter, | Dear Sir,[37]

Thinking that possibly I might be itemised or briefly biographised in the Cyclopaedia I thought I would send you, (or to Mr. Dana,)[38] the accompanying sketch—some authentic statistics, (as I find I am beginning to be noted, & they make sad work of it sometimes.)[39]

Leaving of course the whole thing in your hands, I should like you to get the *statistics*, the *fact-basis*, right—(& should you think proper can be further consulted here, or proof sent, &c.)—My book *Leaves of Grass* as now printed, is in its permanent form—My other Vol. of equal size *Two Rivulets*, (i.e. of Real and Ideal) *will comprise all my other writings, Prose & Verse*, & is now being put into type. I am still prostrated with Cerebral & liver affection, but work occasionally.

Walt Whitman

675. *To Peter Doyle* 5.7. [1875?][40]

ADDRESS: Pete Doyle, | M st. South—bet 4½ & 6th | Washington, D. C. POSTMARKS: Camden | May | 7 | N.J.; Carrier | 8 | May | 8 AM.

431 Stevens st. | cor West. | Camden, | N. Jersey. | May 7.

Nothing special to write about—condition much the same— Yours of last Sunday rec'd—bright here to-day but cool. Love to Mrs. & Mr. N[ash].

WW

36. Rossetti on April 14 (Feinberg) discussed his literary activities, his insertion of notices about WW in the London *Academy*, and his marriage in 1874 to the daughter of Ford Madox Brown, the painter.

37. Robert Carter (1819–1879) was at various times editor of the Boston *Commonwealth*, the Boston *Telegraph*, the Boston *Atlas*, the Rochester *Democrat*, and *Appleton's Journal*. He assisted Dana in editing the first edition of the *New American Cyclopaedia*, and in 1873 he was engaged in the revision.

38. Charles A. Dana (1819–1897) was the owner as well as the editor of the New York *Sun* from 1868 until his death and was at one time co-editor of the *New American Cyclopaedia*. WW permitted Dana to print Emerson's famous letter of 1855.

676. *To Peter Doyle*   *5.14. [1875?]*[41]

ADDRESS: Pete Doyle, | M street South—bet 4½ &
6th | Washington, D. C. POSTMARKS: Camden |
May | 14 | (?); Carrier | May | 15 | (?) AM.

431 Stevens st. | cor West. | Camden, | N. Jersey. | May 14.
Nothing special to write about—I always get the papers, they come
right—letters, cards, &c. the same—Wish I could be with you in Balt[i-
more] to-morrow to spend the day.

                                                        WW

677. *To Peter Doyle*   *5.28. [1875?]*[42]

ADDRESS: Pete Doyle, | M street South, bet 4½ &
6th | Washington, D. C. POSTMARKS: Camden |
May | 29 | N.J.; Carrier | May | 29 | 7 PM.

431 Stevens st. | cor West. | Camden, | N. Jersey. | May 28.
Up & around as usual—but a bad, *bad* time, head, &c—days &
nights—a bad week—papers &c. came all right—will try to send you better
news next time—

                                                        WW

678. *To William J. Linton* (?)   *6.9. [1875?]*[43]

431 Stevens st. | cor West. | Camden, | N. Jersey. | June 9.
Dear friend,
Yours of 5th has reach'd me. Though mainly the same as for a
tedious long while, I have fluctuated (& am fluctuating) through a series of
bad spells—brain & other organs—these current times. My general
strength, however, from fair to middling. Dont feel to leave my anchorage

39. The brief notice in the new edition ignored WW's letter. In 1892, however,
Appleton's printed the "sketch" in facsimile in the *Annual Encyclopaedia*. See *AL*, XXV
(1953), 361–362.
  40. See 667.   41. See 667.   42. See 667.
  43. The account of his ailments makes 1875 a plausible date. Joaquin Miller on
May 27 promised a visit shortly (Feinberg; Traubel, I, 57). As for the recipient, the
reference to the engraving indicates Linton. Furthermore, according to Linton's letter of
May 19 (Feinberg; Traubel, I, 12–13), he was to be in New York on June 5, at which
time he probably renewed the invitation to visit New Haven that he had made in his
earlier letter.

here, just now—but hope yet to take advantage of your affectionate & hospitable offers.

Walt Whitman

The engraving holds its own—satisfies me more & more—Joaquin Miller[44] has visited me here—very pleasant—

679. *To Edmund Clarence Stedman*

431 Stevens st. | cor West. | Camden, | N. Jersey. | June 17, '75.

My dear Stedman,[45]

I have rec'd your kind note, & am pleased that you remember me. I shall select some scrap of my MS. & send you soon. The last fortnight I have had an extra spell of debility & head distress, but feel better to-day.

Should you come to Philadelphia come over here, (by ferry from foot of Market st. Phila., very accessible) & see me, & have a chat. I am leisurely preparing a Volume, 'Two Rivulets,' (i.e. Real and Ideal) all sorts of things, prose & (my) poetry. Won't be out though for five or six months. Pleasant in some respects here, for me—but pretty lonesome.

Walt Whitman

680. *To Peter Doyle*   6.25. [*1875*][46]

431 Stevens st. | cor West. | Camden, | N. Jersey | June 25.

Dear boy Pete,

I have weathered it out pretty well this week—at present moment am sitting here cover'd with sweat, with nothing on but shirt & pants—to-day & yesterday the very *hottest kind*—I suppose you have it too.

Pete, there is nothing new in my case, & no prospect more than usual of anything *sudden*—but it seems pretty clear that there is no substantial recovery probable, (hardly possible,) for me—how long it will last this way it is of course impossible to tell—I take it all without growling—things are steadily growing worse with me—But I must not worry you—& may-be there is something more favorable ahead—

44. Nothing further is known about this meeting with Miller. On August 19 WW spent an evening with Miller in Philadelphia (Feinberg).

45. WW met Stedman during the Civil War; see 89. On June 8 Stedman had requested "one scrap of paper, which you can spare. . . . I am one of those American writers who always look upon you as a noble, original, and characteristic poet" (Donaldson, 214).

I busy myself a little every day writing—I want to fix my books in a little better shape, this summer—partly busy with a new volume—so that they will all be comprised in Two Vols.—(not very much really new matter, but some)—

So you dont come on to Balt[imore], now, (as I take it from your last)—Love to you, dear son.

Walt

Love to Mr. & Mrs. Nash—do you ever see Mrs. O'Connor or Eldridge? Is Tasistro still around?

681. *To Alfred, Lord Tennyson*

ENDORSED: "To Tennyson July 24 '75." DRAFT
LETTER.

July 24 '75.

My dear Mr. Tenn[yson]

Since I last wrote you, (your kind response was duly rec'd)[47] I have been laid up here nearly all the time, & still continue so, quite shattered, but somehow with good spirits—not well enough to go out in the world & go to work—but not sick enough to give up either, or lose my interest in affairs, life, literature, &c. I keep up & dressed, & go out a little nearly every day.

I have been reading your Queen Mary,[48] & think you have excelled yourself in it. I did not know till I read it, how much eligibility to passion, character and art arousings was still left to me in my sickness & old age. Though I am Democrat enough to realize the deep criticism of Jefferson on Walter Scott's writings, (& many of the finest plays, poems & romances) that they fail to give at all the life of the great mass of the people then & there.

But I shall print a new volume before long, & will send you a copy. I send you a paper about same mail with this.[49]

Soon as convenient write me a few lines. (Put in your letter your exact p. o. address.) If you have leisure, tell me about yourself. I shall never see you & talk to you—so I hope you will write to make it up.

46. The allusion to his forthcoming books establishes the year.
47. See 616 and 629. Tennyson replied to WW's letter on August 11.
48. *Queen Mary* appeared in 1875.
49. Probably the Springfield *Republican* of July 23; see 683.

682. *To Anne Gilchrist*

ADDRESS: Mrs. Anne Gilchrist, | Earl's Colne, |
Halsted, Essex, | England. POSTMARKS: Camden |
Jul | 27 | N.J.; Philadelphia, Pa. | Jul | 28 | Paid All;
Halstead | A | Au 13 | 75.

431 Stevens st | cor West. | Camden, | N. Jersey.
U. S. America. | July 27, '75.

Dearest Friend,[50]

Your letter of July 8[51] has reached me, & is comforting, as always.
I must write you at least a line or two. Don't mind my long silences. My
illness has not lifted since I last wrote you, & is still upon me—the last two
or three months the bad spells have been frequent & depressing. Yet I
keep up, go out a little most every day, & preserve good spirits.

I am cheered & pleased by the *friendly & living photographs.* You
did well to send them to me. I shall keep them by me—look at them often—
they do me good.

I have just sent you a paper. When you write, tell me more about your
children—Percy[52] & all. Love to them, & to you, dear friend.

Walt Whitman

Before enveloping my letter, I take a good long, long look at the photographs—with all their silence, cheery & eloquent to me, as I sit here alone
by my open window—A vague impressiveness, a *thought,* not without
solemnity—which you must understand without my writing it—comes
over me, like a little sun-cloud, this vapory day—& with that, & once again
my love, I close.[53]

---

50. Though Mrs. Gilchrist wrote frequently, WW allowed almost two years to
elapse between his replies. In the midst of her prosaic accounts of the activities of her
children, Mrs. Gilchrist reaffirmed her ardent affection. On July 4–6, 1874, she wrote: "I
believe if I could only make you conscious of the love, the enfolding love my heart
breathes out toward you, it would do you physical good. Many sided love—Mothers love
that cherishes, that delights so in personal service, that sees in sickness & suffering such
dear appeals to an answering limitless tenderness—wifes love—ah you draw that from
me too, resistlessly—I have no choice—comrades love, so happy in sharing all . . .
Child's love too that trusts utterly, confides unquestioningly" (LC; Harned, 113). On
September 3 of the same year Mrs. Gilchrist noted that a year ago (see 524) she had
received WW's ring "that put peace and joy and yet such pain of yearning into my heart
—pain for you, my Darling & sorrowing helpless love that waits and must wait useless,
afar off, while you suffer" (LC; Harned, 117). On December 9 she begged: "So please,
dear Friend, be indulgent, as indeed I know you will be, of these poor letters of mine with
their details of my children & their iterated & reiterated expressions of the love and hope
and aspiration you have called into life within me—take them not for what they are, but
for all they have to stand for" (LC; Harned, 120).

683. *To Rudolf Schmidt*

431 Stevens st. | cor. West. | Camden, | N. Jersey.
U. S. America. | July 31, '75.

My dear Rudolf Schmidt,

Your letter of July 17, from near Wiemar has just reached me. I am still here in Camden, & shall probably remain permanently. *I do not recover my health*—for over two months past have been worse than ever, but feel better to-day, as I write—(if it would only continue)—I have pretty much given up all prospect of going out again in the world, as an active worker—& the best I look for is to keep up, by care & moderation, & have the use of my mind as so far, with the partial use of my physical powers, for whatever term of life I have yet to live. I still go out in the open air a little, talk, & keep in good spirits.

I have just sent you a paper with a long piece in, that may give you more particulars about me.[54] Write often as you can—your English I get the meaning of very well, & I am quite lonesome here. (All the letters you have ever sent—& papers, sheets, &c—*have quite certainly reach'd me*— I have a large bundle of them.)

As I write, I sit here by my open window—it is very pleasant, plenty of trees & foliage, (though I live in a street, in a city) warm, but a slight rain, just now—I have been out, this forenoon, riding in a street car—& to the printing office, where I am printing a little book, my War-Hospital *Memoranda* of ten & twelve years since. When finished I will send it to you. Also "Two Rivulets," you see mentioned in the paper.

Your brief words about Wiemar, only made me want *more*.[55] Every

51. This letter is not known.
52. Mrs. Gilchrist had devoted her letter of May 18, 1875, to a recital of Percy's difficulties with his prospective father-in-law (LC; Harned, 126–128).
53. On August 28 Mrs. Gilchrist noted that she had received WW's letter while she tended her dying mother (LC; Harned, 129–130).
54. On July 23 the Springfield *Republican* printed a three-column article entitled "Walt Whitman. | His Life, His Poetry, Himself." Though the article was signed with the initials J. M. S. (James Matlock Scovel), Burroughs observed on July 27: "It is an admirable piece of writing (of course I see your hand) & contains some of the best things about you that have yet been in print" (Feinberg). The New York *Tribune* printed excerpts from the dispatch on July 24; Rossetti quoted from it in *The Academy*, VIII (August 14, 1875), 167, and see *Letters of William Michael Rossetti*, ed. Gohdes and Baum (1934), 96–97; and Scovel utilized most of the material in the *National Magazine*, XX (1904), 165–169.
55. Schmidt described his visit to the tombs of Goethe and Schiller in his letter of July 17 (Feinberg).

thing now going on about literature or authors, or subjects appertaining to them, in the Old World, (Denmark included of course,) is more interesting to me than you might suppose. I have been in hopes of hearing from Elster. I wonder if he got the letter & papers I sent him—If any *Dane you know* is coming to America, (if convenient,) *give him my address here in Camden*—(Philadelphia is on one side of the river Delaware, & Camden immediately opposite on the other—ferries constantly running—I live near the river)—Good bye, my dear Rudolf Schmidt—write often as you can.[56]

Walt Whitman

684. *To Peter Doyle*   8.6. [1875][57]

431 Stevens st. | cor West | Camden, | N. Jersey. | Aug. 6.
Dear Pete, | Dear, dear boy,

Still here, pulling through the summer (I think the winter is better for me)—the hot sunny days are worst for me, an extra bad strange feeling every day in the head, (the doctor thinks probably the result of an old sunstroke 20 years ago—*now* the brain liable to it again in its sensitive condition)—otherwise not much different—*bad enough though*. I still go out a little—(most always feel at the best, for me, evenings, from sundown to 10.)

I still keep a little at work—there is a printing office here,[58] where I am doing my work—they are young men of the right stripe, & very kind & considerate & respectful to me—fix every thing in type, proof, &c. just to suit me—I am leisurely preparing my new Volume.

Mr. Marvin, an Internal Revenue Clerk, a friend of mine, has stopt & paid me a visit on his return to Wash[ington]. Plenty of rain here—hot but pleasant to-day—What has become of Tasistro? Pete, you havn't made that call on Mrs. O'C[onnor] yet. Come when you can, my darling boy. Your loving old comrade & father—

Walt W

papers &c came

56. Schmidt replied at length on August 18 (Traubel, IV, 336–338).
57. The second paragraph establishes the date.
58. *Two Rivulets* was set up in the *New Republic* Print Shop in Camden. Probably the "Walt Whitman Club in Camden" to which the Springfield *Republican* of July 23 referred, if it actually existed, consisted of "mechanics" employed by the local newspaper. Marvin also referred to this "club" in *The Radical Review*, I (1877), 238. Undoubtedly

685. *Alfred, Lord Tennyson to WW* [*8.11.1875*]

TRANSCRIPT.

My dear Walt Whitman[59]

(Somehow the Mr does not come well before Walt Whitman).
I am glad to hear from you again & to learn that at any rate you are no
worse than when you last wrote, & that though your health be shattered
your good spirits flourish up like a plant from broken ground, glad also
that you find something to approve of in a work so utterly unlike your own
as my Queen Mary.

I am this morning starting with my wife & Sons on a tour to the Continent. She has been very unwell for two years, obliged always to lie down
& incapable of any work in consequence of overwork—the case of so many
in this age, yours among others & we are now going into a land of fuller
sunshine in hopes that it may benefit her.

I am in an extreme hurry, packing up & after these few words must
bid you goodbye, not without expressing my hope however that you will
ultimately recover all your pristine vigor. I shall be charmed to receive
your book.

Ever yours

A. Tennyson

686. *To Peter Doyle* 8.20. [*1875?*][60]

ADDRESS: Pete Doyle, | M street South—bet 4½ &
6th | Washington, D. C. POSTMARKS: Camden |
Aug | 20 | N.J.; Carrier | Aug | 21 | 8 AM.

431 Stevens. | cor West. | Camden, | N. Jersey. | Aug 20.
All yours rec'd—Still here—Still about the same—sitting here
by the open window—very bright & sunny, & pretty hot—(bad head to-
day.)

W. W.

WW gave him a copy of the *Republican* during his visit.
   59. This is a reply to 681.
   60. Again (see 667) dating depends upon WW's almost inflexible habit of sending
Doyle a line on Friday. Note also the reference to his "bad head" in this and the following
letter.

687. *To William J. Linton*   [*8(?). (?). 1875*][61]

DRAFT LETTER.

You are entirely welcome to use the eng[raving] as you desire.
I am about as usual—not any worse. Feel, or fancy I feel, relief already as
summer wanes—one of my doctors thinks much of my head trouble the
past three mos. is from the sun. I am almost always easier as day departs.

688. *To Peter Doyle*   *9.4.* [*1875?*][62]

ADDRESS: Pete Doyle | M street South, bet 4½ & 6th |
Washington, D. C. POSTMARKS: Camden | Sep |
(?) | N.J.; Carrier | Sep | 5 | 9 AM.

431 Stevens st. Camden | N. Jersey | Sept. 4.
Nothing new or different with me. Want to come on to Wash-
[ington] before long, for two or three days.

WW

689. *To William J. Linton*   *9.14.* [*1875*]

431 Stevens st. | cor West. | Camden, | N. Jersey. | Sept 14.
My dear Linton,
I rec'd a letter to-day from Moncure Conway (just arr'd here from
England) in which this was enc'd—you being ment'd in it.[63]
I jog on about the same—(frequent bad spells—but still up & around
after a fashion.)
Pleasant September days & nights here—I have just been out for an

61. Linton on August 21 requested permission to use his engraving of WW as a
frontispiece for a volume of American poetry which he was preparing "for *English* publication" (Feinberg; Traubel, II, 201–202). WW wrote this draft on the verso of Linton's
letter.
62. The year is assumed because WW did not seriously plan to return to Washington until 1875.
63. This letter was written on the verso of a letter from William Bell Scott to Conway, dated August 21, 1875. Rossetti had dedicated his edition of WW's poems to Scott.
64. The projected visit to Washington makes the year almost positive.
65. In a letter dated November 16–30, Mrs. Gilchrist referred to a pleasant visit
with Marvin (LC; Harned, 133–136), who had gone to England on official business (see
696). On December 23 Rossetti described to WW a dinner he gave for Marvin which

hour on the river—now, 2 p. m., sitting here by open window, middling comfortable—

Walt Whitman

690. *To Peter Doyle*   10.2. [*1875?*][64]

ADDRESS: Pete Doyle, | M street South, bet 4½ &
6th | Washington, D. C. POSTMARK: Camden | Oct |
2 | N.J.

431 Stevens st. | cor West. | Camden, | N. J. | Oct. 2.

Have had just a slightly more encouraging week—though slightly —strength gets a little more reliable (has been very poor,) will try to send you some definite word soon about coming—

WW

691. *To Anne Gilchrist*

431 Stevens st. | cor. West. | Camden, | N. Jersey
U. S. America. | Oct. 19, '75

Dear Mrs. Gilchrist,

Let me send this to introduce a call from J. B. Marvin, a valued friend of mine[65]—a Yankee born & bred—democratic, literary, married— now briefly visiting London on business.

I still continue here laid up, but working a very little.

Your kind letters received, & welcomed. I was indeed interested in the account of the closing days of your dear mother[66]—surely a calm & beautiful death after a calm & beautiful life.

Best love, dear friend, to you & to your children.

Walt Whitman[67]

was attended by the following "*good Whitmanites*": Mrs. Gilchrist; Joseph Knight, editor of the London *Sunday Times;* Justin McCarthy, a novelist and writer for the London *Daily News;* Edmund Gosse; and Rossetti's father-in-law, Ford Madox Brown (Feinberg).

66. Her letter of August 28 (LC; Harned, 129–130).

67. Fearful after reading a printed account in which Conway reported that WW had given up hope of recovery, Mrs. Gilchrist on December 4 implored: "*Dont give up that hope*, for the sake of those that so tenderly passionately love you" (LC; Harned, 137). She promised to come to America as soon as Percy was married. Meanwhile, on October 19 Mrs. Gilchrist had written to Burroughs to inform him that WW's English admirers were preparing "some tangible embodiment however inadequate" to relieve the poet's financial needs (Boston Public Library; Furness, 244).

692. *To Peter Doyle*   *11.3.* [*1875*][68]

ADDRESS: Pete Doyle | M st. South, bet 4½ & 6th |
Washington, D. C. POSTMARKS: Camden | Nov | 3 |
N.J.; Carrier | Nov | 4 | 8 AM.

431 Stevens st | cor West | Camden, | N. J. | Nov. 3.
All going on about same. I want to come on next Monday (8th
inst) & stay a few days—Would like to stop at Mr. N[ash]'s. (Will write
so you will get particular word Saturday next)—

WW

693. *To Peter Doyle*   *11.5.* [*1875*][69]

ADDRESS: Pete Doyle, | M Street South, | bet 4½ &
6th sts. | Washington, D. C. POSTMARK: Camden |
Nov | 5 | N.J.

431 Stevens st. | cor West. | Camden, | N. Jersey, | Nov. 5.
Dear Son,
I think I shall try to come on to Wash[ington] next Monday, in
the *noon train* from here, W. Phil. (limited express)—Am feeling about
the same—(bad enough at times—but sort o' getting used to it)—

Walt

As I understand it, the train I speak of goes in to your Depot, 6th st.—
must get in some time before dark[70]—

694. *To Ellen M. O'Connor*   *11.9.* [*1875*]

Tuesday, 9th Nov. | 11 a. m.
Dear Nelly,
I am in Washington, stopping at Mr. & Mrs. Nash's, L st. south
east, Navy Yard—am middling well, for me—shall be in pretty sure up

68. See the following letter.
69. The executors dated this letter [1877]. However, November 8 was on Monday
in 1875 (see 692). On November 3 WW had promised Doyle definite word about his
plans by Saturday; this letter was sent on Friday, November 5.
70. Doyle replied on November 7 that he would meet WW at the depot on the
following day, and that Mr. and Mrs. Nash "told me to tell you to come on and they would
do the best they Could to make your Visit pleasant" (Feinberg).
71. On this visit WW attended a public reburial of Poe's remains in Baltimore, and
commented on Poe in an unsigned article in the Washington *Star* on November 18; see
CW, IV, 286–287; and Rollo G. Silver, "A Note about Whitman's Essay on Poe," *AL*, VI
(1935), 435–436.
On November 15, sixteen Washingtonians sent a petition to Benjamin H. Bristow,
Secretary of the Treasury: "We respectfully ask that Walt Whitman, 'the Good Gray
Poet,' may be appointed to a position in the Treasury Department." The docket in the
National Archives reads: "The Secretary says give the applicant a place Jany. 1, '76 if

to 10 a. m. & from 2 to 3 p. m. Am so fixed that it is very convenient for my friends to call—Love to you.[71]

Walt W

695. *To Edwin Einstein*

ENDORSED: "my letter to Einstein | Nov 26 '75."
DRAFT LETTER.

Camden | Nov. 26 '75.

My dear Einstein.[72]

On coming back here, I find your letter of the 20th. It is so kind (bringing up old memories, & making prologue & ceremony unnecessary) that I will at once answer it in its own spirit, & reveal the situation.

My paralysis has left me permanently disabled, unable to do any thing of any consequence, and yet with perhaps (though old, not yet 60) some lease of life yet. I had saved up a little money, & when I came here, nearly three years ago, I bought a nice cheap lot, intending to put on a small house to haul in, & live out the rest of my days.

I had, & yet have, a sort of idea that my books, (I am getting ready, or about have ready, my complete writings, in two volumes—*Leaves of Grass*, and *Two Rivulets*) will yet henceforth furnish me reliably with sufficient for grub, pocket money, &c., if I have my own shanty to live in. But my means, meagre at the best, have gone for my expenses since, & now, while not hitherto actually wanting, (& not worrying much about the future either,) I have come to the end of my rope, & am in fact ridiculously poor. I have my lot yet clear, & it would be a great thing for me to build forthwith a four or five room shanty on it & haul in, snug & quiet, with the sense of security for the rest of my days—for I feel yet about as cheerful & *vimmy* as ever, & may live several years yet—indeed probably will —& may write some—though my days of active participation, & ganging about in the world, are over.[73]

possible." Though WW apparently did not comment on this proposal, Burroughs knew of it, and wrote to Dowden in April, 1876: "We expected he would have a position in one of the Departments at Washington again before this, as it was promised last winter, but nothing seems to come of it yet" (*The Life and Letters of John Burroughs*, I, 183).

72. Edwin Einstein, a tobacconist and a friend from the Pfaffian days of the 1850's, wrote to WW on November 18 from the Union League Club, Madison Avenue and Twenty-sixth Street, New York: "I would not trouble you with this letter, were it not that I saw mentioned in the N. Y. Sun the other day the fact that you were in very needy circumstances, if that is so will you let me know, and myself and a few other of your old friends would be glad to aid you to the best of our ability. If it is not so, (which I sincerely trust may be the case) pardon the liberty I am taking and believe it is only done out of friendship and good will" (Feinberg).

73. Probably the repetitions in this draft were eliminated in the letter itself. As evidenced by the number of stricken passages, WW had difficulty in finding the exact words to describe his lot.

I get out a little nearly every day, & enjoy it, but am very lame—Keep stout & red as ever—grayer than ever—am feeling pretty comfortable as I write—have just returned from a three weeks jaunt to Washington and Baltimore—which has much refreshed me, (the first time I have been away from my anchorage here for nearly three years.) I often recall the old times in New York, or on Broadway, or at Pfaff's—& the faces & voices of *the boys.*

696. *To John Burroughs*   *12.17.* [*1875*]

431 Stevens st. | cor West. | Camden, | N. Jersey. | Dec. 17. Dear John Burroughs,

I have been back here two weeks & over—My Washington jaunt occupied some seventeen or eighteen days, & was a very pleasant one for me—(started out with the idea of a two days visit only)—Am perhaps now lately not so well, but not much different—the gravest trouble is the liver and stomachic business now—Still I keep up about the same, (& get mad at myself for *grunting*)—Your letter of two days since rec'd. Best love to 'Sula, & to Jenny Grant if there—

My new edition is nearly ready—Two Vols—will give you early advice of their appearance—only 100 copies issued—Is the *Winter Sunshine* out?[74] Eldridge call'd to see me on his return home two weeks since. Marvin has gone to England, with a Treas[ury] squad.[75] He has call'd on Mrs. Gilchrist. M. D. Conway[76] called on me. Lord Houghton[77] also.

We have great times in *this house*—a baby has arrived,[78] a fine lusty little fellow, now five weeks old—(he has been named Walt)—just now though he is quite sick, but I opine will get along—The rest all very well, except that my sister, the mother, is part of the time only middling. I

---

74. *Winter Sunshine* appeared in December or January.
75. See 691.
76. Conway published "A Visit to Walt Whitman" in *The Academy*, VIII (November 27, 1875), 554. (The New York *Tribune* noted Conway's article on December 9.) At the same time he informed Rossetti that "Walt is not in need"; see *Letters of William Michael Rossetti*, ed. Gohdes and Baum (1934), 98. At this time Mrs. Gilchrist and Rossetti were contemplating purchasing WW's new volumes and presenting them to libraries; see *Letters*, 95.
77. Richard Monckton Milnes (1809–1885), Lord Houghton, was an intimate of Tennyson and Thackeray as well as a poet. He was a collector of famous people; in DNB he is characterized as "eminently a dilettante." Houghton wrote to Joaquin Miller on September 1 from Chicago: "Please give my best regards to Mr Whitman." On September 5 Miller informed WW that he was trying to arrange a meeting with Lord Houghton. Houghton himself wrote to WW on September 27 and proposed a visit at the end of October or early in November, and on November 3 he asked whether November 6 would be convenient. These letters are in the Feinberg Collection; see also Traubel, I, 360, 364; II, 310; *In Re*, 36; and Blodgett, 141–143.

hear young Walt raising *his* song, in the room overhead as I conclude
my letter—Love to you, as always, my friend—

Walt.

697. *To the Librarian of Congress*

431 Stevens st. | cor West. | Camden, | N. Jersey. | Dec. 20, '75
Librarian Congress: | Dear Sir:

Please furnish me with Copyright for "Two Rivulets," as per title
enclosed. Is the $1 the right sum?

Yours truly

Walt Whitman

If perfectly convenient—& you have a printed slip with Copyright laws,
(latest) please enclose with document.

698. *To an Unidentified Correspondent*[79]

431 Stevens st. | cor West. | Camden, | N. Jersey. | Dec. 30, '75.

Forgive my not writing before. Much of the time, I cannot write,
from paralysis.

Very soon in 1876 I issue a small edition of my complete works in two
volumes. *Leaves of Grass* will be one. The other, *Two Rivulets*, alternations of prose & verse—the themes ab't as diverse as they can be—
poetry, politics, the war, &c—(I kept a diary from 1862 to '65, scenes in
Virginia, Washington, &c. the hospitals, camps, battles, &c. here given
almost verbatim.)

I publish & shall sell the volumes myself, for two good reasons. No
established publisher in the country will print my books, & during the last
three years of my illness & helplessness every one of the three successive
book agents I have had in N. Y. has embezzled the proceeds.[80]

78. Walter Orr Whitman, born November 4, died in the following year.

79. This letter was written either to an editor or to someone who contributed frequently to magazines and newspapers. Since in the fourth paragraph WW exaggerated
the effects of his paralysis, it is doubtful that the letter was sent to anyone like Hinton,
Swinton, Reid, Croly of the New York *Daily Graphic*, the editors of Washington newspapers, Rossetti, Conway, or Dowden, all of whom had some knowledge of his illness.
Perhaps it was sent to the editor of the *West Jersey Press;* see the following note.

80. If added evidence were needed to prove that "Walt Whitman's Actual American Position," in the *West Jersey Press* on January 26, 1876, was written by the poet,
this paragraph is significant when compared with the following in the *Press:* "No established publishing house will yet print his books. Most of the stores will not even sell
them. In fact, his works have never been really published at all. Worse still; for the past
three years having left them in the charge of book agents in New York City, who, taking
advantage of the author's illness and helplessness, have, three of them, one after another,
successfully [and] thievishly embezzled every dollar of the proceeds!" (Furness, 246).
WW referred to O'Kane, Butts, and Somerby.

To sum up the situation at present: My health & strength are probably irrecoverable—still I may endure some years yet—mind unaffected—spirits good—Keep up about one third of the time, prostrated practically or wholly the other two thirds—Pecuniary matters thin & meagre, (but not in want)—shall probably reside steadily here in Camden.

And now good bye, & happy New Year to you, my friend. Though this letter itself is not intended for publication, you are at liberty to use any or all the statements in it, should you have occasion—under your own judgment.

Walt Whitman

One of the first of the proof copies sent out at all shall be to you. A great part of *Two Rivulets*, prose & poetry, is fresh matter, hitherto unpublished.

Undated Post Cards to Peter Doyle,
Probably Written in 1874 or 1875[81]

699. *To Peter Doyle*

ADDRESS: Pete Doyle, | M st. South, bet. 4½ & 6th |
Washington, D. C. POSTMARKS: Camden | Mar | 8 |
N.J.; Carrier | 9 | Mar | 8 AM.

431 Stevens st. | cor West. | Camden. | March 8.
Card rec'd—A bad, bad week—head troubles—hope to send better acc'ts, next time—

WW

700. *To Peter Doyle*

ADDRESS: Pete Doyle, | M street South, bet 4½ & 6th |
Washington, D. C. POSTMARK: Camden | Jul |
30 | N.J.

431 Stevens. | Camden, | N. Jersey. | July 30.
Getting along much the same—feeling pretty fair to-day. Yours
rec'd.

W. W.

701. *To Peter Doyle*

ADDRESS: Pete Doyle, | M st. South—bet 4½ & 6th |
Washington, D. C. POSTMARK: Camden | Sep | 10 |
N.J.

431 Stevens st. | cor West. | Camden, | N. Jersey. | Sept. 10.
I am about as usual—your postal card came to-day—papers
last Monday—As I write (1 p. m.) am having one of my bad mid-day
head spells—but shall probably get as usual toward sundown—dry, warm,
dusty weather here days—fine nights—

WW

81. The following nine post cards cannot be assigned to a specific year for obvious
reasons: the allusions to his health are vague and are in fact applicable to almost any time
between 1873 and 1876; there are no concrete references to events which would make
dating possible. However, all were written on a standard government post card which
was redesigned in 1876.

702. *To Peter Doyle*

ADDRESS: Pete Doyle, | M street South, bet 4½ &
6th | Washington, D. C. POSTMARKS: Camden |
Sep | 1(?) | N.J.; Carrier | 19 | Sep | (?) AM.

431 Stevens. Camden, N. J. | Sept. 18.

Nothing special or new—day after day goes on with me, just about the same—

WW

703. *To Peter Doyle*

ADDRESS: Pete Doyle, | M street South, bet 4½ & 6th |
Washington D. C. POSTMARKS: Camden | Sep |
25 | N.J.; Carrier | 26 | Sep | 8(?) AM.

431 Stevens st. Camden | N. Jersey | Sept. 25.

About the same sort of a week—

WW

704. *To Peter Doyle*

ADDRESS: Pete Doyle, | M street South, bet 4½ & 6th |
Washington, D. C. POSTMARKS: Philadelphia | Oct |
23 | 6 PM | Pa.; Carrier | Oct | 24 | (?).

431 Stevens st. | Cor West | Camden | N. Jersey. | Oct. 23.

Had a very bad fall & shock about 11 days ago—laid me up a week or more—but am around again now—not much different now—bad spells enough—

WW

705. *To Peter Doyle*

ADDRESS: Peter Doyle, | M st. South, bet 4½ & 6th |
Washington, D. C. POSTMARKS: Camden | Oct |
(?)8 | N.J.; Carrier | 29 | Oct | (?) AM.

431 Stevens st. | Cor West. | Camden, N. J. | Oct. 28.

Every thing continues favorable—full as good as any time yet—perhaps rather better than any yet—Letter & paper rec'd.

W. W.

706. *To Peter Doyle*

ADDRESS: Pete Doyle | M street South bet 4½ & M. | Washington, D. C. POSTMARK: Camden | Dec | 16 | N.J.

431 Stevens st. | cor West. | Camden, | N. Jersey. | Dec. 16—3 p. m.

I am *very decidedly better*—very cold here, but bright & pleasant —I go out in it & enjoy it muchly—am now going out on a prowl till dusk—

W W

707. *To Peter Doyle*

ADDRESS: Pete Doyle, | M st. South bet 4½ & 6th | Washington D. C. POSTMARKS: Camden | (?) | (?)9 | N.J.; Carrier | 30 | Dec | 8 AM.

431 Stevens st. | Cor West. | Camden, | N. Jersey
Dec. 29—4 p. m.

Keep along about the same—(thankful to be as well as I am)— have had two days of rainy, cloudy weather—but it has cleared off bright, & I am just going out for an hour or two—O that I had you with me— Happy New Year—

W

Appendix A

A LIST OF MANUSCRIPT SOURCES AND PRINTED APPEARANCES

The locations of the manuscripts transcribed in this volume appear in the following list, through an abbreviation explained in the list of abbreviations in the Introduction. If the version in this edition is based upon a printed source, or is derived from an auction record, the fact is indicated by the word TEXT. Unless otherwise indicated, the manuscripts have not previously appeared in print. I record all earlier printed appearances through the abbreviations CT (Complete Text) and PT (Partial Text). The location and printed appearances, if any, of draft letters are also noted. Occasionally the location of a letter is followed by a reference in parentheses to an envelope in another collection. In this way I have, artificially, restored the manuscript to its original state.

This list is followed by a list of the institutions and individuals whose manuscripts are represented in this volume, in order that scholars may readily tell which letters are to be found in a given collection.

Letters

266. Berg.

267. Draft letter in Feinberg. CT: Traubel, II, 483; Nonesuch, 968.

268. Berg. CT: *CW*, VIII, 219–221. PT: Barrus, 50.

269. Columbia University. FACSIMILE: *Autobiography, Memories and Experiences of Moncure Daniel Conway* (1904), I, 218. DRAFT LETTER (in Feinberg): Traubel, III, 425–426; Nonesuch, 968–970.

270. Draft letter in Feinberg. CT: Traubel, II, 420–421; Nonesuch, 970–971.

271. Draft letter in Library of Congress. CT: Traubel, IV, 190.

272. TEXT: Typescript furnished by Emory Holloway.

273. Mrs. Francis Frederic Phillips. CT: *AL*, XXIII (1951), 344–345.

274. Draft letter in Feinberg.

275. Berg.

276. Mrs. Donald E. Kidd, who provided a transcript. CT: *AL*, XXIII (1951), 346.

277. William E. Barton Estate. DRAFT LETTER (in Feinberg): Traubel, I, 281; Nonesuch, 971.

278. Mrs. Donald E. Kidd, who provided a transcript. CT: *AL*, XXIII (1951), 346–347.

279. University of Texas.

280. Huntington Library. CT: *AL*, VII (1935), 80.

281. Draft letter in Feinberg. CT: Traubel, II, 482; Nonesuch, 971.

282. Draft letter in Feinberg.

283. Draft letter in Feinberg.

284. William Andrews Clark Memorial Library of the University of

California, Los Angeles. CT: *PMLA*, LVIII (1943), 1099.

285. Morgan. CT: Glicksberg, 112–113; Nonesuch, 972–973. PT: *Putnam's Monthly*, V (1908), 166.

286. Berg. CT: *CW*, VIII, 221–222.

287. Draft letter in Feinberg. CT: Traubel, I, 211–212; Nonesuch, 973–974. PT: Esther Shepherd, *Walt Whitman's Pose* (1938), 211.

288. Draft letter in Feinberg. CT: Traubel, III, 244–245; Nonesuch, 974.

289. Pennsylvania. CT: *CW*, VIII, 222–225; Nonesuch, 974–976.

290. Mrs. Joseph R. Perkins, Jr. DRAFT LETTER (in Feinberg): Traubel, III, 454–455; Nonesuch, 976–977.

291. Draft letter in Feinberg. CT: Traubel, III, 329; Nonesuch, 977.

292. Mrs. Francis Frederic Phillips. DRAFT LETTER (in Feinberg).

293. Trent. CT: *CW*, VIII, 225–227.

294. Trent. CT: *CW*, VIII, 227–229.

295. Berg. CT: *CW*, VIII, 229–230.

296. Barrett. CT: *CW*, VIII, 230–232.

297. Trent. CT: *CW*, VIII, 232–233.

298. Historical Society of Pennsylvania. CT: *AL*, VIII (1937), 420.

299. Trent. CT: *CW*, VIII, 234–235.

300. Hanley. CT: *CW*, VIII, 236–237.

301. Morgan. CT: Glicksberg, 113–114.

302. Morgan. CT: *Putnam's Monthly*, V (1908), 167–168; Glicksberg, 114; Nonesuch, 978.

303. Berg.

304. Draft letter in Feinberg. CT: *Calamus*, 35–37; *CW*, VIII, 21–23.

305. Rhode Island Historical Society. CT: *AL*, II (1930), 297–298.

306. Berg. PT: Allen, 400. DRAFT LETTER (in Feinberg).

307. Feinberg. FACSIMILE: George M. Williamson, *Catalogue of A Collection of Books, Letters and Manuscripts* (1903). CT: *WWR*, VI (1960), 72–73.

308. Draft letter in Feinberg. CT: *Calamus*, 37–38; *CW*, VIII, 23–24.

309. Draft letter in Feinberg. CT: *Calamus*, 38–39; *CW*, VIII, 24–25.

310. Draft letter in Feinberg. CT: *Calamus*, 19–20.

311. Draft letter in Feinberg. CT: *Calamus*, 20–21.

312. Berg. DRAFT LETTER (in Trent): Gohdes and Silver, 73.

313. Draft letter in Feinberg. CT: *Calamus*, 39–40; *CW*, VIII, 25–27; Nonesuch, 978–979. PT: Allen, 401.

314. Draft letter in Feinberg. CT: *Calamus*, 41–43; *CW*, VIII, 27–29. PT: William James, *Talks to Teachers on Psychology* (1899), 250–252; F. O. Matthiessen, ed., *The James Family* (1947), 401.

315. Draft letter in Feinberg. CT: *Calamus*, 43–45; *CW*, VIII, 30–31. PT: Allen, 401.

316. Berg.

317. Draft letter in Feinberg. CT: *Calamus*, 45–48; *CW*, VIII, 31–34; Nonesuch, 979–981. PT: Allen, 402.

318. Draft letter in Feinberg. CT: *Calamus*, 48–50. *CW*, VIII, 35–37.

319. Berg.

320. Feinberg. PT: Perry, 192.

321. Morgan. CT: Glicksberg, 114–115.

322. Trent. CT: Gohdes and Silver, 74.

323. Draft letter in Feinberg. CT: *Calamus*, 50–51; *CW*, VIII, 37–38.

324. Missouri Historical Society. CT: *Missouri Historical Society Bulletin*, XVI (1960), 101–102.

325. SOURCE: American Art Association, March 10–11, 1924.

326. NYPL. CT: *AL*, XXIII (1951), 348.

327. TEXT: Traubel, IV, 269–270. PT: Allen, 404.

328. Trent. CT: *CW*, VIII, 237–238.

329. Dartmouth College Library. CT: *Dartmouth College Library Bulletin*, I (May, 1932), 5. DRAFT LETTER (in Feinberg): Traubel, II, 22; Nonesuch, 981–982; Allen, 405.

330. Feinberg.

331. Draft letter in Feinberg. CT: Traubel, II, 22–23.

332. Draft letter in Feinberg. CT: Traubel, III, 499; Nonesuch, 982.

333. Draft letter in Feinberg.

334. Draft letter in Feinberg. CT: Traubel, II, 327; Nonesuch, 982.

335. Ohio Wesleyan.

336. TEXT: *Overland Monthly*, XLIII (1904), 63.
337. Feinberg.
338. Barrett. CT: *SB*, V (1952), 205. DRAFT LETTER (in Feinberg): Traubel, I, 216–217; Nonesuch, 983.
339. Harvard. DRAFT LETTER (in Feinberg): Traubel, II, 326
340. Berg. CT: *CW*, VIII, 238–240. PT: Nonesuch, 983–984.
341. Morgan. CT: Glicksberg, 115–116.
342. Hanley.
343. Feinberg. DRAFT LETTER (in Feinberg): Traubel, IV, 269; *Wake*, VII (1948), 11.
344. Feinberg.
345. Morgan. CT: Glicksberg, 116 (dated July 15).
346. Feinberg. CT: *Calamus*, 53–55; *CW*, VIII, 40–42; Nonesuch, 984–985. PT: Allen, 414.
347. Berg. PT: Allen, 414.
348. Feinberg. CT: *Calamus*, 55–57; *CW*, VIII, 42–45.
349. Feinberg. CT: *Calamus*, 58–59; *CW*, VIII, 45–46.
350. Gilbert S. McClintock.
351. Feinberg. FACSIMILE: Traubel, III, 236. CT: Traubel, III, 237–238; Nonesuch, 986–987.
352. Mrs. Donald E. Kidd. CT: *AL*, XXIII (1951), 349.
353. Pennsylvania. DRAFT LETTER (in Feinberg): Traubel, I, 219–220; Harned, 56–57; Nonesuch, 987–988.
354. Berg.
355. Feinberg.
356. Mrs. Francis Frederic Phillips.
357. Harvard. CT: *MP*, LI (1953), 102–103.
358. Draft letter in Feinberg.
359. TEXT: Typescript in possession of Emory Holloway.
360. Draft letter in Feinberg. CT: Traubel, II, 370; Nonesuch, 988–989.
361. Conway Collection, Columbia University.
362. Feinberg. CT: *Wake*, VII (1948), 11–12.
363. National Archives. CT: *PMLA*, LVIII (1943), 1102.
364. Berg. PT: Allen, 421.
365. Draft letter in Feinberg. CT: Traubel, II, 310–311; Nonesuch, 989.
366. Columbia University Libraries, the gift of Mr. and Mrs. Solton Engel.
367. Feinberg (Envelope: Dr. Max Thorek). CT: *Calamus*, 61–62; *CW*, VIII, 48–50.
368. Berg.
369. Feinberg. CT: *Calamus*, 63–64; *CW*, VIII, 50–51; Nonesuch, 990–991.
370. Feinberg. CT: *Calamus*, 64–66; *CW*, VIII, 51–54. PT: Canby, 197.
371. Feinberg. CT: *Calamus*, 66–67; *CW*, VIII, 54; Nonesuch, 991.
372. Feinberg. CT: *Calamus*, 67–68; *CW*, VIII, 55.
373. Feinberg. CT: *Calamus*, 68–70; *CW*, VIII, 55–57.
374. Feinberg. CT: *Calamus*, 70–71; *CW*, VIII, 57–59; Nonesuch, 991–992.
375. Feinberg. CT: *Calamus*, 71–73; *CW*, VIII, 59–61; Nonesuch, 992–994.
376. Feinberg. CT: *Calamus*, 73–74; *CW*, VIII, 61–62.
377. Feinberg. CT: *Calamus*, 74–76; *CW*, VIII, 62–63.
378. Feinberg. CT: *Calamus*, 76–77; *CW*, VIII, 63–65.
379. Trent. CT: Gohdes and Silver, 74–75.
380. Feinberg. CT: *Calamus*, 77–79; *CW*, VIII, 65–67.
381. Berg.
382. Berg.
383. National Archives. CT: *PMLA*, LVIII (1943), 1103.
384. TEXT: City Book Auction, New York, February 20, 1943.
385. Draft letter in Feinberg.
385.1 Draft letter in Feinberg.
386. Morgan. CT: Glicksberg, 116–117.
386.1 Library of Congress.
387. Yale.
388. TEXT: Thomas F. Madigan Catalog, September, 1937.
388.1 Hanley.
389. Berg.
390. Feinberg. CT: *Calamus*, 81–82; *CW*, VIII, 69–70.
391. Berg.

392. Feinberg. CT: *Calamus*, 97–98; *CW*, VIII, 86–87 (dated 1872).

393. Feinberg. CT: *Calamus*, 82; *CW*, VIII, 70–71.

394. TEXT: Donaldson, 223–224.

395. Feinberg. CT: *Calamus*, 82–84; *CW*, VIII, 71–72.

396. Berg. CT: Nonesuch, 995.

397. Feinberg. CT: *Calamus*, 84–85; *CW*, VIII, 72–73; Nonesuch, 996.

397.1 Barrett.

398. Feinberg. CT: *Calamus*, 85–86; *CW*, VIII, 74.

399. Berg.

400. Feinberg. CT: *Calamus*, 86; *CW*, VIII, 74–75.

401. Yale.

402. Draft letter in Feinberg. CT: Traubel, I, 327; Nonesuch, 997.

403. Draft letter in Feinberg. CT: Traubel, II, 447; Nonesuch, 997.

404. Feinberg. DRAFT LETTER (in Feinberg): Traubel, II, 482; Nonesuch, 998.

405. Library of Congress. CT: Harned, 58–64.

406. Feinberg.

407. Draft letter in Feinberg. CT: Traubel, I, 327–328.

408. Library of Congress.

409. TEXT: Catalog of J. Pearson & Co., London (before 1892).

410. Pennsylvania. FACSIMILE: Holloway, 264. CT: Nonesuch, 998. DRAFT LETTER (in Feinberg): Harned, 67; Traubel, III, 513; Allen, 438.

411. Library of Congress. CT: Harned, 68–71.

412. Royal Library of Copenhagen. CT: *Orbis Litterarum*, VII (1949), 40. DRAFT LETTER (in Feinberg): Traubel, II, 159; Nonesuch, 999.

413. Yale.

414. Morgan (Envelope in Feinberg). CT: Glicksberg, 102.

415. Pennsylvania. CT: Allen, 439.

416. Morgan. CT: *Putnam's Monthly*, V (1908), 164; Glicksberg, 102–103.

417. Morgan. CT: Glicksberg, 101. PT: *Putnam's Monthly*, V (1908), 164.

418. Morgan. CT: Glicksberg, 103–104; Nonesuch, 1000.

419. Morgan. CT: Glicksberg, 104.

420. Morgan. CT: *Putnam's Monthly*, V (1908), 164; Glicksberg, 104–105. PT: Nonesuch, 999 (dated December, 1871).

421. Royal Library of Copenhagen. CT: *Orbis Litterarum*, VII (1949), 41–43. DRAFT LETTER (in Feinberg): Traubel, I, 406–408; Nonesuch, 1000–1002.

422. TEXT: Transcription by Dowden in Berg. CT: Perry, 198–203. DRAFT LETTER (in Feinberg): Traubel, I, 319–321 (dated January 20); Nonesuch, 1002–1004.

423. Morgan. CT: Glicksberg, 105–106.

424. Whitman House, Camden. CT: *AL*, VIII (1937), 420–421.

425. Draft letter in Feinberg. CT: Traubel, III, 316.

426. Lion. DRAFT LETTER (in Lion): Traubel, IV, 58–61.

427. Draft letter in Feinberg. CT: Traubel, II, 463.

428. Draft letter in Feinberg. CT: Traubel, II, 85; Nonesuch, 1004.

429. Pennsylvania. PT: Nonesuch, 1005. DRAFT LETTER (in Library of Congress): Harned, 75.

430. Feinberg. CT: *Calamus*, 87; *CW*, VIII, 76.

431. Feinberg. CT: *Calamus*, 87–89; *CW*, VIII, 77–78.

432. Feinberg. CT: *Calamus*, 89–90; *CW*, VIII, 78–79.

433. Feinberg. CT: *Calamus*, 90–91; *CW*, VIII, 79–80.

434. Berg. CT: Nonesuch, 994 (dated 1871).

435. Feinberg. CT: *Calamus*, 91–92; *CW*, VIII, 80–81.

436. Pennsylvania. CT: Nonesuch, 1005–1006. PT: Barrus, 158.

437. Feinberg. CT: *Calamus*, 92–93; *CW*, VIII, 81–82.

438. Yale.

439. Feinberg. CT: *Calamus*, 93–94; *CW*, VIII, 82–83.

440. Royal Library of Copenhagen. CT: *Orbis Litterarum*, VII (1949), 43.

441. Feinberg. CT: *Calamus*, 94; *CW*, VIII, 83.

442. Feinberg.

443. TEXT: Donaldson, 224–226; Nonesuch, 1006–1007.

444. Trent. CT: Gohdes and Silver, 75.

445. Royal Library of Copenhagen. CT: *Orbis Litterarum*, VII (1949), 43–44.

446. Royal Library of Copenhagen. CT: *Orbis Litterarum*, VII (1949), 45.

447. Feinberg. CT: *Calamus*, 94–95; *CW*, VIII, 83–84.

448. Berg. FACSIMILE: *Nocturne* (Spring, 1955), 10–11. PT: Barrus, 72–73.

449. Feinberg. CT: *Calamus*, 95–96; *CW*, VIII, 84–85.

450. Harvard.

451. Feinberg. CT: *Calamus*, 96–97; *CW*, VIII, 85–86; Nonesuch, 1007–1008.

452. National Archives. CT: *PMLA*, LVIII (1943), 1105.

453. Feinberg (Envelope in Ohio Wesleyan). CT: *Calamus*, 98; *CW*, VIII, 87.

454. Feinberg. CT: *Calamus*, 98; *CW*, VIII, 87–88.

455. Philo Calhoon. PT: Barrus, 73–74; Nonesuch, 1008–1009.

456. Trent. CT: *CW*, VIII, 241–242.

457. Trent. CT: *CW*, VIII, 242.

457.1 Lord Tennyson.

458. Draft letter in Feinberg. CT: Traubel, II, 327.

459. Royal Library of Copenhagen. CT: *Orbis Litterarum*, VII (1949), 46.

460. Yale.

461. Trent. CT: *CW*, VIII, 240–241 (misdated August 13, 1872).

462. Whitman House, Camden. CT: *AL*, VIII (1937), 421–422.

463. Trent. CT: *CW*, VIII, 243.

464. Draft letter in Trent. CT: Gohdes and Silver, 76–78.

465. TEXT: American Art Association, December 12–13, 1938; and *The Collector*, LV (December, 1940).

465.1 Barrett.

466. Trent. CT: *CW*, VIII, 218–219 (erroneously dated 1868).

467. Yale. CT: *In Re*, 73–74. PT: Allen, 448.

468. Yale. CT: *In Re*, 74.

469. Yale. CT: *In Re*, 74–75. PT: Allen, 450.

470. Yale. CT: *In Re*, 75.

471. Yale. CT: *In Re*, 76.

472. Yale. CT: *In Re*, 76; Holloway, 266.

473. Yale. CT: *In Re*, 76–77.

474. Missouri Historical Society. CT: *Missouri Historical Society Bulletin*, XVI (1960), 103.

475. Yale. CT: *In Re*, 77.

476. Yale. CT: *In Re*, 77.

477. Yale. CT: *In Re*, 77–78.

478. Yale. CT: *In Re*, 78–79.

479. Lion. CT: *In Re*, 79.

480. Lion. CT: *In Re*, 79.

481. Lion. CT: *In Re*, 79.

482. Morgan. CT: Glicksberg, 117–118; Nonesuch, 1010.

483. Lion. CT: *In Re*, 79–80.

484. Lion. CT: *In Re*, 80–81. PT: Allen, 448.

485. Whitman House, Camden. CT: *AL*, VIII (1937), 422–423; Nonesuch, 1010–1011.

486. Lion. CT: *In Re*, 81.

487. Lion. CT: *In Re*, 82.

488. Lion. CT: *In Re*, 82–83.

489. Lion. CT: *In Re*, 83.

490. TEXT: *In Re*, 83–84.

491. Ohio Wesleyan.

492. Yale. CT: *In Re*, 84–85.

493. Hanley. CT: *In Re*, 85–86.

494. Hanley. CT: *In Re*, 86–87.

495. Lion. CT: *In Re*, 87.

496. TEXT: American Art Association, March 10–11, 1924.

497. Yale. CT: *In Re*, 87–88.

498. Draft letter in Feinberg.

499. TEXT: *In Re*, 88–89.

500. TEXT: *In Re*, 89; *Wake*, VII (1948), 7–8.

501. Feinberg. PT: Barrus, 81–82.

502. Yale. CT: *In Re*, 89.

503. Yale. CT: *In Re*, 89–90.

504. Feinberg.

505. Barrett. CT: *In Re*, 90–91; *Wake*, VII (1948), 14–15.

506. Lion. CT: *In Re*, 91. PT: Holloway, 266.

507. Yale. CT: *In Re*, 91–92.

508. Fragment in Trent. CT: Gohdes and Silver, 78.

509. Feinberg. CT: *Calamus*, 99; *CW*, VIII, 89.

510. Feinberg. CT: *Calamus*, 99; *CW*, VIII, 89 (dated [1873]).

511. Feinberg. CT: *Calamus*, 100–101; *CW*, VIII, 90–91. PT: Canby, 288.

512. Trent. CT: Gohdes and Silver, 78–80. PT: Barrus, 83–84.

513. Feinberg. CT: *Calamus*, 101; *CW*, VIII, 91–92.

514. Yale. PT: Barrus, 84.

515. Trent. CT: Gohdes and Silver, 80–81.
516. Feinberg. CT: *Calamus*, 102–103; *CW*, VIII, 92–93.
517. SOURCE: American Art Association, February 6, (?).
518. Feinberg. CT: *Calamus*, 103–104; *CW*, VIII, 93–94; Nonesuch, 1011–1012.
519. Feinberg. CT: *Calamus*, 104–105; *CW*, VIII, 94–95.
520. Berg.
521. Feinberg. CT: *Calamus*, 105–107; *CW*, VIII, 95–97.
522. National Archives. CT: *PMLA*, LVIII (1943), 1106–1107.
523. Feinberg. CT: *Calamus*, 109–110; *CW*, VIII, 99–100 (dated August 28–29).
524. Pennsylvania. CT: Nonesuch, 1012–1013. DRAFT LETTER (in Library of Congress): Harned, 94–95 (dated "Summer of 1873").
525. Feinberg. CT: *Calamus*, 107–109; *CW*, VIII, 97–99.
526. Feinberg. CT: *Calamus*, 162; *CW*, VIII, 155–156 (dated 1875).
527. TEXT: Typescript in Berg.
528. TEXT: Barrus, 85.
529. Minnesota Historical Society. CT: Glicksberg, 119.
530. Feinberg. CT: *Calamus*, 110–112; *CW*, VIII, 101–102.
531. Berg.
532. Feinberg.
533. Morgan. CT: Glicksberg, 118. PT: New York *Evening Post*, May 31, 1919.
534. Feinberg. CT: *Calamus*, 112–115; *CW*, VIII, 102–105.
535. Draft letter in Feinberg.
536. Feinberg. CT: *Calamus*, 115; *CW*, VIII, 105–106.
537. Feinberg. CT: *Calamus*, 115–117; *CW*, VIII, 106–107. PT: Allen, 454–455.
538. TEXT: American Art Association, December 12–13, 1938.
539. Mrs. Doris Neale.
540. SOURCE: American Art Association, March 10–11, 1924.
541. TEXT: Barrus, 86.
542. Feinberg. CT: *Calamus*, 117–118; *CW*, VIII, 108–110; Nonesuch, 1013–1015.
543. Berg.
544. Feinberg. CT: *Calamus*, 119–121; *CW*, VIII, 110–112.
545. Historical Society of Pennsylvania. CT: *AL*, VIII (1937), 424.
546. NYPL. PT: Barrus, 86.
547. Feinberg. CT: *Calamus*, 156; *CW*, VIII, 149–150 (dated 1874).
548. Feinberg. CT: *Calamus*, 121–123; *CW*, VIII, 112–114.
549. Berg.
550. Feinberg. CT: *Calamus*, 123–124; *CW*, VIII, 114–115.
551. Feinberg. CT: *Calamus*, 124–125; *CW*, VIII, 115–116.
552. Trent. CT: Gohdes and Silver, 82.
553. Feinberg.
554. Feinberg. CT: *Calamus*, 126–127; *CW*, VIII, 117–118.
555. Feinberg. CT: *Calamus*, 127–128; *CW*, VIII, 118–119.
556. Feinberg. CT: *Calamus*, 128–129; *CW*, VIII, 119–121.
557. Feinberg. CT: *Calamus*, 130–131; *CW*, VIII, 121–122.
558. Draft letter in Feinberg.
559. Feinberg. CT: *Calamus*, 131–132; *CW*, VIII, 122–123.
560. Feinberg. CT: *Calamus*, 132–133; *CW*, VIII, 124–125.
561. Feinberg. CT: *Calamus*, 133–135; *CW*, VIII, 125–126.
562. Feinberg. CT: *Calamus*, 135; *CW*, VIII, 126–127.
563. Draft letter in Trent. CT: Gohdes and Silver, 82.
564. Draft letter in Yale.
565. TEXT: Typescript in Berg.
566. Draft letter in Feinberg.
567. Feinberg. CT: *Calamus*, 137; *CW*, VIII, 129.
568. Feinberg. CT: *Calamus*, 137–138; *CW*, VIII, 129–130.
569. Morgan. CT: *Putnam's Monthly*, V (1908), 168; Nonesuch, 1016–1017.
570. Feinberg. CT: *Calamus*, 138–139; *CW*, VIII, 130–132.
571. Berg.
572. Feinberg. CT: *Calamus*, 139–140; *CW*, VIII, 132.
573. Feinberg. CT: *Calamus*, 140–141; *CW*, VIII, 132–133.
574. Royal Library of Copenhagen. CT: *Orbis Litterarum*, VII (1949), 46–47. DRAFT LETTER (in Feinberg): Traubel, II, 355; Nonesuch, 1017–1018.

575. Feinberg. CT: *Calamus*, 141–142; *CW*, VIII, 133–134.
576. Berg.
577. Draft letter in Feinberg.
578. Feinberg. CT: *Calamus*, 142–143; *CW*, VIII, 135–136; Nonesuch, 1018–1019.
579. Draft letter in Feinberg. CT: Traubel, III, 561.
580. Berg.
581. Feinberg. CT: *Calamus*, 143–144; *CW*, VIII, 136–137.
582. Barrett. CT: Barrus, 105.
583. Feinberg. CT: *Calamus*, 144–145; *CW*, VIII, 137–138.
584. Berg.
585. Feinberg. CT: *Calamus*, 145–146; *CW*, VIII, 138–139.
586. Draft letter in Feinberg.
587. Berg.
588. Morgan.
589. Royal Library of Copenhagen. CT: *Orbis Litterarum*, VII (1949), 47–49.
590. Feinberg. CT: *Calamus*, 146–147; *CW*, VIII, 139–140.
591. Berg.
592. Berg.
593. Feinberg. CT: *Calamus*, 148–149; *CW*, VIII, 140–141.
594. Royal Library of Copenhagen. CT: *Orbis Litterarum*, VII (1949), 49–51.
595. Feinberg. CT: *Calamus*, 149; *CW*, VIII, 141–142.
596. Berg. PT: Asselineau, 226.
597. Berg.
598. Draft letter owned by Oscar Lion, who supplied typescript.
599. Feinberg. CT: *Calamus*, 149–151; *CW*, VIII, 142–143.
600. Feinberg. CT: *Calamus*, 151; *CW*, VIII, 143–144.
601. Berg.
602. Feinberg. CT: *Calamus*, 151–152; *CW*, VIII, 144.
603. Berg.
604. Berg.
605. Draft letter in Feinberg.
606. Berg.
607. Royal Library of Copenhagen. CT: *Orbis Litterarum*, VII (1949), 51–52.
608. Feinberg. CT: *Calamus*, 152–153; *CW*, VIII, 144–145.
609. Berg.
610. Berg.

611. Berg.
612. Berg.
613. Berg.
614. Draft letter in Trent. CT: Gohdes and Silver, 83–84.
614.1 Barrett.
615. Feinberg. CT: *Calamus*, 153; *CW*, VIII, 145–146.
616. Draft letter in Columbia University. CT: Donaldson, 226–227 (dated 1873).
617. Feinberg.
618. Berg.
619. Doheny. PT: Barrus, 90; Nonesuch, 1018.
620. Berg.
621. Berg.
622. Berg.
623. Royal Library of Copenhagen. CT: *Orbis Litterarum*, VII (1949), 52–53.
624. Berg.
625. National Archives. CT: *PMLA*, LVIII (1943), 1107.
625.1 Feinberg.
626. Berg.
627. National Archives. CT: *PMLA*, LVIII (1943), 1108.
628. Berg.
629. TEXT: Donaldson, 227–228.
630. Feinberg. CT: *Calamus*, 154–155; *CW*, VIII, 147–148; Nonesuch, 1019–1020.
631. Berg.
632. Royal Library of Copenhagen. CT: *Orbis Litterarum*, VII (1949), 54–55.
633. Berg.
634. Berg.
635. Berg.
636. Feinberg. CT: *Calamus*, 162; *CW*, VIII, 155 (dated [1875]).
637. Berg. PT: Barrus, 90–91.
638. Berg.
639. Feinberg. CT: *Calamus*, 156; *CW*, VIII, 148.
640. Feinberg. CT: *Calamus*, 163; *CW*, VIII, 156 (dated [1875]).
641. Berg.
642. Mrs. Doris Neale.
643. Feinberg. CT: *Calamus*, 163–164; *CW*, VIII, 156–157 (dated [1875]).
644. Library of Congress. CT: *SB*, VIII (1956), 242.
645. Berg. CT: Nonesuch, 1015 (dated [1873]). PT: Barrus, 91.

646. TEXT: New York *Daily Graphic*, December 19, 1874.
647. Draft letter in Feinberg.
648. Feinberg. CT: *Calamus*, 159; *CW*, VIII, 152–153 (dated [1875]).
649. Feinberg. CT: *Calamus*, 156; *CW*, VIII, 149 (dated August 29, 1874).
650. Feinberg.
651. Berg.
652. Berg.
653. Berg.
654. TEXT: Typescript in Whitman House, Camden.
655. Berg.
656. Berg.
657. Draft letter in Feinberg. CT: Traubel, II, 208.
658. Berg.
659. Yale.
660. Trent. CT: Gohdes and Silver, 84–85.
661. Rollo G. Silver.
662. Berg.
663. Berg.
664. Yale.
665. Barrett. CT: Barrus, 133–134; Nonesuch, 1020–1021.
666. TEXT: *The Academy* (London), VII (April 17, 1875), 398.
667. Berg.
668. TEXT: Typescript prepared by R. M. Bucke, in Trent.
669. Berg.
670. Feinberg. CT: *Calamus*, 160–161; *CW*, VIII, 153–154. PT: Allen, 463.
671. TEXT: *The Academy*, VII (May 29, 1875), 554.
672. TEXT: Transcription by Dowden in Berg.
673. TEXT: American Art Association, November 5–6, 1923. PT: Barrus, 94.
674. TEXT: *AL*, XXV (1953), 361.
675. Berg.
676. Berg.

677. Feinberg.
678. Yale.
679. Berg. CT: Nonesuch, 1021.
680. Feinberg. CT: *Calamus*, 153–154; *CW*, VIII, 146–147 (dated 1874).
681. Draft letter in Hanley. CT: Donaldson, 228–229; Nonesuch, 1022.
682. Pennsylvania (Envelope in Feinberg).
683. Royal Library of Copenhagen. CT: *Orbis Litterarum*, VII (1949), 55–56.
684. Feinberg. CT: *Calamus*, 161–162. *CW*, VIII, 154–155.
685. TEXT: Henkels, October 26, 1899. CT: Donaldson, 229–230 (dated August 16).
686. Berg.
687. Draft letter in Feinberg. CT: Traubel, II, 202.
688. Berg.
689. Yale.
690. Berg.
691. Pennsylvania.
692. Berg.
693. Feinberg. CT: *Calamus*, 169–170; *CW*, VIII, 163 (dated [1877]).
694. Berg.
695. Draft letter in Feinberg. CT: Traubel, III, 408–409; Nonesuch, 1022–1023.
696. Berg. CT: Nonesuch, 1016 (dated 1873). PT: Barrus, 94–95.
697. TEXT: Photostat in possession of Emory Holloway.
698. Yale.
699. Berg.
700. Berg.
701. Feinberg.
702. Berg.
703. Berg.
704. Berg.
705. Berg.
706. Berg.
707. Berg.

Collections

Appendix B

A CHECK LIST OF WHITMAN'S LOST LETTERS

It is sometimes of importance to biographers and critics to know about letters WW wrote, even though the letters themselves are not extant. The entries in this check list include (1) the date, (2) the name of the recipient of WW's letter, and (3) the source of information which makes possible the reconstruction. Many of the dates are approximate because the information is based upon a letter addressed to WW, which simply informs us that the poet had written before the correspondent had replied. I have indicated the date and present location of correspondence addressed to WW. Allusions to lost letters in WW's own correspondence are designated WW and followed by the appropriate letter number. Auction records which contained no text are incorporated into this list, since the letters as of the moment are "lost." The abbreviations are explained in the table of abbreviations in the Introduction.

1868

January 23. To Louisa Van Velsor Whitman. WW 268.

January 23. To Hannah Heyde. WW 268.

February 6. To Louisa Van Velsor Whitman. Letter from Mrs. Whitman, [February 12] (Trent).

February 9(?). To Louisa Van Velsor Whitman. Letter from Mrs. Whitman, [February 12] (Trent).

About February 11. To Thomas Jefferson Whitman. Letter from Mrs. Whitman, [February 12] (Trent).

February 14. To Louisa Van Velsor Whitman. Letter from Mrs. Whitman, [February] 17 (Trent).

February 16. To Louisa Van Velsor Whitman. Letter from Mrs. Whitman, [February] 17 (Trent).

About February 23. To Benton H. Wilson. Letter from Wilson, February 24 (Feinberg).

March 1. To Louisa Van Velsor Whitman. Letter from Mrs. Whitman, [March 3] (Trent).

March 4. To Benton H. Wilson. WW's notation on Wilson's letter, February 24 (Feinberg).

March 9. To Louisa Van Velsor Whitman. Letter from Mrs. Whitman, March 11 (Trent).

March 11. To Abby H. Price. WW 285.

March 12. To Louisa Van Velsor Whitman. Letter from Mrs. Whitman, [March 13] (Trent).

March 19. To Louisa Van Velsor Whitman. Letter from Mrs. Whitman, March [24] (Trent).

March 23. To Louisa Van Velsor Whitman. Letter from Mrs. Whitman, March [24] (Trent).

April 2. To Louisa Van Velsor Whitman. Letter from Mrs. Whitman, April 7 (Trent).

April 6. To Louisa Van Velsor Whitman. Letter from Mrs. Whitman, April 7 (Trent).

April 11. To Benton H. Wilson. WW's notation on letter from Henry Wilson, March 30 (Feinberg).

April 27. To Louisa Van Velsor Whitman. WW 289.

About June 16. To Charles Hine. Letter from Hine, June 17 (Feinberg).

June 19. To Louisa Van Velsor Whitman. Letter from Mrs. Whitman, June 25 (Trent).

June 23. To Louisa Van Velsor Whitman. Letter from Mrs. Whitman, June 25 (Trent).

June 29. To Louisa Van Velsor Whitman. Letter from Mrs. Whitman, July 1 (Trent).

July 6. To Louisa Van Velsor Whitman. Letter from Mrs. Whitman, July 8 (Trent).

July 13. To Louisa Van Velsor Whitman. Letter from Mrs. Whitman, [July 15] (Trent).

August 13. To Hannah Heyde. WW 296.

September 5. To Hannah Heyde. WW 300.

September 18. To Peter Doyle. WW 304.

September 22. To Peter Doyle. WW 304.

September 29. To "No. 6," a streetcar conductor. WW 308.

October 17. To Louisa Van Velsor Whitman. WW 317.

October 25. To (?). Henkels auction catalog, May 25, 1906.

About October 30. To Will W. Wallace. Letter from Wallace, October 31 (Feinberg).

November 1. To Louisa Van Velsor Whitman. Letter from Mrs. Whitman, November 2 (Trent).

November 2. To Louisa Van Velsor Whitman. Letter from Mrs. Whitman, [November 4] (Trent).

November 6(?). To Louisa Van Velsor Whitman. Letter from Mrs. Whitman, [November 11] (Trent).

November 8. To Louisa Van Velsor Whitman. Letter from Mrs. Whitman, [November 11] (Trent).

About November 11. To Charles and Hannah Heyde. Letter from Mrs. Heyde, November 13 (Trent).

November 20(?). To Louisa Van Velsor Whitman. WW 328.

November 25. To (?). Merwin-Clayton Sales Company, January 12, 1906.

December 7. To Louisa Van Velsor Whitman. Letter from Mrs. Whitman, [December 10] (Trent).

1869

January 7. To Messrs. Philp & Solomon, booksellers. *Autograph Prices Current* (London), v (1919–1920), 206.

January 7. To Walter Whitman Reynolds. Letter from Reynolds, June 1, 1870 (Feinberg).

January 10. To Benton H. Wilson. Letter from Wilson, January 24 (Feinberg).

January 11(?). To Louisa Van Velsor Whitman. Letter from Mrs. Whitman, January 12 (Trent).

January 18(?). To Louisa Van Velsor Whitman. Letter from Mrs. Whitman, January 19 (Trent).

January 20. To John Morley. WW's notation on letter from Morley, January 5 (Feinberg; Traubel, 1, 216).

February 15. To Louisa Van Velsor Whitman. Letter from Mrs. Whitman, [February] 17 (Trent).

March 30(?). To Louisa Van Velsor Whitman. Letter from Mrs. Whitman, [March] 31 (Trent).

April 2. To Louisa Van Velsor Whitman. Letter from Mrs. Whitman, April 7 (Trent).

April 12(?). To Louisa Van Velsor Whitman. Letter from Mrs. Whitman, [April] 14 (Trent).

April 19(?). To Louisa Van Velsor Whitman. Letter from Mrs. Whitman, [April 20?] (Trent).

June 22(?). To Louisa Van Velsor Whitman. Letter from Mrs. Whitman, June 23 (Trent).

June 29(?). To Louisa Van Velsor Whitman. Letter from Mrs. Whitman, June 30 (Trent).

August 23. To Peter Doyle. WW 349.

August 25(?). To John Lee. WW 348.

September 27(?). To Louisa Van Velsor Whitman. Letter from Mrs. Whitman, [September 30] (Trent).

October 18(?). To Louisa Van Velsor Whitman. Letter from Mrs. Whitman, October [19] (Trent).

October 29. To Walter Whitman Reynolds. Letter from Reynolds, November 16 (Feinberg).

November 9(?). To Louisa Van Velsor Whitman. Letter from Mrs. Whitman, November 10 (Trent).

December 5. To Louisa Van Velsor Whitman. Letter from Mrs. Whitman, December 7 (Trent).

December 20(?). To Louisa Van Velsor Whitman. Letter from Mrs. Whitman, [December 22?] (Trent).

About December 22. To Thomas Dixon. Letter from Dixon, December 23 (Feinberg).

1870

January 8. To Walter Whitman Reynolds. Letter from Reynolds, February 9 (Feinberg).

January 17(?). To Louisa Van Velsor Whitman. Letter from Mrs. Whitman, January 19 (Trent).

March 21(?). To Louisa Van Velsor Whitman. Letter from Mrs. Whitman, March [23?] (Trent).

March 26(?). To Louisa Van Velsor Whitman. Letter from Mrs. Whitman, [March 28] (Trent).

April 4(?). To Louisa Van Velsor Whitman. Letter from Mrs. Whitman, April 5 (Trent).

April 11(?). To Louisa Van Velsor Whitman. Letter from Mrs. Whitman, [April 13] (Trent).

June 6(?). To Louisa Van Velsor Whitman. Letter from Mrs. Whitman, June 8(?) (Trent).

June 20(?). To Louisa Van Velsor Whitman. Letter from Mrs. Whitman, June 22 (Trent).

July 10(?). To Louisa Van Velsor Whitman. Letter from Mrs. Whitman, [July 12] (Trent).

July 18(?). To Louisa Van Velsor Whitman. Letter from Mrs. Whitman, July 20 (Trent).

December 20(?). To Louisa Van Velsor Whitman. Letter from Mrs. Whitman, December 22 (Trent).

1871

February 3(?). To Louisa Van Velsor Whitman. Letter from Mrs. Whitman, February 8 (Trent).

February 6(?). To Louisa Van Velsor Whitman. Letter from Mrs. Whitman, February 8 (Trent).

About February 8. To John M. Rogers. Letter from Rogers, February 9 (Feinberg).

February 13(?). To Louisa Van Velsor Whitman. Letter from Mrs. Whitman, [February] 14 (Trent).

About February 26. To John M. Rogers. Letter from Rogers, February 27 (Feinberg).

About April 9. To John M. Rogers. Letter from Rogers, April 10 (Feinberg).

About June. To Alfred, Lord Tennyson. WW 443.

June 2. To John M. Rogers. WW's notation on letter from Rogers, June 1 (Feinberg).

December 23(?). To Hannah Heyde. WW 414.

December 23(?). To Martha Whitman. WW 414.

1872

January 22. To Louisa Van Velsor Whitman. WW 423.

January 26. To Hannah Heyde. WW 424.

May 25(?). To Martha Whitman. Letter from Martha Whitman to Louisa Orr Whitman, May 27 (Missouri Historical Society).

August 13. To Louisa Van Velsor Whitman. WW 456.

August 22. To Hannah Heyde. WW 456.

November 7(?). To Hannah Heyde. Letter from Mrs. Heyde to Louisa Van Velsor Whitman, November 15 (LC).

About November 9. To Martha Whitman. Letter from Thomas Jefferson Whitman, November 10 (Feinberg).

December 20(?). To Hannah Heyde. Letter from Mrs. Heyde to Louisa Van Velsor Whitman, January 7–10, 1873 (LC).

December 22(?). To Hannah Heyde. Letter from Mrs. Heyde to Louisa Van Velsor Whitman, January 7–10, 1873 (LC).

December 28(?). To Hannah Heyde. Letter from Mrs. Heyde to Louisa

Van Velsor Whitman, January 7–10, 1873 (LC).

1873

January 10(?). To Martha Whitman. Letter from Thomas Jefferson Whitman to Louisa Van Velsor Whitman, January 14 (Feinberg).

January 12(?). To Mannahatta Whitman. Letter from Thomas Jefferson Whitman to Louisa Van Velsor Whitman, January 14 (Feinberg).

January 20(?). To Martha Whitman. WW 467.

February 5(?). To Thomas Jefferson Whitman. WW 473.

February 5(?). To Hannah Heyde. WW 473.

February 10(?). To Frances B. Felt. WW 498.

February 20. To Hannah Heyde. WW 480.

February 21. To Thomas Jefferson Whitman. WW 481.

February 21. To Hannah Heyde. WW 483.

February 28. To Hannah Heyde. Letter from Mrs. Heyde to Louisa Van Velsor Whitman, March 5 (LC).

March 2. To Louisa Van Velsor Whitman. Letter from Mrs. Whitman, March 4 (Trent).

March 12. To Louisa Van Velsor Whitman. WW 488.

March 19. To Louisa Van Velsor Whitman. WW 490.

March 31. To Thomas Jefferson Whitman. WW 492.

April 3. To Thomas Jefferson Whitman. WW 494.

April 4(?). To Lillie Townsend. WW 494.

April 11(?). To Louisa Van Velsor Whitman. Letter from Mrs. Whitman, [April 12] (Trent).

April 11. To William Michael Rossetti. *Letters of William Michael Rossetti*, ed. Gohdes and Baum (1934), 82.

April 14. To Louisa Van Velsor Whitman. WW 497.

April 28. To Louisa Van Velsor Whitman. WW 502.

About May 8. To Thomas Jefferson Whitman. Letter from Jeff, May 9 (Feinberg).

June 4(?). To Louisa Orr Whitman. Letter from Louisa, June 5(?) (LC).

About June 6. To Hannah Heyde. Letter from Mrs. Heyde, June 7 (LC).

June 7(?). To Peter Doyle. WW 510.

About June 22. To Harry Douglas. WW 512.

June 25. To Mr. Dubarry. WW 513.

June 26. To James M. Edmunds. WW 513.

July 7. To Postmaster, Washington, D. C. WW 515.

About August 16. To Hannah Heyde. Letter from Mrs. Heyde, August 17 (LC).

October 8(?). To Charles W. Eldridge. WW 545.

October 12. To Walter Godey. WW 546.

October 15. To Peter Doyle. WW 548.

December 22. To Peter Doyle. WW 562.

December 29. To Thomas O'Kane. WW 564.

1874

January 7(?). To Walt Whitman Storms. Letter from Storms, January 12 (Feinberg).

February 12(?). To William H. Millis, Jr. Letter from Millis, February 16 (Berg).

February 16. To Thomas O'Kane. WW 605.

About February 27. To Abby H. Price. WW 588.

About March 8. To Walt Whitman Storms. Letter from Storms, March 9 (Feinberg).

About April 16. To J. Hubley Ashton. WW 603.

April 27. To William Stansberry. Letter from Stansberry, May 12 (Trent).

May 28. To Walter Godey. Letter from Godey, June 1 (LC).

June 11. To J. C. Mann. WW's notation on verso of 598.

June 11(?). To J. B. Thayer. WW's notation on verso of 598.

About June 20. To William H. Taylor. Letter from Taylor, June 21 (Feinberg).

About July 28. To Mrs. Isabella A. White. Letter from Mrs. White, July 29 (Feinberg).

About October 6. To John Newton Johnson. Letter from Johnson, October 7 (Feinberg).

About November 6. To John Newton Johnson. Letter from Johnson, November 7 (Feinberg).

About December 14. To Joseph B. Marvin. Letter from Marvin, December 15 (LC).

About December 21. To Whitelaw Reid. Letter from Reid, December 22 (Feinberg).

1875

February 5. To Reuben Farwell. Letter from Farwell, February 11 (Trent).

About February 11. To James Redfield. Letter from Redfield, February 12 (Feinberg).

About February 27. To William H. Millis, Jr. Letter from Millis, February 28 (Berg).

About February 28. To Manvill Wintersteen. Letter from Wintersteen, March 1 (Berg).

About March 4. To Reuben Farwell. Letter from Farwell, March 5 (Trent).

About March 9. To Manvill Wintersteen. Letter from Wintersteen, March 10 (Berg).

About March 11. To Bethuel Smith. Letter from Smith, March 12 (Feinberg).

About March 15. To Charles P. Somerby. Letter from Somerby, March 16 (Feinberg).

March 27(?). To William J. Linton. WW 664.

About April 19. To Walt Whitman Storms. Letter from Storms, April 20 (Feinberg).

April 21. To Bethuel Smith. WW's notation on letter from Smith, March 12 (Feinberg).

April 23. To Manvill Wintersteen. WW's notation on letter from Wintersteen, March 10 (Berg).

April 27. To William H. Taylor. WW's notation on letter from Taylor, June 21, 1874 (Feinberg).

About April 29. To John T. Trowbridge. Letter from Trowbridge, April 30 (Feinberg; Traubel, II, 224 [misdated April 3]).

May 2. To John Newton Johnson. Letter from Johnson, May 10 (Feinberg).

About May 26. To Joaquin Miller. Letter from Miller, May 27 (Feinberg; Traubel, I, 57).

About June 13. To John M. Rogers. Letter from Rogers, June 14 (Feinberg).

July 2. To John Newton Johnson. Letter from Johnson, [August?] 10 (Feinberg).

About July 20. To William Stansberry. Letter from Stansberry, July 21 (Trent).

About July 23. To John M. Rogers. Letter from Rogers, July 24 (Feinberg).

About July 30. To Kristian Elster. WW 683.

August 8. To Manvill Wintersteen. WW's notation on Wintersteen's letter, August 5 (Berg).

About August 8. To Walt Whitman Storms. Letter from Storms, August 9 (Feinberg).

August 13. To John Newton Johnson. Letter from Johnson, November 9 (Feinberg).

About August 15. To Reuben Farwell. Letter from Farwell, August 16 (Trent).

September 24. To Charles P. Somerby. Letter from Somerby, September 25 (Feinberg).

October 19. To William Michael Rossetti. Letter from Rossetti, December 23 (Feinberg).

About November 13. To George Washington Whitman. Letter from George, November 14 (Yale).

About November 13. To George Washington Whitman. Letter from George, November 14 (Yale): "Both of your postals recd."

December 12. To John Newton Johnson. Letter from Johnson, [February 7], 1876 (Feinberg).

Appendix C

This Calendar includes extant letters written to WW. The following information appears in the entries: (1) the date; (2) the name of the correspondent, sometimes with a brief identification in order to indicate the nature of the correspondence; (3) the location of the letter, if known; and (4) appearance in print, if applicable. The letters to WW which are reproduced in this volume are marked WW with the appropriate letter number. Excerpts from many of these letters appear in the notes. Abbreviations are explained in the table of abbreviations in the Introduction.

1868

January 9. From A. Bronson Alcott. Feinberg. CT: Traubel, III, 243–244; Shephard, *Walt Whitman's Pose*, 255.

[January?] 20. From Thomas Jefferson Whitman. Feinberg.

January 20. From William H. Millis, Jr., an ex-soldier. Yale.

February 1. From Moncure D. Conway. Feinberg. CT: Traubel, II, 284.

February 5. To John Camden Hotten. Feinberg. CT: Traubel, II, 285–286.

[February 12].[1] From Louisa Van Velsor Whitman. Trent.

[February] 17. From Louisa Van Velsor Whitman. Trent.

February 24. From Benton H. Wilson. Feinberg.

[February 25?]. From Louisa Van Velsor Whitman. Trent. CT: Gohdes and Silver, 192–194.

February 25. From A. Simpson & Company. Feinberg.

[March 3]. From Louisa Van Velsor Whitman. Trent.

[March] 6. From Louisa Van Velsor Whitman. Trent.

March 11. From Louisa Van Velsor Whitman. Trent.

[March 13]. From Louisa Van Velsor Whitman. Trent. CT: Gohdes and Silver, 194–195.

March [24]. From Louisa Van Velsor Whitman. Trent.

[March 24]. From John M. Binckley. Feinberg.

March 25. From W. C. Church. Feinberg.

March 30. From Henry Wilson, father of an ex-soldier. Feinberg.

March 31. From Louisa Van Velsor Whitman. Trent. CT: Gohdes and Silver, 200–201 (dated 1869?).

April 7. From Louisa Van Velsor Whitman. Trent.

April 8. From John Camden Hotten. Yale. CT: Traubel, IV, 308.

1. The literary executors undertook the difficult task of dating Mrs. Whitman's letters, and for the most part arrived at dates which, if not absolutely certain, are at least plausible. I have not hesitated to alter dates when in my judgment they appeared to be erroneous, but because of difficulties in reading Mrs. Whitman's hand and because of the absence of verifiable material in many of her letters, I cannot guarantee their accuracy.

April 12. From William Michael Rossetti. Feinberg. CT: Traubel, II, 123–124.

April 28. From A. Bronson Alcott. Feinberg. CT: Traubel, III, 245.

May 2. From F. P. Church. Feinberg.

May 3. From Benton H. Wilson. Feinberg.

May 5. From Louisa Van Velsor Whitman. Trent.

May 9. From Moncure D. Conway. Location unknown. CT: Traubel, IV, 10.

[May 14]. From Louisa Van Velsor Whitman. Trent. CT: Gohdes and Silver, 195–196.

May 15. From F. P. Church. Feinberg.

May 16. From Sheldon & Company (for *The Galaxy*). Feinberg.

June 17. From Charles Hine, an artist. Feinberg.

June 25. From Louisa Van Velsor Whitman. Trent. CT: Gohdes and Silver, 196–198.

July 1. From Louisa Van Velsor Whitman. Trent.

July 8. From Louisa Van Velsor Whitman. Trent.

July 12. From Thomas Jefferson Whitman. Feinberg.

[July 15]. From Louisa Van Velsor Whitman. Trent.

[August 19]. From Louisa Van Velsor Whitman. Trent. CT: Gohdes and Silver, 198–199.

September 12. From Byron Sutherland. Feinberg.

September 16. From William D. O'Connor. Feinberg. CT: Traubel, II, 431–432.

September 18. From Peter Doyle. WW 304.

September 23. From Peter Doyle. Typescript in Lion.

September 24. From William F. Channing. Feinberg.

[September 25]. From John Swinton. Feinberg. CT: Traubel, II, 339–340.

September 27. From Peter Doyle. Morgan.

October 1. From Peter Doyle. PT: Swann Auction Galleries, April 4–5, 1951.

October 5. From Henry Hurt. Feinberg.

October 5. From Peter Doyle. Lion.

October 6. From Benton H. Wilson. Feinberg.

October 8. From Byron Sutherland. Feinberg.

October 9. From Peter Doyle. Lion.

October 9. From William D. O'Connor. Feinberg.

October 14. From Peter Doyle. Barrett.

October 16. From Mrs. Henry Reynolds, mother of Walter Whitman Reynolds. Feinberg.

October 31. From Will W. Wallace, an ex-soldier. Feinberg.

November 2. From Louisa Van Velsor Whitman. Trent.

[November 4]. From Louisa Van Velsor Whitman. Trent.

November 8. From Mr. Williamson, probably an ex-soldier. Yale.

After November 10. From Louisa Van Velsor Whitman. Hanley.

[November 11]. From Louisa Van Velsor Whitman. Trent.

November 13. From Hannah Heyde. Trent.

November 17. From Alfred Wise, a jeweler's son. Yale.

[November 18]. From Louisa Van Velsor Whitman. Trent.

November 23. From William D. O'Connor. Feinberg. CT: Traubel, III, 504–505.

November 25. From Louisa Van Velsor Whitman. Trent.

[December 1]. From Louisa Van Velsor Whitman. Trent.

[December 5]. From Louisa Van Velsor Whitman. Trent.

December 5. From James T. Fields. Location unknown. CT: Traubel, II, 22.

[December 10]. From Louisa Van Velsor Whitman. Trent.

[December 14?]. From Louisa Van Velsor Whitman. Trent.

December 14. From James T. Fields. Location unknown. CT: Traubel, II, 211.

[December?] 16. From Louisa Van Velsor Whitman. Yale.

December 27. From Benton H. Wilson. Feinberg.

December 28. From Louisa Van Velsor Whitman. Trent.

1869

January 5. From John Morley. Feinberg. CT: Traubel, I, 216.

January 11. From John Flood, Jr. Yale.

January 12. From Louisa Van Velsor Whitman. Trent.

January 19. From Louisa Van Velsor Whitman. Trent.

January 21. From Thomas Jefferson Whitman. Feinberg.

January 21. From Julius Sing(?), an admirer. LC.

January 24. From Benton H. Wilson. Feinberg.

[February 4]. From Louisa Van Velsor Whitman. Trent.

February 14. From Gabriel Sarrazin. Lion.

[February] 17. From Louisa Van Velsor Whitman. Trent.

[February 18?]. From Louisa Van Velsor Whitman. Trent.

[February]. From Louisa Van Velsor Whitman. Trent. CT: Gohdes and Silver, 199–200.

March 2. From Charles Warren Stoddard. Feinberg. CT: Traubel, IV, 267–268.

March 4. From Louisa Van Velsor Whitman. Trent.

March 4. From W. C. Church. Feinberg.

[March 15]. From Louisa Van Velsor Whitman. Trent.

March 25. From Thomas Jefferson Whitman. Feinberg.

[March] 31. From Louisa Van Velsor Whitman. Trent. CT: Gohdes and Silver, 200–201.

April 5. From Thomas Jefferson Whitman. Feinberg.

April 7. From Louisa Van Velsor Whitman. Trent.

[April] 14. From Louisa Van Velsor Whitman. Trent.

[April 20?]. From Louisa Van Velsor Whitman. Trent.

June 23. From Louisa Van Velsor Whitman. Trent.

June 30. From Louisa Van Velsor Whitman. Trent.

[Summer]. From Louisa Van Velsor Whitman. Trent.

July 14. From Louisa Van Velsor Whitman. Trent.

July 18. From Benton H. Wilson. Feinberg.

July 22. From H. B. Thompson, an ex-soldier. Yale.

August 31. From Meredith R. Brookfield, an admirer. LC.

September 23. From Louisa Van Velsor Whitman. Trent.

[September 30]. From Louisa Van Velsor Whitman. Trent.

October [19]. From Louisa Van Velsor Whitman. Trent.

November 10. From Louisa Van Velsor Whitman. Trent.

November 16. From Walter Whitman Reynolds. Feinberg.

December 7. From Louisa Van Velsor Whitman. Trent.

December 19. From Benton H. Wilson. Feinberg.

[December 22?]. From Louisa Van Velsor Whitman. Trent.

December 23. From Thomas Dixon. Feinberg.

1870

January 9. From William Michael Rossetti. Feinberg. CT: Traubel, I, 379–381.

January 14. From Alfred and John B. Pratt. Feinberg.

January 19. From Louisa Van Velsor Whitman. Trent.

February 8. From Helen A. Horner, an ecstatic admirer. Feinberg.

February 9. From Walter Whitman Reynolds. Feinberg.

March 1. From Mannahatta Whitman. Formerly in the Dorn Collection.

March 15. From John B. and N. M. Pratt, parents of an ex-soldier. Yale.

March 22. From Dr. E. Warner, the doctor who attended Jesse Whitman. Feinberg. CT: Traubel, I, 294.

March [23?]. From Louisa Van Velsor Whitman. Trent.

[March 24]. From Louisa Van Velsor Whitman. Trent. CT: Gohdes and Silver, 201–202.

[March 28]. From Louisa Van Velsor Whitman. Trent. CT: Gohdes and Silver, 202–203.

March 30. From Byron Sutherland. Feinberg.

March. From Jessie Louisa Whitman. LC.

April 2. From Charles Warren Stoddard. Feinberg. CT: Traubel, III, 444–445.

April 5. From Louisa Van Velsor Whitman. Trent.

April 8. From Byron Sutherland. Feinberg.

April 9. From Thomas Dixon. Feinberg.

[April 13]. From Louisa Van Velsor Whitman. Trent.

April 13. From Bret Harte (for *The Overland Monthly*). Feinberg. CT: Traubel, I, 28.

April 26. From Walter Whitman Reynolds. Feinberg.

May 15. From Thomas F. Bainbridge, an ex-soldier. Yale.

May 15. From Benton H. Wilson. Feinberg.

May 28. From Thomas Dixon. Feinberg.

May. From Stephen K. Winant, an ex-soldier. Yale.

June 1. From Louisa Van Velsor Whitman. Trent.

June 1. From Walter Whitman Reynolds. Feinberg.

June 8(?). From Louisa Van Velsor Whitman. LC.

June 13. From Charles L. Heyde. Trent. CT: Gohdes and Silver, 226–228.

June 14. From Mrs. Nellie Eyster, an admirer. Feinberg. CT: Traubel, I, 34–35.

June 22. From Louisa Van Velsor Whitman. Trent.

June 29. From Louisa Van Velsor Whitman. Trent.

[June?]. From Louisa Van Velsor Whitman. Trent.

[July 12]. From Louisa Van Velsor Whitman. Trent. CT: Gohdes and Silver, 203.

July 20. From Louisa Van Velsor Whitman. Trent.

October 19. From John Swinton. Feinberg. CT: Traubel, II, 487–488; Allen, 427.

December 19. From Richard Maurice Bucke. Feinberg. CT: Traubel, II, 6–7.

December 22. From Louisa Van Velsor Whitman. Trent.

1871

February 5. From Thomas M. Woodworth, an ex-soldier. Feinberg.

February 8. From Louisa Van Velsor Whitman. Trent.

February 9. From John M. Rogers, a Brooklyn driver. Feinberg.

[February] 14. From Louisa Van Velsor Whitman. Trent.

February 27. From John M. Rogers. Feinberg.

April 6. From John M. Rogers. Feinberg.

April 10. From F. P. Church. Feinberg.

April 10. From John M. Rogers. Feinberg.

[April 16?]. From Louisa Van Velsor Whitman. Trent.

April 23. From Cyril Flower. Feinberg.

May 16. From Thomas Russell(?). Feinberg.

June 1. From John M. Rogers. Feinberg.

[June 13?]. From Louisa Van Velsor Whitman. Trent.

July 9. From William Michael Rossetti. Feinberg. CT: Traubel, I, 132–133.

July 12. From Alfred, Lord Tennyson. WW 394.

July 16. From Cyril Flower. Feinberg. CT: Traubel, II, 373.

July 23. From Edward Dowden. Feinberg. CT: Traubel, I, 133–135.

July 27. From Thomas Dixon. Feinberg.

August 1. From George Peyton, Charles E. Burd, and James B. Young, for the American Institute. Feinberg. CT: Traubel, I, 326.

August 4. From Mrs. Charles Hine, wife of the artist. Feinberg. CT: Traubel, III, 330–331 (dated August 6).

August 17. From William Black, an autograph seeker. Feinberg.

August 22. From Louisa Van Velsor Whitman. Trent.

August 23. From F. S. Ellis. Feinberg. CT: Traubel, II, 447–448.

August 24. From F. S. Ellis. Feinberg. CT: Traubel, II, 448.

September 3. From Anne Gilchrist. WW 405.

September 5. From Edward Dowden. Feinberg. CT: Traubel, I, 224–225.

September 6. From George Washington and Louisa Orr Whitman. Hanley.

September 10. From Richard J. Hinton. Mrs. Doris Neale.

September 11. From John W. Chambers, for the American Institute. Feinberg. CT: Traubel, IV, 484.

September 13. From Moncure D. Conway. Feinberg. CT: Traubel, III, 111–112.

September 14. From Philip Hale, a youthful admirer. Feinberg. CT: Traubel, III, 533.

[September 30]. From Louisa Van Velsor Whitman. Trent.

September 30. From Joaquin Miller. Feinberg. CT: Traubel, I, 107.

[September?]. From Louisa Van Velsor Whitman. Trent.

October 3–4. From John Burroughs. Feinberg. CT: Traubel, I, 89–90; Barrus, 61–62.

October 7. From John Addington Symonds. Feinberg. CT: Traubel, II, 277–278.

October 8. From William Michael Rossetti. Feinberg. CT: Traubel, III, 376–377.

October 10. From Louisa Van Velsor Whitman. Trent. CT: Gohdes and Silver, 203–204.

October 15. From Edward Dowden. Feinberg. CT: Traubel, III, 41–42.

October 19. From Rudolf Schmidt. LC.

October 20. From Cyril Flower. Feinberg. CT: Traubel, II, 461–463.

October 23. From Anne Gilchrist. LC. CT: Harned, 65–66.

October 30. From John Burroughs. Syracuse University.

November 3. From Roden Noel. Feinberg. CT: Traubel, I, 425–426.

[November 27]. From Anne Gilchrist. WW 411.

1871. From the Census Office, Department of the Interior. Trent.

1872

[January 1]. From Louisa Van Velsor Whitman. Yale.

January 5. From Rudolf Schmidt. Syracuse University. CT: Traubel, IV, 103.

[January 10?]. From Louisa Van Velsor Whitman. Trent.

January 24. From Anne Gilchrist. LC. CT: Harned, 72–74.

January 31. From Matt H. Carpenter. Syracuse University. CT: Traubel, IV, 120.

February 5. From Rudolf Schmidt. Feinberg.

February 7. From John Addington Symonds. Feinberg. CT: Traubel, I, 74–76.

February 18 (not sent until February 14, 1876). From Bram Stoker. CT: Traubel, IV, 181–185.

February 21. From H. Buxton Forman. Feinberg. CT: Traubel, II, 265–266.

February 25. From John Addington Symonds. Feinberg. CT: Traubel, I, 387–388.

February 27. From Rudolf Schmidt. Feinberg.

March 31. From William Michael Rossetti. Feinberg. CT: Traubel, III, 141–145.

April 8. From Pedelia(?) Bates. LC.

April 12. From Anne Gilchrist. LC. CT: Harned, 76–78.

April 25. From Rudolf Schmidt. Feinberg. CT: Traubel, I, 274–275.

May 13. From Walter Whitman Reynolds. Feinberg.

June 3. From Anne Gilchrist. LC. CT: Harned, 79–81.

June 17. From Emil Arctander, acting vice-consul for Denmark. Feinberg.

June 20. From Emil Arctander. Feinberg.

July 14. From Anne Gilchrist. LC. CT: Harned, 82–84.

August 9. From S. W. Green, a printer. Feinberg.

September 3. From Edward Dowden. Feinberg. CT: Traubel, II, 80–81.

September 26. From Grace B. Haight. LC.

November 10. From Thomas Jefferson Whitman. Feinberg.

November 12. From Anne Gilchrist. LC. CT: Harned, 85.

[December 3]. From Louisa Van Velsor Whitman. LC.

December 26. From John M. Rogers, a Brooklyn driver. Feinberg.

1873

January 12. From John Burroughs. Feinberg. CT: Traubel, III, 281–282; Barrus, 80.

January 15. From R. W. Waldo (ordering a book). Feinberg.

About January 20. From Louisa Van Velsor Whitman. Feinberg.

[January] 30. From Louisa Van Velsor Whitman. Trent.

January 31. From Anne Gilchrist. LC. CT: Harned, 86–87.

February 7. From Thomas Jefferson Whitman. Feinberg.

February 11. From Thomas Jefferson Whitman. Feinberg.

[February 12?]. From Louisa Van Velsor Whitman. Trent.

February 24. From Mannahatta Whitman. Formerly in the Dorn Collection.

February 27. From Louisa Van Velsor Whitman. Trent.

[February?]. From Louisa Van Velsor Whitman. Trent.

[March 1]. From Louisa Van Velsor Whitman. Trent.

March 4. From Louisa Van Velsor Whitman. Trent.

March 4. From Hannah Heyde. LC.

[March 10?]. From Louisa Van Velsor Whitman. Trent.

March 10. From George H. Williams. Lion. CT: Traubel, III, 475–476.

March 16. From Thomas Jefferson Whitman. Yale.

March 19. From William F. Channing. Feinberg.

March 21. From Louisa Van Velsor Whitman. Trent.

[March 23?]. From Louisa Van Velsor Whitman. Trent.

March 28. From Sampson, Low & Company. Feinberg.

March 30. From Thomas Jefferson Whitman. Feinberg.

[March]. From Louisa Van Velsor Whitman. Trent.

[March?] Saturday. From Louisa Van Velsor Whitman. Trent.

[April 2?]. From Louisa Van Velsor Whitman. Trent.

[April 3?]. From Louisa Van Velsor Whitman. Trent.

April 4. From Rudolf Schmidt. Feinberg.

[April 5?]. From Louisa Van Velsor Whitman. Trent.

[April 8]. From Louisa Van Velsor Whitman. Trent.

April 11. From John Burroughs. Feinberg.

[April 12]. From Louisa Van Velsor Whitman. Trent.

April 12. From Edward Dowden. Feinberg. CT: Traubel, I, 441–443.

[April 20?]. From Louisa Van Velsor Whitman. Trent.

[April 21]. From Louisa Van Velsor Whitman. Trent.

[May 1]. From Louisa Van Velsor Whitman. Trent.

[May 9?]. From Louisa Van Velsor Whitman. Trent.

May 9. From Thomas Jefferson Whitman. Feinberg.

[May 12?]. From Louisa Orr Whitman. LC.

[May 12?]. From Louisa Van Velsor Whitman. Trent.

May 14. From John Burroughs. Syracuse University. CT: Traubel, IV, 304–305.

[May 15]. From Louisa Van Velsor and Louisa Orr Whitman. Hanley.

[May 17?]. From Louisa Van Velsor Whitman. Trent.

About May 20. From Louisa Van Velsor Whitman. Trent.

May 20. From Sarah Avery. LC.

May 20. From Anne Gilchrist. LC. CT: Harned, 88–90.

June 2. From John Burroughs. Feinberg.

[June 5?]. From Louisa Orr Whitman. LC.

June 7. From Hannah Heyde. LC. CT: *Life in Letters: American Autograph Journal*, II (1939), 103–104.

August 12. From Anne Gilchrist. LC. CT: Harned, 91–93.

August 17. From Hannah Heyde. LC.

September 4. From Anne Gilchrist. LC. CT: Harned, 96–97.

November 1. From Henry M. Alden. Barrett.

November 3. From Anne Gilchrist. LC. CT: Harned, 98–101.

November 10. From Mannahatta Whitman. Formerly in the Dorn Collection.

November 28. From G. A. White, WW's landlord. Feinberg.

December 1. From Henry M. Alden. Feinberg.

December 8–19. From Anne Gilchrist. LC. CT: Harned, 102–104.

December 9. From William Stansberry. Trent.

December 11. From Minnie Vincent, an autograph seeker. Feinberg.

December 12. From Edmund W. Gosse. Feinberg. CT: Traubel, I, 245–246; *Victorian Studies*, I (1957), 181.

1874

January 2. From Rudolf Schmidt. Feinberg. CT: Traubel, III, 361.

January 12. From Walt Whitman Storms. Feinberg.

January 19. From David G. Croly. Feinberg. CT: Traubel, III, 560–561.

February 16. From William H. Millis, Jr. Berg.

[February 25]. From Anne Gilchrist. LC. CT: Harned, 105–107 (dated February 26).

February 28. From Rudolf Schmidt. Feinberg.

March 6. From Leon P. Luckey, President Grant's secretary. Feinberg.

March 9. From Anne Gilchrist. LC. CT: Harned, 108; Holloway, 279.

March 9. From Walt Whitman Storms. Feinberg.

March 20. From J. C. Mann. Oscar Lion.

March 20. From Rudolf Schmidt. Feinberg. CT: Traubel, IV, 356–358.

April 2. From J. C. Mann. Oscar Lion.

April 4. From Rudolf Schmidt. Feinberg.

May 12. From William Stansberry. Trent.

May 14. From Anne Gilchrist. LC. CT: Harned, 109–111.

May 17. From John Burroughs. Feinberg. CT: Traubel, II, 43–44; Barrus, 87.

May 26. From Thomas A. Wilson (a real estate transaction). Feinberg.

June 1. From Walter Godey. LC.

June 21. From William H. Taylor, a former driver. Feinberg.

June 23. From John Swinton. Feinberg. CT: Traubel, I, 24–25 (misdated January 23, 1884).

June 26. From Rudolf Schmidt. Syracuse University. CT: Traubel, IV, 464–465 (misdated January 26).

June 28. From William Stansberry. Trent.

June 30. From George H. Williams. Yale. CT: Traubel, III, 476.

July 4–6. From Anne Gilchrist. LC. CT: Harned, 112–114.

July 6. From George H. Williams. Copy in National Archives.

July 8. From Alfred, Lord Tennyson. WW 629.

July 12. From Edmund Carpenter. Feinberg. CT: Traubel, I, 158–161.

July 15. From Mrs. Jane Stansberry. Trent.

July 28. From Rudolf Schmidt. Feinberg.

July 29. From Mrs. Isabella A. White, WW's landlady. Feinberg.

August 11. From Fred Vaughan, a friend. Feinberg.

August 13. From John Newton Johnson. Feinberg.

August 24. From J. P. Young & Company. Feinberg.

September 2. From Thomas Gibbons, an autograph seeker. Feinberg.

September 3–14. From Anne Gilchrist. LC. CT: Harned, 115–118.

September 8. From Thomas Dixon. Feinberg.

September 13. From John Newton Johnson. Feinberg.

October 6. From Mrs. Isabella A. White. Feinberg.

October 7. From John Newton Johnson. Feinberg.

[November 6]. From Joaquin Miller. Feinberg. CT: Traubel, I, 44–45.

November 7. From John Newton Johnson. Feinberg.

November 16. From Fred Vaughan. Feinberg.

December 9. From Anne Gilchrist. LC. CT: Harned, 119–120.

December 10. From Mrs. Maria Smith, mother of an ex-soldier. Feinberg.

December 15. From Joseph B. Marvin. LC.

December 22. From Whitelaw Reid. Feinberg. CT: Traubel, I, 463–464.

December 28. From Rudolf Schmidt. Feinberg.

December 30–January 1, 1875. From Anne Gilchrist. LC. CT: Harned, 121–122.

1875

February 1. From Mrs. Maria Smith. Feinberg.

February 8. From John Newton Johnson. Feinberg.

February 11. From Reuben Farwell. Trent.

February 12. From James Redfield. Feinberg.

February 16. From Elizabeth Ford, an English admirer. Feinberg.

February 19. From John Newton Johnson. PT: Barrus, 92–93.

February 21–25. From Anne Gilchrist. LC. CT: Harned, 123–125.

February 28. From William H. Millis, Jr. Berg.

March 1. From Manvill Wintersteen, an ex-soldier. Berg.

March 5. From Reuben Farwell. Trent.

March 10. From Manvill Wintersteen. Berg.

March 12. From Bethuel Smith. Feinberg.

March 14. From Mrs. Maria Smith. Feinberg.

March 16. From Mary Van Nostrand. Trent.

March 16. From Charles P. Somerby. Feinberg.

April 3. From John Newton Johnson. Feinberg.

April 4. From William H. Millis, Jr. Berg.

April 14. From William Michael Rossetti. Feinberg.

April 15. From Thomas Dixon. Feinberg.

April 18. From John M. Rogers. Feinberg.

April 20. From Walt Whitman Storms. Feinberg.

April 25. From John M. Rogers. Feinberg.

April 26. From John Newton Johnson. Feinberg.

April 30. From John T. Trowbridge. Feinberg. CT: Traubel, II, 224 (dated April 3).

May 5. From Charles P. Somerby. Feinberg.

May 10. From John Newton Johnson. Feinberg.

May 18. From Anne Gilchrist. LC. CT: Harned, 126–128.

May 19. From William J. Linton. Feinberg. CT: Traubel, I, 12–13.

May 27. From Joaquin Miller. Feinberg. CT: Traubel, I, 57.

May 31. From Will Williams (for *The Pictorial World*). Feinberg.

June 8. From Edmund C. Stedman. Location unknown. CT: Donaldson, 213–214.

June 13. From John Addington Symonds. Feinberg. CT: Traubel, I, 203–204.

June 14. From John M. Rogers. Feinberg.

June 23. From Benton H. Wilson. Berg.

July 5. From Thomas Jefferson Whitman. Feinberg.

July 17. From J. C. Baldwin. Hanley.

July 17. From Rudolf Schmidt. Feinberg.

[July 20]. From John Newton Johnson. Feinberg.

July 21. From William Stansberry. Trent.

July 22. From Frederic R. Marvin (a request to print one of WW's poems). LC.

July 24. From John M. Rogers. Feinberg.

July 27. From John Burroughs. Feinberg.

August 5. From Manvill Wintersteen. Berg.

August 9. From Walt Whitman Storms. Feinberg.

[August?] 10. From John Newton Johnson. Feinberg.

August 11. From Alfred, Lord Tennyson. WW 685.

August 16. From Reuben Farwell. Trent.

August 18. From Rudolf Schmidt. Location unknown. CT: Traubel, IV, 336–338.

August 21. From William J. Linton. Feinberg. CT: Traubel, II, 201–202.

August 28. From Anne Gilchrist. LC. CT: Harned, 129–130.

September 5. From Joaquin Miller. Feinberg. CT: Traubel, I, 360–361.

September 25. From Charles P. Somerby. Feinberg.

September 27. From William H. Millis, Jr. Berg.

September 27. From Lord Houghton (Richard Monckton Milnes). Feinberg. CT: Traubel, I, 364 (dated September 29).

October 4. From Charles P. Somerby. Feinberg.

October 7. From Philip Hale, a Yale admirer. LC.

November 3. From Lord Houghton (Richard Monckton Milnes). Feinberg. CT: Traubel, II, 310.

November 7. From Peter Doyle. Feinberg.

November 9. From John Newton Johnson. Feinberg.

November 14. From George Washington Whitman. Yale.

November 16–30. From Anne Gilchrist. LC. CT: Harned, 133–136.

November 18. From Edwin Einstein. Feinberg.

November 25. From Josie Morse, an autograph seeker. Feinberg.

December 4. From Anne Gilchrist. LC. CT: Harned, 137–138.

December 19. From Thomas Dixon. Feinberg.

December 23. From William Michael Rossetti. Feinberg.

. . . 27. From John Newton Johnson. Feinberg.

1875. From John Newton Johnson. Feinberg.

Undated Letters

February 12. From Ed. C. Stewart, a Washington friend. Feinberg.

November 13. From George D. Cole, a Washington railroad conductor. Yale.

Appendix D

CHRONOLOGY
OF WALT WHITMAN'S LIFE AND WORK

1819	Born May 31 at West Hills, near Huntington, Long Island.
1823	May 27, Whitman family moves to Brooklyn.
1825 - 30	Attends public school in Brooklyn.
1830	Office boy for doctor, lawyer.
1830 - 34	Learns printing trade.
1835	Printer in New York City until great fire August 12.
1836 - 38	Summer of 1836, begins teaching at East Norwich, Long Island; by winter 1837 - 38 has taught at Hempstead, Babylon, Long Swamp, and Smithtown.
1838 - 39	Edits weekly newspaper, the *Long Islander*, at Huntington.
1840 - 41	Autumn 1840, campaigns for Van Buren; then teaches school at Trimming Square, Woodbury, Dix Hills, and Whitestone.
1841	May, goes to New York City to work as printer in *New World* office; begins writing for the *Democratic Review*.
1842	Spring, edits a daily newspaper in New York City, the *Aurora;* edits *Evening Tattler* for short time.
1845 - 46	August, returns to Brooklyn, writes for *Long Island Star* from September until March.
1846 - 48	From March, 1846, until January, 1848, edits Brooklyn *Daily Eagle;* February 1848, goes to New Orleans to work on the *Crescent;* leaves May 27 and returns *via* Mississippi and Great Lakes.
1848 - 49	September 9, 1848, to September 11, 1849, edits a "free soil" newspaper, the Brooklyn *Freeman*.
1850 - 54	Operates printing office and stationery store; does free-lance journalism; builds and speculates in houses.
1855	Early July, *Leaves of Grass* is printed by Rome Brothers in Brooklyn; father dies July 11.
1856	Writes for *Life Illustrated;* publishes second edition of *Leaves of Grass* in summer and writes "The Eighteenth Presidency!"
1857 - 59	From spring of 1857 until about summer of 1859 edits the Brooklyn *Times;* unemployed winter of 1859 - 60, frequents Pfaff's bohemian restaurant.
1860	March, goes to Boston to see third edition of *Leaves of Grass* through the press.
1861	April 12, Civil War begins; George Whitman enlists.

1862	December, goes to Fredericksburg, Virginia, scene of recent battle in which George was wounded, stays in camp two weeks.
1863	Remains in Washington, D. C., working part-time in Army Paymaster's office, visits soldiers in hospitals.
1864	Mid-June, returns to Brooklyn because of illness.
1865	January 24, appointed clerk in Department of Interior, returns to Washington; meets Peter Doyle; witnesses Lincoln's second inauguration; Lincoln assassinated, April 14; May, *Drum-Taps* is printed; June 30, is discharged from position by Secretary James Harlan but re-employed next day in Attorney General's office; autumn, prints *Drum-Taps and Sequel*, containing "When Lilacs Last in the Dooryard Bloom'd."
1866	William D. O'Connor publishes the *Good Gray Poet*.
1867	John Burroughs publishes *Notes on Walt Whitman as Poet and Person*; July 6, William Rossetti publishes article on Whitman's poetry in London *Chronicle*; "Democracy" (part of *Democratic Vistas*) published in December *Galaxy*.
1868	William Rossetti's *Poems of Walt Whitman* (selected and expurgated) published in England; "Personalism" (second part of *Democratic Vistas*) in May *Galaxy*; second issue of fourth edition of *Leaves of Grass*, with *Drum-Taps and Sequel* added.
1869	Mrs. Anne Gilchrist reads Rossetti edition and falls in love with the poet.
1870	July, is very depressed for unknown reasons; prints fifth edition of *Leaves of Grass*, and *Democratic Vistas* and *Passage to India*, all dated 1871.
1871	September 3, Mrs. Gilchrist's first love letter; September 7, reads "After All Not to Create Only" at opening of American Institute Exhibition in New York.
1872	June 26, reads "As a Strong Bird on Pinions Free" at Dartmouth College commencement.
1873	January 23, suffers paralytic stroke; mother dies May 23; unable to work, stays with brother George in Camden, New Jersey.
1874	"Song of the Redwood-Tree" and "Prayer of Columbus."
1875	Prepares Centennial Edition of *Leaves of Grass* and *Two Rivulets* (dated 1876).
1876	Controversy in British and American press over America's neglect of Whitman; spring, begins recuperation at Stafford Farm, at Timber Creek; September, Mrs. Gilchrist arrives and rents house in Philadelphia.
1877	January 28, gives lecture on Tom Paine in Philadelphia; during summer gains strength by sun-bathing at Timber Creek.
1878	Spring, too weak to give projected Lincoln lecture, but in June visits J. H. Johnson and John Burroughs in New York.
1879	April 14, first lecture on Lincoln in Philadelphia; September, makes trip to Colorado, long visit with brother Jeff in St. Louis.
1880	January, returns to Camden; summer, visits Dr. R. M. Bucke in London, Ontario.

1881	April 15, gives Lincoln lecture in Boston; returns to Boston in late summer to read proof of *Leaves of Grass*, being published by James R. Osgood; poems receive final arrangement in this edition.
1882	Osgood ceases to distribute *Leaves of Grass* because District Attorney threatens prosecution unless the book is expurgated; publication is resumed by Rees Welsh in Philadelphia, who also publishes *Specimen Days and Collect;* both books transferred to David McKay, Philadelphia.
1883	Dr. Bucke publishes *Walt Whitman*, biography written with poet's co-operation.
1884	Buys house on Mickle Street, Camden, New Jersey.
1885	In poor health; friends buy a horse and phaeton so that the poet will not be "house-tied"; November 29, Mrs. Gilchrist dies.
1886	Gives Lincoln lecture in Philadelphia.
1887	Gives Lincoln lecture in New York; is sculptured by Sidney Morse, painted by Herbert Gilchrist, J. W. Alexander, Thomas Eakins.
1888	Horace Traubel raises funds for doctors and nurses; *November Boughs* printed; money sent from England.
1889	Last birthday dinner, proceedings published in *Camden's Compliments*.
1890	Writes angry letter to J. A. Symonds, dated August 19, denouncing Symonds's interpretation of "Calamus" poems, claims six illegitimate children.
1891	*Good-Bye My Fancy* is printed, and the "death-bed edition" of *Leaves of Grass* (dated 1892).
1892	Dies March 26, buried in Harleigh Cemetery, Camden, New Jersey.

Index

Index

THIS BOOK is set in Monticello, a Linotype face designed after what was perhaps the first native American type face of real quality, cut by Archibald Binney probably in 1797. Printed on S. D. Warren Paper Company's University Text, the book was manufactured in its entirety by Kingsport Press, Inc.

The design and typography are by Andor Braun.